D1557559

IBERIA BEFORE THE IBERIANS

IBERIA BEFORE THE IBERIANS

The Stone Age Prehistory of Cantabrian Spain

LAWRENCE GUY STRAUS

University of New Mexico Press

Albuquerque

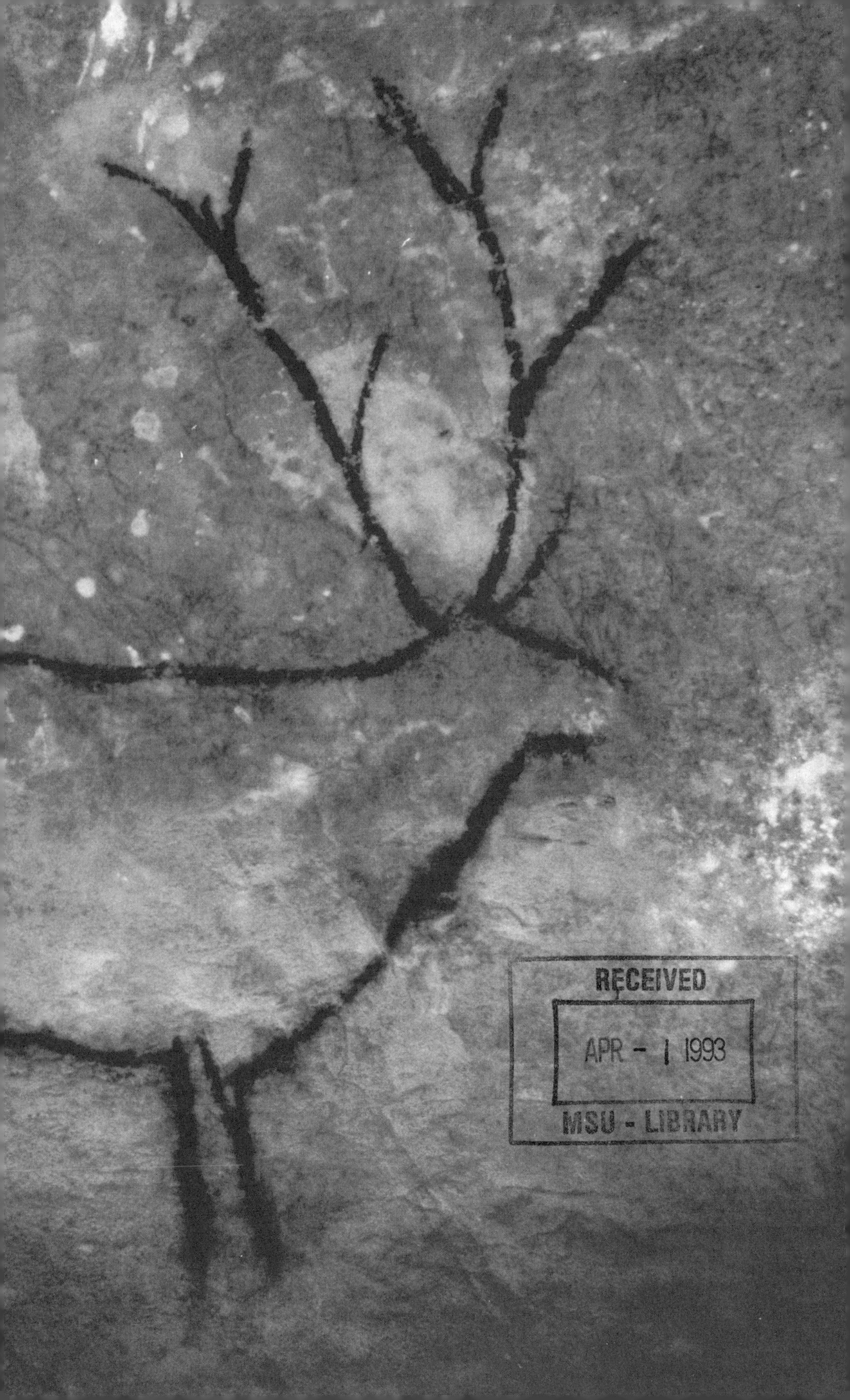

Library of Congress Cataloging-in-Publication Data

Straus, Lawrence Guy.
    Iberia before the Iberians : the Stone Age prehistory of
Cantabrian Spain / Lawrence Guy Straus. — 1st ed.
        p.   cm.
    Includes bibliographical references and index.
    ISBN 0-8263-1336-1
    1. Man, Prehistoric—Spain—Cantabria. 2. Excavations
(Archaeology)—Spain—Cantabria—History. 3. Paleoecology—Spain—
Cantabria. 4. Cantabria (Spain)—Antiquities. 5. Spain—
Antiquities. I. Title.
GN836.C33S77   1992
936.6—dc20   91-39171
                                                              CIP

CONTENTS

FIGURES

ix

TABLES

APPENDICES

IBERIA BEFORE THE IBERIANS

PREFACE

IT is never possible to present *the* definitive prehistory of any region. For one thing, the data base grows daily and new discoveries may invalidate even some "factual" aspects of such a work. More importantly, each scholar brings to such an attempt at synthesis his or her own paradigmatic biases: he or she "reads" the data in his or her own way, conditioned by his or her own theoretical perspectives and experiences. My biases are those of an American positivist, materialist, "processual archeologist" trained at the University of Chicago as well as the University of Michigan and field schools such as the Field Museum's Southwest Expedition on the Carter Ranch in Arizona and Northwestern University's Lower Illinois Valley Project at Kampsville. My professorial career so far has been exclusively at the University of New Mexico, certainly as much a hotbed of "processual archeology," cultural evolution, and functionalism as were Michigan and Chicago in the 1960s and early 1970s. These "radical" influences were moderated somewhat by my unusual ancestry: both my great-grandfather (Louis Magnant) and my grandfather (Guy Magnant) were serious amateur prehistorians in southwestern France. And I had been "digging" since my early teenage years, both in France and throughout the United States. While I firmly believe that paleo-anthropology can be directed toward the elucidation and explanation of prehistoric adaptive change, I am a field archeologist with a healthy respect for the empirical record and its problems of excavation, analysis, and interpretation.

This book owes its origins to my mentors, Prof. Leslie Freeman of the University of Chicago and the Reverend Dr. Joaquin González Echegaray of the Museo Etnográfico de Cantabria (formerly of the Museo de Prehistoria de Santander and the Museo y Centro de Investigación de

3

Altamira). They tried to teach me the rich Paleolithic prehistory of the Cantabrian region; if they failed in this, the fault is mine. Dr. Jesus Altuna (Sociedad de Ciencias Aranzadi) and Prof. Geoffrey Clark (Arizona State University) have been constant sources of help, advice, information, and useful criticism over the twenty years that I have been working on the problems of northern Spanish prehistory. Prof. Karl Butzer (University of Texas, formerly University of Chicago) has tried to educate me in matters geomorphological, paleo-environmental, and paleo-ecological. Prof. Richard Klein (University of Chicago) provided valuable faunal data as well as wise advice and support over the years.

Spanish colleagues who have generously provided me not only with insights, data, counsel, and assistance but also with hospitality and friendship are innumerable. Among the archeologists are Professors E. Aguirre, J.M. Apellániz, I. Barandiarán, J.M. de Barandiarán, F. Bernaldo de Quirós, V. Cabrera, M.S. Corchón, M. Escortell, J. Fernández-Tresguerres, J. Fortea, M.A. Garcia Guinea, M.R. González Morales, M.C. Márquez A. Moure, P. Utrilla, and P. Arias, A. Baldeón, C. González Sainz, M. de la Rasilla, and M.F. Sánchez Goñi, members of the "younger generation," have been most helpful by sending me copies of their recent publications. I trust that none of my Spanish or Basque colleagues and friends will find that I have distorted their data or ideas too greatly. I hope that this book can serve some useful purpose even in Spain, whose patrimony I have dared to try to synthesize and interpret partially from my own point of view. Other wonderful friends who have both made me feel at home in Cantabrian Spain and taught me a great deal about its modern, historic, and prehistoric lives include Ricardo Duque de Estrada and Paz Herrera (the present Condes de la Vega del Sella), J.M. García Cáraves, and Felipe Puente who, as Chief Cave Guide for the Province of Santander and along with his fellow guides Alfredo and Chema, initiated me into their underground world. ¡Para todos, un abrazo muy fuerte—y gracias!

My work in Spain (as well as in France and Portugal) would not have been possible without the financial support of the National Science Foundation, the L.S.B. Leakey Foundation, the National Geographic Society, and the University of New Mexico.

My thanks go to Diana Mercer and especially Mary Kay Day for their skill in word processing the manuscript for this book. Several people, notably Charles Carrillo and Ron Stauber redrafted figures. The photos are mine. The La Riera artifact drawings are by J. Fernández-Tresguerres; plans by G.A. Clark. Suggestions from reviewers and J. Grathwohl were of great help in revising the manuscript.

My parents, Drs. David A. and Clotilde Magnant Straus, have always supported and inspired my career as an archaeologist. I owe an immense debt to them, as I do to my late parents-in-law, Tita Errazti and Gregorio Rapado of Santander.

Finally, this book is dedicated to my modern-day Cantabrians, Mari Carmen and Eva. They have lived through many of the years of my archae-ological obsession, patiently—at least most of the time. ¡Para ellas, este pequeño libro está dedicado con mi amor!

Chapter 1

INTRODUCTION

Why a Book on the Stone Age Prehistory of Cantabrian Spain?

THIS book is intended for English-speaking students of paleo-anthropology and all others interested Stone Age prehistory. It was written with two fundamental, related goals in mind: 1) to produce a synthesis of our current understanding of the course of hominid adaptations throughout the Stone Age in a particularly well-defined and well-studied *region* of southwestern Europe; and 2) to provide a counterweight to the preponderant French (particularly Périgord) bias in the presentation, in the United States and Britain, of the Paleolithic record.

Basically, there are three perspectives from which the Stone Age record of the Cantabrian region could be interpreted: humanism, natural science, and social science. At the risk of oversimplification, I would argue that until recently the viewpoint of most Spanish prehistorians has been humanistic, whereas French and some Basque specialists directly involved in the study of the Cantabrian region are essentially natural scientists (sedimentologists, palynologists, paleontologists). The Spaniards are heirs to a distinguished intellectual tradition in the universities of Castile *and* to the centennial tradition of phylogenetic interpretation in prehistory, developed in France and both imported by Spaniards and exported by French to Spain since the last quarter of the nineteenth century. Much of the emphasis in Cantabrian "prehistoriography" until very recently has been on attempting to fit particular artifact assemblages, site sequences, and, indeed, the regional record as a whole into the ideal model developed by French prehistorians (from E. Lartet and G. de Mortillet, through H. Breuil and D. Peyrony, to D. de Sonneville-Bordes and F.

Bordes), based on type collections, levels, and sites in southwestern France, notably in the Périgord (Dordogne). The accent has been on increasingly detailed, well-documented description and comparison of objects and assemblages, in a manner akin to that of art history.

My approach (and, I think, that of other American researchers who have worked in the Cantabrian region) has been to build on the impressive archeological record established mainly by Spanish prehistorians since the early decades of this century and to use the more recent results of natural science analyses by French, Basque, American, and some Spanish colleagues in order to explore the adaptations of human groups to the changing environments of the region over the course of the Upper Pleistocene and early Holocene. By "environments," I mean not only physical but also demographic and social environments.

A major premise of this book is that the prehistory of the Cantabrian (or any) region has to be understood on its own terms. *Comparisons* with the adaptive systems of other regions are most instructive and valid, but *fitting* the record of this region into that of another (such as the Périgord) has become a rather unproductive enterprise at this stage of research.

Especially since most of this book concerns hunter-gatherer adaptive systems that were more or less territorially extensive, the focus is on the *region* with subregional differences in lithology and topography taken into account. That the inhabitants of the region were in contact, directly or indirectly, with contemporary human groups, particularly in the French Pyrenees and beyond, is acknowledged. This regional focus in the study of Cantabrian prehistory, long the perspective of both Spanish archeologists and "the Chicago school," is line with the new emphasis being given to regional studies in Paleolithic prehistory (e.g., Bailey 1983; Gamble 1986; Soffer 1985, 1987; Soffer and Gamble 1990; Gamble and Soffer 1990; Straus 1986a). Hunter-gatherer studies (more than studies of agriculturalists, which, because of greater sedentism, can be more "local" in scale) must deal with adaptations to environment on the scale of natural regions. These are usually larger than the modern administrative units or provinces into which Cantabrian Spain currently is divided (Asturias, Santander, Vizcaya, and Guipúzcoa), and which are among the smallest in Spain.

Although a major aspect of the monograph *La Riera Cave: Stone Age Hunter-Gatherer Adaptations in Northern Spain* (Straus and Clark 1986) is a comparative study of the Upper/Epi-Paleolithic and Mesolithic prehistory of Cantabrian Spain, it does not cover the scantier Middle or Lower Paleolithic or the Neolithic records for the region and is written for specialists. There has been no synthesis of Cantabrian prehistory in

English since 1924 when the only such synthesis was published: H. Obermaier's *Fossil Man in Spain*. Such syntheses are rare even in Spanish and are either encyclopedic tomes covering all of Spain or studies of the entire prehistory of individual provinces (e.g., Jordá 1977, Blas and Fernández-Tresguerres 1989 for Asturias; González Sainz and González Morales 1986 for Santander; Altuna 1975 for the Basque Country) or of particular periods throughout part or all of the region (e.g., Rodríguez 1983 for the Acheulean; Freeman 1964, 1970 for the Mousterian; Bernaldo de Quirós 1982 for the Early Upper Paleolithic; Straus 1983b for the Solutrean; Utrilla 1981 for the Lower Magdalenian; González Sainz 1989 for the Upper Magdalenian; Fernández-Tresguerres 1980 for the Azilian; Clark 1976 and González Morales 1982a for the Asturian; Altuna 1980, and Blas 1983 for the Neolithic). The period synthesis books, along with numerous monographic site reports, usually are highly technical in nature and are derived in almost all cases from doctoral dissertations.

In contrast to the Cantabrian situation (many excellent but highly specialized reports and partial syntheses, mostly in Spanish), Anglophone nonspecialist readers have been saturated with syntheses of the prehistory of France—a subject dominated by the record from the Périgord, a small, enormously rich region drained by the Isle, Vézère, and Dordogne rivers. In great part, the reason for this has been a long attraction of British and American scholars to France, with many early, strong relationships between such figures as the Abbé Breuil and M. Burkitt, D. Garrod, H. Kelly, C.G. McCurdy, H. Field, and A. Pond (but see Straus 1979d, for discussion of the early involvement of Americans in Santander with Obermaier, Breuil, and Carballo). The "French connection" grew stronger in the post-World War II period, notably by the involvement of several prominent British, Canadian, and American archeologists (including G. Daniel, J.G.D. Clark, P. Mellars, C.B.M. McBurney, H. Movius, F.C. Howell, A. Jelinek, J. Sackett, H. Bricker, N. David, P.E.L. Smith, L.R. and S.R. Binford) in southwestern France. Many worked in association with F. Bordes who influenced the teaching of Paleolithic prehistory in America not only as a result of the translation of his well-known textbooks *The Old Stone Age* and *A Tale of Two Caves* into English but also by his frequent, extended, and far-flung lecture tours in the United States. Articles in English by Bordes (1961) and D. de Sonneville-Bordes (1963) in *Science* and by both of the Bordes (1970) in *World Archaeology* (as well as other articles and book chapters) were of great importance in emphasizing the Périgord record to the Anglophone audience, as was the famous Bordes-Binford debate. The excellent book by Laville, Rigaud, and Sackett (1980), *Rockshelters of the Périgord*, continues to make the Périgord record accessible to American and British students—at the risk of emphasizing this region as "typical" of the Paleolithic of Europe. Even the Neolithic of France has won widespread familiarity in Britain and America as a result of books by Phillips (1975) and Scarre (1983).

Ironically, prehistoric archeological research began in Cantabrian Spain (and in Portugal) only a few decades after the earliest serious excavations in France and, indeed, not long after the epochal work by Lartet and Christy. And the first recognition of Paleolithic cave art, by M. Sanz de Sautuola (1880) at Altamira in 1879, came well before acknowledged scientific discoveries were made in France (see full account in Bahn and Vertut 1988:18–25). Indeed, Spain—particularly Cantabrian Spain—was the cornerstone of the research program established by Prince Albert I of Monaco for (and even before) his Institut de Paléontologie Humaine (IPH) in Paris during the five years immediately preceding World War I. This research program, including cave art discovery and documentation and monumental excavations in El Castillo as well as in other caves in Santander, involved the close collaboration of Spaniards H. Alcalde del Rio and L. Sierra with Breuil, Obermaier (an expatriate German living first in France, later Spain, and finally in Switzerland), and J. Bouyssonie (Madariaga 1972). Participants in the Castillo excavations included P. Teilhard de Chardin and P. Wernert of France, A.C. Blanc of Italy, N.C. Nelson of the United States, and M. Burkitt of Britain. Castillo was a major culture-stratigraphic sequence in the construction of the modern Paleolithic subdivision scheme by Breuil and Obermaier, but lack of definitive publication (because of the outbreak of World War I and its consequences) prevented Castillo from playing as critical a role as did Périgord sites such as Le Moustier, La Ferrassie, or Laugerie (but see Burkitt 1933). After the war, which had abruptly ended the IPH's collaborative research in Spain, Obermaier—a real internationalist and now under the patronage of the Duke of Alba—excavated in Altamira and became the first Professor of Prehistory at the University of Madrid. Through his relationship with H.F. Osborne of Yale (who gave a prominent place to Spanish finds in his own widely read book, *Men of the Old Stone Age*), Obermaier published the English version of *El Hombre Fósil* under the auspices of the Hispanic Society of America.

Then the disaster of the Civil War befell Spain; prehistoric research ended and did not really get under way again in the Cantabrian region until the mid-1950s. Isolated from the international community, Spain turned inward. Even its prehistory, once so widely known and influential, became more strictly "peninsular" and parochial—despite some efforts to the contrary. The Périgord record came to represent the archetypical model for western Europe in the eyes at least of the archeological communities of Britain and North America.

Meanwhile, in part from the stimulus of the major international research project at Cueva Morín with its classic sequence from the Middle Paleolithic to the Epipaleolithic (González Echegaray and Freeman 1971, 1973, 1978), there came a flood of syntheses of individual culture-stratigraphic units (see references above) and of old excavations (e.g., La Paloma by Hoyos et al. 1980; El Pendo by González Echegaray 1980; El Castillo by Cabrera 1984). And an impressive number of new excavations, with modern collection and recording standards and multidisciplinary analyses, not only have been carried out but also have been *monographically* published. These include Tito Bustillo (Moure 1975; Moure and Cano 1976), El Rascaño (González Echegaray and Barandiarán 1981); Las Caldas (Corchón 1981); Ekain (Altuna and Merino 1984); Erralla (Altuna et al., 1985); Piélago (Garcia Guinea 1985); El Juyo (Barandiarán et al. 1985); La Riera (Straus and Clark 1986); Amalda (Altuna et al. 1990)—an enviable publication record by any standard, including that of France. Other major monographs include the comprehensive tomes by I. Barandiarán (1967, 1972) and M.S. Corchón (1986) on bone implements and on mobile art, respectively. And the corpus of descriptions, redescriptions, and analyses of Cantabrian rupestral art has not ceased to grow, especially since the 1960s, with notable monographs on Las Monedas (Ripoll 1972), Las Chimeneas (González Echegaray 1974), Chufín (Almagro 1973), Altxerri (Altuna and Apellániz 1976), Ekain (Altuna and Apellániz 1978), Llonin (Berenguer 1979) and Altamira (Freeman et al. 1987), as well as syntheses (e.g., Almagro and Garcia Guinea 1972; UIMP 1978; Almagro 1980; Apellániz 1982; Garcia Castro 1987) and several substantive articles by Balbín and Moure (1981a,b, 1982) on Tito Bustillo.

Given this extraordinary accumulation of data and analyses, and given my own preliminary attempts at interpretation (e.g., Straus 1977b, 1985a, 1986b; Straus and Clark 1986), it would seem that the time is ripe to attempt to present an overview of the Stone Age prehistory of this extremely rich region (*pace* González Echegaray 1984). Such a synthesis would outline the essential facts and sketch a set of models from my perspective—that is, the perspective of one who has participated in the construction of the data base and in the debates of the past fifteen years. My interpretations of the Cantabrian record are given comparative perspectives by my research experiences in the northern Meseta of Castile, in the western French Pyrenees, and in central and southern Portugal.

Thus, this book represents a stock-taking, an attempt to render some coherence to the state of our knowledge of the Stone Age prehistory of Cantabrian Spain, a region of the world where the data are rich and dense enough to permit going beyond classification and chronology and to construct various interpretive or explanatory scenarios. What follows is such an attempt at interpretation. Although it tries to be factual, it is certainly neither complete nor exhaustive. It approaches the subject matter explicitly as a case study in the evolution of human adaptations at the regional scale.

The Cantabrian Region: Location and Topography

Cantabrian Spain is a narrow, mountainous, coastal strip extending along 43° north latitude between 2° and 7° west of the Greenwich Meridian (Figure 1.1). Situated in the middle latitudes on the Atlantic facade of southwestern Europe, the study area is a natural region bounded to the north by the Bay of Biscay (Cantabrian Sea), to the south by the Cantabrian Cordillera, and to the east by the western end of the Pyrenees. Although open to Galicia in the west, Cantabrian Spain is different topographically and lithologically from the Galician shield rock region at the northwestern corner of the Iberian Peninsula. The absence of calcareous bedrock, and hence of caves (and good preservation conditions), results in a nearly total void in the known distribution of Stone Age sites in Asturias to the west of the Rio Nalón and in Galicia.

Whereas eastern Galicia and western Asturias are composed principally of early Paleozoic quartzites and slates, further east there are bands of mid-Paleozoic sandstones and limestones. Central and eastern Asturias is dominated by Carboniferous limestones that make up the Picos de Europa. However, most of Santander is composed of Cretaceous limestones. The lithology of the Basque Country also is fundamentally Mesozoic but with significant Paleozoic outcrops in the Pyrenees *per se* of eastern Guipúzcoa. Cretaceous limestones predominate in most of Guipúzcoa as well as in Vizcaya (Terán and Solé Sabarís 1968).

From east to west, the Cantabrian region is divided into the provinces of Guipúzcoa and Vizcaya (which, together with Alava, constitute the autonomous administrative region of Euskadi—(part of the historic Basque Country that includes the separate region of Navarra and the three French Basque provinces of Labourd, Basse-Navarre, and Soule), Santander (formerly part of Old Castile; now the autonomous region of Cantabria, a term not used in the political sense here to avoid confusion with the larger natural region), and Asturias (now an autonomous principality within the federated Spanish nation state). The capitals and chief cities of the four provinces are, respectively, San Sebastián (Donostia), Bilbao (Bilbo), Santander, and Oviedo.

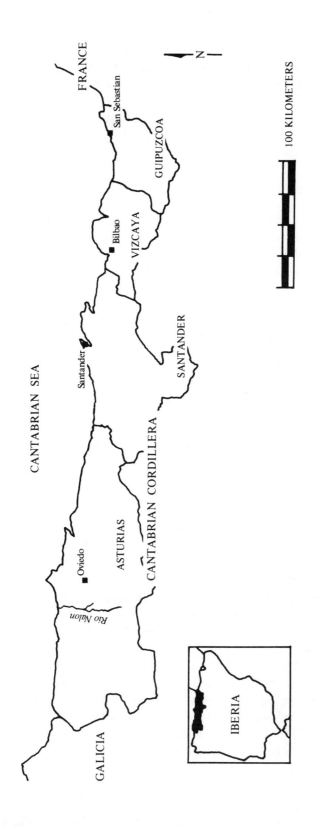

Figure 1.1. *Cantabrian Spain, showing provinces of Asturias, Santander, Vizcaya, and Guipúzcoa. Asturias and Santander (now called Cantabria) are "autonomous regions"; Vizcaya and Guipúzcoa (together with Álava) make up the "autonomous region" of Euzkadi. (After Straus and Clark 1986.)*

FIGURE 1.2. *Picos de Europa seen through the Río Bedón pass from the coastal plain of eastern Asturias at Posada de Llanes, near La Riera and Cueto de la Mina.*

It is about 350 km (200 miles) from lower Río Nalón in central Asturias (where the limestone bedrock ends at Peña de Candamo, the Upper Paleolithic art and habituation cave site) to Río Bidasoa at the French border (not far from the easternmost Cantabrian Upper Paleolithic art and archeological karstic complex of Alkerdi-Berroberría, actually in the Nivelle drainage). The distance between the present shore and the crestline of the Cordillera is never more than 30 to 50 km. The separate Picos de Europa chain in western Santander and eastern Asturias is even closer (25 km) to the coast (Figure 1.2). Under full glacial conditions, such as existed in the middle of the Upper Paleolithic at 18,000 B.P., sea level was about 120 m lower than it is at present. However, because of a narrow continental shelf that descends steeply to a trench running parallel to the Cantabrian coast, full glacial conditions exposed only an additional 4 to 12 km of coastal plain at the very most. Thus, this is a small, well-defined, elongated, narrow, and topographically highly circumscribed region with high relief and a definite geographic identity. The area involved totals about 14,000 km² (Figure 1.3).

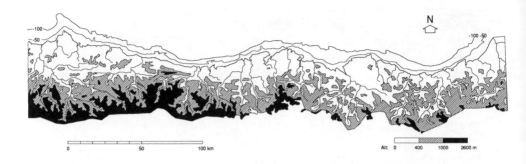

FIGURE 1.3. *Simplified relief map of Cantabrian Spain, showing coastal lowlands, foothills, Cantabrian Cordillera/Picos de Europa, and − 50 and − 100 m isobath contours that correspond, respectively, to Late Tardiglacial and Pleniglacial coastlines. (Redrawn after González Sainz 1989.)*

The Cantabrian region is distinct from the high tablelands ("Meseta del Norte") and Ebro valley to the south in terms of elevation, relief, climate, vegetation, and modern settlement. The Cordillera that separates the northern coastal strip of Atlantic Spain from the rest of the Peninsula is essentially a westward prolongation of the Pyrenees, uplifted as a result of the same alpine orogenic processes in the early Tertiary. The two chains merge at the modern Franco-Hispanic border in Navarra, and the Basque Pyrenees continue westward to Mont Rhune where the seacoast turns north. The Basque sector of the Cordillera is relatively low (scarcely ever over 1,500 m, even in its highest massifs such as Gorbea, Aralar, and Aitzkorri—and generally no more than 1,000 m). But it runs very close to the ocean and steeply separates the coastal Basque provinces from the low, broad expanses of the Ebro basin whose ancient interior Basque lands drain into the distant Mediterranean and are subjected to climatic, vegetative, and cultural influences more from that maritime region than from the Atlantic world.

The Cordillera rises toward the west, attaining summits of 1,500 to 2,000 m in Santander. Here, the Cordillera drops very steeply down to the coastal zone but to the south it is abutted by the high, barren, inhospitable Meseta of Burgos whose elevation is usually around 1,000 m and sometimes is more. Further westward, the Cordillera continues, with peaks of 1,500 to 2,000 m, until it descends and ends in Galicia. As noted above, the Picos de Europa, one of the steepest, most spectacular mountain chains in Europe, lies between the Cordillera and the coast, in a 40-km east-west line between Santander, León, and Asturias. Rising essentially from sea level, its peaks well surpass 2,000 m—the tallest exceeds 2,600 m, nearly as high as the summits of the central Pyrenees.

In eastern Asturias and most of Santander the relief is quite regularly structured. Running along the shore is an uplifted coastal plain, usually narrow but widening in several areas to as much as 10 km (such as around the city of Santander). In some areas this coastal zone is made up of platforms at various elevations and is punctuated by low lines of hills parallel to the coast and often harboring caves. Throughout Asturias and Santander, foothills of the Cordillera or Picos de Europa ascend steeply from the southern edge of the coastal zone, and in some sectors (notably between Ríos Sella and Deva in Asturias and at the head of the Bay of Santander) there are precipitous, high (600 to 1,300 m) ranges running parallel to the shore. South of these are definite intermontane valleys also oriented east-west. Immediately to the west of the mouth of the Río Sella in Eastern Asturias, in all of eastern Santander, and in most of the coastal Basque provinces (except for the coastal valleys—now estuaries—around Bilbao and Guernica in Vizcaya and at San Sebastián/Pasajes in Guipúzcoa), mountains plunge directly into the sea from summit elevations frequently exceeding 600 m (and occasionally more than 1,000 m).

Even under maximal glacial conditions of sea level regression, there would have been only the narrowest of coastal plains in many sectors of the region. In general, the relief of Asturias and the bulk of Santander is more regularly structured, with easier, more direct avenues of communication (provided by both north-south and east-west trending valleys and a broader coastal plain) than is the case in the Basque Country. The latter, located at the convergence of the Pyrenees and Cantabrian Cordillera, is more ubiquitously hilly with many small, steep-sided, closed valleys, even if the summits are lower than those to the west.

As a consequence of its steep relief and the short distance between the Cordillera and the coast, the Cantabrian region is drained by a large number of short, closely spaced, fast-flowing rivers that run essentially northward. These rivers have carved a series of valleys critical to communication between the coast and hinterland sectors of the region. They include, from west to east: the Nalón, Sella, Bedón, Deva of Asturias, Nansa, Saja, Besaya, Pas, Miera, Asón, Nervión, Deva of Guipúzcoa, Urola, Oria, Urumea, and Bidasoa. Some of these rivers (notably the Nalón) have east-west trending stretches in valleys between coastal ranges and the Cordillera. Particularly in Asturias, Santander, and central Vizcaya, where such intermontane valleys are prominent, there are major east-west tributary rivers. These longitudinal avenues of communication include Ríos Nora, Piloña, Güeña, Cares, Pisueña, Carranza, Cadagua, and Ibaizabal. The lattice of north-south and east-west valleys, together with the coastal plain (where present), create the chief patterns of munication, settlement, and land use in the past, as in

The Present Climate

The present climate of the Cantabrian region is strikingly different from that of the remainder of Spain, fundamentally because of its location on the Atlantic coast. The region is characterized today by seasonal equability and high humidity. Obviously, temperatures are lower and snow is far more abundant in the Cordillera and Picos de Europa than in the low valleys and coastal plain to which most meteorological records pertain. Microclimates are notable in some of the mountain valleys such as Liébana in the Picos de Europa of western Santander. (This fact is important to keep in mind when interpreting synchronic variability among Last Glacial pollen diagrams.)

In general, precipitation is higher along the coast (and there, higher in the extreme eastern [Basque] end of the region) than behind the coastal hill ranges. However, the highest (albeit poorly measured) annual average precipitations are in the high mountains (1,500 to 2,000 mm or more). The montane environments are obviously far colder on average than the low coastal ones. Table 1.1 lists the annual average precipitation and temperature for several major cities, all on the coast except for Oviedo (near interior) and Reinosa (Santander) and Gasteiz (Alava); the latter two cities both are montane and just south of the Cordillera, at about 800 to 900 m. The variation between summer and winter temperatures is far higher in the highlands than on the coast, the winters being very extreme in places like Reinosa. Although it snows heavily in the mountains (where, although there are no glaciers, the snow on north-facing slopes often does not completely melt until late summer), it virtually never snows on the coastal plain. It is common to be able to see the snow-covered Cordillera and Picos de Europa from the warm coastal strip in spring and summer.

The Present Vegetation

It is often difficult to reconstruct mentally the natural Holocene vegetation of the Cantabrian region because of the effects of extensive, long-term pastoralism and of equally extensive but more recent industrial siviculture. Dairy cattle pastoralism, a major economic factor throughout most of the region (much more so than farming, which is impractical and, at most, small-scale in this mountainous environment) has

Table 1.1 Cantabrian Annual Average Precipitation and Temperature

City	Precipitation (mm)	Temperature (C)
Gijón	1,034	13.8
Oviedo	940	
Santander	1,172	13.6
Reinosa		9.1
Bilbao	1,142	14.3
Guernica		15.1
San Sebastián	1,397	13.7
Gastiez (Vitoria)	828	11.0

Source: Terán and Solé Sabarís (1968)

historically eliminated the dense, mixed deciduous woodlands that would have characterized Cantabria since early Holocene times, replacing them with carefully tended, bright green pastures. Ironically, earlier in this century, when many of the great cave art and archeological discoveries were made, goat pastoralism in the upper elevations had stripped the steepest slopes of arboreal vegetation, making it easier to detect and to reach cave mouths than it is now (see photographs in Alcalde del Rio et al. 1911).

Not only has goat pastoralism been abandoned in the post-War period but, also in recent years, economic forces and the attractions of modernity have led pastoralists (often traditionally transhumant) to abandon their higher montane cattle pastures in order to concentrate herds closer to roads and towns in the lower slopes and valleys. A consequence of these developments has been the reforestation of the hill and mountain slopes—but usually not with native trees. Fast-growing eucalyptus (introduced by M. Sanz de Sautuola, discoverer of Altamira) and pines are planted even on the steepest of slopes for use in manufacturing paper and fabrics, thereby completely changing the vegetative aspect of the region.

From relic stands and historical accounts, it can be deduced that the lower elevations of the region would be characterized by oak woods, including a number of *Quercus* species (*robur, pyrenaica, lusitanica, ilex*), depending on local conditions of soil, humidity, temperature, slope orientation, shade/sunlight, etc. The region was once well-known for its chestnut trees; poplars, hazels, willows, maples, lindens, and alders lined watercourses. The upper elevations were dominated by beech forest, leaving only the cliffs bare and the highest mountain slopes covered with alpine meadow plants. The contrasts to glacial conditions could not be more striking. One point of similarity, however, is the existence today not only of "artificial" grasslands in the coastal lowlands and valleys but also of ericaceous heathlands and "matorrales." These open vegetation communities, dominated by various species of *Erica*, *Calluna*, and *Ulex*, are partly the product of human activities but, according to pollen analyses, existed naturally along the glacial coast. For details on the extensive local variability that makes up the modern vegetational mosaics in the Cantabrian region, see Terán and Solé Sabaris (1968), Mayor and Diaz (1977), Houston (1967), Lautensach (1964), Polunin and Smythies (1977), and Guinea Lopez (1953), among others.

The modern large to medium-size mammalian faunas of the Cantabrian region are much less abundant and diverse than those of the Pleistocene, as a result of environmental change plus human density and activity. Present native big game species include red deer, roe deer, chamois, ibex (reintroduced), boar, brown bear, wildcat, lynx, genet, common fox, wolf, various mustelids, hare, and rabbit (Noval 1976; Van den Brink 1968; Corbet 1966). Despite massive industrial and urban pollution, the salmon and sea trout that once were abundant in all Cantabrian rivers and estuaries still survive in the Cares-Deva, Asón, and a few other streams (Netboy 1968). Trout continue to be abundant (as a result of stocking) in mountain streams throughout the region; the coastal sea fish are extremely abundant and include many species accessible in estuaries and shallow shore waters (see Bauchot and Pras 1982). The terrestrial and aquatic avifaunas are also rich and varied (see Peterson et al. 1982).

Ice Age Environments

Most of the human societies dealt with in this book—except those of the Last Interglacial (which are very poorly represented in the prehistory of the region) and those of the early Holocene Interglacial Mesolithic and Neolithic—existed under environmental conditions of the Last Glacial, far different from those of the present. Both "middle-aged" Mousterian and "middle-aged" Upper Paleolithic societies coped with full glacial ("stadial" or Pleniglacial) conditions in Cantabrian Spain. The latter is well dated and well described here; although the Lower Pleniglacial is poorly known, it can be assumed by analogy that its conditions were generally similar to those of the Upper Pleniglacial. It must be remembered that the remainder of the period between about 115,000 and 10,000 years ago was characterized by variable climatic conditions that were intermediate between those of an interglacial and those of a glacial maximum (Table 1.2).

Table 1.2 Late Quaternary Chronostratigraphic Schemes

Age in 10³ yr B.P.	Oxygen isotope stages	Alpine glacial divisions	General glacial division	European pollen zones*	Age in 10³ yr B.P.
				Subboreal	5–3
				Atlantic	8–5
	1	Holocene	Postglacial	Boreal	9–8
				Preboreal	10–9
10					
				Dryas III	
			Tardiglacial	Alleröd	11.8–10.8
			(~13–10 × 10³ B.P.)	*Dryas II*	
				Bölling	13–12.4
		Würm IV	Upper Pleniglacial	*Dryas Ic*	
				Prebölling	14.5–14
				Dryas Ib	
				Angles	15.5–15
				Dryas Ia	
			(Last Glacial Maximum	Lascaux	18–16.5
			at ~19–18 × 10³ B.P.)	Laugerie	20–19
	2				

(continued)

Table 1.2 Late Quaternary Chronostratigraphic Schemes *(continued)*

Age in 10³ yr B.P.	Oxygen isotope stages	Alpine glacial divisions	General glacial division	European pollen zones*	Age in 10³ yr B.P.
				Tursac	24–23
		Würm III		Kesselt	29–27
30–35					
	3	Würm Interstadial (38–34 × 10³ B.P.)	Interpleniglacial	Arcy	31.5–30
				Cottés	36–34.5
				Hengelo	40–38
				Moershoofd	~50
61					
	4	Würm II	Lower Pleniglacial (maximum at ~65 × 10³ B.P.)		
73					
	5a	Würm I	Early Glacial	St. Germain II	
	5b				
	5c			St. Germain I	
	5d				
118					
	5e	Riss/Würm	Last Interglacial	Eem	
128					
	6	Riss III	Penultimate Glacial		
190					

*Named cold periods are italicized.

Specific environmental reconstructions (insofar as they can be made from existing data sources) will be presented in each chapter; however, some general statements about Ice Age Cantabrian Spain should be made at the outset. Sources of information relevant to this region include: classic glaciological studies; geomorphological analyses of cave, rock-shelter, and slope deposits and of river terraces; palynology (to date mostly conducted in archeological cave sites in this region, with a limited number of mountain and coastal bog cores); paleontology and malacology; and, most recently, oxygen isotope analysis of deep-sea cores drilled in the Cantabrian Sea and off the coasts of Galicia.

It has long been known that various sectors of the Cordillera and the Picos de Europa were glaciated during the late Pleistocene. Although the exact chronology of these mountain glacial centers is not yet worked out, it would seem reasonable to assume that the ice caps were maximal or at least very great during the Würm Pleniglacials (central dates about 65 to 70 and 18 Ka B.P., oxygen isotope stages 4 and 2, respectively). Traces of Cantabrian mountain glaciation include moraines, U-shaped valleys, striated rocks, cirques, serrate ridges, etc. From east to west, glaciers existed in the Sierra de Aralar (terminal moraines at 825 m above sea level, 25 km from the present coast), Castro Valnera (terminal moraines 600 m above sea level, 30 km from the present coast), Montes de Reinosa (down to within 30 km of the present coast), Picos de Europa (terminal moraines as low as 750 to 650 m above sea level, within 25 km of the present coast), and several centers in the Cordillera of central Asturias with terminal moraines from 1,600 to >1,000 m above sea level. These glaciers were generally oriented toward the north or east. Obviously, such low glaciers so far south required not only low annual temperatures but also abundant solid precipitation. Estimates of the limit of the permanent snow line at the time of glacier formation range from 1,650 to 1,025 m above sea level. Details can be found in Obermaier (1914), Hérnandez Pacheco (1944), Lötze (1962), Nussbaum and Gygax (1952), Butzer (1973), Kopp (1965), Alonso Otero et al. (1982—cited in González Sainz 1989).

Besides the glaciological evidence, which is not precisely dated, there are numerous data on periglacial geomorphological processes (cryoturbation, congelifraction, solifluction) from cave and rockshelter contexts that are dated either chronometrically by radiocarbon analysis or indirectly with reference to archeological assemblages. These (as well as geomorphological indicators of milder—interglacial or interstadial—conditions such as paleosols, flowstones, corrosion, and weathering) are discussed specifically in the context of the environments of the successive climatic and cultural periods discussed in the bulk of this book. The point here is that there is abundant evidence, even within the protected environment of cave mouths, of significantly colder climatic conditions during much of the Last Glacial in the Cantabrian region than exist at present; these are marked by geomorphological processes not operative, at least on the coast, under Holocene conditions.

Similarly, the chapters on individual periods will utilize pollen data, mostly for the Upper Paleolithic and Mesolithic, to document the changes in local and regional vegetation within the late Upper Pleistocene and early Holocene. Suffice it to say here that, under glacial conditions, arboreal pollens are rare in many diagrams and are almost exclusively pollens of pine during glacial maxima, a fact that may be of little local meaning because *Pinus* produces copious amounts of highly aerodynamic pollen that can be wind-borne over long distances. It is also the case that pollen grains have percolated downward in cave sediments, contaminating Pleniglacial spectra with Holocene taxa (Turner and Hannon 1988). Nonetheless, the complex relief and southerly location of the Cantabrian region made it a refuge for many relatively thermophile taxa of trees and plants. This causes some interesting mixtures of pollen types in many diagrams, suggesting complicated vegetative mosaics under all but the most severe glacial conditions. By Atlantic times (postglacial optimum) many changes in pollen spectra can be attributed to anthropogenic, as opposed to climatic, causes (deforestation, disturbance, revegetation).

Mammalian paleontological evidence (notably from the work of J. Altuna [1972 et seq.]) has limited paleoclimatic/paleo-environmental value because many of the species are tolerant of a wide variety of conditions (notably, the ubiquitous red deer). In the region, there is a long-term trend toward the disappearance of archaic Pleistocene species feebly represented in the faunas of the older archeological sites (mainly in caves): mammoth, rhinoceros, giant deer, primitive forms of bear, etc. And there were a number of extinctions, extirpations, or reductions at or near the end of the Last Glacial that probably were related to environmental changes. The presence of small numbers of remains of reindeer, arctic fox, and Nordic vole in certain deposits of Last Glacial age is an indication of climatic conditions far colder than those of the present, while the relative abundance of remains of bison and horse suggest the existence open grasslands that disappeared with the onset of the Postglacial. On the other hand, the increase in finds of roe deer and boar in deposits dating to the Pleistocene–Holocene boundary is, at least in part, evidence of the growth of wooded habitats.

Marine mollusks have provided limited climatic data in the form of "northern visitor" species such as *Cyprina islandica* and in changing relative frequencies of sea snails with different tolerances for cold water (*Littorina littorea* versus *Monodonta lineata*). These data are concordant with land-based evidence of long-term climatic changes by showing that water temperatures in the Cantabrian Sea went from very cold in Upper Plenigalcial times (about 25,000 to 16,000 B.P.) to warm under Holocene conditions with the presence of a branch of the Gulf Stream. The trend took thousands of years during the course of deglaciation in the late Last Glacial. Under early Holocene conditions, the presence of land snails (*Helix*) in many cave sites is evidence of warm temperatures and high humidity.

Finally, the drastic nature of the temperature depression in the Cantabrian region during Last Glacial Maximum (about 18,000 B.P.) has recently been dramatically confirmed by deep-sea data analyzed by the CLIMAP group (CLIMAP 1976; McIntyre et al. 1976; Gates 1976). The CLIMAP results in the waters off northwestern Spain, which show some of the greatest temperature gradients recorded anywhere in the world at 18,000 B.P., can be assumed to apply to the Lower Pleniglacial, which is relevant to the Middle Paleolithic occupation of the Cantabrian region. The CLIMAP reconstructions show Cantabrian Sea surface water temperatures to have been 10 to 11 degrees C lower at 18,000 B.P. than today. Subsequent Late Glacial (16,000 to 10,000 B.P.) deep-sea core oxygen isotope results have documented the details of temperature fluctuations and a long-term increase in the Cantabrian Sea. These studies generally coincide with geomorphological and palynological results but with some interesting differences in terms of the varying degrees to which the different methods detect subtle climatic signals that may be of regional rather than worldwide scale (Duplessy et al. 1981; Ruddiman and McIntyre 1981).

Despite its relatively southerly location, the Cantabrian region underwent very significant climatic changes throughout the course of the Pleistocene, much more so than did southern regions of Atlantic Iberia or Mediterranean Spain in general. In fact, the CLIMAP data point not only to severely lower temperatures both in summer and winter but also to very stormy conditions along the Cantabrian and Galician coasts during the Last Glacial Maximum because of the extremely steep gradient in ocean surface water temperatures at precisely this latitude in this part of the Atlantic. Not far (about 500 km) to the south, off southern Portugal, Pleniglacial surface water temperatures were only slightly cooler (2–3 degrees C) than those of today, the Gulf Stream having been displaced to the south by polar waters in the Cantabrian Sea.

Chapter 2

THE DEVELOPMENT OF PREHISTORIC RESEARCH IN CANTABRIAN SPAIN

Altamira

CANTABRIAN prehistoric studies can be divided into four periods of which the first three are distinctly separated. The first period concerns the work of a limited number of local amateur prehistorians—notably Marcelino Sanz de Sautuola of Santander—in the last quarter of the nineteenth century. The second concerns the archeological "boom" years from 1902 until 1914 (for major foreign involvement, until the outbreak of World War I) or 1936 (for research by local Spaniards, until the start of the Civil War). The third period began around 1955 with the work of a few Spaniards (sometimes collaborating with foreigners). It gradually became the fourth period in the late 1960s to early 1970s when those same Spaniards, their disciples, and several more foreigners began excavations and synthetic studies on a much larger scale.

Systematic interest in prehistoric antiquities in Spain and Portugal coalesced in the 1860s with the creation of the Comisiones Provinciales de Monumentos and of the Commissão Geologica de Portugal and with the work of Casiano del Prado and J.F. Nery Delgado, respectively. The founding of anthropological and prehistoric societies in Madrid occurred in this same period, centered on Juan Vilanova y Piera, Professor of Geology at the University of Madrid.

At the regional level, the history really begins in 1876, in Santander Province, when Sanz de Sautuola, a gentleman landowner with a summer house in Puente San Miguel between Torrelavega and Santillana del Mar, explored the cave of Altamira. This cave had been discovered by a hunter in about 1868, on a hillside above the latter town. By 1860, Sanz de Sautuola, a natural scientist with a particular interest in agronomy, was already a well-known collector of antiquities in the province (Madariaga 1972, 1975, 1976). Sanz de Sautuola (1880) found black drawings and engravings on the walls of Altamira and apparently collected artifacts and bones in his first and subsequent visits to it before traveling to Paris to attend the Universal Exposition in 1878. He was one of several Spaniards (including Vilanova) to visit the Anthropology Pavilion where he viewed the prehistoric archeological collections (including objects of mobile art recently dicovered in southwestern France) assembled by Gabriel de Mortillet. He also met Paul Broca, Emile Cartailhac, Edouard Piette, and Henri Martin (Sanemeterio 1976; Bahn and Vertut 1988).

By his own description (Sanz de Sautuola 1880:1), this visit further sparked his enthusiasm for archeological exploration. In 1879, he conducted excavations in the vestibule of Altamira. He found lithic and bone artifacts, pieces of red ochre, and faunal remains but, as he notes, no ceramics; these were described in his 1880 pamphlet, *Breves Apuntes sobre algunos Objetos Prehistóricos de la Provincia de Santander*. It is here that Sanz de Sautuola also reported his discovery of the paintings of bison and other large ungulates on the ceiling of a hall to the side of the vestibule, actually first noticed by his eight-year-old daughter María. Sanz de Sautuola made the intellectual association between the artifacts and bones in the archeological deposit in Altamira and the works of mobile art discovered in France on the one hand and the paintings (some of animals no longer living in Spain, notably bison) on the ceiling of Altamira on the other hand. From this he tentatively concluded that the art was the work of Stone Age people.

Altamira was not Sanz de Sautuola's only site; in association with Eduardo Pérez del Molino and Eduardo de la Pedraja, he also dug in Paleolithic deposits in the caves of Camargo, Cobalejos, El Cuco, and El Pendo near the city of Santander, all in 1878 and 1879. Digging in El Pendo continued in 1880 in the company of Vilanova who visited Altamira at this time (González Echegaray 1980; Sanemeterio 1976). In 1880, Pedraja, who made the first reproduction of the Altamira paintings, discovered the Paleolithic cave site of Fuente del Francés east of Santander (Madariaga 1972). Beginning in 1880 in a series of lectures and at the epochal IX International Congress of Anthropology and Prehistoric Archeology in Lisbon, Vilanova publicized and repeatedly defended Sanz Sautuola's report of Stone Age paintings at Altamira to a largely skeptical and often frankly hostile scientific community (Madariaga 1972, 1976; Sanemeterio 1976). Chief among the doubters were the deans of the nascent science of prehistory in France, Gabriel de Mortillet and Emile Cartailhac, who, according to Bahn and Vertut (1988:21–22), were afraid that the paintings were forgeries perpetrated by "anti-evolutionist Spanish Jesuits" to discredit prehistory. Few prominent prehistorians of the time even deigned to visit Altamira, but in 1881 Mortillet and Cartailhac dispatched Edouard Harlé, who visited the cave and published (in the Mortillet-Cartailhac journal *Matériaux*) his opinion that the paintings were recent (Harlé 1881). Although Piette and Henri Martin, as well as Vilanova, supported him (Bahn & Vertut 1988:23), when Sanz de Sautuola died in 1888, his honor was still tainted by the implication of being either a forger or a dupe (Delporte 1989).

Meanwhile, other amateur prehistorians had begun to dig in a number of caves throughout the region, including Justo del Castillo in Collubil, and S. Soto Cortés possibly in La Paloma (both in Asturias) (González Morales 1974, 1978), and the Conde de Lersundi in Aitzbitarte (Guipúzcoa) (Barandiarán 1961). But the importance of the Cantabrian record really (and unfortunately) became widely manifest only after the accumulation of discoveries of cave art in France (at Chabot, Figuier, La Mouthe, Pair-non-Pair, Marsoulas, Les Combarelles and Font de Gaume).

After visiting Marsoulas in 1902 soon after its discovery, accompanied by the recently ordained Abbé Henri Breuil (as artist-copyist), Cartailhac finally went to Altamira. Now a believer, Cartailhac had published his famous posthumous apology to Sanz de Sautuola earlier in the same year, " 'Mea culpa' d'un sceptique," in *L'Anthropologie* (Bahn and Vertut 1988; Madariaga 1972; Sanemeterio 1976). With these developments began the second period in the investigation of Cantabrian prehistory: the "heroic" period.

Prewar Cantabrian Prehistory: The Heroid Period

Swept up in the delayed recognition of Sanz de Sautuola's discovery, a professor in the vocational school of Torrelavega, Hermilio Alcalde del Río, worked with Cartailhac and Breuil in their month-long study of Altamira (Sanemeterio 1976). Alcalde del Rio then went on to discover the cave art in El Castillo, Hornos de la Peña, and Covalanas in 1903, in Santian in 1905, in La Clotilde (with Breuil) in 1906, in El Pendo and La Meaza in 1907 (all in Santander), in El Pindal, La Franca, Balmori, and (with Breuil and L. Mengaud) La Loja in 1908, in San Antonio in 1912 (all in Asturias), and in Atapuerca (Burgos) in 1910 (Madariaga 1972, 1975). In this same period, Father Lorenzo Sierra, a teacher in a Paulist school in eastern Santander and a friend of Alcalde del Río, discovered several important Paleolithic cave sites on his side of the province, including El Valle, El Mirón El Salitre, El Rascaño, El Otero, Venta de la Perra, Sotarriza, etc. (Madariaga 1972).

In 1906 Alcalde del Río published *Las Pinturas y Grabados de las*

Cavernas Prehistóricas de la Provincia de Santander in which he described not only rupestral art in a number of sites but also excavations he conducted in Altamira (clearly distinguishing the Solutrean and Magdalenian strata, with their different stone and antler projectile points, respectively) and in the uppermost ("Neolithic," Azilian, and Magdalenian) deposits at El Castillo. Much to Alcalde's credit, the latter cave was to turn out to contain the most complete culture-stratigraphic sequence in the entire Cantabrian region—still unrivaled today. Furthermore, Alcalde del Río contributed a chapter on the archeology of Altamira to the book *La Caverne d'Altamira, à Santillane, près Santander* also published in 1906 by Cartailhac and Breuil with the patronage of Prince Albert I of Monaco.

Alcalde del Río was the first to attempt to apply systematically de Mortillet's scheme of prehistoric archeological subdivisions, based on temporally diagnostic artifact types, to the Cantabrian region. In 1908, Sierra published a very interesting but now little known work, "Notas para el Mapa Paletnográfico de la Provincia de Santander"—a precursor to settlement pattern studies. He was able to demonstrate a dense scatter of known Paleolithic sites along the river valleys and on the coastal plain of the province.

Beginning in 1906, Prince Albert I of Monaco became the patron of prehistory in the Cantabrian region, first with the signing of contracts in that year and in 1909 with Alcalde del Río for the funding of excavations and publications (to be done in collaboration with Breuil and Sierra) (Madariaga 1972 *contra* Breuil 1951). After visiting Santander and the caves of Altamira, El Castillo, and Covalanas with Alcalde del Río, Breuil, and Obermaier in 1909, Prince Albert founded the Institut de Paléontologie Humaine (IPH) in Paris in 1910; Marcellin Boule was its first director and its first field work began immediately under the direction of Breuil, Father Hugo Obermaier, and Father Jean Bouyssonie, in collaboration with Alcalde del Río and Sierra at El Castillo, Hornos de la Peña, and El Valle.

While the monumental IPH excavations were just getting under way at El Castillo in 1911, Alcalde del Río, Breuil, and Sierra published the equally monumental *Les Cavernes de la Région Cantabrique*, funded by Prince Albert. Unequaled today as a detailed description of the known cave art sanctuaries of an entire region, *Les Cavernes* consists of 250 pages of text and 100 plates (large format photographs and Breuil's watercolor copies of cave paintings). Also during the course of the Castillo excavation in 1911, Obermaier and his assistant, Paul Wernert, discovered magnificent complexes of rupestral art in the adjacent cave of La Pasiega. With remarkable speed, this discovery resulted in another fully illustrated, folio-size volume, this one by Breuil, Obermaier, and Alcalde del Río (1913) and again funded by Prince Albert (this time under the imprint of the IPH).

This publication project would end virtually on the eve of the Spanish Civil War with unsurpassed folio editions in Spanish and English (the latter, like Obermaier's *Fossil Man in Spain*, co-published by the Hispanic Society of America) of Breuil's definitive (if not flawless) restudy of the cave art of Altamira. This book also contained Obermaier's report on his 1924–1925 excavations in the vestibule of Altamira, where Sanz de Sautuola and Alcalde del Río had conducted their pioneering digs, 50 and 20 years earlier, respectively. This volume (Breuil and Obermaier 1935) and Obermaier's research (as well his Chair at the University of Madrid, and the Altamira Museum) were funded by a new patron, the Duke of Berwick and Alba. Such good fortune in publication did not befall the IPH excavations in El Castillo.

Under Obermaier's direction and with an international cast of future stars of early scientific archeological research, virtually the entire vestibule of the huge cave at El Castillo, with a 16- to 18-m deep stratigraphy, was excavated in five seasons between 1910 and 1914, ending abruptly with the start of World War I. From bottom to top, the Castillo infilling was composed of one or more horizons each of (in modern terminology) Acheulean, Mousterian, Aurignacian, Gravettian, Solutrean, Lower Magdalenian, Upper Magdalenian, Azilian, Bronze Age, and Medieval: the whole prehistoric sequence of Europe! But because of the war, the collections and the excavators were dispersed (Obermaier and Wernet went into exile in the Nueva, Asturias, palace of the Conde de la Vega del Sella—one of the many prestigious participants in the excavation [Conde de la Vega del Sella, pers. comm.]) and the ambitious publication plans never came to fruition. All that the principals published was a series of short progress reports on IPH research in *L'Anthropologie* (Breuil and Obermaier 1912, 1913, 1914) and various other brief summaries and topical articles in that and other journals and congress proceedings as well as Obermaier's summaries in the successive editions of *El Hombre Fósil* (1916, 1924, 1925).

Not until the 1970s when M. Almagro Basch, Director of the Museo Arqueológico Nacional in Madrid and Commissioner of the Archeological Excavations in Spain, was able to repatriate the IPH collections and the excavation notes (notably those kept by Wernert) could a complete study of El Castillo be undertaken. This was done by Victoria Cabrera and published 70 years after the unexpected end of that excavation (Cabrera 1984).

Asturias was not to be overshadowed by the IPH work in nearby Santander. Here two Spaniards, one a great noble landowner and the other a professional geologist—both associated with the Comisión de Investigaciones Prehistoricas y Paleontologicas in Madrid—conducted numerous excavations of Paleolithic cave sites (including some with critical stratigraphic sequences) and studied cave art sites. They produced several major monographic publications. While working essentially alone or occasionally in collaboration with one another, Ricardo Duque de Estrada, the Conde de la Vega del Sella and Eduardo Hernández-Pacheco did get help (for better or worse) directly from Obermaier or indirectly through Wernert. (Obermaier and Wernert were wartime refugee guests in the Conde's palace at Nueva in Asturias [Vega del Sella, pers. comm.].)

Vega del Sella had been interested in prehistoric archeology since the late nineteenth century, having dug at the Dolmen de Santa Cruz (Cangas de Onis, Asturias) in 1891 and visited Lersundi's excavation in Aitzbitarte in 1892 (Barandiarán 1961). However, his remarkable series of excavations, mostly in caves within a short radius of his palace in highly karstic eastern Asturias, took place essentially in the period 1912 to 1922 and centered on five years of intense activity between 1915 and 1919 (Márquez Uría 1974). Vega del Sella's work primarily covered the Upper Paleolithic and Mesolithic, based on his excavations at Penicial, Cueto de la Mina, La Riera, Balmori, and Cueva Morín (where he took turns [!] in the excavation of this famous cave with a local Santander prehistorian, Father Jesus Carballo [1923]) (Vega del Sella 1914, 1916, 1921, 1930).

Besides these published excavations, Vega del Sella dug at many other sites, leaving at his death in 1941, unpublished manuscripts or extensive notes on Collubil (a high mountain Magdalenian ibex hunting site) and Cueva del Conde (Mousterian and Aurignacian) in particular (Márquez Uria 1974). He also published on cave art he discovered at El Buxú (Obermaier and Vega del Sella 1918) and was involved with Obermaier, Wernert, and Hernández-Pacheco in the discovery of the Peña de Candamo cave art site (Vega del Sella 1929). His 1915 article, "Avance al estudio del Paleolitico superior en la región asturiana," was the first synthesis of the region's Upper Paleolithic sequence and was based on his own empirical observations (especially at Cueto de la Mina, with its sequence of Aurignacian, Gravettian, Solutrean, Lower and Upper Magdalenian, Azilian, and/or Asturian levels), not on a model imposed from France. Already showing a great interest in Pleistocene climates in this early work, Vega del Sella later published a volume on climate change (1927). And, based on his excavations at Penicial, La Riera, and a large number of other (unfortunately scantily published) caves in eastern Asturias, he correctly defined the post-Pleistocene "Asturian" culture (Vega del Sella 1923), later often mistaken for a Lower or Middle

Paleolithic industry because of its simple cobble picks and other crude, heavy-duty stone tools. Vega del Sella also excavated and published a few megalithic monuments.

A very careful, observant excavator on his own (witness his description of hearths in Cueto de la Mina [Vega del Sella 1916:42–43]), a perceptive typologist and faunal analyst, and an impeccable author, Vega del Sella seems to have come under the influence of the "professional," Obermaier. A clear example comes from revisions in Vega del Sella's interpretation of the significance of heavy-duty lithic artifacts found in Upper Paleolithic contexts. In publishing Cueto de la Mina, Vega del Sella (1916:51 and Fig. 36) had no problem ascribing a series of seven quartzite macrolithic tools (atypical for the Upper Paleolithic, he said) to the Upper Magdalenian, in which layer they were found in a niche in the cave wall. In fact, he described them as "non-portable artifacts belonging to the permanent domestic effects of the occupation site"— anticipating Binford's notion (1978) of "site furniture" by some 60 years! However, by the time he had gotten around to publishing La Riera in 1930, long after his excavations of 1917–1918, orthodoxy seems to have been imposed on his interpretations of similar phenomena. To explain a small number of similar quartzite macroliths found in the midst of his Magdalenian levels, Vega del Sella (1930:9,29,31,45–46) postulated the existence of a (hypothetical) Acheulean open-air site on the slope above the cave mouth, from which clay deposits had slid into La Riera in late Last Glacial times. This explanation "made the artifacts fit" into the standard normative scheme, one that had been established in regions where quartzite was not a significant raw material for tool manufacture. Obermaier in 1924 (p. 175), citing himself as having explored La Riera with Vega del Sella, provided the "slipped Acheulean" explanation not only for that cave but also for the "hand axes" inthe Magdalenian of Cueto de la Mina! (We found a similar biface and other heavy-duty quartzite tools in a clayey layer in association with classic Magdalenian artifacts at the rear of the La Riera vestibule, far from any possible landslide from the exterior [Straus and Clark 1986].)

Obermaier's *ex cathedra* pronouncements were not reserved only for the "amateur" Vega del Sella. He minimized the work of Hernández-Pacheco who dug a number of sites throughout eastern and central Asturias and studied the cave art of Candamo (Hernández-Pacheco 1919, 1923, 1959). Obermaier (1924:175–178) consistently listed his assistant Wernert as co-excavator of all of Hernández-Pacheco's sites and concluded that the rich Magdalenian sequence at La Paloma was "completely disturbed," making it impossible to "establish a clear and trustworthy stratigraphic succession" (p. 177). This conclusion was reversed recently in a detailed restudy of La Paloma by Hoyos et al. (1980) who found the Hernández-Pacheco excavation, stratigraphy, and Magdalenian cultural sequence to be valid and of great importance for the establishment of the regional Tardiglacial scheme.

Another important contributor, not only to the prehistory of Asturias but also to cave art studies and Paleolithic archeology throughout Spain in the latter years of the "heroic" period of discoveries, was Juan Cabré (e.g., 1915, 1934).

Among the Santander cave sites dug by Jesus Carballo besides Morin (rather more haphazardly than by his Asturian contemporaries) was the vast, exceptionally rich El Pendo. Carballo, who founded the Museum of Prehistoric Archeology of Santander, collaborated with a number of other prehistorians including Prof. George Grant McCurdy of Yale's American School of Prehistoric Research. Carballo dug in El Pendo during the 1920s and early 1930s. Chauvinistic in many aspects of his publications, Carballo (e.g., 1960) argued that the Azilian had a Cantabrian origin.

Basque prehistory in the "heroic" period (and in subsequent periods to the present) was dominated by Father Jose Miguel de Barandiarán who in 1989 celebrated his one-hundredth birthday and was still active (see Altuna 1990a,b for biographies). In 1916, a Basque research triad composed of Telesforo de Aranzadi (Professor of Physical Anthropology at the University of Barcelona), Enrique de Eguren (Professor of Geology at the University of Oviedo), and Barandiarán (Professor of Physics [!] at the Seminary of Vitoria) was formed and undertook the excavation of Santimamiñe and Lumentxa caves in Vizcaya. Rupestral art had just been discovered in Santimamiñe near Guernica, and it was first studied by Aranzadi et al. (1925) soon after Breuil's visit to the cave. Barandiarán, who began lecturing on Basque prehistory as early as 1917, was in contact with Breuil since then, with whom he would study at the IPH in 1923 to 1924 (Altuna 1990b:12).

The sites of Santimamiñe and Lumentxa, dug by the triad over the course of a decade (Aranazdi et al. 1931, Aranzadi and Barandiarán 1935) contained long sequences of Upper Paleolithic, Epi-Paleolithic, and Neolithic materials, still important to the Vizcayan data base despite somewhat confusing descriptions of the stratigraphies. In addition to large numbers of megalithic discoveries and excavations in the Basque mountains, Barandiarán in collaboration with Aranzadi also excavated other Paleolithic cave sites, notably Ermittia (Aranzadi and Barandiarán 1928) and Urtiaga. This excavation was abruptly terminated by the outbreak of the Civil War and the invasion of Guipúzcoa by Nationalist troops in July 1936. Barandiarán soon had to flee by boat from Motrico to Saint-

Jean-de-Luz. The "heroic" period of Cantabrian prehistory had ended. Barandiarán's exile would last 17 years; meanwhile, Aranzadi and Eguren would die.

In Nueva, Asturias, the monarchist son and heir of the Conde de la Vega del Sella (himself a respected political moderate and President of the Provincial government) was dragged from the palace and murdered by thugs. Vega del Sella did no more archeology and died in 1941. Father Sierra, whose collections apparently were lost when his school in Limpias was used as a field hospital during the Civil War, died within two months after Alcalde del Río in 1947 (Madariaga 1972). Obermaier—by now a Spanish citizen and the country's most respected prehistorian internationally—fled from Fascist Spain, refusing to take the new required oath of allegiance to Franco, and died, once again in exile, in Switzerland in 1946 (Breuil 1946).

Breuil had been an agent for French Naval Intelligence while doing prehistoric research in southern Spain and Gibraltar during World War I. With the Castillo "alumnus" Teilhard de Chardin, Breuil did research at Choukoutien in the 1930s after considerable time spent on French cave art and on the Lower Paleolithic of northern France in the 1920s. Breuil became Professor of Prehistory at Collège de France in 1929 (Broderick 1963). After seeing the just-discovered Lascaux in 1940, he spent the years of World War II in Portugal and Africa; he died in Paris in 1961. His early years in Spain had been irreversibly formative in his career, even if it was the record of southwestern France, not the equally rich and complete Cantabrian one, that he so forcefully and universally imposed on the prehistoric science he dominated for over a half century through such seminal works as "Les subdivisions du Paléolithique supérieur" (1913).

The Postwar Period: New Beginnings

Father Jose Miguel de Barandiarán returned from exile in the French Basque Country (where he had been conducting archeological and ethnographic research) in October 1953 and soon picked up where he had left off in 1936: excavating the important Tardiglacial and early Postglacial site of Urtiaga in Guipúzcoa. In 1956 and in 1960, Barandiarán undertook long-term excavations of the sites of Lezetxiki and Aitzbitarte IV, with long Middle and Upper and Upper Paleolithic sequences, respectively, which he published in the form of numerous articles in *Munibe* (the journal of the Sociedad de Ciencias Aranzadi) during the course of the 1960s (see re-editions in J.M. Barandiarán, *Obras Completas* ([1976–

1978]) (Altuna 1990a,b). The Sociedad de Ciencias Aranzadi began to serve as an institutional base for Basque prehistory (and natural sciences), with its headquarters in San Sebastián's Museo de San Telmo. Barandiarán began to train the three individuals who would play central roles in Quaternary archeozoology, cave art studies, and prehistoric archeology, respectively, not only in the Basque Country but throughout the Cantabrian region as a whole and in western Europe in the following (present) period. These scholars are Jesus Altuna, Jose Maria Apellániz, and Ignacio Barandiarán, all former priests or friars.

Similarly, in Santander, Father Carballo was informally training his scientific heir, another young priest, Joaquin González Echegaray, who today is the "dean" of Upper Paleolithic specialists in Spain. In 1953 and for four more years, Prof. J. Martínez Santa-Olalla directed large-scale excavations in El Pendo. Along with González Echegaray, the participants in the new El Pendo research included the prominent French prehistorians André Cheynier, André Leroi-Gourhan, and Arlette Leroi-Gourhan. The last did the first palynological analysis of a Cantabrian Paleolithic cave site at El Pendo, thereby beginning a long, fruitful involvement in the study of Pleistocene vegetations in the region. Together with El Castillo, El Pendo contains the most complete chronostratigraphic sequence in the entire region (Mousterian through Azilian), and it suffered the same sorry fate. Its collections were poorly curated and it remained essentially unpublished at the time of Santa-Olalla's death in 1972. It was González Echegaray who, in collaboration with I. Barandiarán and L. Freeman, "rescued" the information gathered by the international excavation of the 1950s, publishing a comprehensive monograph on El Pendo in 1980 (González Echegaray 1980).

In the mid-1950s, González Echegaray also collaborated with a Belgian, Paul Janssens, in the excavation and publication of what would become a key early Magdalenian site near El Pendo: El Juyo (Janssens and González Echegaray 1958). In collaboration with Garcia Guinea, Beginés, and Madariaga, González Echegaray dug two Magdalenian sites in eastern Asturias in 1962 and 1963: La Chora and El Otero (González Echegaray et al. 1963, 1966). At the latter site, Leroi-Gourhan also did a pollen analysis. These excavations applied the then-new lithic tool typology for the Upper Paleolithic developed in France by de Sonneville-Bordes and Perrot. The first radiocarbon dates in the region were done at Altamira and El Juyo by Crane and Griffin (1960).

The long hiatus of Paleolithic research in Asturias after the retirement and then death of Vega del Sella was ended by the arrival in 1951 of Francisco Jordá as head of the provincial Archeological Research Service and with the holding of the V International Quaternary Association Congress in Asturias in 1957 (Hernández-Pacheco et al. 1957). Jordá published his thesis on the Spanish Solutrean in Oviedo in 1955. In 1956, he excavated the Magdalenian site of La Lloseta (now known to be the same site as "El Río," dug by Hernández-Pacheco) in eastern Asturias. The slim, conventional monograph on La Lloseta (Jordá 1958), with no natural science studies, was the only one Jordá published on his many excavations in Asturias throughout the course of the 1950s and 1960s. However he did produce many important syntheses of the Upper Paleolithic art and archeology and, having become Professor of Prehistory at the prestigious University of Salamanca in the late 1960s, trained several students who would become major figures in present-day Paleolithic research in Asturias.

The 1950s witnessed a miniature explosion of major cave art discoveries, all due to the systematic efforts of Alfredo Garcia Lorenzo of Santander, who found the sanctuaries of Las Monedas and Las Chimeneas (adjacent to El Castillo and La Pasiega) and (with González Echegaray) La Cullalvera (Madariaga 1975). Cave art, still rare in the Basque Country, was discovered at Altxerri and Ekain in Guipúzcoa in 1963 and 1969, respectively (Altuna and Apellániz 1976, 1978).

Modern Research

The 1968–1969 excavations in Cueva Morín near the city of Santander marked a significant milestone in the history of Paleolithic research in the Cantabrian region. With financial support from the Ford Foundation and the National Science Foundation, the close collaboration of González Echegaray and Freeman accomplished meticulous, large-scale excavations. The collaboration of numerous natural scientists (including Altuna, Leroi-Gourhan, and Karl Butzer) produced thorough faunal and paleo-environmental analyses and a radiocarbon record, all essentially unprecedented in the whole region. The collaboration was a marriage of necessary Old World concerns for stratigraphy and typology with a New World ecological focus on reconstructing prehistoric adaptations and a concern for archeological explanation approached through multivariate statistical analyses.

Besides providing spectacular discoveries (i.e., Aurignacian burials and structures; a possible Mousterian structure) and a sequence spanning the Middle and most of the Upper Paleolithic (including the rare transitional "Chatelperronian" period), Morín was a training school for many members of the next generation of American and Spanish Paleolithic prehistorians and a model of multidisciplinary and interdisciplinary research. And it was rapidly and fully published (González Echegaray and Freeman 1971, 1973, 1978). The series of doctoral dissertations and of major excavations done by Spaniards and Americans in the past 20 years, whose publications are cited in the introduction of this book, represent the healthy dialectic between the traditional but valid concerns for description and classification and the processual perspectives on archeological explanation and on cultural evolution produced by the "archeological revolution" in the late 1960s in the United States. The dissertations of the late 1960s to the 1980s were essential exercises in pattern recognition, whether from a normative or from an adaptationist perspective.

The successors of the Cueva Morín project have been a series of multidisciplinary and interdisciplinary research projects all more or less focused on going beyond individual site stratigraphies to contextual studies of sites in regions. This reorientation of research has been accomplished by the steady increase in the use of radiocarbon dating of deposits and assemblages (at least from Upper Paleolithic and more recent times), thus freeing artifacts to be interpreted functionally rather than strictly as temporal markers. It has also been accomplished by the much increased emphasis on thorough faunal analysis, with its potentials for determining not only diet but also subsistence strategies and tactics, seasonality, and human mobility patterns. This has been the product of the analyses of mammalian remains by Jesus Altuna and his associates Koro Mariezkurrena and Pedro Castaños and by Richard Klein—together with syntheses and hypotheses put forward by Freeman, Bailey, Clark, and Straus.

The malacological studies by Madariaga and Ortea have also had an important effect in showing what can be learned, beyond species lists, from molluscan archeofaunas. And, whether explicitly or implicitly, the increased number and sophistication of paleo-environmental interpretations in the Cantabrian region (from sedimentology and palynology) have forced even fairly traditional prehistorians to ask questions about human adaptations. This has been largely the work of Butzer, Mary, Laville, Hoyos, Leroi-Gourhan, Boyer-Klein, and Dupré.

In addition, questions asked by Freeman (1978d), Conkey 1978, 1980), and others, about the roles or "purposes" of Paleolithic art have helped lead local specialists to think more about the art in archeological context rather than as a separate phenomenon. In fact, throughout the course of the late 1960s to the 1980s, many discoveries of rupestral art were made and many of these were in caves that were either already known to be or were later determined to be Upper Paleolithic habitation sites. Such newly found art-plus-habitation caves include La Riera, Balmori,

El Otero, La Viña, La Lluera, Tito Bustillo, Coimbre, Los Canes, Chufín, Ekain, Arenaza, and El Juyo. Many other cave art discoveries were also made in the past two decades, with a definite renaissance of systematic prospection particularly in the last few years. Future testing may also reveal the existence of archeological deposits in at least some of these sites (see summaries of discoveries in González Echegaray 1978; Garcia Castro 1987; ACDPS 1986; Fortea 1981; Arias et al. 1981).

Prehistoric archeological research in the Cantabrian region has been greatly enhanced in recent years and given continuity with the strengthening of old institutions such as the Sociedad de Ciencias Aranzadi in San Sebastián, the Museo Histórico de Vizcaya in Bilbao, the Museo Arqueológico de Alava in Gasteiz, and the Department of Prehistory and Archeology of the University of Oviedo and with the creation of new institutions such as the Departments of Prehistory and Archeology at universities in the Basque Country in Gasteiz, in Deusto in Bilbao, and in Cantabria in Santander, the Centro de Investigación y Museo de Altamira in Santillana, and the Instituto de Investigaciones Prehistóricas in Santander and Chicago. The days of the solitary researcher are quickly fading, as all archeological research is now of a multidisciplinary, collaborative nature, requiring adequate funding and infrastructure. These finally are becoming available in the reorganized, federated, modernized Kingdom of Spain.

The 1970s and 1980s have seen two kinds of major Paleolithic research projects in the Cantabrian region: 1) excavations of *single* sites that also are important cave art sanctuaries (Tito Bustillo [Moure 1975, 1989; Moure and Cano 1976]; Chufín [Almagro et al. 1977; Cabrera 1977]; El Castillo [re-excavation of remnant stratigraphy under way—see Cabrera and Bischoff 1989]; Berroberría-Alkerdi [I. Barandiarán 1979]; and 2) broader projects. The latter have a regional focus, either by the kinds of analyses and interpretations done (e.g., The La Riera Paleoecological Project [Straus and Clark 1986]), or because several temporally and geographically related sites have been excavated and studied together by a team (e.g., The Guipúzcoa Paleolithic Project; Ekain [Altuna and Merino 1984], Erralla [Altuna et al. 1985], Amalda [Altuna et al. 1990] and Aitzbitarte III [Altuna 1987]; the Central Santander Magdalenian Project: El Rascaño [González Echegary and Barandiarán 1981], El Juyo [Barandiarán et al. 1985] and Altamira [re-excavation of remnant deposits—see Freeman 1988]; the Middle Rio Nalón Project [Fortea 1981, 1983; González Morales 1989; Fortea et al. 1990]). These and other recent, modern-quality projects such as the Azilian excavations at Los Azules (Fernández-Tresguerres 1980, 1983), Arenaza (Apellániz and Altuna 1975) and El Piélago (Garcia Guinea 1985), provide the principal empirical bases for the synthetic interpretations presented in the remainder of this book. And because excavations and analyses are ongoing in all parts of the Cantabrian region (including a renaissance of Paleolithic research in Vizcaya, with work by Apellániz and his students in Arenaza, Laminak, Lumentxa, Santa Catalina, and Kurtzia), many of my conclusions are inevitably provisional and subject to revision in the future.

Chapter 3

THE LAST INTERGLACIAL AND EARLY LAST GLACIAL (OXYGEN ISOTOPE STAGES 5, 4, AND EARLY 3):
The Lower and Middle Paleolithic

ARCHEOLOGICAL evidence of late Middle and early Upper Pleistocene occupation of the Cantabrian region is relatively scarce, poorly dated, and poorly contextualized. The Acheulean is particularly rare and poorly known, especially in comparison with the rich record of Lower Paleolithic sites in eastern, southern, and central Spain and in Portugal (Freeman 1975; Santonja and Villa 1990; Villa 1990). With the exception of the basal deposit in El Castillo cave, supposed Acheulean finds in the Cantabrian region are restricted mainly to isolated surface occurrences (some of which actually may date to the Mousterian which, in this region, is known for its bifaces and especially cleaver flakes) and a few possible open-air sites (Figure 3.1). The situation for the Mousterian (Middle Paleolithic) is somewhat better, notably because assemblages from stratified cave contexts are known (and well studied)—from El Conde (Asturias), El Castillo, El Pendo, and Morin (Santander), Axlor (Vizcaya), Lezetxiki and Amalda (Guipúzcoa)—as well as from Olha and Isturitz in the adjacent French Basque country together with other caves and a number of open-air localities. However, the Mousterian too is poorly dated and has few paleo-environmental indicators, making it much more difficult to interpret than the subsequent Upper Paleolithic. On the other hand, faunal analyses by Altuna (summarized in 1989) and interpretations by Freeman (1973b, 1981) and Straus (1977b, 1982) now provide a fairly large amount of information about the subsistence activities of Middle Paleolithic hominids (and contemporary carnivores) in the Cantabrian region.

A basic chronological framework for the major culture-stratigraphic units in Cantabrian Spain is given in Table 3.1. The dates are approxi-

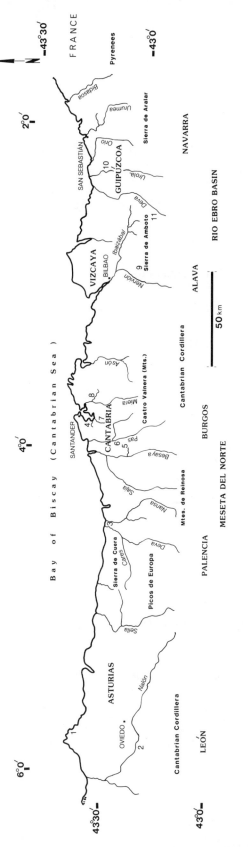

FIGURE 3.1. *Distribution of Acheulean and Mousterian sites. 1, Bañugues; 2, El Conde; 3, Unquera; 4, El Pendo, Cobalejos, El Ruso; 5, Hornos de la Peña; 6, El Castillo, La Flecha; 7, Morín; 8, Fuente del Francés; 9, Axlor; 10, Amalda; 11, Lezetxiti. (Bañugues is Acheulean; Castillo is Acheulean and Mousterian; all other sites are Mousterian.)*

Table 3.1 Simplified Chronological Framework for
Stone Age Cantabrian Spain

Approximate radiocarbon age (10^3 yr B.P.)	Traditional culture–stratigraphic units
	Pastoral Neolithic
6	
	Asturian or Geometric Mesolithic
9	
	Azilian
11	
	Late Magdalenian
13.5	
	Early Magdalenian
16.5	
	Solutrean
20.5	
	Gravettian
27	
	Aurignacian
	Chatelperronian
40	
	Mousterian
90*	
	Acheulean

*Uranium-series date.

mations, and there is considerable overlap between adjacent pairs of
traditional cultural periods.

The Acheulean of El Castillo

It is becoming increasingly clear from recently excavated and dated sites
in France (e.g., Biache, Vaufrey) that the archeological taxonomic units
"Acheulean" and "Mousterian" intergrade arbitrarily and that assemblages of "Mousterian" appearance can date not only to the Last Interglacial (128,000–118,000 B.P.) but also to the so-called "Riss Glacial"
(oxygen isotope stage 6 and before). This makes it difficult to support
an *absolute* distinction between the two culture-stratigraphic units or,
indeed, even to confirm the existence of a "classic" Acheulean in Canta-

FIGURE 3.2. *Monte Castillo in Puente Viesgo, Santander, showing locations of the caves of El Castillo, La Pasiega, Las Chimeneas, and Las Monedas (along the mountain face road).*

brian Spain where, as Butzer (1981:166) has noted, rough bifaces had been made not only in the Mousterian but also in the Upper Paleolithic and Mesolithic. Even the excavators Obermaier and Breuil had doubts about attribution of these basal assemblages. On the basis of a recently acquired chronometric date, one can now be fairly confident that the basal levels at El Castillo antedate the Last Glacial, as argued below.

Nonetheless, many assemblages of the undoubtedly Cantabrian Mousterian (of early-mid Last Glacial age) are characterized by the presence of cleaver flakes, with few true bifaces (Freeman 1971, 1973, 1980; Cabrera 1983). The rare Mousterian bifaces are not of forms characterized of the "Acheulean" (viz., amygdaloid, bottle-shaped, etc.) and are always small. The cleaver flakes, probably linked to the utilization of specific nonflint lithic raw materials such as ophite, are minimally and unifacially retouched. Other assemblages, demonstrably older than the classic Mousterian in the Castillo stratigraphy (and *presumably* also older in other contexts), have many true bifaces, some rather large and with classic Acheulean shapes. Cleaver flakes may be present but rare (one at Castillo, versus thirteen bifaces [Cabrera 1984]). If anything, these bifaces may be a useful, albeit arbitrary and imprecise, temporal marker. On the basis of the presence of classic bifaces, one can hypothesize that the basal levels at El Castillo may be labeled "Acheulean" for convenience sake; and they may antedate the Last Glacial, as argued below. By analogy, other true biface-rich assemblages and isolated finds of classic bifaces may be considered "Acheulean" by definition (*pace* Butzer 1981). The unresolved question is the significance of the disappearance of large "Acheulean"-type bifaces near the beginning of the Last Glacial.

Following Cabrera's (1984:109–139) nomenclature and description, there are four levels at El Castillo below the oldest, undoubted Mousterian, level: Levels 26–23 (Figure 3.3). Level 26 actually is a complex of levels totaling about 0.75 m in thickness and containing both a lithic assemblages and a faunal assemblage, the latter apparently dominated by cave bear (*Ursus spelaeus*) together with some red deer (*Cervus elaphus*), horse (*Equus caballus*), bovines (*Bos/Bison*), ibex (*Capra pyrenaica*), lion (*Panthera leo* [?]), leopard (*Panthera pardus*), fallow deer (*Dama dama*), and reindeer (*Rangifer tarandus*). (The last two identifications are problematical; the correct modern scientific names are given here.) The lithic assemblage (of which Cabrera could only find 55 surviving artifacts—of which 19 are retouched tools) was dominated by quartzite flakes, followed by indurated limestone flakes and a few quartz and flint pieces. In Cabrera's sample there are six sidescrapers, five denticulates/notches, two naturally backed knives, and one chopper, chopping tool, partial biface, and discoid each—mostly made on quartzite, followed by limestone. The excavators noted the presence of charcoal in Level 26.

Level 25b groups a number of units defined by varying depths during the 1913 and 1914 seasons of excavations at El Castillo, basically making up a unit about 30 cm thick. Again, the industry described in notes by Obermaier is dominated by quartzite and limestone flakes, plus flake tools and a few heavy-duty tools of the same materials. Cabrera found and classified 117 artifacts, including 1 Levallois flake and point, 6 sidescrapers, 8 backed knives, 24 denticulates/notches/Tayac point, and 2 choppers, bifaces and discoids each—also mostly in quartzite, followed by limestone and flint. The Level 25b fauna, as compiled from notes by Cabrera, include cave bear, wolf (*Canis lupus*) and/or dhole (*Cuon alpinus*), bovines, red deer, rhinoceros (*Dicerorhinus*), horse, and chamois (*Rupicapra rupicapra*).

Level 25a was about 20 to 25 cm thick and was characterized, at least in part, as "stony." Again, quartzite flakes were said to dominate the

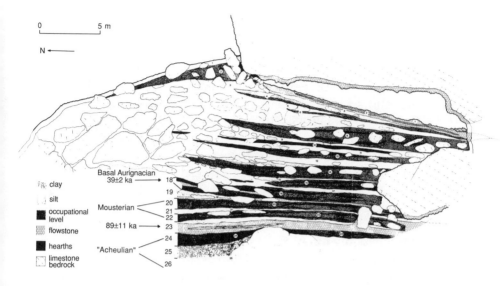

0   5 m

N ◄──────

clay
silt
occupational level
flowstone
hearths
limestone bedrock

Basal Aurignacian 39±2 ka ──► 18

Mousterian

89±11 ka ──► 23

"Acheulian"

19
20
21
22
24
25
26

FIGURE 3.3. *Transversal stratigraphic section of El Castillo Cave Vestibule Infilling (Obermaier Excavation: 1910–1914). Stratigraphy according to Cabrera (1984): Levels 26–24, Acheulean; 23–20, Mousterian; 19–16, Aurignacian; 15–12, Gravettian; 11–10, Solutrean; 9–6, Magdalenian; 5–4, Azilian; 3–1, Bronze Age. (From Bischoff et al. 1991.)*

lithic assemblage, followed by limestone artifacts and a few quartz and ophite ones. Cabrera counted a total of only 111 pieces, almost half of which are tools including 3 Levallois flakes/points, 20 sidescrapers, 13 denticulates/notches, 1 chopper, and 4 bifaces. One of the bifaces is a large, subtriangular type, not common in the regional Mousterian. In this level, the surviving flake *tools* are equally divided between quartzite and flint; the heavy-duty tools are divided between quartzite and limestone. The fauna from this level was the same as in Level 25b plus marmot (*Marmota marmota*). The Level 25 fauna is notable for the variety of large carnivores (felids and canids) as well as for the abundance of cave bear remains.

Cabrera's Level 24 is what the excavators called the Acheulean (or "Micoquian") level *per se*, 10 cm thick (in the center of the vestibule) to 30 cm thick (toward the cave mouth). This silty deposit included many reddened blocks and areas of burning as well as abundant ochre and faunal remains, according to the excavators' notes. Although quartzite continued to dominate the lithic assemblage, flint was a close second, followed by limestone, quartz, and ophite. Cabrera found only 146 artifacts in the museum collections, fewer than half the number counted by Obermaier. Among the tools are 19 Levallois points/flakes, 24 side-scrapers, 18 denticulates/notches, 7 bifaces, and 1 chopper, chopping tool, and cleaver each. One of the bifaces is a large amygdaloid piece typical of the Acheulean but rare in the Mousterian of Acheulean Tradition. Flint dominates these flake tools; the cleaver is ophite; all of the bifaces are quartzite and both the chopper and the chopping tool are limestone. Cabrera (1984: Fig. 35.4) illustrate one excellent prismatic blade from this level.

The fauna is like that of the underlying levels but with fewer cave bear remains, more rhinoceros (including several young individuals), and the addition of scarce remains of *Hyaena spelaea* and one femur fragment of elephant (*Elephas* sp.). There is a problematical citation of fallow deer. According to Vaufrey's analysis (cited by Cabrera 1984:135), the bovines (possibly bison) had a mininum of 19 individuals and the red deer, 29—not surprising for a stratum of fairly great thickness excavated over large area. This probably is a major "palimpsest" of many occupations of the cave by both hominids and carnivores (cave bear, wolf, and hyena).

Above Level 24 was an archeologically sterile layer that was subdivided by Cabrera (1984:142) into Level 23c (a level with cave bear remains), Level 23b (a flowstone deposit with weathered cave bear bones), and Level 23a (a phosphatic breccia with cave bear and hyena remains). These levels correspond to Butzer's (1981:162–168) units 5e–a, which, on the basis of his sedimentological analyses, he ascribed to warm conditions with cooling at the top of the series. The underlying main Acheulean level (Obermaier's [1924: 164] Level b; Cabrera's Level 24; Butzer's unit 4) was, according to Butzer (1981), formed under generally cool to cold conditions with a very cold climate at the time of the deposition of a layer of eboulis (spall). The abundant rhinoceros remains in Level 24, originally classified as *"Rhinoceros mercki"* (= *Dicerorhinus kirchbergensis*), are now considered to pertain to *D. hemitoechus*, a related form that was more adapted to open, grassland conditions than to wooded ones—implying a relatively cold climate in the Cantabrian region at the time (Butzer 1981; Altuna 1972).

Below Level 24, Butzer found evidence of warmer episodes corresponding to Obermaier's basal clay and Cabrera's Levels 25 and 26. Butzer [1981:73] hypothesized that the flowstone (Level 23) was formed during one of the warm phases of the Early last Glacial (O.I. stage 5c or, according to Butzer's [1981:73] hypothesis, 5a). This interpretation finds support in a recent long-count uranium-series date of the travertine near the base of Level 23: 89,000 + 11,000/ − 10,000 B.P. (Bischoff et al. 1991). If there are no depositional hiati, the cold conditions of Level 24 could pertain to a cold interval at the beginning of the Last Glacial (O.I. Stage 5d or, more likely, 5b). Level 25a could also pertain to the cold conditions of O.I. Stage 5b, Level 25b to O.I. Stage 5d, and Level 26 to O.I. Stage 5e—the Last Interglacial *sensu stricto*. Thus, Castillo would have no deposits pertaining to the Penultimate Glacial (= "Riss III" = O.I. Stage 6). Other than Freeman's (1975:716–718) conclusion that the artifacts from these levels are quite crude and unlike those of the regional Mousterian of Acheulean Tradition, there are a few arguments for a "long" chronology at El Castillo, despite Butzer's reticence.

An earlier sedimentological analysis of the basal Castillo deposits and correlations to neighboring river terraces by Fernández Gutierrez (1969) led to the conclusion that the alternation of warm and cold climates below the Mousterian antedates the Last Glacial. The marmot remains in Levels 24 and 25a, an indicator of cold climate, are of a morphologically primitive form (sometimes called *M. primigenia*) and were judged by Chaline (1966:419) to be "among the oldest in Europe (Riss?)." But these arguments seem to be superseded by the new uranium-series date.

Little can be said about the lithic industries other than to note the heavy use of local quartzite and even limestone (and ophite), especially for large tools such as choppers and bifaces. As will be shown later, El Castillo is located in central Santander at a point where the bedrock lithology changes from the ubiquitous Cretaceous limestone with the abundant good flint of the Basque Country and eastern Santander to a more complex situation with Carboniferous (as well as some Jurassic and Cretaceous) limestones bearing small nodules often of rather poor-quality flint and bands of quartzite together with volcanic outcrops of ophite. Both nodule size and stone toughness (resistance to shattering) may have led the Acheulean (and Mousterian) inhabitants of Santander and Asturias to use these materials (and hard limestone itself) for such heavy-duty tools. The small size and poor quality of locally available flints also are factors in the apparently very low use of the Levallois technique (Levallois typological index = 1.4% for Levels 24–26 and 5.5% and 2.2%, respectively, for Mousterian Levels 22 and 20 [Freeman 1975]). There is no evidence of utilization of nonlocal lithic raw materials, and there are no marine mollusks, despite the relatively short distance, 20 or 25 km, to the interglacial or glacial coast, respectively. Little else can be said about the nature of Acheulean adaptations, given the extant data base from the Obermaier excavation in El Castillo.

Simple fires seem to have been made, and red ochre possibly was used (although it could be naturally occurring in the cave, given the iron-rich limestones of the area, because Obermaier does not mention any fashioning of the pieces he found). Although hominids could have acquired some of the game by simple hunting, it is also very possible that they scavenged, particularly the larger forms. A proboscidian is represented by only one bone fragment, but the rhinos are represented fairly abundantly; unfortunately anatomical element data are not available. The cave seems to have been used mostly by a number of large carnivores before and after hominid occupation, so many of the ungulate remains may have been brought in by them rather than by hominids, a situation like that of several of the Mousterian deposits in the Cantabrian region (see Straus 1982a).

Bañugues and Other Possible Acheulean Occurrences

The only other significant stratified find of materials attributable to the Acheulean is on the central Asturias coast at Bañugues on the northeastern side of Cabo de Peñas. Studied by Rodríguez and Flor (1979, 1983), Rodríguez (1978, 1983), and by M. Hoyos (in Jordá 1977:20–21), this site on the littoral of an estuary has a 2.6-m section exposed by wave action. Denticulates, notches, "knives," flakes, a biface, a cleaver, a sidescraper, a chopper, and a spheroid (almost all quartzite), like those originally found eroding onto the beach surface, were recovered in an excavation from two brecciated sandy gravel deposits atop bioturbated clays of Aptian (Cretaceous) age.

The two breccias with industrial remains (but no fauna) are separated by a 20-cm layer of light-brown sandy silt. The breccias are interpreted as cold-climate phenomena, the results of solifluxion. They are followed by a marine (estuarine) transgression that deposited a layer of clayey silt (also with a few artifacts of Lower Paleolithic typology). This in turn is capped by aeolian clayey silts thought to date to the early Last Glacial and then by more recent aeolian, colluvial, and beach sediments. Near the top is the source of Asturian (Mesolithic) picks, frequently mistaken for Lower Paleolithic artifacts. The cold conditions under which the artifact-bearing breccias were formed (solifluxion, cryoturbation) were very tentatively assigned by Rodríguez and Flor to what, with modern terminology, would be called O.I. Stage 5d, 5b, or 4. It is not clear if the artifacts could have been derived from significantly older shoreside deposits (viz., Last Interglacial, O.I. Stage 5e). There seems to be little basis for making any particular chronological placement other than the aspect of the stone tools, of which some are said to have been produced by the soft hammer technique, implying an "Upper Acheulean" at the oldest.

Rodríguez (1983) reported on a large number of other finds of bifaces, cleavers, choppers, and other pebble tools, both in similar (but generally unstratified) coastal contexts and on river terraces throughout Asturias. Similar finds are fairly common in these types of settings in Santander (Freeman 1975:715), and isolated objects assigned typologically (and thus problematically) to the Lower Paleolithic have been found in river terrace deposits in Alava and in marine terrace contexts in the French Basque Country (Baldeón 1990a).

Butzer (1981:177) argued that by Middle Pleistocene times at least the Santander caves he studied had already been long open and that, perhaps repeatedly, they had been infilled and cleared of sediments by erosion. Any Middle Pleistocene Acheulean materials in such caves thus would have been lost. If any of the widespread surface occurrences do indeed date to before the Last Glacial, they would indicate a low-density hominid population (possibly of unspecialized foragers) in the Cantabrian region, perhaps living under both temperate and glacial conditions with simple use of fire and a generalized, multi-purpose lithic (and no doubt wooden) technology based on utilization of readily available local materials. However, at this time we have no further data nor any way of ascertaining the time of earliest hominid occupation of the region. This was nonetheless likely to have been in the middle or late Middle Pleistocene, by analogy with sites in Castile (Aridos, Torralba, Ambrona, La Maya, etc. [see Santonja and Villa 1990]). In the cave of Atapuerca, 110 km south of El Castillo, in Burgos, several homonid fossils (mostly cranial and mandibular fragments) have been found in loose association with Acheulean artifacts preliminarily assigned by uranium-series dating to ≥300,000 B.C. (Aguirre et al. 1989).

There is no indication of any abrupt break in technology, settlement, or subsistence between the "Acheulean" and the "Mousterian" (Figure 3.4). However, the lack of dates does not permit us to assert complete continuity in human occupation of the Cantabrian region throughout and between these periods.

Chronostratigraphy of the Mousterian

The only data available on early Last Glacial (O.I. Stages 5d–a[?] and 4) chronostratigraphy and paleo-environments in the Cantabrian region come from Butzer's (1971, 1973, 1980, 1981) analyses of fairly long stratigraphic sequences of sediments associated with Mousterian artifacts in the central Santander caves of El Castillo, Morín, and El Pendo. In addition, Butzer attempted to fit short sequences with Mousterian artifacts from the nearby caves of La Flecha, Hornos de la Peña, and Cobalejos into the overall scheme based on the first three sites, but this is a tenu-

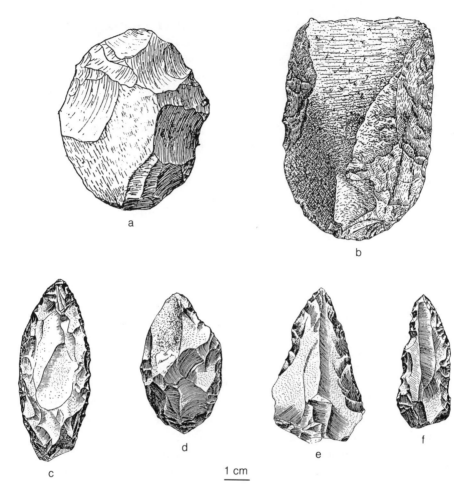

FIGURE 3.4. *Acheulean and Mousterian artifacts: a, Acheulean oval partial biface from El Castillo; b, Mousterian cleaver flake from Cueva Morín; c–f, Mousterian sidescrapers, "point," and denticulate from El Castillo. (a, c–f, from Obermaier 1924; b from Vega del Sella 1921.)*

ous procedure, particularly in the absence of any radiometric dates. There are no pollen analyses for this time period and no precise temporally diagnostic faunal forms.

The situation improves somewhat in the latter part of the Interpleniglacial (O.I. Stage 3). There are available pollen spectra from the terminal Mousterian levels in Cuevas Morín and Otero (Santander) (Leroi-Gourhan 1966, 1971) as well as stratigraphically isolated spectra, probably of similar age (also with Mousterian assemblages), from El Pendo (Leroi-Gourhan 1980) and Amalda (Guipúzcoa) (Dupré 1990). And there are *terminus ante quem* dates for the late Mousterian provided by radiocarbon dates: on charcoal from the basal Aurignacian level at Castillo (40,000, 38,500, and 37,700 B.P., all ± 2,000 years [Cabrera and Bischoff 1989]); on charcoal from the Chatelperronian level at Morín (36,000 ± 7,000 B.P. [Stuckenrath 1978]); on bone from right below a possible Chatelperronian level at Ekain (30,000 B.P. [Altuna 1984]); and on travertines apparently overlying the Mousterian in both El Castillo and La Flecha (31,500 ± 1,000 B.P. [Butzer 1981]). In neighboring Burgos south of Santander, the uppermost Mousterian level in Cueva Millán dates to 37,000 ± 700 B.P. (Moure and Garcia 1983). At Peña Miel Cave in La Rioja (south of Alava) the uppermost Mousterian level (C) dates to 39,900 ± 1,500 B.P. and the middle level (E), to 45,000 + 1,400/ − 1,200 B.P.; the lowest level (G) gave an infinite reading of >40,000 B.P. (Utrilla 1986; Baldellou and Utrilla 1985).

It is as yet unresolved as to whether the earliest Cantabrian Mousterian dates back to O.I. Stages 5a–d (or older) as Butzer (1981) argued. A sedimentological analysis of the deep infilling of Lezetxiki Cave (Guipúzcoa) by Kornprobst and Rat (1967) revealed the existence of a number of oscillations in temperature and humidity. A major warm, wet phase at the base of the sequence (Level VIII: clay with travertine and phosphates) was tentatively assigned, by extrapolation from their work, to the "Riss-Würm Interglacial" (Altuna 1972:1388). The overlying Mousterian levels (VII–IV) were assigned to the classic French Würm I and II stages. It would be possible to read the curves of Kornprobst and Rat as representing O.I. Stages 5e to 3 for the Mousterian and pre-Mousterian levels.

Recent uranium-series dates (done on bone by Y. Yokoyama) of about 300,000 B.P. for Level VII and 200,000 B.P. for Level VI (Altuna 1990c:230) need to be confirmed before being taken into serious consideration. A date of 70,000 ± 9,000 B.P. for Level V does make sense for O.I. Stage 4 (however, there is another date, 186,000 + 164,000/ − 61,000 B.P. for the same level!). Altuna (1990c) noted that Levels VIII and VII yielded remains of *Ursus deningeri*, an ancestral form of cave bear that elsewhere in Europe evolved into *U. spelaeus* in or before O.I. Stage 6, a fact that might support the early uranium-series dates, as does the presence of an archaic form of *Equus (ferus) caballus* in Level VI (Altuna 1972, 1990c). The presence of *Dicerorhinus kirchbergensis* (true Merck's rhinoceros) in Level VIII is an indicator of temperate, wooded conditions, supportive of an interglacial climate. In any event, any hypothetical chronological ordering of the Mousterian for the Cantabrian region as a whole, or for just the Basque country (as attempted by Baldeón 1990b), is highly risky at this point.

Paleo-environmental Evidence for the Early Last Glacial

The chronological issue is partially semantic: the supposed "distinction" between Upper Acheulean and Mousterian. Aside from this, it is clear that a significant portion of the Mousterian occurred during the course of O.I. Stage 4, beyond the rage of radiocarbon dating. Butzer (1981) characterized the onset of this phase as "glacial": cold with increasing aridity. There is abundant evidence of congelifraction with the deposition of considerable spall in the caves. Succeeding O.I. Stage 3 is even more abundantly represented by Mousterian-bearing deposits. Butzer (1981:176) characterized this as a period of cool, frequently wet conditions with slope soil instability and winters like those of Iceland today.

The pollen spectra support the existence of open pine woodlands during the late Mousterian. At Morín, a pollen sample (with a very small *n*) from Level 12 (the penultimate Mousterian layer) has an arboreal pollen (AP) fraction of 50%, almost exclusively pine pollens (with a few hazel and oak pollens). Pollens of Gramineae and fern spores are abundant, suggesting relatively humid conditions. Leroi-Gourhan (1971) Leroi-Gourhan and Renault-Miskovsky (1977) assigned this spectrum to the second part of the Hengelo interstadial, with an age estimated at around 37,000 to 38,000 B.P. At nearby El Pendo, the stratigraphically isolated, simplified, but statistically valid pollen diagram from the penultimate Mousterian level (IX) gives the same picture as that of Morín: AP = 50% (almost all pine, with traces of hazel and oak). Graminineae and Cichoriae are equally represented here, and there are some fern spores (Leroi-Gourhan 1980).

At El Otero in eastern Santander, the terminal Mousterian (represented by two samples), has the "least-cold" spectra of the entire cave sequence (the rest being Upper Paleolithic). The AP values are low (but the samples are very large) and are dominated almost completely by pine with small numbers of birch followed by traces of juniper, hazel, and alder. In contrast to Morín and El Pendo, Cichoriae outnumber Gramineae, and fern spores are only moderately represented (Leroi-Gourhan 1966).

Further east, in Amalda Cave, there are three stratigraphically isolated pollen samples (of small to moderate size) from the unique Mousterian level (VII) which is separated from the overlying Gravettian layer (27,400 B.P.) by a depositional hiatus. The Mousterian pollen samples have among the highest AP fractions of the site sequence but are composed again almost exclusively of pine (one has a trace of oak). Fern spores are abundant (Dupré 1990). Sedimentologically, this level is characterized as relatively cold and humid (Areso et al. 1990), but its age is unknown despite Baldeón's (1990) placement of it early.

Pollen analyses of Levels VI and Va in Lezetxiki, associated with "Mousterian" artifacts, yield high AP values, including thermophile taxa. Level VIb shows a sharp decline in trees (Sánchez 1991). In combination with the new Th/U and ESR dates, these results could suggest a Late Middle Pleistocene age and the existence of "Mousterian" culture under temperate conditions.

The general picture painted by the paleo-environmental analyses is of a rather severely cold and often relatively dry condition in the early Mousterian at O.I. Stage 4 (Lower Pleniglacial), followed by a somewhat more temperate, but by no means warm, especially humid, and fluctuating O.I. Stage 3 (Interpleniglacial). At best, the vegetation could be characterized by open pine woods with isolated oak, hazel, and birch trees or groves in sheltered microhabitats (such as south-facing slopes away from the open coast). North-facing and higher or steeper slopes may have been denuded and frequently unstable geomorphologically. Much of the landscape of the coastal plain and river valley floors would have been covered by grasses—rich pasture for herds of bison, red deer, and, especially in the drier times, horses and rhinos.

Macromammalian faunas provide further data on Middle Paleolithic environments. Aside from the Merck rhino underlying the oldest Mousterian level at Lezetxiki, there are remains of the same species (*Dicerorhinus kirchbergensis*) in Levels VII, VI, and IVa, but there also may be elements of the more open grassland species, *D. hemitoechus*. Reindeer is present in Level IV and marmot, another indicator of cold climate, was found there and in Level VI + V. Reindeer was found in Levels IV and III of Axlor, but Amalda Level VII lacked specific cold-indicator species (Altuna 1990c). Reindeer is absent at all other known Mousterian levels in the Cantabrian region; however, *D. hemitoechus* has been identified (at least tentatively in some cases) in Levels 22 and 17 at Morín, in Mousterian Levels Beta and Alpha at El Castillo, and in the Mousterian at Cobalejos (a site near El Pendo in Santander) (Altuna 1971, 1973). Also, there is an old identification of the woolly rhino (*Coelodonta antiquitatis*) at the open-air Mousterian site of Unquera in western Santander (Altuna 1972). This is not the only citation of this extreme cold-adapted, steppe tundra-dwelling rhino in the Cantabrian region, but it is rare and the others are either undated paleontological finds or Upper Paleolithic finds at Lezetxiki (as well as Mousterian ones at Olha and Isturitz in the French Basque Country and Upper Paleolithic ones at the latter site). The relative abundance of bison and horse in the Mousterian will be commented on later.

Mousterian Settlement

Mousterian sites are rare. This fact may be only partly due to destruction by erosion or invisibility caused by deep burial. Excavations in several sites have encountered sterile basal clays below the Upper Paleolithic
levels, and then bedrock. On the other hand, two fairly definite open-
air Mousterian sites have been found so far (Kurtzia in Vizcaya and
Unquera in Santander), and there have been many surface finds of isolated artifacts or small "assemblages" that typologically resemble the
Mousterian, despite steep gradients, high rainfall, and swift rivers. The
fact that more than a century of prospection and excavation in the
Cantabrian region has not revealed more Mousterian sites suggests that
the number is, and was, truly small, even if some (particularly open-air
sites) may have been destroyed. Most of the Mousterian sites known at
present in Asturias and Santander are the same ones that were known
by about 1914, despite intensive research since the 1950s. One new site,
El Ruso Cave near El Pendo, had sidescrapers and cleavers but was looted
before it could be studied (Gavelas 1986).

   In Asturias there is only one definite Mousterian site: la Cueva del
Conde, located on a tributary of the broad, low Río Nalón valley in the
interior of the central part of the province, about 30 km from the present shore and about 10 km north of the first Cordilleran mountain ranges.
Western Santander has only the isolated (now apparently destroyed) open-
air site of Unquera, revealed by a railroad trench near the present shore
in the beginning of this century. Most of the Mousterian sites (all are
caves) of the Cantabrian region are in central Santander, in the drainages
of Ríos Besaya, Pas, and Miera/Bay of Santander: El Pendo, Cobalejos,
Fuente del Francés, and Cueva Morín on or at the southern edge of the
broad coastal plain (which is relatively broad [10–12 km] in this sector);
and Hornos de la Peña, El Castillo, and La Flecha on hillsides at relatively low elevations (280 and 190 m for the Monte Castillo caves), dominating broad river valleys in the interior, about 10 km from the edge of
the Cordillera but not far from the coastal zone. El Otero Cave, in eastern Santander, is on the low coastal plain, close to the present shore at
the Río Asón estuary.

   Westernmost of the Basque country sites, Kurtzia is a multi-component open-air site (apparently a flint source/workshop) near the shore,
on the relatively broad, low coastal platform near Bilbao, whereas Axlor
Cave is on the southern edge of the low Ibaizabal valley—the only broad
interior valley of Vizcaya, also near Bilbao. Amalda is in low hills at 205
m above the present sea level, within 7 km of the shore, in a tributary
valley of Río Urola. Of all the Mousterian sites, only Lezetxiki is really

in mountainous terrain, albeit at only 375 m above sea level and only 20 m above the valley floor of a tributary of Río Deva in Guipúzcoa (Altuna 1972:133). At 30 km, it is not much farther from the present coast than El Castillo, La Flecha, or Hornos de la Peña.

The Basque sites form a geographically less-clustered ensemble than the central Santander sites: the distance from Kurtzia in the west to Amalda in the east is 60 km, whereas the maximum distance in the Santander group—between Hornos and Fuente del Francés—is only half that. Between the Basque sites and those of central Santander is only El Otero. It is about 60 km from Fuente del Francés to Kurtzia, and between El Otero and Kurtzia, steep, high mountains plunge directly into the sea. There is no coastal plain in the border area between Santander and Vizcaya. Unquera and El Conde, the western sites, are, at least at present, quite isolated, although some of the surface finds of bifaces and cleaver flakes in Asturias might date to the Mousterian time range rather than to the Acheulean (?).

The observation by Freeman (1973b:39) that the Mousterian sites are located more or less centrally, relative to the coast (especially to the *glacial-age* coast) and to the Cordillera, is generally valid, although the sample size is quite small and Lezetxiki is in a more mountainous context than the Santander sites he analyzed. There are no Mousterian sites on steep cliffs. Sites seem to have been placed primarily in order to exploit the resources of the coastal plain or of fairly broad interior valleys, with no suggestion of specialization. The sites seem to be camps from which foraging was conducted in limited, favored parts of the Cantabrian landscape. Most of the same sites were also used later, in the Upper Paleolithic, but by at least the beginning of the Last Glacial Maximum (about 20,000 B.P.), other kinds of places also were being selected for use, notably high mountain ibex-hunting sites (logistical camps). Evidence of these is totally absent in the Mousterian. Some form of central-based foraging, perhaps involving residential mobility within the scope of an area the size of the modern province of Santander, may have been characteristic of the Middle Paleolithic adaptations to this region.

Cave Sites and Carnivores in the Early Last Glacial

The quantified faunal assemblages from modern excavations of Cantabrian Mousterian deposits are summarized in Appendix A1. One of the striking features of many of the faunal assemblages from deposits also containing Mousterian artifacts is the large number and diversity of carnivore remains. Among the older Mousterian faunal collections, leopard and hyena were noted in Castillo B, wolf in Castillo A and B and La Flecha, fox in Castillo A, and cave bear in Castillo A and B, Hornos de la Peña, and La Flecha (Cabrera 1984; Freeman 1973). I (Straus 1982a) studied the role of carnivores in the cave sites by tabulating the numbers of remains and of species of carnivores and calculating the carnivore/ungulate ratios for the quantified data available a decade ago. The data base for the Mousterian has changed only insofar as there are new facts from Amalda and further stratigraphic precision for Axlor (Altuna 1989). Calculated in terms of minimum numbers of individuals (MNI), as I did in 1982, the carnivore/ungulate ratio for Amalda Level VII is 38.8%.

I suggested in 1982 that some of the caves (notably Lezetxiki—and Isturitz in Basse-Navarre, for which quantitative data are lacking) had been major dens of large carnivore in early Last Glacial times and that human use thereof had been relatively modest, alternating with carnivore use. Among other uses, the caves served as hibernation sites for cave and brown bears, but other large or medium-size species common or present in Mousterian-age deposits include hyena, lion, leopard, lynx, wildcat, wolf, dhole, fox, and badger. Altuna (1990c:156–157) has replied that: 1) calculation of the carnivore/ungulate ratio in terms of MNI tends to exaggerate the relative importance of the carnivores that usually are rare; and 2) cave bears, the most abundant carnivores in Lezetxiki, probably were mostly vegetarian.

Both points are valid. However, there is still a marked contrast between most Mousterian deposits and Late Upper Paleolithic (21,000 to 10,000 B.P.) deposits in terms of the numbers, diversity, and kinds of carnivores present. The large carnivores are very rare in archeological deposits of the Late Upper Paleolithic, whereas smaller species (mustelids, foxes) are often common and may have been trapped by humans (for their pelts?). The frequent presence of such undoubtedly large predators as hyena and wolf (together with the less frequent presence of dhole, leopard, and cave lion as well as smaller felids, fox, and the scavenger-predator badger) suggest that parts of the faunal assemblages in the Mousterian were not solely accumulated or consumed by hominids. The frequent presence of cave bear, especially in certain "favorite" caves, indicates that those caves were used by hominids only sporadically in this period, perhaps on an ephemeral basis. In this regard it is interesting that there is clear evidence of *summer* occupation of Amalda Level VII on the basis of the presence of nine young ungulates (Altuna 1990c:162). There is no evidence for or against winter death of ungulates. But perhaps the site was occupied in winter by the bears (?), an idea that was contested by Altuna (1990c:162,166) on the basis of the rarity of bear thoracic bones, at least in the front part of Amalda that was excavated. Unfortunately we lack seasonality data for the other Mousterian levels in the region.

More work on bone damage marks of the type conducted by Altuna (1990c:157) at Amalda is needed to decipher the relative importance of carnivore versus hominid actions with respect to ungulate carcasses throughout the region in all time periods. In Amalda Level VII there are both cut marks and marrow-cracking impact fractures caused by humans on the one hand and many bite marks on many ungulate bones caused by carnivores on the other. But this evidence does not prove which predator-scavenger (hominid or animal) procured each ungulate or by which method: predation or scavenging. And, although largely vegetarian, modern brown bears do kill and eat animals. Grizzly and polar bears are notorious carnivores. Carnivory by cave bears cannot be ruled out entirely.

Subsistence

Until the debate over the role of carnivores in the accumulation of at least some of the Mousterian ungulate faunas is resolved, it will remain unclear as to how meaningful the "associations" of animal bones with Mousterian artifacts are. Nonetheless, the following patterns emerge from the ungulate faunal data presented in Appendix A1.

1. None of the ungulate faunal assemblages from the relatively thin archeological levels defined in modern excavations are very large; both numbers of identifiable specimens (NISPs) and MNIs usually are very low, even for the red deer extremely abundant in Late Upper Paleolithic levels. Even when the MNIs appear to be relatively high (*Cervus* and Bovini in El Pendo Level XVIa [Fuentes 1980]—if the numbers are not typographical errors, which would not be surprising given the other errors in the source tables), the NISP/MNI ratios are very low, signifying that individual carcasses are represented by only one or a very few bones or teeth. Otherwise, most ungulates seem to have been procured singly or in numbers of individuals rarely exceeding three to five. The one clear, major exception to this is the case of 16 chamois represented by 536 remains in Amalda Level VII.

2. Bovines and, to a lesser extent, horse are consistently represented relatively abundantly in a pattern very different than that of Late Upper Paleolithic archeofaunas in the region. It is hard to see how this might be the result of some environmental factor because the Late Upper Paleolithic and especially the Middle Paleolithic spanned wide varieties of

"stadial" and "interstadial" climatic conditions, with episodes of extreme cold and dryness and dominant open grasslands versus others of more moderate temperatures with higher humidity and more woodlands. Red deer, the dominant game species of the Late Upper Paleolithic, is a highly flexible, catholic species in terms of its diet and habitat (from grassland grazer to woodland browser) (Straus 1981a), making it unlikely that it was substantially rarer for some reason of habitat difference in early Last Glacial times than in the late Last Glacial. Unfortunately, aurochs and bison usually cannot be distinguished on the basis of most bones, especially fragmentary ones, and thus some potential ecological data are lost. However, even the wild horse, which supposedly preferred open grassland, survived into early Holocene times in this region and in southern France under forest conditions. Roe deer (*Capreolus capreolus*), true woodland denizens, are present in many of the Mousterian levels with many bovines and horses. Thus, I would interpret the relative abundance of bovines and horse in the Mousterian archeofaunas to be more a result of human selective factors than a reflection of a particular environment.

3. The dangerous, swift boar (*Sus scrofa*) is virtually absent from Mousterian archeofaunas and the swift, wary ibex—especially adapted to steep rocky slopes and cliffs—is rare, only being represented consistently, but usually slightly, in sites of the hilly Basque country (see Freeman 1973b, 1981; Straus 1977b).

4. Mollusks and remains of fish and birds are virtually absent from Mousterian levels, in sharp contrast to the situation in the Late Upper Paleolithic, often in the same caves. The seacoast would have been no farther in the Mousterian than in the Late Upper Paleolithic and, indeed, much of the time (O.I. Stage 3) it would have been closer than during the Upper Pleniglacial, when shellfish become some abundant in archeological sites of the region.

While there is little doubt that the Neanderthal inhabitants of Cantabrian Spain probably killed such animals as red deer, roe deer, and chamois on a fairly regular basis, they generally seem to have done so one animal at a time. There is no evidence of mass kills by such methods as drives or surrounds. Evidence of the means used to kill such medium-small ungulates is lacking, but no so-called Levallois or Mousterian "points" from this region have obvious evidence of hafting, although microwear studies of at least flint specimens of these types have not yet been done. Wooden thrusting spears may be a possibility, particularly given the enormous physical strength of the Neanderthals (Trinkaus 1986) and the microwear evidence (from France) that many Mousterian tools very often were used to work wood (Beyries 1987). Neanderthals may have selected targets that were young or crippled by old age, disease, or injury, but solid evidence for this hypothesis is still lacking.

One of the striking aspects of the large ungulate faunas (the bovines and horses) is the relative abundance of fractured long bones, with many diaphysial fragments. Freeman (1971, 1978c, 1980) interpreted many of these bones in the Mousterian of Morín and El Pendo as "flaked tools." Many of those are identifiable as bovine and, to a lesser extent, horse. The many unidentifiable ones are often of large size and consistent with those taxa. In an analysis of the Morín and Lezetxiki bovine bone counts from the Mousterian (and of other materials), I argued that the evidence of systematic "flaking" on the long bones suggests marrow bone cracking rather than tool manufacture (Straus 1976). At Morín (and at El Pendo [Fuentes 1980:236]), the large ungulates are only partially represented by their anatomical parts, whereas at Lezetxiki the bison are notable for the complete representation of the skeletons. At the latter site there are not only many fractured long bones but also many head and thorax parts. Whether killed or scavenged near Lezetxiki, much of the carcasses made it into the cave and were then thoroughly processed for removal of all parts having food value, including brains and marrow. At Morín (and El Pendo), marrow-rich long bones were brought to (or left at) the sites for processing, although it cannot be said definitely that this was the result of the scavenging of parts left over by non-bone-crushing carnivores such as big cats. The remains of rhinoceros found in numerous Mousterian levels (including old collections from Unquera, El Pendo, Cobalejos, and El Castillo, where they are said to be abundant [Freeman 1973; Cabrera 1984] also might have been parts scavenged by the hominids from carnivore kills or natural death occurrences.

Neanderthal subsistence seems not to have involved the systematic exploitation of fast, elusive, or dangerous animals, steep cliff habitats, or aquatic habitats. An opportunistic mix of simple hunting and scavenging may have been practiced. Once acquired, by whatever method, carcasses generally were consumed fully and significant use was made of marrow and brains. Evidence of use of plants for food is lacking, although it can be argued that, at least during the colder periods, there were few plants in the region that were edible by humans. Nonetheless, stone tools such as bifaces, cleavers, and choppers well could have been used for root digging as well as for shaping wood. During more temperate intervals, as indicated by pollen diagrams, there would have been hazels and acorn oaks and probably some berry bushes. A picture of generalized foraging from centrally situated cave residential sites seems to emerge from these data, but much more remains to be learned before we can confidently reconstruct Neanderthal subsistence strategies in this or any other region.

Lithic Raw Material Exploitation

The only part of Mousterian technology that has survived in this region
(and in most regions except Germany, where a 2-m wooden "spear" was
found at Lehringen) is lithic. The Cantabrian Neanderthals seem to have
used strictly local rocks for the manufacture of their tools. Thus, in the
Basque country, rich in good-quality flint, almost all the Mousterian
tools and debris (85.4%) at Amalda are of that material. Even the few
quartzites, ophites, and other rocks that were used could have come from
sources within one to two hours' walk of the cave (Baldeón 1990b; Viera
and Aguirrezabala 1990).

On the other hand, in central Santander—unless there is a complex
lithology including abundant quartzite, ophite, and quartz formations
as well as areas of Carboniferous and Cretaceous limestone that bear
flints of various nodule sizes and qualities—the Mousterian lithic assemblages are much more heterogeneous in raw material composition,
although all the rocks used are also locally available. Differences among
the individual sites probably reflect variations in strictly local lithology. In analyzing the flake tools and debris from Morín, El Castillo,
Hornos de la Peña, and El Pendo statistically, Freeman (1964, 1971, 1973,
1980; see also Cabrera 1984; Benito 1976) found no *general* preferences
for making specific types of artifacts with specific types of rock although
in individual assemblages there are some statistical tendencies to make
certain artifacts more often with one kind of rock than with others.

The "preference" for producing (generally rare) Levallois flakes with
ophite in several cases is simply due to the fact that ophite cobbles are
large enough to be worked with an elaborate core preparation technique,
whereas the local flint nodules are not. There is sometimes (but not
always) a "preference" for making denticulate edges on quartzite and
scraper edges on flint. No cleaver flakes are made on flint; they are made
on tough ophite and coarse quartzite. There is not such absolute avoidance
of flint for making true bifaces, although these are relatively rare. One
consistent finding by Freeman is that quartzite is under-represented in
terms of flaking debris, although the reasons for this are unclear. They
might include the initial working of the large cobbles of this material
to a greater degree at the sources, such as river beds, than in the caves,
perhaps to reduce transportation effort.

Finally, in the Mousterian levels at El Conde in central Asturias, where
flint outcrops are rare and the dominant local bedrock is quartzite, all
the flaked tools are quartzite (Freeman 1977).

The Neanderthals did not even go short distances to acquire flint. These data all reinforce the impression that Neanderthals foraged within relatively restricted radii of residential camps with no indication of "logistical" mobility (the provisioning of base sites by means of specialized, long- distance expeditions to secondary sites). The Neanderthals seem to have moved among a series of fairly similar sites within a subregion, perhaps whenever game resources seemed to be diminishing or harder to acquire.

Mousterian Stone Tools

In the 1960s, armed with the typology, technical indices, and descriptive statistical methods devised by François Bordes for the Lower and Middle Paleolithic and with the factor analysis technique, whose application to archeology he was pioneering at Chicago with L.R. and S.R. Binford and J. Brown, Leslie Freeman analyzed all the Cantabrian Mousterian lithic assemblages available at the time.

Given the small number of collections studied and the strong influence of Bordes, it is not surprising that Freeman "found" evidence of the existence of several of the classic "Mousterian facies" (assemblage types) in the Cantabrian region: Denticulate, Quina Charentian, and, sometimes partly because of the presence of cleaver flakes in lieu of bifaces, Mousterian of Acheulean Tradition (Freeman 1964, 1966, 1970). But already with the first results from his own new excavations in Cueva Morín, Freeman was beginning to find assemblages that combined tools characteristic of more than one "facies." He suggested that this fact constituted a proof of the validity of the "functional" explanation for Mousterian inter-assemblage variability being argued by the Binfords in opposition to Bordes' "ethnic" explanation (e.g., Bordes 1961; Binford and Binford 1966).

Such assemblages of "mixed" composition would represent site occupations during which broad combinations of activities—otherwise separated—took place. It was becoming clear that the presence of at least some cleaver flakes cut across the variability in the flake tool fraction of Cantabrian lithic assemblages. This regionally characteristic tool type, which is always made on ophite or quartzite, was the basis of the creation by Bordes (1953, 1981) of a special type of Mousterian, the "Vasconian", present in Santander and in the French Basque country (see discussion in Cabrera 1983).

However, with further excavation and analyses of the Mousterian at

Morín and his analysis of the then newly available Mousterian assemblages from El Pendo, Freeman began changing his mind. First, he was obliged to reclassify some assemblages from Charentian to Mousterian of Acheulean Tradition, while continuing to argue for much compositional intergradation among different assemblages and while pointing out the artificiality of Bordes' facies pigeonholes, particularly in a non-Périgord context (Freeman 1971, 1973). Finally, after a Kolmogrov-Smirnov analysis of all the large Mousterian collections from Morín, El Pendo, and El Castillo, Freeman (1980) concluded that the assemblages form an unbroken gradient between ones with very many denticulates (up to 40%) and very few sidescrapers on the one hand and ones with very many sidescrapers (up to 66%) and few denticulates on the other.

This polar dichotomy and intergradation between denticulate-rich and sidescraper-rich assemblages was confirmed by Freeman's analyses of Hornos de la Peña, La Flecha, and El Conde as well by Baldeón's (1990a,b) analyses of the assemblages from Amalda, Axlor, and Lezetxiki. Cleavers and, rarely bifaces can be associated with assemblages across the entire spectrum of denticulate/sidescraper ratios.

Basic data on the composition of major Cantabrian Mousterian assemblages are presented in Appendix A2. It can be seen that, between them, sidescrapers and denticulates make up an average of 70% of the Bordesian flake tools ($n = 28$; $SD = 13.2$). (Despite the fact that they are made on large flakes in this region, cleavers are counted separately with the bifaces and "core" tools in the Bordesian system. Notches are not included in the denticulate index; if they were, that index would be much higher in several cases.) That Mousterian interassemblage variability mostly can be accounted for statistically by the denticulate/sidescraper ratio also has been recognized for French collections by Rolland (1981, 1988), although he saw temporal trends in the statistical relationship, something not (yet?) apparent in Cantabrian Spain. Butzer (1986) saw no evidence of directional change among the so-called Mousterian facies in the Cantabrian region but showed that sidescraper-rich and denticulate-rich assemblages were "contemporaneous," at least at the level of his climatic phases.

At the two ends of Freeman's continuum of sidescraper and denticulate percentages may lie assemblages that represent functionally highly specialized site occupations or major differences in terms of lithic economization or stone tool "curation," as measured by the extent of edge retouching ("high" in the case of sidescrapers—especially multi-edge and "Quina" types made by step scalar retouch on thick blanks—and "low" in the case of the very simple denticulates) (see Dibble 1987,

1988). Intuitively, it would seem unlikely that the same activities that were done with smooth, "strengthened" scraper edges could be carried out equally as well with serrate edges, although microwear analyses might be useful (particularly for flint artifacts, if unpatinated) in trying to prove the "functional" argument. There is some tendency for quartzite-dominated assemblages to have high denticulate indices and for flint-dominated ones to have relatively low denticulate indices, but this tendency is far from absolute. However, as a group the Basque country assemblages (all-flint) do have relatively few denticulates, compared with many of the assemblages from Santander and Asturias (flint-poor).

The compositionally intermediate assemblages (with moderate percentages of both denticulates and sidescrapers) may represent either functionally more complex occupations or major palimpsests of many occupation residues, or both. Because of their size and morphology, the cleaver flakes clearly had a different range and type of function, one for which tough, nonbrittle raw materials, found in fairly large "package sizes," were imperative. One general characteristic of the Cantabrian Mousterian that can be related directly to the raw materials is the very low use of the Levallois technique, even in a flint-dominated assemblage like Amalda VII, because the Guipúzcoan flint nodules, although of good quality, are small. As noted above, if the Levallois technique was used, it often was on the large cobbles of ophite or quartzite.

Mousterian Structures

A clue to the nature of the observed interassemblage variability is provided by Freeman's discovery and description (1973a:64–65, 1978a:96–111, 1978b:122–124) of a possible structure in Level 17, near the bottom of the Mousterian sequence of strata in Cueva Morín. Running more or less diagonally across the middle of the cave vestibule for nearly 4 m was a rough line of stones 5 to 25 cm in diameter (mostly 10–20 cm). At one end, this alignment is truncated by the old excavations of Carballo and Vega del Sella; the other end was left unexcavated by Freeman. There is a mass of other stones toward the side of the "wall" that faces the cave exterior, but apparently few large stones toward the interior. Similarly, almost all the bones of the abundant Level 17 faunal assemblages lie to the exterior of the "wall," where there is a bone "breccia" in sediments deep reddish brown in color, probably caused by decomposition of carcass remains; to the interior of the "wall," the sediments are gray or light cream color.

It is this bone breccia that produced the large number of systematically fragmented long bones, interpreted as "tools" (by Freeman) or as evidence of marrow extraction. The map of this feature (Freeman 1978a: Fig. 4) shows 11 cleaver flakes within the area of the bone breccia bounded by and rich in stones. These include all but one of the cleavers found in the whole level.

A factor analysis (Freeman 1978b) demonstrated that one group of intercorrelated tools is more densely distributed in the area to the exterior of the "wall" (within the bone breccia, near the cave mouth); besides cleavers, these tools include choppers, chopping tools, discs/picks, backed knives, Levallois flakes/points, and a few other flake tool types plus some bifaces. The constituents of another group are more abundantly distributed toward the cave interior, beyond the wall; these include almost uniquely a wide variety of sidescrapers plus endscrapers, notches, and perforators. It looks very much as if there was a distinct separation of activities between the front area and the rear area of the vestibule, perhaps delineated by some sort of wall (?).

Such a neat spatial pattern, supported by multivariate correlation analyses, would seem to belie the importance of deposit mixing or compounding, at least in the case of Morín Level 17. And, significantly, as Freeman pointed out, if one were to do a Bordesian analysis of the two areas of this level separately, as opposed to lumping the two areas (as is standard practice prescribed by Bordes despite his own recognition of "activity areas" or tool clusters within such caves as Pech de l'Azé), one probably would assign the "exterior" assemblage in Morín 17 to a Mousterian of Acheulean Tradition and the "interior" one, to a Charentian Mousterian. This is a strong case arguing for the functional explanation of Mousterian interassemblage variability, even if we can still only speculate as to the exact nature of the functions performed with these tools.

Although no clear Mousterian hearths were observed in Cueva Morín (except for a depression in Level 11 associated with calcined objects [Freeman 1971:98]), this is not surprising, as none was found in the recent excavations of Amalda either (Altuna 1990c). The term "hearth" is used to describe evidence of fire in Levels VIII and V at Axlor, whereas simple traces of "combustion" are cited for other levels there, as well as at Lezetxiki and Amalda (Baldeón 1990a:20). The presence of ashes is cited only for Level XIV at El Pendo (González Echegaray 1980:26); however, the field notes from El Castillo describe abundant "hearth" layers (i.e., widespread lenses of ash and charcoal—not apparently constructed hearths) in both Mousterian strata (Cabrera 1984:142–143). Burnt bones occur, but rarely.

In sum, while there is fairly common evidence for the use of fire by Cantabrian Neanderthals, it seems to have been simple: perhaps mostly bonfires used for cooking, light, and, significantly, protection of caves from carnivores (with no stone or dugout structures and no earth ovens or roasting pits). Whatever the deliberate, man-made structural significance of the stones in Morín Level 17 (if any), there does seem to have been a definite partitioning of activities in the vestibule of that cave. And if they were a structure, this seems to have been a rare exception. Neanderthals in this region deliberately modified their living spaces little or not at all.

No Neanderthal burials have been discovered in the Cantabrian region, which in this respect differs, together with the rest of the Iberian Peninsula and the French Pyrenees, from the Charente-Corrèze-Périgord region, central Italy, and Israel which are relatively rich in such burials. Like other parts of Spain, Gibraltar, and Portugal, the Cantabrian region has yielded only isolated Neanderthal skeletal remains. These include a robust humerus of an adult (possibly female), with notable muscle markings, from the basal level at Lezetxiki and two taurodont teeth from Mousterian levels in the same cave. There also are five taurodont teeth from upper Mousterian levels at Axlor, all studied by J.M. Basabe (Rua 1990). This scarcity of Neanderthal remains is peculiar, given the excellent faunal preservation and the large areas of Mousterian deposits excavated at El Pendo, Morín, and, most of all, El Castillo. Indeed, no more-or-less complete human skeletons (which would suggest actual *burials*) show up in the Cantabrian record until the Epipaleolithic/Mesolithic, about 8,000 to 10,000 years ago.

Conclusions

Neither the "Acheulean" nor the "Mousterian" records from the Cantabrian region are extremely rich, but there is a definite increase in the numbers of sites and in the amount of information in the early Last Glacial than before that time. There seems to have been some increase in the regional populations, but this may still have consisted of no more than a very few bands throughout the whole region at any one time. One preferred center of habitation was the coastal plain and lower river valleys of central Santander, and another was in the central coastal part of the Basque country in the Ibaizabal, Deva, and Urola drainages. Less-abundant data (El Conde and open-air finds) suggest at least some use of lowland areas of Asturias. A separate center of Mousterian habitation seems to have been in the French country (Isturitz, Olha, and several open-air sites). The scarcity of skeletal finds also point to a very low population density. Large areas of the region may have been unoccupied or only occasionally used; whole habitats (mountains, riverine, littoral) were exploited only slightly or not at all.

Mousterian settlement systems may have resembled the model of "residential mobility" (Binford 1980, 1982) or the similar "circulating" settlement model (Marks and Friedel 1977). Missing from the Mousterian record are special-purpose, "logistical" sites (such as high-mountain, ibex hunting camps, common in the Cantabrian Cordillera and Pyrenees in the Late Upper Paleolithic). Lithic procurement seems to have been strictly local and the technology, fairly simple. However, there is a suggestion that some assemblages are dominated by more heavily worked tools than others, suggesting some relative degree of longevity of site occupation *or* reuse of (scavenged?) tools. The dichotomy between sidescrapers and denticulates may have something to do with some fundamental functional difference, as yet unexplained by microwear studies or by spatial or correlational analyses. If the unique Cueva Morín Level 17 living floor analysis may be generalized, cleavers and other heavy-duty tools may have been used for butchering carcasses and breaking the marrow bones of large animals, although they may also have been used to cut wood and to dig.

Subsistence activities seem to have been unspecialized, simple, and opportunistic. There is little or no evidence of sophisticated, mass hunting, although the small-medium size ungulates probably were killed individually, the Neanderthals perhaps especially targeting vulnerable individuals. Hunting may have been done with simple untipped wooden thrusting spears, clubs, rocks, etc., and the Neanderthals made use of their great strength and endurance. (Traces of supposed human tooth marks on faunal bones from the Mousterian of El Castillo [Cabrera 1984:422] would, if confirmed, lend weight to the paramasticatory hypothesis of Neanderthal tooth use [Trinkaus 1986]. The largest animals found in the Mousterian archeofaunas (bovines, rhinos, horses) may have been scavenged; heavy use was made of marrow bones by the Neanderthals. The presence of many large carnivores in several of the Mousterian strata suggests that the hominids were not the only agents of ungulate bone collection and that they were not yet the sole users of the chosen habitation caves. When available, particularly under the frequent interstadial conditions of the early Last Glacial, plant foods such as nuts, roots, and berries may have been used, but they do not seem to have been processed with any technology that has survived in the record. Nor have plant remains been found.

The overall picture suggests a simple but effective and long-lived adaptation, flexible enough to survive the climatic vicissitudes of the stadial and interstadial phases of the first two-thirds of the Last Glacial. Replacement of the archaic but millennial stone flake and core tool technology of the Lower and Middle Paleolithic by the lithic blade and bone implement technologies of the Upper Paleolithic and of Neanderthal by *Homo sapiens sapiens* some time around 40,000 years ago in this region remains one of the most controversial issues in paleo-anthropology.

Chapter 4

THE EARLY UPPER PALEOLITHIC
(Late Oxygen Isotope Stage 3)

The Late Interpleniglacial

THE approximate period from 60,000 to 30,000 B.P. was one of generally moderate, interstadial temperatures, with significant reforestation at times. Although it was not a period of uniformly more temperate climate, this 30,000-year interval nonetheless was a major interruption of pleniglacial conditions, globally meriting the term "interpleniglacial." The optimal conditions of this period were attained between 38,000 and 34,000 B.P., an episode now known as "the Würm Interstadial" by French specialists and acknowledged as a subdivision of the Last Glacial that was more bipartite than quadripartite (Laville et al. 1984; see also Raynal and Guadelli 1990). What is interesting from the point of view of trying to explain the "transition" to the Upper Paleolithic and to the modern human anatomy are the facts that the most severe glacial conditions of the first half of the Last Glacial in Europe were experienced around 65,000 years ago (in O.I. Stage 4) and that late Middle Paleolithic times often enjoyed relatively benign conditions, intermediate between full glacial and interglacial. The transition took place during a time not of climatic stress, but of moderation.

Early Upper Paleolithic Chronology

Dates for the end of the Middle Paleolithic and for the beginning of the Upper Paleolithic in and near the Cantabrian region are given above. They are rare and of low precision because 40,000 B.P. is at least about the present maximum of the radiocarbon method (even in its accelerator-mass spectrometer [AMS] version). In that regard, the AMS C-14 dates recently obtained by Bischoff (Cabrera and Bischoff 1989) on three charcoal samples from the lowest Upper Paleolithic level (early Aurignacian) at El Castillo are of great significance. These dates are in correct stratigraphic order within Level 18 of Cabrera's new excavation, separated from the uppermost Mousterian level (20) by a 0.5-m archeologically sterile layer. The dates are: 40,000 ± 2,100, 38.500 ± 1.800, and 37,700 ± 1,800 B.P. (average, 38,700 ± 1,900 B.P.). They coincide with Bischoff's multiple uranium-series dates on travertine, about 40,000 B.P. (± 1,500) for the terminal Mousterian at the Abric Romaní in Barcelona at the Mediterranean end of northern Spain (Bischoff et al. 1988). The Castillo dates agree with Bischoff's AMS dates on charcoal from the uppermost Mousterian level and from the lowest Upper Paleolithic level (also early Aurignacian) at L'Arbreda Cave, Gerona (also in Catalonia). The terminal Mousterian dates there are 41,400 ± 1,600, 34,100 ± 750, and 39,400 ± 1,400 B.P. (average, discounting the middle date, 40,400 ± 1,400 B.P.); and the Aurignacian ones are 38,700 ± 1,200, 39,900 ± 1,300, 37,700 ± 1,000, and 37,700 ± 1,000 B.P. (average, 38,500 ± 1,000 B.P.) (Bischoff et al. 1989).

If confirmed by determinations from these and other sites in Spain, Bischoff's dates mean that the Mousterian technology as a unique, integral phenomenon ceased to be made around 40,000 years ago in at least some parts of northern Spain and that a fully Upper Paleolithic technology, based on blade production and new bone-working techniques, came into use not long thereafter—about 38,500 to 39,000 years ago. If correct, these are the oldest dates for the transition of Middle to Upper Paleolithic in western Europe (as old, in fact, as those in central and southeastern Europe).

If the transition was the result of an *east-to-west* migration or flow of genes, artifacts, and ideas, then all the conventional radiocarbon dates from central and southeastern Europe may be too young. Alternatively, the development of the Upper Paleolithic in western Europe may not have been a product of introduction via migration or diffusion but rather a case of independent invention. Nonetheless, wherever hominid remains have been found in association with "Aurignacian" artifacts, they have been remains of anatomically modern humans.

The Fossil Record of the Neanderthal–
Cro-Magnon Transition

The recent discoveries of a Neanderthal skeleton associated with a Chatelperronian artifact assemblage at Saint-Césaire in southwestern France (Lévêque and Vandermeersch 1980) and of possible Neanderthal teeth also in the Chatelperronian at La Grotte du Renne in north-central France (Leroi-Gourhan and Leroi-Gourhan 1964) clearly suggest that the anatomical transition to *Homo sapiens sapiens* and the technological transition to the Upper Paleolithic were mosaic phenomena. Neanderthals may have tried to adapt, to keep up with a changing situation, by making changes in their technology—including some of their first unmistakable attempts at personal adornment in the form of perforated teeth (Taborin 1990). The (undated) interstratification of Aurignacian and Chatelperronian artifacts at le Roc de Combe and le Piage in southwestern France (Bordes and Labrot 1967) and at El Pendo in Santander (González Echegaray 1980), and the chronostratigraphic argument for a late-surviving Mousterian and Neanderthals in southeastern Spain (Vega-Toscano et al. 1988; Vega-Toscano 1990), also suggest a long, complex period of change in western Europe, perhaps spanning more than 5,000 years—roughly from 40,000 to 34,000 years ago during the late Interpleniglacial.

The Banyolas Neanderthal mandible in Catalonia, once thought to be very old, has recently been shown to be young—perhaps not much older than about 45,000 B.C., according to uranium-series dating of travertine matrix adhering to the bone (Julià and Bischoff 1991). Neither Mousterian technology nor Neanderthal anatomy became extinct instantaneously in all places and regions, even in such a relatively small subcontinental area as western Europe. Unfortunately hominid remains are rare in Cantabrian Spain: Obermaier (1924:288) found fragments of a child's jaw and skull plus an adult's molar and three robust skull fragments in the basal Aurignacian level (Level 18) at El Castillo (Garralda 1989). No Neanderthal traits were noted on these specimens or on the anatomically modern skullcap found in the "Aurignacian" level at nearby Camargo Cave by Sierra (Obermaier 1924:288).

Paleo-environmental Evidence

Aside from El Castillo and El Pendo, there are few sites in the Cantabrian region that have archeological levels pertaining to "the transition" (notably Morín, El Conde and Ekain). Among them, only one other has paleo-environmental evidence: Cueva Morín. Sedimentological data from the basal Aurignacian at El Castillo were interpreted by Butzer (1981) as having been deposited under cool, moist conditions. At Morín, he interpreted those of the Chatelperronian and overlying oldest Aurignacian as cool and then temperate. The sequence of early Aurignacian, Chatelperronian, and early Aurignacian at El Pendo was interpreted by Butzer

(1981) as cold and then temperate. Arlette Leroi-Gourhan's (1971) pollen analysis of the Chatelperronian (Level 10) and basal Aurignacian (Level 9) layers at Morín shows a marked increase in arboreal pollens relative to the terminal Mousterian (up to 75%), but these are mostly pine with only traces of birch, hazel, and alder. Graminaceous grass pollens and fern spores are abundant, so it was humid although cool. She assigned these levels to what now would be called the Les Cottés (Hengelo II) Interstadial, which, albeit with fluctuations, continued through the course of Morín Level 8 (also early Aurignacian, with three radiocarbon charcoal dates of about 27,500 B.P. [Stuckenrath 1978]—all possibly too young). Open grasslands with pine thickets seem to have characterized the vegetation of this period which was neither extremely cold nor extremely warm.

Butzer indicated somewhat of a warming, drying trend in the upper levels of the early Aurignacian at the trio of sites he analyzed. Conditions rapidly degenerated, however, according to both Butzer (1981) and Leroi-Gourhan (1971), in the Typical (later) Aurignacian, with cold, virtually treeless conditions setting in. There is an improvement in Level 6 times at Morín (still Typical Aurignacian), with a short increase in aboreal pollens (mostly pine with some hazel, birch, juniper, alder, and even oak), assigned by Leroi-Gourhan (1971) to the Arcy Interstadial. However, because underlying Level 7 has radiocarbon dates of 28,700 ± 900 and 27,200 ± 1,500 B.P. and the Level 7/6 interface has a date of 31,600 ± 900 B.P. (Stuckenrath 1978—corrected to Libby half-life), this interstadial could be "Kesselt," which is controversial. This episode does not show up in the sedimentological analyses except for some decrease in frost weathering (Butzer 1981). No pollen analysis has yet been published for a supposed Chatelperronian level (IX) with mammoth and wooly rhinocerous remains in Labeko Cave (Guipúzcoa), but a higher level (VIII), attributed to the "Aurignacian 0," has palynological evidence of open vegetation characteristic of cold climate, possibly the stadial between Hengelo and Denekamp (Sánchez 1991).

The mammalian faunas associated with the transition are not very expressive climatically except in that classic cold climate forms, such as reindeer, are *absent* from the relevant Chatelperronian and early Aurignacian levels at El Castillo, Morín, and El Pendo. On the other hand, there are small quantities of remains of roe deer in all three sites and of boar in El Castillo and Morín, suggesting the presence of woods or at least substantial thickets. There are also "abundant" remains of "Merck's rhino" in the lowest Aurignacian level (Level 18) at El Castillo (Cabrera 1984:236); if correctly identified and equivalent to *Dicerorhinus kirchbergensis*, this would also be an indicator of the existence of some wooded areas (Freeman 1973; but see Altuna [1972:397] for a different tentative interpretation of these remains). "Merck's rhino" also has been cited from the old excavations of the basal Aurignacian at El Conde in Asturias (Altuna 1972). A tooth of a sperm whale was found in the same basal Aurignacian level at El Castillo, which, aside from demonstrating human visits to the shore, is an indicator of temperate coastal waters in the Cantabrian Sea at the time (Cabrera 1984:236). This level also yielded a few remains of *Elephas antiquus*, which, according to some specialists, may have included parklands or woodlands among its habitats (Freeman 1973).

The sum of the sedimentological, palynological, and paleontological data indicates that the transition from Middle to Upper Paleolithic in the Cantabrian region took place under fluctuating but generally moderate climatic conditions. Parkland environments dominated much of the time during the Interpleniglacial, but the proportions and the compositions of wooded areas varied as functions of temperature and precipitation as well as strictly local conditions of soil and exposure.

The Technological Transition

A word on archeological systematics is needed before the Middle-to-Upper Paleolithic transition is discussed. Whereas the Mousterian was divided by Bordes (1953) into "facies" that were supposedly not time-successive, much of the variability of the Upper Paleolithic—defined on the basis of the southwestern French stratigraphic sequences by Breuil (1913), Peyrony (1933), and Sonneville-Bordes (1960)—was accommodated within a temporal, "evolutionary" scheme with one instance of "parallel cultural phyla"—the Perigordian and the Aurignacian—evolving contemporaneously. Each of the many temporal "phases" of the Perigordian, Aurignacian, Solutrean, and Magdalenian (plus Azilian) "cultures" was defined by the presence or relative frequency of specific lithic or osseous "fossil director" artifacts (Figure 4.1).

Until recently, a major goal of Upper Paleolithic studies in western Europe has been to try to trace the origins of these cultures—hence, the term "phylogenetic paradigm" used to describe the dominant French school of prehistory. In the traditional scheme, the "Perigordian" cultural phylum was thought to have evolved from the French Mousterian of Acheulean Tradition and to have passed through a number of phases, beginning with Perigordian I (Chatelperronian) defined by the presence of a form of curved backed knife, other tools made on blades such as burins and endscrapers, and many Middle Paleolithic tool types. The Aurignacian is generally believed to be an allochtonous phenomenon

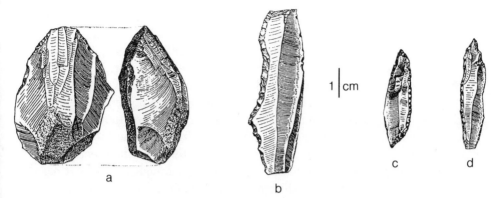

FIGURE 4.1. *Early Upper Paleolithic artifacts from Cueva Morín: a, "Aurignacian" keeled endscraper; b, retouched blade; c, Chatelperron knife; d, Gravette point. (Vega del Sella 1921.)*

in western Europe; once arrived, it too went through a series of developmental stages (Aurignacian 0–V), defined mainly by bone point styles as well as the presence of distinctive retouched blades, thick, nosed and keeled endscrapers, etc. The validity of the Perigordian and Aurignacian subdivisions and the contemporaneity of the two supposed cultural phyla recently have come under considerable criticism. Many prehistorians have returned to the idea of a Chatelperronian industry *per se* (probably contemporary with the earliest Aurignacian [Phase 0] in western Europe), followed by the bulk of the Aurignacian and then by the Gravettian— breaking the "Perigordian" phylogenetic linkage that had no real stratigraphic basis in fact (for reviews, see Laville et al. 1980; Straus 1987c).

Because of significant perceived differences in technology, environments, and adaptations between the Chatelperronian, Aurignacian, and Gravettian on the one hand and the Solutrean, Magdalenian, and Azilian on the other, prehistorians now tend to speak of an Early Upper Paleolithic (EUP) prior to the Last Glacial Maximum (the downslide into it was under way before 20,000 B.P.) and a Late Upper Paleolithic (LUP). This is extended to western Europe as a whole (Campbell 1977; Straus 1983a; Hoffecker and Wolf 1988).

Unfortunately, prehistorians in Cantabrian Spain have tried to fit local assemblages into the numbered phases of the basic Upper Paleolithic culture-stratigraphic units as defined in southwestern France. Yet beyond type sites, even these subdivisions may have limited value. In the absence of independent dating, these borrowed subdivisions traditionally used in Cantabrian Spain must be taken with a grain of salt and are generally avoided in what follows.

The differences between the Middle and Upper Paleolithic have been characterized and discussed at length in a number of publications (e.g., Mellars 1973, 1989, 1990; White 1982; papers in Bordes 1972, Trinkaus 1983, Hoffecker and Wolf 1988, Farizy 1990, Mellars and Stringer 1989). Many textbook characterizations based on the record from the Périgord (e.g., Bordes 1968; Laville et al. 1980) stress the importance of stone blades, endscrapers, and burins as well as bone, antler and tooth, or ivory artifacts in distinguishing the Upper Paleolithic from the Mousterian. These descriptions usually are careful to note that the Chatelperronian industry is at least partially a hybrid of both, although generally it has been definitely classified within the *Upper* Paleolithic (e.g., Bordes 1968; Harrold 1981, 1983, 1986, 1989)—the Saint-Césaire discovery in 1979 having raised the possibility of Neanderthal "acculturation."

That issue aside, how different is the Mousterian from the Chatelperronian and the Aurignacian? Part of the problem of comparison lies in the use of the typology of Bordes for Mousterian assemblages and the automatic use of the typology of Sonneville-Bordes and Perrot for assemblages thought to be Upper Paleolithic. Another aspect has to do with the effect of different lithic raw materials. Appendix B1 shows the relative frequencies of "Middle Paleolithic" tool types (notches, denticulates, and sidescrapers) in EUP assemblages. The overall mean is 24.7% (SD = 18.0) but, in general, the percentages are highest in the oldest levels of each series—including *both* Chatelperronian and early Aurignacian ones. There is a tendency for these archaic tool types to be made on quartzite or other nonflint materials (although ophite, so popular for heavy-duty tools in the Mousterian of the Santander caves, virtually disappears in the EUP) (Straus and Heller 1988). Even at Amalda Cave, in flint-rich Guipúzcoa, nonflint materials were used to make many of the archaic tool types in the 27,000 B.P. "Perigordian V" level (Baldéon 1990b). On the other hand, Appendix B2 shows the relative frequencies of typical Upper Paleolithic tool types in Cantabrian Mousterian ssemblages. The mean percentage is 16.8% (SD = 4.95).

The cross-over effect can be significant in both directions, showing that the distinction between Middle and Upper Paleolithic is far from absolute. Nor is there a multisite trend for Upper Paleolithic tool types to become more common through time in Middle Paleolithic levels (Straus and Heller 1988). Within the EUP of Santander and Asturias, there is a correlation between the heavy use of quartzite and the high representation of endscrapers in assemblages such as Castillo 18 and El Cierro 7. Appendix B3 compares lithic raw material use in EUP and Mousterian assemblages. Coarse-grained materials, such as quartzite and ophite, where abundant in the local environment, do become less important with time although the decrease generally is gradual, not abrupt at the "transition." In the long sequences from the Santander sites of Morín, El Castillo, and El Pendo, the percentages of flint increase irregularly from 40% to 60% in the Mousterian to 90% to 98% in the late Aurignacian or Gravettian. Where there is little or no flint in the local lithology (i.e., around El Conde), quartzite continues to be the sole raw material source; humans did not go any distance to procure flint in central Asturias, even in the Aurignacian. The decrease in utilization of rocks other than flint in "Gravettian" contexts probably is related to the domination of these late EUP technologies by small or even "microlithic" backed blades and bladelets, difficult to manufacture from coarse-grain materials.

In terms of nonlithic artifacts, the Chatelperronian of both Morín and El Pendo (as well as the possible Chatelperronian of Ekain, which consists only of a Chatelperron knife, a backed bladelet, and a sidescraper [Merino 1984]), totally lacks bone tools or perforated teeth. There are bone points in the earliest Aurignacian of El Castillo (including 10 split-base, 1 lozenge-shaped, and 1 leaf-shaped point in Level 18 [Cabrera 1984:219–225]) and Cueva Morín (1 possible tip fragment). El Pendo's "Aurignacian 0", however, has none. Later Aurignacian levels at all three sites do have varying quantities of different types of bone or antler points, as do the undated Aurignacian levels at El Conde (Vega del Sella excavations) and El Otero (Straus and Heller 1988). Osseous technology thus is not necessarily abundant or even present in the earliest Upper Paleolithic levels in the Cantabrian region although, when present, it does serve to distinguish them from Middle Paleolithic, fundamentally suggesting changes in weaponry.

However, the Aurignacian assemblages of this region are very poor in objects of adornment (i.e., engraved or perforated pieces)—not much richer than the Chatelperronian ones (with none). This is in sharp contrast to the relative wealth of the Aurignacian levels in Gatzarria and Isturitz, just across the Pyrenees. The Cantabrian pieces with credible Aurignacian provenance total no more than a small handful of perforated teeth, mostly from later Aurignacian levels (Straus and Heller 1988). The only mobile art objects said to come from this period are of problematical provenance. Again, one cannot claim an abrupt, sharp transition or "punctuation event" in the case of the beginning of the Cantabrian EUP, which may have had a substantial element of *in situ* development as opposed to replacement. While there do seem to be differences between several assemblages labeled "Aurignacian" and others labeled "Gravettian" in the Cantabrian region in terms of osseous artifacts, generally there is considerable overlap between the two culture-stratigraphic units in terms of lithic artifact composition—more than would be expected

Table 4.1 "Aurignacian" and "Perigordian" Tool Group Indices From Chatelperronian, Aurignacian, and Gravettian Assemblages

Tool type*	Chatelperronian assemblages (n = 2)		Aurignacian assemblages (n = 24)		Gravettian assemblages (n = 9)	
	Average	SD	Average	SD	Average	SD
GA	6.2	0.2	16.4	9.4	8.8	3.7
GP	6.9	0.8	3.4	2.4	19.0	12.5

*GA, all characteristically Aurignacian; GP, all characteristically Perigordian.

in the ideal characterizations developed in southwestern France (Straus and Heller 1988).

To show this overlap, Appendix B4 lists the tool group indices developed by Sonneville-Bordes and Perrot (1953) to distinguish different culture-stratigraphic units as applied to the Cantabrian region. The percentages are derived from the original site reports or from reanalyses presented in Bernaldo de Quirós's (1982) dissertation on the Cantabrian EUP.

In some of the assemblages, the indices do not clearly discriminate between the classic taxa, and may even violate the expected relationship. *Overall*, however, the "Aurignacian" and "Perigordian" indices do differ between the groups of Aurignacian and Gravettian assemblages in the Cantabrian region (Table 4.1), although there is a degree of circularity in this observation. A supposed Aurignacian fossil director, the alternately, semi-abruptly retouched Dufour bladelet, does not discriminate between the two supposed cultural taxa in the Cantabrian region, as can be seen in Appendix B5. And Chatelperron knives, Gravette points, and Noailles burins occasionally appear in "Aurignacian" assemblages. (The presence of so-called Aurignacian assemblages at the top of the El Pendo EUP sequence is anomalous within the now-accepted phylogenetic scheme, since the idea of the French "Aurignacian V" has been abandoned by one of its inventors, Sonneville-Bordes [1982], but it does highlight the existence of significant interassemblage variability even in the late EUP.) Clearly, the assignment of individual assemblages to one "culture" or the other often is a circular exercise fundamentally semantic in character.

These facts might call into question the ultimate validity of the "Aurignacian" and "Perigordian" culture concepts in the Cantabrian region. The two Chatelperronian assemblages from the region are composed of tools characteristic of the Perigordian, Aurignacian, *and* Mousterian types of industries. The "Aurignacian" and "Perigordian" indices are equal (about 7%) in both Chatelperronian assemblages, and the index of Mousterian tool types ranges from 40% to 60%.

Nonetheless, there does seem to be a series of assemblages (generally early, where this has been demonstrated stratigraphically or radiometrically) characterized by relatively many endscrapers (especially thick, heavy-duty ones) and relatively few backed implements or (usually) burins. Some of the assemblages do have classic "Aurignacian" bone "points," although the weapons function of all of these is not demonstrated. On the other hand, after about 27,000 B.P. and stratigraphically high in such sites as Morín, El Pendo, and El Castillo, there are assemblages that tend to have many backed blades, bladelets, and lithic points together with many burins (especially Noailles burins) and fewer endscrapers. These differences suggest a reorientation of technology, including the use of composite weapons with stone tips, barbs, or cutting edges (often incorporating very small lithic elements affixed to wooden or antler shafts). Thus, the terms "Aurignacian" and "Perigordian" or "Gravettian" are used here in a strictly descriptive sense, to facilitate communication but with no implication of ethnicity.

Site Numbers and Settlement Pattern

It has already been seen that the only two definite Chatelperronian levels in the Cantabrian region occur above Mousterian sequences in Santander (at Morín and at El Pendo—where there is an intervening early Aurignacian level). (There are levels with isolated Chatelperron points in Ekain and Labeko in Guizpúcoa.) Most of the few other demonstrably or arguably early Aurignacian levels also occur at sites that had been occupied earlier during the Mousterian (e.g., El Castillo, El Conde). There is no change in the low number of at least residential sites or in settlement patterns at the time of the transition. El Castillo, El Pendo, and Morín all continued to be occupied regularly throughout the course of the EUP and into the LUP. However, many other sites had their first EUP occupation later in time, either having never been substantially used before by humans (as at Cueto de la Mina) or after a hiatus in occupation (as at Amalda).

Altogether, there are as many as 26 known or possible EUP sites in Cantabrian Spain. In 20 of these, the EUP levels were stratified below Solutrean or Magdalenian deposits or both, although in several cases the attribution to the EUP is based essentially on this stratigraphic position only and not on any distinctive characteristics of the assemblages in question (i.e., they might be "Solutrean"/Last Glacial Maximum in age but lacking foliate points). Alternatively, some rather nondescript assemblages from basal levels at sites like Rascaño or La Riera might be assigned, on the basis of radiocarbon dates, to late within the EUP before the Last Glacial Maximum. Otherwise, many of the putative EUP assemblages are very small and undated; some are stratigraphically isolated and may be labeled "Aurignacian" or "Perigordian" by default, in the absence of Solutrean points or Magdalenian harpoons. In no more than nine of the sites were multiple EUP levels found during excavation. At five of these, both Aurignacian and Perigordian levels were defined, although, as noted above, some of the attributions are tenuous even within the framework of normative definitions borrowed from southwestern France. All but one of the known Cantabrian EUP sites are in caves, and the attribution of the one open-air site (Kurtzia in Vizcaya) is problematical (Barandiarán et al. 1960)—although this may be clarified by current excavations directed by J.M. Apellániz. Realistically, there may be no more than 21 credible EUP sites in the region, with perhaps 47 archeological levels among them representing some 20 millennia, clearly a small sample even if human populations were very low in the region.

The only major EUP sites in the region are Cueto de la Mina (Asturias), Lezetxiki, and, especially in terms of numbers and richness of levels, El Castillo, El Pendo, and Morín; only the last was excavated and analyzed with modern methods. There have been no significant EUP excavations in the region since the late 1960s, until the recent, ongoing reopening of the Aurignacian levels at El Castillo by V. Cabrera (unpublished) and the excavation of the newly discovered but chronologically rather late Perigordian in Amalda by Altuna et al. (1990). In contrast to the small number of EUP sites, there are now 44 known Solutrean sites in the same region, even though Solutrean technology spanned a maximum of 4,000 years as opposed to the 20,000-year span of the combined Aurignaco-Perigordian technology.

Some of the possible or certain EUP sites are located in the mountainous interior of the Cantabrian region on steep slopes (e.g., Lezetxiki, Bolinkoba, El Salitre, and Rascaño), but it is only with the Solutrean and especially the Magdalenian/Azilian that such sites became common and were frequently utilized (principally for ibex hunting as at Bolinkoba, Rascaño, El Piélago, Chufín, and Collubil). As pointed out by Freeman (1973b) for the Mousterian, most of the EUP sites are also located in the coastal zone (or in the hills not far from the shore in Guipúzcoa, which is virtually lacking in a coastal plain). They often are centrally located in sheltered spots (e.g., south- or west-facing lower

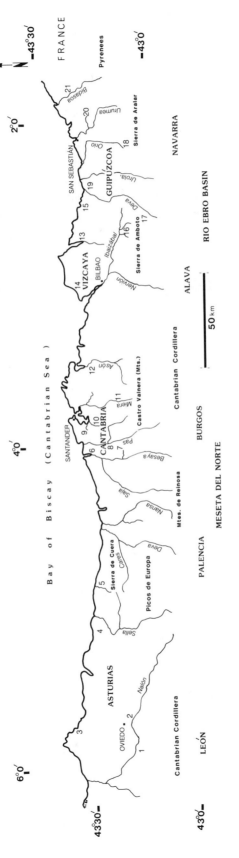

FIGURE 4.2. *Early Upper Paleolithic Cantabrian sites: 1, El Conde; 2, La Viña; 3, Cueva Oscura de Perán; 4, El Cierro; 5, Cueto de la Mina, La Riera, Arnero; 6, El Cudón; 7, Hornos de la Peña; 8, El Castillo; 9, El Pendo, Camargo; 10, Cueva Morín; 11, El Salitre, El Rascaño; 12, El Otero; 13, Santimamiñe; 14, Kurtzia; 15, Lumentxa, Atxurra; 16, Bolinkoba; 17, Lezetxiki, Labeko; 18, Usategi; 19, Ekain, Amalda; 20, Aitzbitarte; 21, Lezia.*

slopes of ridges or dolinas) between the Last Glacial shore and the north-ernmost Cordilleran ranges, just as in the Mousterian (Figure 4.2). This suggests little change in the hypothesized centrally based foraging strat-egy of the earlier period. In the EUP, bands may have engaged in resi-dential mobility in order to support their subsistence needs within fairly limited territories. No evidence has been found to date for nonlocal lithic raw materials, and the faunal data (discussed below) point to limited use of logistical strategies (i.e., specialized ibex hunting on cliffs, late in the Gravettian, or expeditions to the not-very-distance seacoast to gather shellfish), even toward the end of the EUP.

Later EUP Chronology

Although there are several (often contradictory) radiocarbon dates for the beginnings of the Cantabrian EUP (notably the "old" accelerator series from El Castillo and the "young" conventional series from Morín), there are few dates for the later period of the EUP. The Cueva Morín dates for the Aurignacian (noted above) are generally out of stratigraphic order and may be too young. At about 27,000 to 28,000 B.P. they overlap with a date from Level 7 in nearby El Rascaño (27,240 ± 950/ – 810 B.P.). The latter level has only 13 banal tools', it overlies a sterile deposit and then basal Level 9 (dated to >27,000 B.P.) characterized as a possible Aurignacian on the basis of the presence of several large retouched flint blades together with quartzite sidescrapers and a notch (González Eche-garay 1981). The Morín Aurignacian dates also overlap with two identical dates, 27,400 ± 1,000 or 1,100 B.P., from Level VI at Amalda; this level is attributed to the Upper Perigordian and is very rich in Noailles burins (and with several backed pieces, as well as significant numbers of "Aurig-nacian" types of endscrapers and blades).

After 27,000 B.P. there is a large hiatus in the Cantabrian radiocarbon dates, the next cluster being at the beginning of the Last Glacial Maxi-mum in association with assemblages that are either clearly Solutrean by normative definition (i.e., there are Solutrean points) or possibly late Gravettian/Perigordian (i.e., there are no Solutrean points but there are many backed pieces and often Noailles burins), or something else that does not fit the normative definitions of industries supposedly charac-teristic of this time. Level 5 (upper) at Morín, with a classic Gravetian assemblage, is dated to 20,100 ± 350 B.P. At La Riera Cave in Asturias, basal Level 1—below the long Solutrean sequence—has three dates: 20,860 ± 410, 20,360 ± 450, and 19,620 ± 390 B.P. But the overlying Level 4, with Solutrean points, has a date of 20,970 ± 620 B.P. (Straus and Clark

1986). Like Rascaño Level 9, La Riera Level 1 has 14 large retouched blades that come close to the definition of Aurignacian blades, 2 thick endscrapers, a Dufour bladelet, and several large dihedral burins but no Gravetian tool types.

Lezetxiki Level IIIa, with a C-14 date of 19,340 ± 780 B.P., has a rather nondescript Upper Paleolithic assemblage and no credible Solutrean pieces. Ekain Level VIII, with a date of 20,900 ± 450 B.P., yielded only 27 tools: backed bladelets, a few burins, truncations, and sidescrapers (Altuna and Merino 1984) Amalda Level V, whose based has been dated to 19,000 ± 340 B.P. and whose middle has been dated to 17,880 ± 390 B.P., is rich in burins, backed bladelets, and points but lacks Solutrean points despite its age. Although assigned to the "Perigordian VII" (Baldeón 1990b)—showing the problematic nature of the phylogenetic approach in the face of independent chronometric dating—this assemblage is considered later in this book in the context of the Last Glacial Maximum which corresponds chronologically to the Cantabrian Solutrean.

Paleo-environments

Butzer (1981) characterized the environments of the late Aurignacian and Gravettian of the Santander caves as "cool, with moist summers." Hoyos and Laville (1983) cautioned that this part of the El Pendo stratigraphy has been seriously affected by erosion. The basal levels (8 and 9) of Rascaño (Santander) were formed under cold conditions and Level 7, under cool, wet conditions, according to the sedimentological analyses by Laville and Hoyos (1981). As in these deposits, there is a great amount of cryoclastic spall in basal Level 1 at La Riera, interpreted as evidence of cold conditions—followed by more temperate, humid ones during which (Laugerie "interstadial") clays containing a fairly high arboreal pollen (AP) percentage were deposited (Laville 1986; Leroi-Gourhan 1986). The sediments of Amalda Level VI are interpreted as having been deposited under cold, humid conditions (Areso et al. 1990).

Arlette Leroi-Gourhan (1971) described evidence of a cooling trend after the "Arcy Interstadial," believed to be registered in Middle Aurignacian Level 6 of the Morín stratigraphy, with low but fluctuating arboreal pollen percentages in the terminal Aurignacian and Gravettian. Most of the few trees are pines, with some birches, hazels, and junipers and only occasional traces of surviving thermophile taxa. The AP is also very low in the isolated samples that refer to this time period at El Pendo (Leroi-Gourhan 1980). As at Morín, the presence of ferns and graminaceous grasses suggests fairly high humidity. The Amalda pollen diagram (Dupré 1990) suggests cold conditions during the "Noaillan" (or Upper Perigordian) of Level V, with virtually no arboreal pollens (save a few pine and traces of hazel, birch, and oak). Fern spores are abundant as are, at times, grass pollens (along with Cichoriae).

The presence of reindeer remains in El Castillo Level 14 and Amalda Level VI, both Gravettian, is another indicator of conditions colder than in the early part of the Cantabrian EUP. As yet, no analyses have definitively shown the existence in the Cantabrian region of the "Tursac Interstadial" (ca. 23,000 B.P.), as identified in caves in southwestern France, and its very existence is now being questioned (Turner and Hannon 1988; Sánchez 1990).

In sum, the later part of the EUP, corresponding to the development of industries labeled "Gravettian" or "Upper Perigordian," took place against a backdrop of declining temperatures and increasingly open grassland habitats, as global conditions moved into the Last Glacial Maximum around 25,000 years ago.

Cultural Developments

While works of mobile art are absent in the Chatelperronian and early Aurignacian in the Cantabrian region and pendants are very rare in the latter, there does seem to be an increase in such nonutilitarian objects in the later Aurignacian and especially in the Gravettian. The sample still remains extremely small, in contrast with contemporaneous periods in southwestern France. (The Aurignacian provenance of a horse engraved on a horse frontal bone from Hornos de la Peña—important to Breuil's scheme for "dating" cave art [Alcalde de Río et al. 1911:207–8]—is highly doubtful according to I. Barandiarán [1972:133–134]). There are engraved stones in the Gravettian levels of El Castillo (one with a possible animal figure) and Morín (one with an anthropomorph, plus another nonfigurative engraved and perforated stone) (see Barandiarán 1972; González Echegaray and Freeman 1971). In addition to a few perforated red deer canines and other teeth, there are at most one or two perforated shells per level in the Gravettian of Morín, Bolinkoba, and Amalda (Barandiarán 1972; González Echegaray and Freeman 1971; Baldeón 1990b). There is only scant, equivocal evidence for rupestral art dating to the EUP in the Cantabrian region (Straus 1987a); this is further discussed below.

Changes that do occur in technology during the course of what archeologists call the EUP—namely, formal distinctions between "the Aurignacian" and "the Gravettian"—primarily seem to involve developments in weapon tips, as noted above. The Aurignacian is classically distinguished by a relative abundance of *sagaies* (bone "points"), whereas the Perigordian has few. In contrast, the Perigordian is characterized by a number of sharp, small-to-medium-size stone "points": Gravettes, microgravettes, and backed bladelets (on the basis of microwear studies, widely believed to be barb or cutting edge elements of composite weapons tips). There is an exception to the bone point/stone point dichotomy in that some late Perigordian assemblages in France have so-called *sagaies d'Isturitz*, an antler point with transverse lines engraved across the base. Despite the proximity of the great EUP (and LUP) type site of Isturitz, such pieces are rare in Cantabrian Spain: one in Level F at Bolinkoba (Upper Perigordian with Noailles burins and at least one Solutrean point), one in Level G at Cueto de la Mina (nonetheless called "Aurignacian" by Bernaldo de Quirós [1982:71] despite its position *above* a level he calls "Perigordian" on equally weak grounds), and one in the otherwise poor, little-known site of Usategi Cave in Guipúzcoa (Altuna et al. 1982:81–82). The significance of these technological changes may be better appreciated in light of the subsistence evidence.

Early Upper Paleolithic Fauna and Subsistence

There are not enough quantified faunal assemblages from EUP levels to permit detailed discussion of Chatelperronian/Aurignacian and Gravettian archeofaunas separately. Appendix B6 presents the currently available data in terms of minimum numbers of individuals (MNIs), a statistic that tends to underestimate abundant taxa and to exaggerate the relative importance of rare taxa but nonetheless gives a fairly clear comparative picture of faunal composition.

In comparison with the Mousterian, EUP archeological levels are somewhat less richly populated with large carnivore remains. Cave bear apparently still made use of a few of the cave sites in the absence of humans (notably at Lezetxiki, Ekain, Amalda, and, to a lesser extent, El Pendo [Altuna 1972, 1990c; Altuna and Mariezkurrena 1984; Fuentes 1980]). Even in richly "anthropogenic" deposits, such as Amalda Level VI or Morín 5, hyena (*Crocuta crocuta*) and especially wolf (*Canis lupus*) remains are still fairly common. Even lion (*Panthera leo* and *P. spelaea*) and leopard (*P. pardus*) remains appear with some regularity in EUP levels, and dhole (*Cuon alpinus*; "Himalayan hunting dog") can be present, too. However, the smaller carnivores are now generally more prominent in the archeofaunas: fox (*Vulpes vulpes*), mustelids, and small felids. Although it is entirely likely that carnivores continued to use the same caves as humans (on a "time-sharing" basis) and that at least some of the ungulate remains in the caves may have been brought there by carnivores, the increase in small fur-bearers may indicate human hunting or trapping for pelts as well as food. Cutmark studies would be of use in determining this.

In any event, there is not an abrupt break between Middle and Upper Paleolithic faunas in terms of the representation (and possible ungulate carcass acquisition agency) of carnivores—notably large canids, felids, and ursids. Carnivore/ungulate ratios often run as high as 15% to 30%—without even including the extremely high values, >50%, at Lezetxiki (Straus 1982a; Altuna 1990c).

Appendix B6 also shows that red deer, bovines (aurochs or, more likely, bison), and horse all are consistently represented in EUP assemblages but never in very large numbers. (If the count of 216 *Cervus* "individuals" from basal Aurignacian Level 18 [Cabrera 1984:236] is correct and if it indeed does refer to MNIs as opposed to numbers of remains, it is an extraordinary number; however, perhaps it is explainable by the great thickness [up to 65 cm], internal complexity [at least three major lenses], and vast area over which this stratum was dug.) Ibex, chamois, and, to a lesser extent, roe deer also were frequent constituents of the EUP game bag—again, usually as single animals or in very small quantities. A notable exception to this, as in the Mousterian level of the same site, is Level VI of Amalda with 2,769 remains from a minimum of 59 chamois (Altuna 1990c). Clearly, there was something about the habitat directly around Amalda that made it a good place for chamois to inhabit and to be killed (and then carried more or less whole to the cave).

Another case of specialization is Bolinkoba, a site high on a steep cliff on the edge of the Sierra de Amboto, dominating a strategic gorge. This site was first occupied in the Gravettian (undated) and is one of the first instances of a true mountain site in the Cantabrian Upper Paleolithic. Level F (= VI, with many Noailles burins and one Solutrean point probably mixed into the layer from the overlying Solutrean levels) has a moderate size faunal assemblage with 83% ibex remains and only a smattering of remains of six other species (Altuna 1990d). The same is true of the basal (EUP) levels of Rascaño, also a cliff-side mountain site whose LUP levels, like those of Bolinkoba, are heavily dominated by ibex remains (Altuna 1981).

One of the most striking changes in human subsistence activities toward the end of the EUP is this new, systematic hunting from specialized mountain sites of the fast and elusive cliff-dwelling ibex (Straus

1977b). This is a phenomenon that grew in importance in the Solutrean and especially Magdalenian, both in the Cantabrian mountains and in the Pyrenees (Straus 1987b).

However, the EUP archeofaunas lack the large quantities of red deer remains so common even in thin LUP levels from limited excavations of sites in the coastal zone (notably El Juyo, Altamira, La Riera, and Tito Bustillo). Mass drives or surrounds of *Cervus* do not seem to have been part of the normal repertoire of EUP hunting strategies. In addition, boar remains are extremely rare in the EUP assemblages, which could be the result of unfavorable environments (although roe deer, also a species preferring wooded habitats, are present fairly consistently) or avoidance of the most dangerous game, or both.

EUP deposits are devoid of significant quantities of marine (or terrestrial) mollusks (El Castillo's uppermost Gravettian level [12] being a possible exception, although the "very abundant, large" limpets there are quantified [Cabrera 1984:276]). Shellfish only become consistent major components of archeological deposits (and presumably of human diets) in the LUP, when the coast was no closer (and perhaps a bit further during the Last Glacial Maximum) from the cave sites. Nor are fish ever more than very rare finds in EUP levels (e.g., four bones in Amalda Level VI [Morales and Roselló 1990]), again in contrast to the LUP. Nonetheless, the presence of at least a few shellfish, fish bones, aquatic birds, and a whale tooth in EUP deposits (the last two categories found in the Aurignacian of El Castillo) clearly indicates that human groups living at times in the interior also lived at other times near (or visited) the coast, which could be as far away as 25 km.

The question of hunting or netting birds in the EUP is an interesting one in light of the large, diverse collections of bird bones from El Castillo. Many of the species may have inhabited the vast mouth of this cave while others may have been taken by raptors who were among the cave dwellers, but others (notably marine birds) seem hard to explain other than by human action (Cabrera 1984). Small numbers of bird bones appear in a few other EUP levels, notably Amalda Level VI where Eastham (1990) identified 53 remains, of which over half are of chough, which would have lived on the rocky cliffs around the cave mouth. Many of the other birds are raptors, which could explain the choughs as their prey. Detailed examination of the bird bones for cut or scrape marks might help determine whether and to what extent humans were involved in their capture and butchering.

Unfortunately, evidence of utilization of plants as food is absent, although heavy-duty stone tools that might have had a role therein are occasionally present in EUP assemblages and, as noted above, side-scrapers, denticulates, and notches can at times be frequent. Nut-bearing and other trees and bushes would have been more common in Aurignacian times than in Gravettian ones, perhaps helping to explain the shift away from assemblages dominated by thick scrapers and large retouched blades (woodworking tools?) and toward tools dominated by often much more delicate lithic elements of possible hunting weapons and small burins (possibly in part used to work antler and hide) along with thin endscrapers on blades (for working hide).

Again there are indications of both continuity and change across the Middle Paleolithic–UpperPaleolithic transition and throughout the EUP. Humans have not yet totally excluded the large carnivores from their chosen caves, suggesting less human presence, or less human continuity. On the other hand, the presence of large carnivores is diminished, suggesting a possible human role in trapping small fur-bearing carnivores. Mass kills of red deer do not seem to have been conducted as they commonly would be in the LUP. As in the Middle Paleolithic, bovines and horse continued to be major food sources. There is no apparent environmental reason for their *relative* decline in numerical importance in LUP archeofaunas because both bison and horse can easily be open country species. The occasional kill of a single bison or horse often seems to have sufficed for EUP band subsistence for long periods of time. On the other hand there is some evidence of specialized chamois and ibex hunting, the latter requiring elaborate strategies, tactics, weapons, and, for the first time, utilization of high mountain, cliff-side sites: logistical camps. Boar, even though especially present under interpleniglacial conditions, were avoided, however. The coast was visited, and shells were collected, probably mostly for ornamentation as well as "snacks," but marine (or estuarine or riverine) resources were not exploited at all systematically (at least not to the extent of being transported back to residential sites). Similarly, birds sometimes may have been taken (notably at El Castillo), but this seems to have been a rare activity.

EUP subsistence seems to have been intermediate in many respects to that of the Mousterian and that of the regional LUP, both of which were characterized by intensification through both overall diversification *and* situational specialization. The EUP, particularly in the late phase (i.e., Gravettian), shows indications of increasing intensification, representing the early phase of LUP subsistence strategies. This may have been related to the onset of pleniglacial environmental conditions after about 25,000 B.P.

Early Upper Paleolithic Structures and Burials

A novel but rare aspect of the Cantabrian EUP is the evidence from Cueva Morín of considerable human modification of the interior of a cave mouth by digging and possible construction. The rich structural and burial evidence from Morín was described by Freeman and González Echegaray (1970; also Freeman 1971; González Echegaray and Freeman 1973, 1978). Dating to the early Aurignacian (Level 8a: at least 27,000 to 28,000 B.P.), there is a large rectangular dugout, a line of holes, and a series of three apparent tombs containing "sediment casts" of possible human corpses. The shallow rectangular dugout measures about 2.6 m long and at least 1.7 m wide (having been cut through by the Carballo–Vega del Sella trench). It contained a shallow, oval-shaped basin, measuring 35 by 40 cm and filled with charcoal-blackened sediments, burnt stones, and bones. A short, shallow trench extends from this basin hearth in a southeastwardly direction (away from the cave entrance and beyond the limits of the dugout). This feature is reasonably interpreted as a draft trench. The dugout floor was covered by thin lenses of fine sediments interpreted as trampling laminae, suggesting repeated use of the structure although not necessarily over a long period of time. Extending in a line continuing the axis of the longest surviving wall of the dugout toward the back of the cave is a line of holes: one group of two, one of three, and one single hole for a total of six. All holes are marked by darker stained sediments standing out against the generally light color of the surrounding dirt. When sectioned, the vertical sides and flat bottoms of these features suggest postholes in which posts 12 to 19 cm in diameter had been left to rot. Traces of digging stick marks were preserved at the side of the triple posthole group.

Further to the southeast (toward the cave interior) two elongated, subparallel mounds of dark sediments were discovered, excavated, and found to cap separate trenches. One measured 210 by 52 cm and the other 168 by 47 cm. The smaller trench contained no organic remains or traces, but digging stick marks were revealed at its base. The larger trench contained a putative human-shaped "pseudomorph" together with a mold of what may have been a small ungulate. A small pit connected to the main trench, near the "foot" end, contained pieces of ochre and burnt bone. A similar pit with similar contents was found toward the foot end of the smaller (empty) trench. The sediments of the larger trench contents were jacketed in plaster, cut from the underlying sediments, flown to the Smithsonian Institution, indurated, and turned over for excavation from the underside. During this process, a third "burial" was apparently cut into, revealing part of a second pseudomorph.

It is hard to determine which objects in the rich midden fill surrounding the trenches might be grave-offerings. Two knives and a bifacial scraper are interpreted as possibilities, not only because of their locations either in the small connected pit of the smaller trench or in the larger trench in contact with the pseudomorph but also because they are typologically unusual. Ochre was found on the larger of the two mounds, as was a small dug-out hearth full of ash and burnt bone and underlain by burnt sediments.

The one curious aspect of these burials is that no supposed human bone or tooth survived, whereas faunal preservation in the surrounding level is good. This might have been due to microtopographical differences that affected preservation adversely but enabled gradual replacement of body tissue by fat-wax and then conversion into a sedimentary mold. Due to a high calcium content, the mold fluoresces under ultraviolet light.

The individual in the larger trench is believed to have been decapitated and to have had his legs severed, perhaps to lessen the amount of tomb digging and to make him fit. The head is interpreted as having been placed at the side of the body. Estimates of the individual's height range from 185 to 195 cm, which is in line with other very tall early Cro-Magnon males in western Europe.

All of these structures in Cueva Morín were dug from the early Aurignacian Level 8a down into the uppermost Mousterian deposit. They represent a considerable amount of effort at modification of the living space and, presumably, care for the dead. The facts that such effort was expended, that the dugout seems to have been used repeatedly, that the some of the postholes seem to have been replaced, and that at least three individuals may have been buried (and not all at the same time, since the large, complete pseudomorph overlaid the remnant of a second one) all suggest a degree of permanency (or at least repetitiveness) of human occupation of Morín at this time—possibly by a single band with a degree of temporal continuity. Unfortunately, these finds are unique for the EUP of the Cantabrian region.

Amalda, a recent and meticulous excavation, yielded only a concentration of charcoal-rich sediments and burnt bones with no structure in its Level VI (Altuna 1990c). Citing Obermaier's rather vague descriptions, Cabrera (1984:93–94) mentions "hearths" in the Aurignacian and Gravettian levels of El Castillo, but most of these designations may simply refer to organic-rich lenses with no specific descriptions of dugout or stone-lined hearths in the strict sense. Similarly, Vega del Sella (1916) speaks of "hearths" in the basal "Aurignacian" level at Cueto de la Mina, but with no specific description. Regrettably, there is no description of

features in El Pendo. EUP humans obviously constructed fairly elaborate features on occasion, but these are by no means as frequent as in
the LUP. Notably, roasting pits or floors (accumulations of fire-cracked
rock) do not seem to have been common features of EUP living areas.

If the interpretation of the Morín trenches is correct, burial of the
dead made its appearance in the Cantabrian region early in the EUP.
Unfortunately, the Morín case is unique. The only actual human remains
from the EUP in the Cantabrian region (the Camargo skullcap and the
Castillo mandible) were lost long ago and were never thoroughly described
or studied (but see Garralda [1989] for some details from H. Vallois'
unpublished description of the Castillo remains). Although complete
burials are absent in the region until the Azilian and Asturian, isolated
human remains (teeth, fragments of bones) are relatively common in
Solutrean and Magdalenian cave site deposits, perhaps an indication of
an increased regional population in the LUP.

Conclusions

The Early Upper Paleolithic of the Cantabrian region bears a general,
and some specific, similarity to the Chatelperronian, Aurignacian, and
Gravettian of adjacent regions of southwestern France. Several osseous
and lithic fossil director artifact types characteristic of different so-called
cultures and phases of the French EUP are found in the Cantabrian region,
although not necessarily in large quantities or in the "correct" cultural
or temporal slot. Such peculiar, technically complex types as split-base
and lozenge-shaped bone points, *sagaies d'Isturitz*, or Noailles burins
suggest the existence of direct or "down-the-line" contacts between
Cantabrian and French, perhaps as part of widespread mating networks
necessitated by low population density in the long, narrow, physically
circumscribed Cantabrian region (Wobst 1974, 1976). The Cantabrian
EUP was definitely a part of the wider EUP world, but with the following clear regional differences.

1. Although blades/bladelets and tools made on them (endscrapers,
burins, perforators, backed elements, points) are significant elements of
the Cantabrian lithic technologies, raw material considerations, especially in flint-poor, quartzite-rich Santander and Asturias, resulted in
significantly "archaic" looking EUP (and LUP) assemblages in many sites.
Large, presumably hand-held tools such as sidescrapers, denticulates,
notches, choppers, and bifaces continued to be made and used. A more
fully leptolithic technology developed only in the later EUP, but, even
then, Gravettian assemblages contain significant numbers of "Middle

Paleolithic" elements. In the Basque Country, the abundance of good-quality flint (albeit usually in much smaller nodules than are common in the Périgord) may have been at least partly responsible for the development of rather microlithic late EUP industries with many backed bladelets and small Noailles burins—indicative of hafting systems for fairly elaborate compound tools/weapons.

2. There was no "explosion" of "artistic" or "ornamental" activity with the onset of the Upper Paleolithic in the Cantabrian region. There is no such evidence for the Chatelperronian, and only gradually through the course of the EUP do engraved stones and bones at perforated teeth and shells seem to increase ever so slightly. This is in sharp contrast to the situation even in Isturitz just on the other side of the low Basque Pyrenees. Representative art was virtually absent in Cantabrian Spain at this time, and there is only the most scanty evidence of rupestral art possibly dating to the EUP in this region. Whatever purposes of marking may have been served by Upper Paleolithic art and ornamentation, group identification, information storage, or magico-religious expression, such possible "causes" were apparently not yet very important to the *Cantabrian* situation in the EUP. If "artistic and ornamental activity" was a density-dependent phenomenon, at least in part, its scarcity in the Cantabrian EUP relative to the LUP would be understandable in terms of the low regional population in the former period.

3. The EUP settlement pattern does not differ markedly from that of the Middle Paleolithic because site numbers increased only marginally and EUP levels often are found in the same caves as the Mousterian ones. However, there is evidence that, by the late EUP, some caves in steep, rocky habitats in the mountains of the near interior of the Cantabrian region were being used as logistical camps for ibex hunting. Human population levels may not have been markedly larger than in Mousterian times; large stretches of the region are totally lacking in EUP sites, and only certain "preferred" sectors (notably central Santander) seem to have been used substantially over long periods of time.

4. At least occasionally, EUP inhabitants did build dug-out hearths and structures, including possible graves, but these were rare phenomena and a far cry from the contemporaneous structures and burials of the Moravian EUP, for example. The use of fire in general seems to have been less sophisticated than in the Cantabrian LUP.

5. Humans apparently were beginning to gain the upper hand over large carnivores but may still have been "sharing" certain caves with them on an alternating basis. Some of the ungulate remains in those caves may still have been brought in by carnivores. On the other hand, humans may have begun to exploit smaller carnivores for pelts.

6. Subsistence practices in the Cantabrian EUP involved presumed hunting of the same ungulate species as in the Middle Paleolithic—notably red deer, bison, and horse procured individually or in very small groups—but with the consistent addition of ibex. The ibex remains suggest the development of fairly sophisticated, organized, cooperative activities, perhaps including logistical hunting expeditions to mountain sites used to supply lowland residential camps. They also may imply the development of propelled weapons, tipped by the Gravette points or edged with backed bladelets. Trips to the coast also seem to have been made fairly regularly from major sites located centrally in areas like the coastal plain/foothill ecotone in Santander. Nonetheless, marine resources were not exploited systematically, nor were boar, which are dangerous. Some birds seem to have been captured, but again not consistently. The lack of exotic lithic raw materials suggests that territory sizes may have been relatively restricted and that contacts with distant human groups may have been on a fairly infrequent, low-level basis. Some aspects of EUP subsistence hark back to the Middle Paleolithic; others seem to presage the sophistication and complexity of the intensified subsistence of the regional LUP.

In sum, the whole EUP in Cantabrian Spain constituted a long, irregular, and, in many domains, gradual transition from Middle Paleolithic adaptations to the "classic Upper Paleolithic" adaptations of the better known LUP of this region. Under way since at least 40,000 years ago, the changes in the EUP were a mosaic. Data are lacking on the timing and nature of the anatomical shift from *Homo sapiens neandertalensis* to *Homo sapiens sapiens* in this region. The cultural data do not support an abrupt, punctuation event in terms of adaptations. This contrasts with other regions of Europe. So, even though adjacent to and undoubtedy in some degree of contact with hominid groups living in France, the bands inhabiting Cantabrian Spain adapted to the conditions of the Interpleniglacial and beginnings of the Upper Pleniglacial on their own terms, given their own physical environmental and demographic conditions and resources. The EUP of the region leads into the LUP with evidence of both considerable continuity and significant change in conditioning factors at the outset of the Last Glacial Maximum.

Chapter 5

ADAPTATIONS TO THE LAST GLACIAL MAXIMUM: "The Solutrean"

Solutrean Chronology

THE "Solutrean" is one of the most exotic and controversial subdivisions of the Upper Paleolithic of France, Spain, and Portugal. This is due in large part to the period's innovative, beautiful, and relatively short-lived mastery of leaf-point manufacture, sometimes by invasive pressure retouch. Generations of prehistorians have tried to explain "Solutrean origins" through migrations or *in situ* phylogenetic development. Here, I combine and add to both approaches to suggest that an expanded regional population adapted to changing demographic and physical environments by adopting new weapons and by intensifying this food quest.

The cultural period typified by the general presence of Solutrean leaf-shaped or shouldered stone points in archeological assemblages spans the traditional Würm III/IV interstadial and the beginning of the Würm IV stadial. Credible radiocarbon dates of levels with Solutrean points range from 20,970 ± 620 to 16,090 ± 240 B.P. (Appendix C1), although there are also three stratigraphically incoherent dates of slightly under 16,000 B.P. from the La Riera Cave sequence (probably too young). In addition there are dates in the range 20,000 to 21,000 B.P. for levels lacking Solutrean points at La Riera (Level 1), Ekain (Level VIII), Cueva Morín (Level 5sup.), and Lezetxiki (Level IIIa); these levels have been attributed variously to the "Upper Perigordian," "Aurignacian," or "Solutrean". At the opposite end of the time range, Urtiaga Level F, dated to 17,050 ± 140 B.P. generally has been labeled "Lower Magdalenian," although there is now a report that it actually contains a few Solutrean pieces (Sánchez 1990). Amalda Level V (dated to 19,000 ± 340 and 17,880 ± 390 B.P.) has anomalously been called "Perigordian VII" or "Protomagdalenian" (Baldeón 1990b). The next oldest dates for the Cantabrian

"Lower Magdalenian" are from La Riera Levels 19 and 20 (16,420 ± 430 and 17,160 ± 440 B.P., respectively), Ekain Level VIIb (16,510 ± 270 B.P.), and Rascaño Level 5 (16,430 ± 130 B.P.). These overlap with dates from levels with Solutrean points.

In both of the recently excavated, long, radiocarbon-dated Solutrean stratigraphic sequences (La Riera and Las Caldas), there are levels without Solutrean points, highlighting the variability among lithic artifact assemblages dating to this period. The purely cultural nature of the supposed differences between the Solutrean and Aurignaco-Perigordian assemblages on the one hand and the Lower Magdalenian ones on the other hand has been seriously challenged recently (e.g., Straus 1975b, 1979a,b, 1983b, 1986c,d, 1987c). Aside from the presence of points, some "Solutrean" assemblages resemble "Gravettian" ones and others are similar to "Cantabrian Lower Magdalenian" assemblages in composition.

Environments of the Last Glacial Maximum

According to CLIMAP (1976; McIntyre et al. 1976), the Gulf Stream was shifted southward during the Last Glacial Maximum and did not flow into the Cantabrian Sea as it does today. Instead, it ran into the western coast of the Iberian Peninsula. The southern edge of polar waters was situated at 42° N, causing an exceptionally steep thermal gradient at Galicia. August and February water temperatures at the surface of the Cantabrian Sea thus would have been about 10 and 11 degrees C colder, respectively, than they are now, and there would have been pack ice on the sea. At this time, the Cantabrian coast experienced cold, stormy conditions, despite its low latitude and relatively high degree of insolation.

Butzer (1981) divides the 21,000 to 17,000 B.P. time range among his regional climatic phases 36, 37, and 38, principally developed in the Santander caves of Morín, El Castillo, and El Pendo. These units are parts of a generalized glacial maximum period (Oxygen Isotope Stage 2) of severe cold, increasingly dry conditions, and unstable slope soils. Phase 36 is characterized as somewhat more humid and temperate than the succeeding phase 37, which had dry, cold conditions with less runoff. Phase 38, at the end of the Solutrean time range, witnessed only a moderate increase in runoff. The currently unglaciated Cantabrian Cordillera and Picos de Europa had significant centers of mountain glaciation sustained by periods of abundant snowfall, with permanent snow lines averaging 1,500 m in elevation (Butzer 1973, 1981; Straus 1983b:24–26 with references). Periglacial phenomena attributable to the period include cryoturbation, solifluxion, screes, and frost weathering in caves.

Figure 5.1. *La Riera Cave (Posada de Llanes, Asturias).*

Few detailed sedimentological studies of archeological sites in the region are available for this period; however, a general picture of significant climatic fluctuations is beginning to form. At Cueva Morín (Santander), undated (but probably late) Solutrean Level 3 includes angular frost weathering products, indicating the existence of cold climatic conditions (Butzer 1971). Similar observations were made by Butzer (1981) at the Santander caves of El Castillo, Cobalejos, and Hornos de la Peña.

The extensive, detailed analyses by Laville (1981, 1986; Straus et al. 1981) of the deposits in La Riera Cave (Asturias, Figure 5.1) show that the Solutrean sequence began (Levels 2 and 3) under humid conditions, possibly at the end of the Laugerie oscillation (old "Würm III/IV interstadial") as defined in southwestern France. Levels 4 through 8, with abundant éboulis, however, were deposited under decidedly cold conditions, corresponding to the glacial maximum at the beginning of "Würm IV." Levels 9 through 17 show evidence of wetter, moderating conditions, with clayier sediments containing fewer (more corroded) éboulis (except in Level 16). These conditions—equivalent to the Lascaux oscillation—continued into the earliest Lower Magdalenian levels at La

Riera and at Rascaño (Santander) (Laville and Hoyos 1981). The major climatic subdivisions would seem to correspond to Butzer's (1981) phases 36 through 38.

At Las Caldas (Asturias), Hoyos (1981) developed a paleoclimatic scheme based on his sedimentological analyses; it now is associated with eight radiocarbon dates (Jordá et al. 1982). The basal Solutrean levels (19 and 18) are said to have been deposited under generally temperate, humid conditions, interrupted by a colder, drier episode (Levels 17 through 15). This was followed by a return to relatively temperate, humid conditions in Levels 14 through 10, with an increase in frost weathering products in Level 12. Levels 9 through 3 were formed under generally cold conditions, with more moderate episodes in Levels 6 and 3 and especially intense cold in Levels 7 and 4. This sequence is claimed to span the full period from the Laugerie interstadial to the early Dryas I stadial (Jordá et al. 1982), despite obvious contradictions in the radiocarbon dates (Straus 1986c). Nonetheless, Hoyos' (1981) work at Las Caldas corroborates the existence of cold, albeit fluctuating, climatic conditions with oscillations particularly in the amount of available moisture during the 3,000- to 4,000-year period of the Solutrean in this region.

In the radiometrically late Solutrean Level IV of Amalda (Guipúzcoa), the sediments were deposited under very cold conditions with variable humidity. There are abundant large and small éboulis. The coldest, driest conditions occurred at the beginning of the level's formation (Areso et al. 1990). At the base of this level there are very few arboreal pollens and almost all are pine. Other trees (including oak) make minor appearances in the upper part, and fern spores increase. Cichoriae pollens are generally abundant. Dry, open grasslands and hearths dominate, with an increase in humidity at the end. This period could be assigned to inter-Laugerie/Lascaux and to the beginning of Lascaux, or it could date to early Dryas I (Dupré 1990). Sediments and pollen agree in showing the extreme rigor of conditions of this time.

Arlette Leroi-Gourhan analyzed pollen from Level 3 at Cueva Morín (1971) and from Solutrean Levels 2 through 17 at La Riera (1986; Straus et al. 1981). With an AP of about 18%, the former spectrum indicates the existence of open, steppe-like vegetation with small thickets in sheltered areas. The basal Solutrean levels at La Riera have few tree pollens and contain high percentages of heather pollens. Cool but humid conditions are suggested. These were followed by dry and even colder conditions (through Level 8); the vegetation is characterized as an Atlantic heath and is devoid of trees. Tree pollens, including those of some thermophile deciduous taxa, increased somewhat in Levels 9 through 15. Conditions were more temperate and humid, with the development of localized thickets. However, beginning at the top of Level 16, dry steppe-like vegetation replaces the heath. But at the end of the Solutrean and beginning of the Magdalenian at La Riera, deciduous trees again increase. AP never exceeds 6% at La Riera, even during the so-called Lascaux interstadial.

An isolated pollen spectrum that can be correlated with the end of the La Riera Solutrean sequence by radiocarbon dates (i.e., about 17,000 B.P.) is available from Cueva Chufín, a site located in a sheltered interior valley of eastern Santander. In contrast to the more exposed, coastal plain sites of Cueva Morín and La Riera, the Chufín AP reaches as high as 55%. However, much of this is composed of pine, an overrepresented taxon because of its high production of very aerodynamic pollen. However, there are also many alder pollens as well as those of other deciduous trees (Boyer-Klein 1980). Local development of woods with abundant ferns in sheltered, well-watered habitats is indicated for the Lascaux interstadial in the vicinity of Chufín. The end of this relatively temperate, humid episode is also seen in the pollen spectrum for the basal Magdalenian (Level 5c) at Rascaño (Boyer-Klein 1981).

Even two isolated pollen spectra from different parts of the Solutrean sequence at Las Caldas analyzed by M-M. Paquereau (Hoyos 1981) demonstrate a range of vegetation types, with AP of 22% and 35% composed mostly of pine pollens. Inferred conditions ranged from cold/dry to more temperate/humid. These differences in humidity are particularly well demonstrated by dramatically different ratios of composites to grasses. Other relevant pollen spectra include those of the Solutrean stratum at Isturitz (Pyrénées-Atlantiques, France) (Leroi-Gourhan 1956) and various coastal bogs in Asturias and Galicia dated to this period (Mary et al. 1975, 1977a,b). All show vegetations nearly devoid of trees, with open areas ranging between steppe-park and heath.

In sum, the presence of trees, always limited compared with pre-agricultural Holocene climax vegetation, was variable both in time and space during the Würm Upper Pleniglacial and was dependent on localized conditions of moisture and shelter from strong, cold ocean winds. The overall vegetation of the region was heath or grassland, with the proportions of heathers, Gramineae, Compositae, and ferns principally dependent on available moisture as well as on soils. There were periods of great coldness and dryness when ground cover was incomplete, thereby favoring slope instability.

The ungulate faunas associated with Solutrean levels are generally banal from a climatic standpoint, but all the major species (bison, horse, and red deer) could thrive in open vegetations (despite the frequent erroneous interpretation by archeologists of *Cervus* as a woodland indicator [Straus 1981a]). Reindeer were present throughout the region at this time but always scarce. This is best represented in Basque sites nearest to France, where reindeer was the dominant ungulate at this time. Those Basque sites with reindeer are Amalda, Aizbitarte, Ermittia, and Santimamiñe, but it also has been identified at Altamira and Cueto de la Mina to the west (see Appendices C2 and C3). *Rangifer* seems to have been somewhat more abundant (albeit still scarce) in Magdalenian contexts. Ibex and, to a lesser extent, chamois are present in many Solutrean levels, particularly in or near steep, rocky slopes. Their presence near the coast, as at La Riera which is near a low but very steep coastal mountain range, could have been caused in part by displacement from the then-glaciated Cordilleran summits and high valleys.

The only climatically indicative micro-mammal present in Cantabrian Solutrean contexts (and indeed common at Amalda [Pemán 1990]) is the Nordic vole (*Microtus oeconomus*), today not found south of the Netherlands. This rodent inhabits cold, humid habitats (Altuna 1972, 1986; Straus et al. 1981). The presence of the arctic mollusk *Cyprina islandica* in the Solutrean of El Castillo is an indicator of the very cold ocean waters referred to above. However, the absence of the periwinkle *Littorina littorea* in the middle levels (9 through 15) of the Solutrean sequence at La Riera coincides with the Lascaux oscillation and may indicate somewhat more moderate ocean temperatures after 18,000 B.P. (Straus et al. 1981).

In general terms, the Last Glacial Maximum environments, coinciding with the Solutrean in northern Spain, included an open, somewhat broader coastal zone adjoining a cold, stormy sea to the north. The mountainous interior to the south, with high relief, provided some habitats adequately sheltered from the north sea winds (e.g., sunny, south-facing slopes) and, at times, receiving enough water to permit the development of local thickets and woods composed of pines and various deciduous taxa, particularly during relatively temperate oscillations. The high mountain crests and some upper river valleys were glaciated, and snowfall may have been abundant at times due to the proximity of the coast. Steep, north-facing slopes were probably denuded and many slopes underwent active solifluxion. While rigorous, these environments were rich in game as well as some fish and shellfish and must have been attractive to hunter-gatherer groups, compared with the far less productive, far harsher environments of northern Europe or even the Spanish Meseta during the Last Glacial Maximum.

The Nature of the Archeological Record

The archeological materials from the Solutrean period are found in discrete sites, almost exclusively under rockshelters or within caves (generally cave vestibules), except for an open-air site (la Vega de Corao) said to contain Solutrean remains (Blas and Fernández-Tresguerres 1989:46). Interpretive problems related to this archeological signature are addressed below. Recent excavations in such sites as Cueva Morín, La Riera, Cueva Chufín, Las Caldas, Amalda, and Cova Rosa show the Solutrean levels to be discrete horizons with considerable integrity. Features (hearths, pits, manuport clusters, etc.) are sometimes found on surfaces that probably represent individual "living floors." However, true sterile zones between levels generally are absent, and even so-called single-component Solutrean sites (Chufín, Morín Level 3) may represent palimpsests formed of residues from several separate, albeit penecontemporaneous, occupations. "Levels" defined during modern excavations clearly have greater behavioral integrity than the major "cultural" strata often characterizing older excavations, although Vega del Sella (1916) made five subdivisions of the important Solutrean sequence at Cueto de la Mina (unfortunately, not consistently preserved during subsequent curation of the collections).

Site Numbers, Locations, and Settlement Pattern

Prima facie evidence of Solutrean occupations—the presence of Solutrean points (laurel-leaf, unifacial, shouldered, and concave base types)—has been found at 44 sites to date, although the materials from a few of these locations (dug in the early years of prehistorical research in the region) have been lost (e.g., Sel, Bona, Carranceja, Salitre). The sites are listed by province in Table 5.1 and mapped in Figure 5.2.

For the first time in Cantabrian prehistory, the sites are distributed throughout the entire region from the French border in the east to the end of limestone bedrock in central Asturias in the west and from the present coast to the edge of the Cordillera and Picos de Europa, with no major gaps in site distribution. The 44 sites represent about 11 sites per millenium for the Solutrean period, in contrast to only about 1.3 sites per millennium for the Aurignacio-Perigordian period. Thus, despite likely major loss of even Solutrean sites, due to erosion and burial, the record from 20,500 to 16,500 B.P. probably presents a significant portion of the actual settlement pattern, especially in terms of large- and medium-scale occupation loci. Another first-time occurrence in the record is the presence of many minor sites, possibly special-purpose, "logistical"

Table 5.1 Solutrean Sites in the Cantabrian Region as of 1985

Navarra	19. La Pasiega
1. Abauntz	20. Hornos de la Peña
Guipúzcoa	21. Peña de Carranceja
2. Aitzbitarte III & IV, Torre	22. Altamira
3. Amalda	23. Cueva Chufín
4. Ermittia, Urtiaga	*Asturias*
Vizcaya	24. Cueva del Sel
5. Santimamiñe	25. Balmori
6. Atxeta	26. Tres Calabres
7. Atxuri	27. La Riera
8. Bolinkoba	28. Cueto de la Mina
Santander	29. Coberizas
9. El Mirón	30. El Buxú, Corao
10. La Haza	31. Sulamula, Aviao
11. El Salitre	32. Cova Rosa
12. La Bona (Rascaño)	33. El Cierro
13. Fuente del Francés	34. Cueva Oscura de Perán
14. Cueva Morín	35. La Viña
15. El Pendo	36. La Lluera
16. Cobalejos	37. Las Caldas
17. Camargo, El Ruso	38. Peña de Candamo
18. El Castillo	

camps or foraging way stations (e.g. Atxeta, Atxuri, Torre, Bona, El Ruso, Carranceja, Buxú, Aviao, Sulamula, Tres Calabres, Coberizas, Oscura). Noteworthy in this category is the appearance of a Solutrean point in the basal level (below a sequence of Magdalenian strata) at Abauntz cave *in northern Navarra.* This is evidence of human penetration of the high country to the south of the Cordillera, perhaps only in summer, if we can extrapolate back from the seasonality evidence from the main Magdalenian level at this site (Utrilla 1982). However, the recent discovery of a Solutrean deposit (dated to 19,700 ± 310 B.P. [GrN–12681]), as well as Magdalenian levels (dated to 12,660 ± 70 and 12,020 ± 350 B.P. [GrN–14561 and 12682]) in Chaves Cave in Huesca, points to at least some Upper Pleniglacial and Tardiglacial human occupation of the Ebro Basin and contacts between the Vasco-Cantabrian and Mediterrean worlds along the *southern* flanks of the Pyrenees (Utrilla 1989).

An increasingly dense human settlement of the region is also suggested by the fact that many caves and rockshelters were apparently first occupied during the Solutrean period. These include Abauntz, Ermittia,

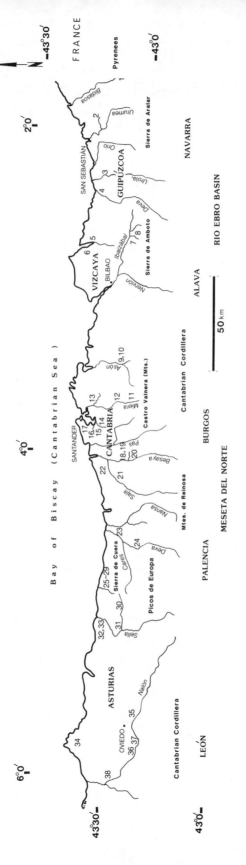

FIGURE 5.2. Solutrean sites (see Table 5.1 for site names).

Atxeta, Altamira, Balmori, Coberizas, Tres Calabres, Cova Rosa, La Lluera, La Viña, Cueva Oscura, and others. Some Solutrean point-bearing deposits are underlain by strata containing banal industries assignable either to the Aurignacian/Perigordian or to a Solutrean without points (e.g., La Riera, Aitzbitarte). (Because bedrock was not attained in many of these excavations, it is conceivable that pre-Solutrean levels might exist at some of these sites.) As noted below, there are also several sites at which the only Paleolithic deposits are of Solutrean attribution. Despite the brevity of the Solutrean period, it is exceptionally well represented in the Cantabrian region, in part undoubtedly reflecting a more substantial human population at the height of the Last Glacial Maximum.

It is probably not simply coincidental that at this time, as a consequence of the extreme cold, drought, and glacial advances of the Last Glacial Maximum, northern and northwestern Europe was abandoned. The northerly parts of the human range were progressively less used as conditions worsened so that, by around 20,000 B.P., human habitation or utilization of England, northern France, Belgium, Netherlands, Germany and Poland was ephemeral at best (Campbell 1977; Fagnart 1988; Schmider 1990; Otte 1990; Weniger 1990; Kozlowski 1990). The range had contracted southward, and, after passage of time, more people were living in the southern parts of western Europe—south of the Loire. Not a migration, this cumulative increase in human population in southwest Europe may be part of the explanation for the dramatically larger site numbers in the "Solutrean" of Cantabrian Spain and for the need to intensify human subsistence strategies in this region (Straus 1977b, n.d.c.; Straus and Clark 1986; Clark and Straus 1983).

The regular pattern in distribution of Solutrean sites along the length of the Cantabrian region is clearly evident in Figure 5.2. The salient feature of this pattern is the alignment of sites along major river valleys. In Asturias there are four sites along (and one site adjacent to) the valley of the Río Nalón, six along the Río Sella drainage (including Ríos Piloña and Güeña), and five in the lower drainage basin of Rios Calabres and Bedón (connected by a pass to the middle Sella). In Santander there are three sites in the Saja-Besaya drainage, three in the Río Pas valley, four in the immediate drainage of the modern Bay of Santander (where there probably was a fluvial system under conditions of full glacial sea level regression), at least three sites along the Río Miera valley above its estuary at the Bay of Santander, and two in the Río Asón drainage. Vizcaya has four sites along the valleys of the Ría de Guernica-Río Oca and upper Río Ibaizábal, all of which are joined by a low pass. There are three sites in the Río Urumea drainage in Guipúzcoa. So far, the other major river valleys in the region have yielded only one Solutrean site each: Río Deva of Asturias and Santander, Río Nansa, Río Deva of Guipúzcoa, and Río Urola (although in the last case the Solutrean site of Amalda may be accompanied by Ekain, where Level VIII yielded a small, diagnostically banal Upper Paleolithic industry and a radiocarbon date of 20,900 ± 450 B.P. [Altuna and Merino 1984]). Further archeological reconnaissance and cave testing undoubtedly will add to this list of sites and will fill in some of the blanks in their distribution along the main river systems. (At least 11 sites have been discovered in the decade since I did my dissertation research on the Solutrean [Straus 1975a].)

With the exception of Abauntz, which is located in high piedmont surrounded by peaks higher than 1,000 m (outliers of the Cantabrian and Pyrenees mountain chains, which join to the north of the site), no known Solutrean site is at an elevation of more than 500 m above present sea level (600 m above Upper Pleniglacial sea level). (The site of Cueva del Sel may lie as high as 600 m above present sea level in high mountain terrain above the Hermida Gorge of Río Deva on the Santander–Asturias border. However, it has not been relocated with absolute certainty and the original references to this Solutrean site are imprecise.) Nonetheless, Solutrean sites located in the interior are regularly surrounded by peaks 500 to 800 m in elevation within a radius of 1 km. Within a 5-km radius there are peaks ranging from 900 to 1,400 m high.

Several sites are located on very steep cliff faces at high elevations in rugged terrain (e.g., El Buxú at 350 m, Hornos de la Peña at 280 m, Bolinkoba at 350 m, Atxuri and La Haza at 280 m, El Mirón at 300 m, El Salitre at 500 m, and La Bona/Rascaño at 240 m). Others, although not high in absolute terms, are on steep mountain slopes (e.g., Aitzbitarte, Santimamiñe, El Castillo, La Pasiega, Cueva Chufín, Peña de Candamo, La Viña), generally with commanding views of major valleys. Although three or four of these "mountain" sites were occupied in earlier times, notably in the Aurignaco-Perigordian (Castillo and Hornos also have Mousterian levels), never before had there been such a significant human utilization/occupation of the mountain zones (particularly the very flanks of the Cordillera and Picos de Europa). In terms of both absolute (and relative) numbers and distribution of sites, the Solutrean settlement pattern represents a major change in the prehistory of the Cantabrian region from earlier patterns, although it is presaged in the Gravettian, notably by Bolinkoba.

Types of Sites and Problems of Preservation

As noted earlier, almost all the known Solutrean sites in the Cantabrian region are caves. There is only one case (Corao) of isolated surface finds of supposed Solutrean artifacts (plus a rather peculiar group of seven laurel-leaf points *said* to have been found in the field right in front of La Riera Cave [Pradel 1979]. Because it is unlikely that in this period humans deposited artifacts only in caves, a significant part of the archeological record is missing. This is due to erosion (by streams, surface runoff, solifluxion, etc.) or through burial under deep fluvial or colluvial sediments. The very steep gradients in this region also mean that surface archeological materials of substantial antiquity stand little chance of preservation or visibility.

Caves thus provide excellent containers for archeological deposits; they are contexts in which deposition often outweighs erosion as the dominant geomorphological process. In addition, under conditions of extreme cold, caves were logical places for different types of human occupations. This is particularly true of caves facing south, southwest, or west—the preferred range of orientations among the known Solutrean sites (except some mountain sites where the strategic view may have outweighed solar exposure as the chief consideration for selection). In a region where caves are abundant, they were the obvious choice for all sorts of living sites (not just major "base camps"), and humans could be very selective in the caves they did occupy. Naturally, during the past 110 years of searching in this region archeologists perhaps have selectively discovered *cave* sites at the expense of the less-visible, less-"rich," open-air loci. However, even cave sites can become invisible if the deposits eventually reach the ceiling at the entrance and are then covered by dense vegetation. Such was the case for La Riera, discovered by accident by the Conde de la Vega del Sella during his 1916 excavation of nearby Cueto de la Mina. Many of the Solutrean (and other) sites were found around the turn of the century when goats still actively grazed the hills and mountain slopes of the region, making cave mouths far more visible than they are today.

At Cueva Chufín, it is probable that the small, surficial Solutrean deposit under the cave mouth overhang was a mere *remnant* of an originally much larger site that had been entirely eroded by running water (possibly from within the karst). The Solutrean remnant deposit had been held in place by a natural retaining wall of limestone blocks fallen from the overhang. However, many Solutrean levels are thin, single-component deposits, possibly representative of short, ephemeral occupations or actual single occupations. Some Solutrean sites, therefore, are "minor" in terms of the quantity of residues and the magnitude of human occupations.

In contrast, a few Solutrean sites are multicomponent, even when the excavations were conducted with old methods that did not distinguish thin levels or lenses. Sites with obviously multiple Solutrean strata indi-

Chapter 5 / 102

cating repeated human occupation include Aitzbitarte, Bolinkoba, Altamira (where the Solutrean was unfortunately not divided at all in the old excavations despite substantial thickness), Cueto de la Mina, La Riera, Cova Rosa, Las Caldas, and La Viña (Figure 5.3). Consequently, the artifact and faunal collections from these multicomponent ones (particularly from old excavations) may represent palimpsests formed by occupations and disposal modes of different types. The collections from the minor Solutrean occupations may be more indicative of brief occupations and limited sets of activities, although we lack good information on many of these sites. The "major" sites usually are located in places with both good solar exposure and shelter from sea winds, generally on the lower slopes of valleys, ridges, or dolinas. Protection and comfort were significant factors in the selection of these (residential) sites, as opposed to some of the minor (logistical) sites, particularly those in the mountains.

Raw Material Sources and Evidence for Mobility and Territories

There is no evidence of long-distance transportation of raw materials within the Cantabrian region or between it and other regions in the Solutrean period. This does not mean that objects or people did not move along the coast of the Bay of Biscay and into southwestern France. Indeed, there are indications of such movements, or at least contacts—e.g., the presence in the Basque Country and the French Pyrenees of a few concave-base foliate points whose center of distribution is central Santander/central Asturias. Likewise, there are a few points in Cantabrian sites that resemble the unusual asymmetrical, broad-shouldered points found at Montaut and Tercis in Les Landes (southwestern France) (Straus 1977c,d, 1978, 1983b).

The lithic raw materials used in the Solutrean for the manufacture of artifacts mostly include a variety of flints and quartzite. As noted above, this region, like the Pyrenees, lacks large flint nodules or blocks. Most of the flint occurs in stream beds or breaches in the form of small nodules often of poor quality. However, there is a clear east–west gradient in the relative importance of flints in the archeological assemblages (Straus 1980). In Solutrean assemblages of the French and Spanish Basque Country, flint (albeit of relatively small unit size) makes up nearly 100% of the lithics. This is a direct reflection of the nature of the Cretaceous limestone bedrock of this area. Moving westward, however, the lithology changes, with the inclusion of quartzite-bearing sandstones in Santander. In corresponding fashion, the Solutrean lithic assemblages

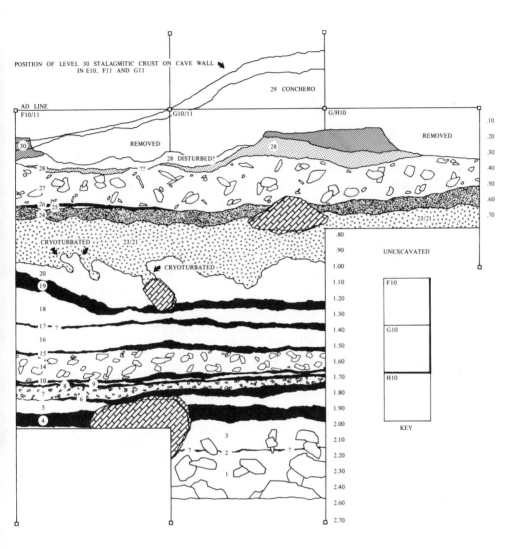

FIGURE 5.3. *Stratigraphic section of La Riera Cave. Levels: 1, pre-Solutrean; 2–17, Solutrean; 18–25, Magdalenian; 26–28, Azilian; 29–30, Asturian. (From Straus and Clark 1986.)*

contain small percentages of quartzite artifacts in this area. Carboniferous limestone, with poor-quality flints, occurs in Asturias but the farther west one goes, the greater the proportion of quartzites. Quartzite bands increasingly dominate the bedrock as one approaches the lower Río Nalón basin. Correspondingly, quartzites become increasingly important among the Solutrean lithic assemblages of Asturias, as one samples them from east to west.

The relationship between the proportion of quartzite in archeological assemblages and the changes in bedrock would seem to be a clear indication of use of local lithic sources by prehistoric human groups. The flints also are of local origin (e.g., in areas where distinctive flint types such as "Griotte" flint from "Caliza de Montaña" are present in stream beds, they are the types found in the artifact assemblages despite poor quality in this example). At La Riera Cave, where petrographic analyses and some local lithic prospection (Straus et al. 1986) were conducted during the course of the excavations, it is clear that the flints and quartzites are of local origin. The few "exotics" in Solutrean Levels 4 through 5 are associated with specialized use of the cave as an ibex hunting camp and are exotic only by comparison with the more usual types of lithics found throughout the rest of the sequence. Their sources, still unknown, are not likely to be far off, and their absolute quantities are relatively small. Because of the scarcity of cores or primary debitage in these exceptional assemblages, dominated instead by points and small chipping debris, it appears that blanks were carried to the site to be worked into Solutrean points (Straus et al. 1981; Straus and Clark 1986).

Concave-base points were made preferentially on quartzite. These large, heavy points, probably spear tips, are found mainly in central and eastern Asturias and the western half of Santander where quartzite is abundant but where flints are at least present locally. On the other hand, the small, light-shouldered points found throughout the whole region are almost exclusively made of flint, even in areas where this was a rare material and where quartzite dominates the lithology and the rest of the Solutrean lithic assemblages. These points may have been tips for darts propelled by spear thrower or atl-atl (or even for arrows shot by bow). Lithic raw material availability *and* functional factors both operated in determining point materials. The quartzite pieces probably were useful for withstanding shock when used in thrusting spears; the flint pieces were sharp and useful for penetration after long-distance propulsion (Straus 1990b, n.d.a,b).

Sea shells, other possible indicators of human mobility, are found in interior Solutrean sites (e.g., El Castillo), but even these sites were no more than 25 to 30 km from the Pleniglacial coastline and none of the mollusks in question could not have been collected along the *Cantabrian* strand at the time. There are no known instances of strictly Mediterranean taxa in Cantabrian sites. Nor are there any fossils or objects known to derive from the Spanish Meseta, from Aquitaine, or from other regions.

Wood for fuel and construction may have been in short supply, particularly under the most severe climatic conditions in the coastal zone where most of the major Solutrean occupation sites are located. Although bone sometimes may have been burned for heat, wood gathering must have been a major activity, taking people to thickets and woods in sheltered habitats. Cyclical abandonment of sites (and of whole habitual settlement areas like the southern face of La Llera ridge, where there are four Solutrean sites within a 1-km stretch, or Monte Castillo where there are two) may have been caused by exhaustion of the local wood supply. Such abandonments and reoccupations after wood regrowth could have caused lateral shifts in the human utilization of different sectors of the coastal zone, particularly for major base camps.

Finally, there is no need to propose long-distance transport to explain the rare occurrences of remains of reindeer and seals in Cantabrian Solutrean contexts. Reindeer were clearly occasional visitors to this region from the adjacent Aquitaine where they were a dominant ungulate game species. Beached seals may have been procured by human groups visiting the shore during mollusk-gathering expeditions.

The implication of the lack of evidence of significant movement of goods to the Cantabrian region from other regions during the Solutrean period is that human groups were not extremely wide-ranging in their annual rounds and that their territories may have been relatively small compared with those of hunter-gatherer groups on the North European Plain or even in the Aquitaine Basin during the Magdalenian. Individual bands may have had territories larger than individual river drainages and their corresponding stretches of the coastal zone, but these do not seem to have been moving between Asturias and Aquitaine or from Vizcaya to Valencia, for instance. There must have been contacts among human groups in Cantabria and Aquitaine, as suggested by similarities in overall artifact technology and form within the Solutrean, as well as by the few instances of apparently imported point types (or point design ideas), as mentioned above. Furthermore, it is likely that some of the cave art in both southwestern France and Cantabrian Spain dates to the Solutrean period. If so, the general similarities in style, themes, and techniques would be further indications of at least occasional human contacts. But the overall impression is one of regional self-sufficiency and of limited territories, made possible by a rich, variegated set of environments in which short altitudinal and lateral movements would have permitted access to a wide variety of resources without the need for long-distance migrations. This same rugged topography would have discouraged such movement and was home to several major ungulate species (notably red deer and ibex) not known for lengthy migrations, unlike those of the barren ground reindeer or caribou.

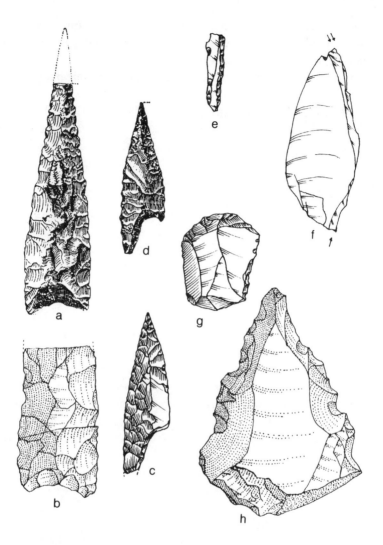

Bone and Stone Artifacts

Due to problems of earlier erosion and excavation and the necessary partial sampling of sites, no Solutrean site has been excavated *entirely* by modern methods. Thus, comparative data on assemblage size and density are unavailable. No systematic microscopic use-wear studies of Solutrean lithics in this region have yet been conducted, although under ×20 magnification it is clear that Solutrean points and a substantial proportion of chipping debris ("unretouched" flakes, blades, etc.) as well as formal tools were used (Straus 1975a; Straus and Clark 1986) (Figure 5.4). Most of the Solutrean points that have been found are broken; the

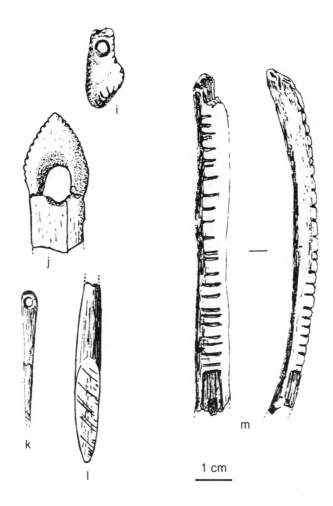

FIGURE 5.4. *Solutrean artifacts: a,b, concave base points; c,d, shouldered points; e, backed bladelet; f, multiple dihedral burin; g, endscraper on blade; h, denticulate; i, perforated red deer canine with engravings; j, bone pendant; k bone needle; l, antler point ("sagaie"); m, engraved rib; a and d from Cueto de la Mina (Vega del Sella 1916); all others from La Riera (Straus and Clark 1986).*

breaks include many hinge fractures, pseudo-burins, and other signs of impact fracture (Straus n.d.c).

Antler implements and weapon tips ("sagaies") are present in Solutrean contexts, although they are less numerous than in the Magdalenian of this region (as in other regions of Western Europe). Before the recent reexcavation of La Riera (and new Solutrean excavations at Las Caldas, La Viña, Amalda, etc.), a count of the extant collections gave a total of about 380 sagaie fragments from the entire region. Most are undecorated (except for lines on the basal segment to facilitate hafting) and cross sections are predominantly circular, semicircular, or oval with sizable numbers of quadrangular and centrally flattened types as well. The 16 Solutrean levels from the new excavation of La Riera yielded a total of only 33 sagaie fragments. Again, most are circular or oval in cross section with single-bevel bases and "anti-skid" hafting lines but otherwise undecorated (González Morales 1986). The only level at Amalda with Solutrean points (Level IV) yielded seven whole or fragmentary sagaies including one with longitudinal grooves along two sides, presumably for mounting microlithic cutting edge or barb elements (Baldeón 1990b). The dozen Solutrean levels at Las Caldas produced only three sagaies—all plain (Corchón 1981). Thus, antler points continue to seem to be of secondary importance *vis à vis* stone points in the Solutrean. (This relationship is reversed in the subsequent Magdalenian.) Other bone/antler artifacts in the region include eyed needles (which make their first appearance in the Solutrean) and so-called wands, awls, pins, spatulas, retouchers, etc. There are also a few decorated "bâtons de commandement"—less frequent than in the Magdalenian—and notched hyoid and rib segments, engraved shoulder blades (as in the Magdelanian), perforated and sometimes engraved teeth, etc.; these are discussed below in the section on Solutrean art. No antler objects have yet been definitely identified as atl-atls in the Solutrean of northern Spain, but one recently was described by Cattelain (1989) from the Solutrean of Combe Saunière in southwestern France. Of course, atl-atl hooks also could have been made of wood.

Detailed information on the regional and La Riera Solutrean lithic assemblages has been published (Straus 1977a, 1983b; Straus and Clark 1986). Reliable tool:debris ratios and volumetric data are available only for thin levels from modern excavations at La Riera, Amalda, and Cueva Morín. They are presented in Appendix C4. The density of artifacts per square meter (perhaps in part reflecting variability in the intensity or frequency of occupation) ranges from 43.4 in La Riera Level 2 to 439.8 in Morín Level 3.

There also are wide variations in ratios of primary to secondary debitage, cores to debitage, and tools to debris at these and the other sites that have major (albeit more selective) collections. At La Riera, at least, it is clear that the changing ratios and densities of lithic artifacts reflect changing uses of the cave throughout the course of 3,500 years and many human occupations, from the very specialized to the very generalized. Lithic tool manufacture was a major activity in some, but not all, of the occupations of the cave area excavated.

Analyses of the Solutrean assemblages of formal tools (e.g., Straus

Table 5.2 Summary of Major Tool Indices for the Cantabrian Solutrean (n = 30 assemblages)

Tool Group	Range	Average Percentage	SD
Solutrean points	0–31.8	8.9	8.5
Endscrapers	4.2–35.0	15.9	9.4
Burins	4.6–36.4	12.7	6.8
Denticulates + notches	4.3–56.9	22.2	13.2
Sidescrapers	0–13.7	5.7	3.5

1975a, 1983b; Straus and Clark 1986) have shown them to be quite variable also. Appendix C5 lists tool group indices (percentages) for the modern Solutrean excavations (Las Caldas, La Riera, Chufín, Morín, and Amalda) and for the more important of the older excavations where screening and careful curation may have been less systematic. Basic information on Solutrean assemblage variability is given in Table 5.2. Solutrean points make up between 0 and 32% of the tools (both extremes occurring at La Riera where there were no excavation biases in the collection of lithics). In the La Riera stratified sequence (and in isolated, but chronometrically late, Amalda Level IV), it is possible to argue that backed bladelets *replaced* the large, single-unit Solutrean points in weapon tips (see Straus and Clark 1986; Straus 1990b; Rasilla 1990), although both are rare at the top of the Las Caldas Solutrean sequence. Certainly, virtually the sole criterion for differentiating many "Lower Cantabrian Magdalenian" assemblages (rich in backed bladelets) from "Solutrean" is the *absence* of foliate and shouldered points in the former (Straus 1975b; see also Utrilla 1984–85). Repeated microwear analyses of backed bladelets in France and in northern Europe (e.g., Moss 1983; Keeley 1981; Dumont 1986; Geneste and Plisson 1986), as well as in Cantabria (Keeley 1988), have shown these to have often been used as "armatures"—weapon tips, edges, or barbs set into antler (or wooden?) axial point elements.

Earlier I observed that Solutrean assemblages with relatively many backed bladelets tended to be the ones associated with many ibex or chamois remains in sites of the mountainous Basque Country (including the old collection from Ermittia with a backed bladelet index of 16.4% and 40% ibex [Straus 1975a]). Both old and modern Basque Solutrean assemblages are consistently very poor in Solutrean points (Straus 1974, 1975a, 1990a), despite good availability of flint raw material—probably because they were functionally replaced by composite weapons with microlithic elements. With the addition of the La Riera data, the caprid/backed bladelet relationship is less clear, although Levels 4 through 6, with moderately high backed bladelet indices *and* many Solutrean points also have many ibex remains (Straus and Clark 1986). Cabrera (1977) states that Chufín is rich in caprids, a fact not surprising given this site's steep, rocky surroundings. It remains possible that caprid hunting was facilitated by use of some kind of light projectile weapon tipped or barbed with these microliths. Certainly, the recent discovery of large numbers of chamois at Amalda IV, nearly half of whose tools are backed bladelets, adds support to this functional hypothesis, although red deer and other small to medium size ungulates were certainly hunted with sagaies and microliths, both in "Solutrean" and, especially, "Magdalenian" times.

Other aspects of Solutrean variability include the fact burins outnumber endscrapers in the Basque sites and that many of these burins are of the Noailles type, supposedly diagnostic of the late Perigordian in southwestern France. Here, however, whether as a product of the abundant, good, but small size, Basque area flint nodules or for some functional reason, Noailles burins are even found in at least one "Magdalenian" (Tardiglacial) context. The relationship between burins and endscrapers is more variable among the assemblages of sites in Santander and Asturias—even within the sequence at La Riera where burins often equal or outnumber endscrapers (not a classic, *normative* Solutrean characteristic any more than is the presence of many backed bladelets). Large, "archaic" tool types, notably sidescrapers, denticulates, notches, and thick endscrapers (as well as choppers, bifaces, etc.) are particularly abundant in assemblages with much quartzite and are often made of that material (especially in Asturias). Perhaps as a result of some functional relationship (heavy hide scraping?) or as a case of equifinality, the scraper-rich assemblages of Santander and Asturias are usually associated with large quantities of red deer remains. These sites are often on the coastal plain or in broad lower valleys that were good *Cervus* habitat.

Traditional claims that the French scheme for subdividing the Solutrean on the basis of point types (based on the unique stratigraphic sequence of Laugerie-Haute in Périgord) could be applied to the Cantabrian Solutrean have been shown to be incorrect (Straus 1975a, 1983b, 1986c; Straus and Clark 1986). At La Riera, chronometrically *old* (about 20,000 B.P.) levels at the *base* of the stratigraphic sequence have yielded so-called *Upper* Solutrean fossil director types (shouldered and concave-base points) but no classic laurel leaves, whereas higher, more recent levels have produced laurel-leaf points but no shouldered or concave-base points. This is the exact reverse of the Laugerie-Haute scheme. I would not presume to generalize the La Riera sequence, as I believe that the presence, absence, and relative frequency of points are determined largely by site function and sampling error. However, at Chaves in Huesca, 8 shouldered points and 21 backed bladelets—types traditionally indicative of an *Upper* Solutrean—have been found in a level radiocarbon dated to about 20,000 B.P., as noted above (Utrilla 1989). At Vale Almoinha (Portuguese Estremadura), willow and shouldered points are associated with a radiocarbon date of 20,380 ± 150 B.P. (ICEN–71)—as are more traditionally "Middle" Solutrean laurel leaf points (Zilhão 1984, Zilhão et al. 1987). And in Caldeirão Cave in the same province, there are shouldered and tanged points dated as old as 20,400 ± 270 (OxA-1938) (Zilhão 1987, 1990a). Thus La Riera is not alone on the Iberian Peninsula in suggesting that functional and sampling variability—not "time"— may be responsible for Solutrean diagnostic type representation in particular site deposits. The lithic points are only temporally diagnostic in the broadest sense (i.e., 21–16,000 B.P.) (Straus 1991b). Clearly, *lithic* weapons (both foliate/shouldered points and microlithic armatures) were important in the technology of the Last Glacial Maximum when hunting effectiveness and efficiency had become critical to human survival.

Subsistence

We have no evidence of plant foods from the Cantabrian Solutrean. Although at times there probably were small numbers of nut-bearing trees in the region (particularly during the Laugerie and Lascaux oscillations), the open heaths and grasslands were unlikely to have provided substantial food for humans.

The main sources of food were five taxa of ungulates (*Cervus elaphus*, *Capra pyrenaica*, *Rupicapra rupicapra*, *Equus caballus*, and Bovini), supplemented at times by small numbers of *Capreolus capreolus*, *Sus scrofa*, *Rangifer tarandus*, and perhaps seal (*Phoca* cf. *vitulina*) (Appendices C2 and C3). In addition, Solutrean levels (principally at La Riera but also at El Castillo, Altamira, Cueto de la Mina, Cova Rosa, et al.) for the first time contain substantial marine mollusks, notably large *Patella vulgata* and some *Littorina littorea*. The small area of Solutrean deposits dug by us at La Riera produced about 5,500 shells of edible mollusks (Ortea 1986). The shellfish may have served as a winter "tiding-over" resource, although attempts at determining seasonality by oxygen isotope analysis have been unsuccessful so far. There also are limited quantities of fish remains (mostly salmon, trout, and sea trout [*Salmo* spp.]) at a number of Solutrean sites. The Solutrean Levels at La Riera yielded 67 salmonid bones (Menéndez et al. 1986).

Some sites, notably Amalda (Eastham 1990), have a small number of bird remains. These, along with rodents, lagomorphs, and insectivores found at some sites may not necessarily have been entirely the result of capture by humans. (The rodents in particular may be intrusive in most cases.) There also are small numbers of small carnivores (particularly *Vulpes vulpes* and Mustelidae) in most Solutrean contexts: these were probably trapped for their pelts. A few remains of bears and wolves do occur in some Solutrean levels, but big cats and hyena are now virtually absent (and single identifications of these taxa at El Castillo and Cueto de la Mina, respectively, are old and possibly problematical).

Detailed discussions of Solutrean faunas have been published elsewhere (e.g., Straus 1983b; Altuna 1972; Straus et al. 1981; Straus and Clark 1986). There are two salient aspects to subsistence developments during the Solutrean time period that contrast sharply to patterns typical of the Middle and Early Upper Paleolithic periods in this region: diversification, and specialization. Together, these indicate significant intensification in the food quest (Straus 1977b; Straus et al. 1980; Clark and Straus 1983). Diversification is evidenced by the now consistent hunting of alpine caprines (ibex and chamois), animals essentially unexploited by Neanderthals and even by most Early Upper Paleolithic humans and particularly well adapted to steep, rocky slopes where they can escape unsophisticated hunters by their speed and agility. Diversification is also shown by the occasional hunting of boar, a very fast, dangerous animal almost totally absent from the earlier faunas in this region (despite the existence of earlier climatic phases in which thickets—preferred boar habitat—would have been at least as abundant or more abundant than during Solutrean times) (see Freeman 1973; Straus 1977b). Finally and most importantly, diversification is evidenced by the appearance of aquatic resources (shellfish and fish) in Solutrean deposits. These resources had been entirely unexploited before and appear in sites that in Solutrean times would have been 8 to 10 km farther from the sea than they are today. At La Riera, humans were transporting substantial amounts of limpets over a two-hour walk from the pleniglacial shore, creating virtual shell middens of some of the thin archeological levels in the cave. This fact suggests that, if many Pleniglacial coastal sites today are inundated, marine resources may have been even more significant as dietary supplements than the present evidence would indicate.

Under certain circumstances (e.g. seasonal need, ability, human or animal aggregation), specialized hunting methods (such as drives or surrounds) were used to kill substantial numbers of the two most important ungulate species, red deer and ibex, beginning in Solutrean times. Bolinkoba Levels E and D yielded remains of at least 11 and 16 individual ibex, respectively; the small Ermittia Solutrean level yielded 8. Both sites are on steep cliffs. Thin Levels 4 through 6 at La Riera yielded a total of 28 ibex individuals; Level 7 had as many as 14. La Riera is within 1.5 km of the steep, cliff-like north face of the Sierra de Cuera-Peña Llabres and seems to have served as a specialized ibex hunting camp at the time of deposition of at least Levels 4 through 6. Chamois seem to have been systematically hunted near the hill-country sites of Amalda (MNI = 16 in Level IV), Aitzbitarte IV (MNI = 6 in Level 3), and El Buxú (MNI = 17 in the Solutrean level from four small test pits), although red deer also are abundant in all three assemblages—a fact not incompatible with the wooded habitats sometimes inhabited by both species.

Old collections from the Solutrean levels at Altamira (a fairly thick stratum but one whose faunal collection has obviously suffered many losses since 1924) and El Cierro (a fairly restricted deposit) have red deer MNI of 20 and 21, respectively. There are a dozen in the small Solutrean deposit from La Pasiega (sampled by only a restricted pit) and relatively large numbers at such sites as Aitzbitarte, Cueto de la Mina, Las Caldas, etc. Under the carefully controlled, complete recovery conditions at La Riera, despite the very limited surface areas dug in the Solutrean, large MNI of red deer have been found: 34 in Level 7, 16 in Level 8, 14 in Level 9, 10 in Level 10, 13 in Level 11, 20 in Level 14, 15 in Level 15, 27 in Level 16, and 16 in Level 17. The red deer could have been taken in such large numbers by surrounding female-led herds (in winter yards, for example). Cul-de-sac valleys, water crossings, gorges, cliff sides, and even snowdrifts could have been used to help trap numbers of driven deer. Several Solutrean sites are located near topographic features that could have been used advantageously in the mass slaughter of hind herds. There are age and sex data from the Solutrean (and Magdalenian) in the region that suggest that such tactics may have been used. However, stags also were taken (and freshly shed antlers were collected) because many sites do have quantities of antler, both worked and unworked (Altuna 1976; Klein et al. 1981; Clark and Straus 1983; Straus and Clark 1986). Mass ibex drives could have involved beaters driving the animals toward hidden hunters at the crest lines, taking advantage of their natural defensive flight reaction pattern.

Analysis of body parts (Altuna 1972, 1986, 1990c) indicates heavy marrow cracking of bones in the Solutrean period; this includes breaking even of phalanges of deer and ibex. Sites such as La Riera generally lack the sorts of parts that normally would have been left at the kill sites (e.g., heads) and probably represent locations where secondary processing, cooking, and consumption occurred. At Amalda, the small chamois carcasses were brought back to the site more or less whole. La Riera and other sites (Las Caldas, Amalda, Abauntz, Cueto de la Mina, etc.) have yielded hearths, possible roasting pits and surfaces (with quantities of fire-reddened and -cracked cobbles and limestone rocks together with burnt bones), and roasting surfaces probably related to the cooking of meat. Further analysis of body parts will be required to determine exact butchering and usage patterns and practices. Preliminary studies of bones from La Riera and Amalda indicated regular placement of cut marks derived from the butchering process (see Altuna 1986, 1990c).

Hearth Features

As stated above, all known Solutrean sites in Cantabrian Spain are in the mouths of caves that provided natural shelter. Caves with major occupation residues (implying repeated, large-scale human habituation) generally are located in protected spots, as discussed above. To date, no evidence of postholes or other definite indication of superstructures have been found in Solutrean sites. However, there is some evidence of hearths and other combustion features in a few of the sites. At Cueto de la Mina, Vega del Sella (1916) noted three semicircular hearths with quartzite or sandstone cobbles, one in each of three layers of his Stratum E within the small cave sector of this rockshelter/cave site. Unfortunately, other than to note that with time the hearths were built closer to the rear of the cave, he provided no details on these features.

As in many Solutrean sites, repeated, generalized evidence of fire (charcoal, ash, burnt clay, fire-cracked/reddened stones) was found among the levels at La Riera, some of which are fire lenses. There also are localized, constructed hearths in a few La Riera Solutrean levels. In Level 7 there is a circular pit, maximally 25 cm deep and 80 cm wide, located on the right side of the interior cave vestibule near the cave wall (Figure 5.5). The base and sides of the basin-shaped pit were lined with small limestone rocks and the interior was also mostly filled with such rocks, of which many are fire-cracked and burnt. At the top of the pit there were bones, shells, and charcoal-black sediments of the sort that were widespread in overlying Level 8. However, the pit fill *per se* did include 89 bones and teeth of red deer and 77 of ibex, including cranial elements, suggesting the roasting of heads in this pit. There are several pieces of lithic chipping debris and a denticulate.

Level 11 yielded three apparent hearths, again in the cave interior (the only remaining area of intact sediments left to excavate in 1976–1979). In square E5 there is a charcoal patch lined by small-medium size limestone rocks and burnt sediments. A cluster of seven stone tools is on one

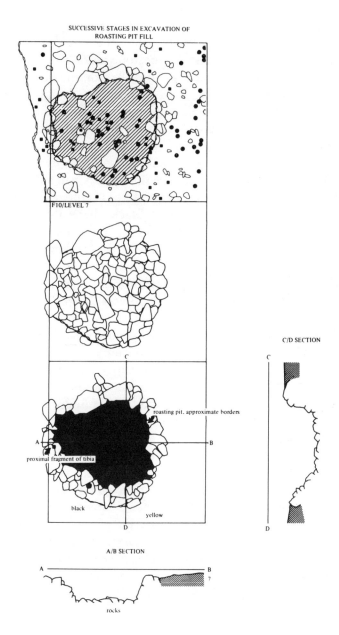

FIGURE 5.5. *Plan and sections of a Solutrean roasting pit, La Riera (dug into Level 7). Each side of square equals one meter. (From Straus and Clark 1986.)*

side of the hearth and a cluster of limpet shells is on the adjacent side. In square E8, there is a more formal, dug-out pit hearth of triangular shape, about 55 cm long, 50 cm wide, and 12 cm deep. It abuts a large rock outcrop (like a more informal hearth in the lowest Solutrean level [Level 2]) and is partially lined with limestone rocks. The surface is covered with charcoal. Unlike the Level 7 pit hearth, the fill of this pit is not rich; there is a sandstone "anvil" among the "lining" stones but few other artifacts or bones. The third charcoal area, in square E7, is less definite and may represent a localization of hearth cleaning debris.

Level 14 at La Riera also contains several features associated with localized fire. In square E7 there is a small (10 by 7 cm) patch of ash surrounded by small stones, mostly to one side; it is associated with several artifacts, jaw fragments, and ribs. In E8 there is another ash patch (8 by 7 cm) at one end of a rectangular area of black, charcoal-rich sediments measuring at least 40 by 25 cm. Neither stone-lined nor dug-out, this possible hearth (or hearth-fill dump area) is adjoined by one area with clustered artifacts and faunal remains and another area free of objects. There is a similar feature (albeit, more oval in shape) in F9 (only partially excavated); it is full of bones and artifacts. Level 14 yielded over 7 kg of fire-cracked sandstone cobbles, suggesting considerable roasting during this occupation of the cave. Level 15 has generalized scatters of charcoal and large quantities of burnt sandstone but no formal hearths, although in E7-E8 there is a shallow, irregular, charcoal-filled depression. Level 16, a very rich, thick stratum, has a well-defined living floor at its base. In E6 there is a small ring of rocks outlining a charcoal concentration; near it in E6-E7 is a pit filled with ash and debris (probably from the cleaning of the hearth). The uppermost Solutrean level (Level 17) only has generalized charcoal scatters and large quantities of burnt sandstone but no features *per se*, at least in the area excavated.

In sum, while the evidence of features in most of the La Riera Solutrean levels consists of generalized fire evidence (charcoal, burnt sediments), some levels had definite hearths or roasting pits in the interior of the cave, at least 10 m back from the present cave mouth overhang (Straus and Clark 1986). Amalda Level IV has a hearth consisting of half a dozen large stones surrounding a dense cluster of burnt bones and cobbles in a concentration of charcoal-rich sediment (Altuna 1990e).

Development of Artistic Activity

All substantial Solutrean artifact collections in this region contain at least some decorated bone, antler, or tooth objects, but these are fewer than in levels dating to the subsequent Magdalenian period. The decoration of mobile art works is also far more elaborate in the Magdalenian, which represents the culmination of the development of artistic traditions in the Upper Paleolithic in the Franco-Cantabrian region. The famous Altamira red deer scapulas, engraved with images of hinds, supposedly were found in the Solutrean deposit, although they are extremely similar to others from the Lower Magdalenian of El Castillo and to parietal engravings in both those caves (Almagro 1976). This similarity implies that the rock engravings were made in the "Solutrean" and "Magdalenian," and it reinforces the other evidence of complete continuity between these two archeological subdivisions. An extraordinary cave bear canine pendant carved into the three-dimensional figure of a bird (a spotted crake?) was found in the Solutrean layer of El Buxú, a small site and cave art sanctuary on a cul-de-sac high above the intermontane valley of eastern Asturias (Menéndez 1984). Otherwise, figurative mobile "art" is virtually nonexistent in the Solutrean.

One characteristic form of Solutrean decorated bone consists of rib (or other element such as hyoid) segments with notches ("tally marks") cut along their edges; examples of these have been found at La Riera, Cueto de la Mina, Las Caldas, Aviao, Altamira, etc. But such objects (possibly pendants) are not exclusive to the Solutrean; for example, a few have been found in apparently pre-Solutrean assemblages, as at Riera (Barandiarán 1972; González Morales 1986). Perforated (and sometimes engraved) teeth and perforated shells are common, though not abundant, in Solutrean assemblages. The mammoth molar fragments found in the late Solutrean of Cueto de la Mina (Castaños 1982) and La Caldas (Corchón 1981) probably were collected from dead animals (or even from "fossils") and were used as material for ornaments. No other skeletal parts are present.

It is impossible to determine whether or how much of the well-known Cantabrian cave art was created during the period of the Solutrean. It can be noted, however, that several cave art sanctuaries have yielded *only* Solutrean cultural materials in their sedimentary deposits: El Buxú, Peña de Candamo, Cueva Chufín, La Pasiega, and La Haza. Because Magdalenian deposits physically overlie parietal engravings at La Viña and at Isturitz, it is likely that the art was created during the Solutrean period amply represented at both sites. There are many other cave art localities with Solutrean deposits as well as others, another indication of probable artistic activity between 20,500 and 17,000 B.P. These sites include La Lluera, Coberizas, Cueto de la Mina, La Riera, Balmori, Altamira, Hornos de la Peña, El Castillo, El Pendo, Cueva Morín/Oso, El Salitre, Atxuri, Santimamiñe, and possibly Ekain.

One peculiar motif may be associated with the Solutrean in a restricted area of western Santander and eastern Asturias: natural cavities in cave walls outlined with ochre or red dots in La Riera, Chufín, and Mazaculos (Straus 1982b). (As indicators of the age of the art, La Riera was a major "Solutrean" site and Chufín has only a "Solutrean" archeological level. But the pre-Mesolithic deposits at Mazaculos have not yet been dug, so the existence of a Solutrean level there is unknown at present.)

The rather late "explosion" of "artistic" activity in Cantabrian Spain in relation to southwestern France, raises the question of cause. If personal adornment and rupestral art were in some way related to demographic, social, and economic factors involving marking, identification, and cybernetic behavior, then the development of mobile art and at least some cave art in northern Spain may have accelerated during the Last Glacial Maximum in relation to an increased regional population living under stressful conditions with limited margins for error. Territorial boundaries, ethnic identification, and the storage and dissemination of long-term survival skills may have become critical at this time (Conkey 1978, 1980; Gamble 1982; Jochim 1983; Mithen 1988; Straus 1987a). The Late Upper Paleolithic art phenomenon is further discussed in a subsequent chapter; however, it is clear that full-blown artistic behavior did not occur instantly or everywhere in southwestern Europe with the so-called "Middle–to–Upper Paleolithic transition." Each kind of phenomenon that *we* call Paleolithic art and each region must be understood on its own terms and in its own context.

Human Remains

The only human remains found in association with Solutrean artifacts are two cranial fragments and a molar from La Riera Levels 7, 14, and 16, respectively (Garralda 1986) and a deciduous tooth from Level 3 at Morín (Altuna 1971). A human phalange and molar from El Buxú might be from the Solutrean (Soto 1984). There are no known burials from this region or time period, and, in fact, there are very few human remains known from the Solutrean in all of Spain, France, or Portugal.

Conclusions

Under fluctuating but generally cold, stormy conditions at the height of the Würm Upper Pleniglacial, human populations were relatively high along the narrow region between the Cantabrian Sea and Cordillera. This may have been due in part to the cumulative growth of the regional population present since the Lower Paleolithic and, especially, to a gradual influx of people from northern parts of Europe toward a relatively more livable condition, with rich, varied food resources, in Cantabrian Spain during the Last Glacial Maximum (see Jochim 1987). Exploitation of those resources reached new levels of efficiency in the Solutrean period. This is seen in the further development of specialized technologies—particularly weapon tips (foliate and shouldered stone points, backed bladelets, sagaies) probably delivered on spears, darts, or even arrows and propelled by the unaided arm, atl-atl, or bow. A wider variety of food resources was exploited (including fish and shellfish for the first time), and key ungulate species were taken by new mass hunting techniques. For the first time there was a significant exploitation of littoral, estuarine, riverine, and montane habitats. Some sites were located on steep, rocky mountain slopes (ibex habitat) and other sites, at about a two-hour walk from the now inundated Pleniglacial coast, contain real shell middens.

Although the main species exploited for food by Solutrean hunters (red deer and ibex) are usually migratory, their migrations were certainly much more limited in scale than those of the reindeer, so important to Solutrean subsistence in southwestern France. In this region of high relief, with geographical barriers to both the north and south (including mountain glaciers), migratory range would have been limited and altitudinal in character. Humans could have access to the resources of the lower slopes of the Cordillera/Picos de Europa, the intermontane valleys, the coastal mountain ranges and hills, the coastal plain, the shore, and the intertidal zone, all within no more than a day or two on foot from any central location. Figure 5.6 shows the location of Solutrean and Magdalenian sites in eastern Asturias, centered on La Riera and the other sites of La Llera ridge.

The evidence of the Solutrean settlement pattern that survives today suggests the way in which this region was exploited. Sites are aligned along all the major river valleys, but the major occupations were clearly in the coastal zone, in well-oriented, sheltered caves and often within a relatively short distance of the mouths of important estuaries at the time. The sites of the hinterland are generally small, with very limited Solutrean deposits and assemblages. Subsistence strategies probably combined aspects of Binford's (1980) forager and collector types. Major sites such as Aitzbitarte, Altamira, the La Llera ridge group (Balmori, Tres Calabres, La Riera, Cueto de la Mina, plus Coberizas), Cova Rosa, and Las Caldas may have been base camps used at times by relatively large groups composed of both sexes and all ages for significant periods of

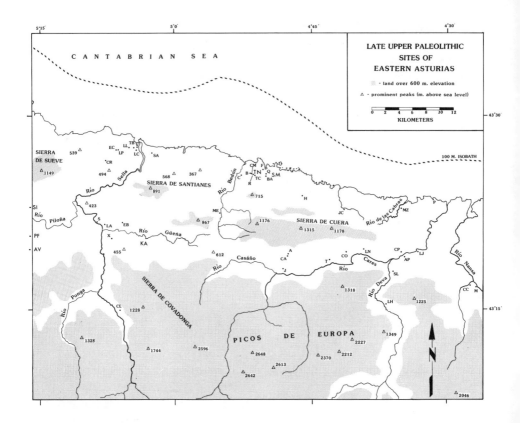

FIGURE 5.6. *Solutrean (S), Magdalenian (M), and Late Upper Paleolithic cave art (C) sites in eastern Asturias. Abbreviations: AV, Aviao (S); PF, Peña Ferrán (M); SI, Sidrón (C); CL, Collubil (M); X, Xuëlga (M?); EB, El Buxú (S,C); LA, Los Azules (M); S, Sulamula (S); CR, Cova Rosa (S,M); EC, El Cierro (S,M); LP, Les Pedroses (C); LL, La Lloseta (M,C); TB, Tito Bustillo (M,C); V, Viesca (M); LC, La Cuevona (M,C); SA, San Antonio (M,C); C, Coberizas (S,M,C); B, Bricia (M); CM, Cueto del la Mina (S,M,C); R, La Riera (S,M,C); TN, Tebellín (C); TC, Tres Calabres (S); F, Fonfría (M): Q, Quintanal (C); BA, Balmori (S,M,C); SM, Samoreli (C); H, Herrerías (C); JC, Juan Covera (M); MZ, Mazaculos (C); P, El Pindal (C); LJ, La Loja (M,C); AP, Abrigos de Panes (M?); CP, Cueva de la Peña (M?); SL, Sel (S?); LH, La Hermida (M?); LN, Llonín (M,C); CO, Coimbre (M,C); T, Trauno (C); J, Jabiana (M?); CA, Los Canes (C); A, Arangas (M?); KA, Corao (S); CC, Cueva Chufín (S,C); M, Micolón (C).*

time, such as a season. Segments of the population probably foraged for food and fuel within an approximate two-hour radius of such sites on a daily basis, at the same time gathering information on the state and distribution of other resources. From these sites, longer-range specialized expeditions could have left to hunt ibex in the mountains or red deer in the upland valleys. But the sites along the coastal zone need not have been used strictly in winter (and in fact were not, as shown by some of the La Riera levels with seasonality indicators).

A mechanistic, transhumant model of human use of this region is not realistic because of the proximity of different resource zones. In the aggregate, the 16 Solutrean levels at La Riera represent occupations during all seasons, although individual levels or blocks of levels seem to have been principally or exclusively formed during different seasons (see Altuna 1986). Seasonality data from hinterland sites are scarce but, even there, specialized winter occupations (to procure ibex on their low pastures) are as likely as summer occupations (to procure red deer on their high pastures). El Buxú seems to have been used at least in the period from spring to fall (Soto 1984), and Amalda was at least used in summer, but no more precise seasonal specification is possible (Altuna 1990c). Caves like La Riera were used not only as full-scale base camps but also as specialized, ephemeral camp sites, with corresponding differences in artifact and faunal assemblages and in features. The variability observed within the Solutrean is certainly due mostly to differences in the functions and scale of occupations rather than to abstract techno-evolutionary trends.

The annual territory of an individual band may well have corresponded roughly to a river drainage and its associated stretch of the then enlargened coastal zone. Yet with depletion of food and fuel, lateral moves along the coast and among adjacent valleys were undoubtedly necessary, perhaps on a rather cyclic basis. In such a circumscribed region, and under conditions of relatively high population density, territorialism was probably useful to ensure access to adequate food resources, particularly because those resources were not very mobile. On the other hand, labor, information, mating, and back-up resource requirements ("insurance") certainly necessitated intergroup contacts within the framework of the regional macroband, perhaps formalized in a ritual context associated with centrally located cave art sanctuaries (e.g., Altamira [Straus 1976–77; Conkey 1980]). Multiband aggregations could have facilitated and been facilitated by collective activities such as major game drives. Here, art may have served in part as a social identifier and territorial marker; major sanctuaries may have functioned as landmarks on the human territorial landscape. Thus, beyond technological and tactical advances, the efficient exploitation of this region and the continued successful adaptation of an enlarged human population may have depended on a more elaborate form of social organization and communication involving a delicate balance between sharing and partitioning access to regional resources.

Chapter 6

THE MAGDALENIAN OF THE CANTABRIAN LATE GLACIAL

LIKE all the cultural subdivisions of the Cantabrian Paleo-lithic, the next archeological period goes by a name borrowed from a French "type site," La Madeleine. Early Spanish suggestions (by Alcalde del Río and Fathers Sierra and Carballo) that at least the early part of this time slot be locally called the "Altamiran" might not have been bad ones, given the need for consensual descriptive labels. Such a solution certainly would have helped in later years during the interminable discussions as to which numbered phases of the French Magdalenian are represented in the Cantabrian record. Also, use of the term "Altamiran" to refer to assemblages (like that of the upper cultural stratum at Altamira) without antler harpoons and dating to the still climatically rigorous period immediately after the Last Glacial Maximum would help to distinguish more clearly the adaptations of this early Last Glacial phase from those of the period of fluctuating but generally warming conditions after about 13,000 B.P. As it is, the entire complex set of quickly changing technologies, settlement patterns, subsistence strategies, and artistic activities of the dynamic period between 17,000 to 16,500 B.P. and 11,000 to 10,500 B.P. is grouped under the label "Magdalenian."

Perhaps because it is closer to the present and represented by so many sites, levels, and assemblages (so many of which have been excavated and studied in recent times), the variability internal to this archeological construct, "the Magdalenian," seems far greater than that of the Middle and Early Upper Paleolithic and even than that of the Solutrean. The complexity and internal variability of cultural physical and demographic environments of the Tardiglacial are real—not just products of sampling bias due to the relative recency and stratigraphic accessibility of the Magdalenian. The synchronic and diachronic variations archeologically observed within this span of 5,000 to 6,000 years represent the cumulative effect of millennia of technological inventions as well as the selective adoption of strategies or precise techniques and tactics for survival under specific, ever-changing conditions.

A recent attempt to study the "Upper and Final Magdalenian" of the Cantabrian region by individual climatic phases (González Sainz 1989) shows one direction in which detailed future analyses need to go. However, neither the precision (or density) of available radiocarbon dates nor the specificity of extant climatic phases (mainly pollen zones adapted from those of northwestern Europe and France) are great enough yet to guarantee the detailed validity of such an approach. This work will side-step the arguments over the presence of (or distinctions between) the "Lower" and "Middle" Magdalenian in northern Spain; indeed, the Magdalenian sequence even in the French Pyrenees differs significantly from that of the supposed "classic" region of the Périgord (Clottes 1976,1989). It will divide the Cantabrian Magdalenian into two essentially temporal phases: early (16,750 ± 250 B.P. to about 13,000 B.P.) and late (about 13,000 B.P. to 10,750 ± 250 B.P.). Assemblages in the early period lack harpoons; many (but not all) of those in the late period contain at least one or a few (and sometimes many) harpoons.

Because the archeological record in the Cantabrian region is absolutely continuous throughout the time that archeologists have artificially subdivided into "Solutrean," "Magdalenian," and "Azilian," there are some considerable temporal overlaps.

1. Assemblages with foliate/shouldered points called "Solutrean" overlap with assemblages with neither such points nor harpoons, called "Lower Magdalenian," in the radiocarbon time range of 17,000 to 16,000 B.P. (Straus 1975b, 1983b; Altuna 1990c).

2. There is overlap of assemblages dating to between 14,000 and 13,000 B.P. without and with round cross-section harpoons (early and late Magdalenian) (Utrilla 1981; González Sainz 1989).

3. Assemblages with round cross-section harpoons overlap those with flat cross-sections harpoons, called "Azilian," in the radiocarbon time range of 11,000 to 10,500 B.P. (Fernández-Tresguerres 1980; Straus 1985b; González Sainz 1989).

Thus, the fossil director artifact types in question (significantly, all are weapon tips) do have some real temporal value, *when factors of site role, artifact function, and sampling cause them to be found in excavations.* However, at the temporal boundaries of their existence, their usefulness in dating is blurred during periods of technological change. The issue of debate should no longer be precisely when a particular culture-stratigraphic unit or subdivision began or ended or if a particular subdivision is present in the region. Such questions assume in advance that these units are somehow real. They are, to the contrary, abstractions or simplifications of extensive interassemblage variability, shorthand useful for description and comparison. The debate should focus on how and why human adaptive strategies changed throughout the course of the Late Glacial.

Magdalenian Chronology

Appendix D1 lists radiocarbon dates for the Cantabrian Magdalenian, defined with the caveats outlined above. It is apparent that the period assigned by prehistorians to the Magdalenian spans a bit more than 6,000 years and includes the Late Glacial climatic phases (defined palynologically): Dryas I (with further subdivisions), Bölling, Dryas II, Alleröd, and possibly part of Dryas III. The invention of the antler harpoon serves to divide the Magdalenian culturally into early and late stages.

The earliest dated harpoon is from Level 1c of Tito Bustillo: 13,870 ± 220 and 13,520 ± 220 B.P. Levels 1b and 1a in this eastern Asturias cave art and occupation site so far have yielded two harpoons each. Level 1a has a series of four controversial dates ranging from 15,400 to 14,200 B.P. (Moure and Cano 1976; González Sainz 1989). Before the harpoons were discovered, this deposit had been assigned to the Lower Magdalenian, which goes to show how similar the lithic assemblages of the early and the late Magdalenian can be in this region. The basal part of Tito Bustillo Level 1c is dated to 14,930 ± 70 B.P. (The inversions in these dates are not surprising because Level 1 is a fairly thin, superficial level subdivided into lenses that are not separated by sterile zones.) The next oldest dated harpoons are from Level 2b at Rascaño (Santander): 12,900 B.P. The overlap in radiocarbon dates between early and late Magdalenian assemblages is so complete and pervasive as to suggest that 1) the lithic industries overlap fully in composition (here there are no lithic fossil directors for the late Magdalenian, as there supposedly are in southwestern France—where even these are now called into question [Laville et al. 1980]); and 2) harpoons were "invented" sometime between 15,000 and 13,500 B.P. but did not become widespread elements of the common technology until after about 13,000 B.P. Even then, their presence or abundance was highly dependent on functional factors (i.e., fishing near the sites [for discussions of harpoon use, see Julien 1982 and González Sainz 1989, with references]).

Furthermore, the distinction between unilaterally and bilaterally barbed harpoons is not a very useful chronological marker. The former occur in all periods of the late Magdalenian, whereas the rarer bilateral harpoons occur in the most recent dated levels. But the absence of the latter does not necessarily make an otherwise undated assemblage old. And there are geographical differences in the distribution of the two types, the bilateral harpoons being far more common in the Basque country than in the west (González Sainz 1989). These differences could be stylistic, but alternatively they could be practical or functional. It is conceivable that some of the unilaterally barbed pieces (those that lack clear basal attachment elements: holes or flanges) were actually elements of leisters, whereas others (with such lanyard attachment features) and the bilaterally barbed pieces were actual harpoons. Increasingly, radiocarbon dating should serve as the basis for comparing diachronic and synchronic Late Glacial archeological assemblages but, at present, the corpus of data still includes many important, undated collections from old excavations. Also, there are problems with the precision or accuracy of many of the extant radiocarbon dates as well as issues of circular reasoning in their application.

Tardiglacial Environments

The earliest "Magdalenian" assemblages—like the youngest "Solutrean" ones—relate to the so-called Lascaux oscillation. This is manifested sedimentologically at Rascaño (Levels 6 and 5 base) with evidence of flooding due to karstic rejuvenation and with an absence of cold climate phenomena (Laville and Hoyos 1981). A similar set of observations and interpretations apply to the Solutrean–early Magdalenian transitional levels (Levels 17 and 18) at La Riera: humid and moderate (cool, not cold) (Laville 1986). Areso (1984) concludes that the sediments of the base of Level VII at Ekain were deposited under conditions of high humidity with temperate to cool temperatures. High humidity also is suggested granulometrically or with evidence of erosion in Level VI at Erralla (Hoyos and Fumanal 1985), Level 3 at Las Caldas (Hoyos 1981), and Levels 9 through 2 at La Paloma (Hoyos 1980). The oldest Magdalenian at Rascaño has arboreal pollen percentages reaching 17% and including not only pine, juniper, and birch but also willow, hazel, and alder, as well as ferns, all of which are indicators of humidity (Boyer-Klein 1981). Similar evidence of a brief, limited growth of woods is also found at the beginning of the Magdalenian sequence (Level VII base) at Ekain (Dupré 1984). At La Riera there also is a slight upward inflection of the AP curve with small quantities of pine, birch, oak, hazel, willow, juniper, and alder pollens. This period is especially marked at this coastal plain by the development of a heathland (Leroi-Gourhan 1986). That the Lascaux oscillation (ca. 17,000 B.P.) was by no means balmy in Cantabrian Spain is indicated by the presence of Nordic vole in Rascaño Level 5 (Altuna 1981). But there are no reindeer remains from assemblages dated to this period. Recent critical reviews of the pollen data question the existence of the Laugerie and Lascaux "interstadials" and suggest that pleniglacial conditions were unbroken (Turner and Hannon 1988, Sánchez 1991).

Dryas I is marked by a return to severely cold temperatures with some decrease in humidity. Cryoclastic spall is abundant in Levels 5 and 4.2 of Rascaño, with some decrease in Level 4.1 (perhaps attributable to the Angles oscillation) (Laville and Hoyos 1981). Colder, drier conditions culminating in cryoturbation at La Riera (Levels 19 through 21) may be assignable to Dryas I, depending on which radiocarbon dates are valid (Laville 1986; Straus 1986d). Sediments of the upper part of Ekain Level VII are interpreted as having been deposited under cold, humid conditions (Areso 1984)—of course, humidity in caves is partly a very local phenomenon. The sediments of Erralla Level V are interpreted as having been deposited under very cold and dry conditions (Hoyos and Fumanal 1985).

The AP decreases at Ekain, although there occasionally still are traces of trees other than pine. Composites dominate the non-arboreal pollen, and ferns decrease. There is a hint of a brief amelioration in the midst of Level VII, perhaps attributable to pre-Bölling (Dupré 1984). Erralla Level V has very low AP percentages—mostly pine, but with one or two oak and alder "spikes" that might be attributable to Angles or pre-Bölling. Graminaceous grasses are rare *vis à vis* Cichoriae, testifying to relative dryness (Boyer-Klein 1985). Arboreal pollens are rare and almost totally dominated by pine throughout Level 4 at Rascaño. Ferns spores are few, and the few willow pollens reflect the adjacent riverine habitat along Río Miera. There may be a more temperate oscillation in the midst of this period (Boyer-Klein 1981).

At nearby El Juyo, in a more sheltered, lowland setting, a significant, if subtle, interruption of Dryas I conditions is suggested by pollen spectra predating 14,400 B.P., with low, fluctuating AP percentages including oak and traces of walnut, ash, and elm. Heathers are abundant and ferns moderately so. Even Mediterranean species of pine and oak are represented slightly in this period which is followed by a return to cold, drier conditions at the end of the early Magdalenian sequence at El Juyo (Boyer-Klein and Leroi-Gourhan 1985). In the time range radiocarbon dated to Dryas I times at La Riera, the AP is very low (generally <5%), but with one minor spike (12%), including some birch and elm in addition to the omnipresent pine pollens. There are few ferns or Graminae

(Leroi-Gourhan 1986). In general, the plants suggest cold, dry conditions. The basal pollen spectra at Urtiaga are virtually treeless, suggestive of rather brutally cold, open conditions during Dryas I along the Basque coast (Sanchez 1990).

Bison priscus—presumably a grassland grazer—has been definitely identified among the bovines of La Riera Level 16, which, like most of the La Riera levels, is nonetheless heavily dominated (80%) by red deer remains. Nordic vole is present in Ekain Level VII (Zabala 1984), in Level 4a at Rascaño (Altuna 1981), and in Level V of Erralla (Pemán 1985). Reindeer is present in Erralla Level V (Altuna and Mariezkurrena 1985), La Paloma Level B (Castaños 1980), Urtiaga Levels F and E (Altuna 1972), and the early Magdalenian level at Ermittia (Altuna 1972). *Cyprina islandica*, an Arctic mollusk, is present in the early Magdalenian Level Beta Level (8) of El Castillo (Cabrera 1984). The existence of small woods or thickets, at least, but not necessarily exclusively, during in the temperate oscillations within Dryas I is suggested by the sporadic presence of remains of boar and roe deer at some sites including El Juyo (Klein and Cruz-Uribe 1985).

The Bölling oscillation (ca. 13,000 B.P.) marks the real end of full glacial conditions in southwestern Europe. In analyses of oxygen isotopes of deep core samples from the Cantabrian sea, the Bölling and Alleröd phases show up as a single major warming period, truncated by the short, sharp Dryas III episode that closes the Pleistocene (see Duplessy et al. 1981). It is marked by erosion in several Cantabrian cave sites such as La Riera (Laville 1986), Rascaño (Laville and Hoyos 1981), Erralla (Hoyos and Fumanal 1985), and possibly Ekain and El Juyo.

The lower part of Rascaño Level 3 shows a marked increase in arboreal pollens and fern spores with some hazel, juniper, oak, birch, and willow, suggesting higher humidity and moderating temperatures (Boyer-Klein 1981). At Tito Bustillo Level 2, an increase in the AP with trace quantities of several thermophile trees and high percentages of Graminae and ferns is interpreted as pertaining to Bölling (Boyer-Klein 1976). However, this attribution is contradicted by the date, 14,890 ± 410 B.P., from this level (possibly early Magdalenian) as well as by the seven overlying dates. Thus, the oscillation in question might in reality be pre-Bölling (about 15,000 to 14,500 B.P.). Instead of being Dryas II, the sharp reduction (or disappearance) of trees in Tito Bustillo Level 1c would be late Dryas I, with a slight moderating trend possibly beginning at the top of Level 1b (Boyer-Klein 1976). Reindeer remains are present in Level 1b (Altuna 1976).

As noted above, Dryas II (ca. 12,500 to 12,000 B.P.) has not been identified in deep-sea cores off the Cantabrian coast. However, it is recognized palynologically in several late Magdalenian deposits. At Rascaño, after the erosive episode, Level 2.1 has almost no trees (only pine and hazel) or Graminae, but ferns continue to be abundant, at least locally (Boyer-Klein 1981, 1984). The sediments suggest cold and humid conditions with some frost weathering (Laville and Hoyos 1981). Berroberría, on the French and Guipúzcoan borders of Navarra, also shows a downward deflection of the AP with virtually no trees except pines at this time (Boyer-Klein 1984). The same is true at La Riera, although there are difficulties in interpreting the dates (i.e., whether to choose the "old" or "young" dates for Levels 20 through 24). In any event, Level 24, interpreted by Laville (1986) as the product of cold, humid conditions, contains reindeer as does Level 22 (Altuna 1986), which falls within the period assigned by Leroi-Gourhan (1986) to Dryas II at La Riera. Dryas II is well dated and marked palynologically at Ekain, with almost no trees except some pines and virtually no Graminae (in contrast to many Compositae and xerophiles) (Dupré 1984). This level (Level VI) is characterized sedimentologically as cold and dry (Areso 1984) and reindeer is present (Altuna and Mariezkurrena 1984). Level 2 at Morín (late Magdalenian) is undated but it is virtually without tree pollen except traces of pine, hazel, beech, and alder. There are many composites but relatively few ferns. This level may be reasonably assigned to Dryas II, although stratigraphically isolated (Leroi-Gourhan 1971). This would concur with Butzer's (1971) interpretation of cold conditions with evidence of frost shattering.

Reindeer is present in this level at Morin, as in both Magdalenian strata at El Castillo. The equally isolated and undated late Magdalenian level (Level II) at El Pendo is palynologically similar: very few trees, traces of pine, hazel, juniper, and alder, and few ferns (Leroi-Gourhan 1980). Butzer's (1980) sedimentological interpretation of Level II is cold and relatively dry.

Although Levels II and III at Erralla are assigned to the Alleröd, and the pollen and sediments seem to suggest a humid condition and relatively moderate temperatures (Hoyos and Fumanal 1985; Boyer-Klein 1985), Level III dates to 12,310 ± 190 B.P. In fact, most of the trees in that level are pines, with AP fluctuating between 14% and 30%. Trees, in particular thermophile taxa, do become abundant in Level II (undated), so perhaps it alone should be assigned to Alleröd. Levels II and III are considered as a cultural unit to be late Magdalenian and not Azilian (Baldeón 1985). Reindeer is present, but it is not indicated as to whether in Level II or III (Altuna and Mariezkurrena 1985). Reindeer is relatively abundant in the late Magdalenian at Urtiaga, whose dating is problematical (Altuna 1972). Both "Magdalenian" and "Azilian" assemblages are found in Alleröd in the Cantabrian region. This temperate and especially humid period will be discussed in Chapter 8 because many of the assemblages from this period, when the transition seems to have occurred, are classified as Azilian.

The palynological, sedimentological, and paleontological data all point to a Tardiglacial that can be characterized as a rising, sawtooth curve of temperatures, each successive cold period perhaps less severe than the last. Conditions were generally quite humid—not surprising, given the coastal location—with some exceptions in the still very severe Dryas I. Woodlands were still scarce and limited in extent and diversity, even during the ever-more moderate oscillations. Most of the area was covered with open vegetation. Frost weathering was still occurring, especially in Dryas I, but the glaciers must have been substantially melted by the end of Bölling. However, sea levels had not yet come up significantly, so the coast was still one to two hours' walk farther north than it is today. Cold climate fauna such as Nordic voles and reindeer were still present until the end of Dryas II. By the end of this period, conditions were far more benign than at the beginning. However, reforestation really got under way substantially in the Alleröd, only to be cut short by Dryas III—in the midst of the development of the "Azilian," a form of "epi-Magdalenian" (Straus n.d.d).

Sites, Population, and Settlement Pattern

Given the vagaries of normative culture-stratigraphic attributions of individual, undated assemblages, it is difficult to come up with very accurate counts of early and late Magdalenian sites. Many assemblages (particularly from old excavations or casual discoveries) that lack harpoons or foliate/shouldered points *and* dates may be erroneously classified as early Magdalenian (i.e., >13,000 B.P.). Thus, the present count of 52 early Magdalenian sites in the Cantabrian region, derived from Utrilla's (1981) dissertation and updated with new discoveries in the Nalón valley of Asturias (Fortea 1981) and in the Basque Country (Utrilla 1990), may be slightly inflated relative to the count of late Magdalenian sites. The latter list is derived from González Sainz's (1989) dissertation plus the review by Arribas (1990) of the Basque late Magdalenian; it contains 45 entries. Because the early Magdalenian, as defined here, lasted some 3,500 years (16,500 to 13,000 B.P.), the site count translates into an average of almost 15 sites per millennium, a slight increase relative to the Solutrean. Assuming a duration of 2,500 years (13,000 to 10,500 B.P.) for the late Magdalenian, its average is 18 sites per millennium which, with many caveats, may be interpreted as evidence for a continuing increase in regional population—but nothing like the jump that occurred between the Gravettian and Solutrean (i.e., at the Last Glacial Maximum, coinciding with the transition between the Early Upper Paleolithic and the Late Upper Paleolithic).

Naturally, the caveats concerning the use of site numbers as approximate measures of *relative* population changes have to do with the greater preservation, visibility, and stratigraphic accessibility of the more recent Magdalenian materials and the fact that with more elaborate "logistical" systems of resource procurement more small, specialized sites are "created" on the landscape than in simpler systems more heavily dependent on "residential" mobility. On the other hand, the early and the late Magdalenian, like the Solutrean, are extremely short periods (4,000 to 2,500 years) in the geological time scale. There was thus less time for the production of sites that would survive in the archeological record, compared with the long Gravettian and Aurignacian periods (ca. 7,000 and 13,000 years, respectively) or the vast span of the Mousterian (at least 50,000 years in this region).

In the absence of burial populations that would permit the construction of life tables and the absence of residential structures that would permit the application (also questionable) of cross-cultural, ethnographically derived formulas relating house area to population size, and completely mistrusting the use of population calculations based on potential meat weight or calorie counts from archeofaunal remains from what are inevitably palimpsest deposits, the site counts provide at least some way of comparing different periods in terms of the critical variable of relative population density. This measure of the demographic environment is probably not much less precise than the reconstruction of the physical environment from sediments, pollen, or animal bones: each measure is subject to many sources of error, but we currently lack better alternatives and must use these measures in conjunction with one another and with common sense.

Just as there are now enough generally concordant data to permit reconstruction of the main lines of climatic and vegetative changes throughout the Last Glacial, I would argue that we do have data suggestive of a rather sudden population increase during the Pleniglacial followed by continued, more gradual growth throughout the course of the Tardiglacial and into the Postglacial (Straus 1977b,1981b; Straus and Clark 1986; Clark and Straus 1983).

The settlement patterns of the early and the late Magdalenian did not differ fundamentally from the pattern of the Solutrean (Figure 6.1). In fact, in at least 23 or 24 sites, early Magdalenian levels overlie Solutrean

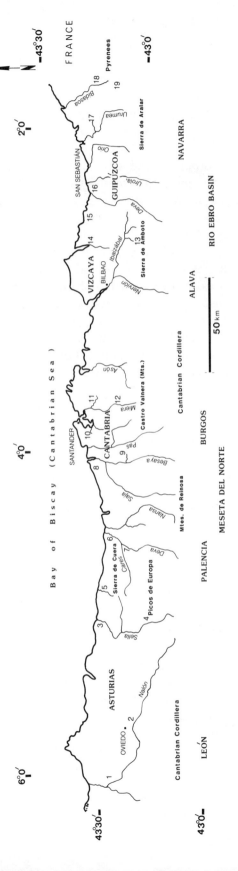

FIGURE 6.1. *Early Magdalenian sites: 1, Candamo, Ancenia, La Paloma, Sofoxó, Las Caldas, La Luera; 2, La Viña, Entrefoces; 3, Cova Rosa, El Cierro, La Cuevona, La Lloseta, San Antonio, Tito Bustillo, Viesca; 4, Collubil; 5, Coberizas, Cueto de la Mina, La Riera, Balmori, Fonfría; 6, Juan de Covera, La Loja, Cueva de la Peña; 7, Coimbre, Trauno, La Hermida; 8, Altamira, Cuco; 9, Hornos de la Peña, El Castillo, La Pasiega; 10, El Juyo, Loreto, El Pendo, Camargo; 11, Fuente de Francés, Truchiro; 12, El Rascaño, El Salitre, La Bona; 13, Sailleunta, Bolinkoba; 14, Santimamiñe; 15, Atxurra, Lumentxa; 16, Ermittia, Urtiaga, Ekain, Erralla; 17, Aitzbitarte IV; 18, Berroberría, Sorquinen; 19, Abauntz. This includes some little-known or problematic early Magdalenian sites. Because numbers of sites are large, numerals represent approximate centers of site clusters.*

ones (usually without stratigraphic separation) and in 3 other sites a hiatus separates the Solutrean deposit from a late Magdalenian level. At least 22 sites have both early and late Magdalenian strata. However, only 9 sites have Solutrean and early and late Magdalenian levels; these include such major residential sites as Cueto de la Mina and neighboring La Riera, El Castillo, El Pendo, Santimaniñe, and Aitzbitarte, all of which also have Early Upper Paleolithic deposits. These sites were clearly chosen again and again by humans for occupation because of ideal location, exposure, shelter, or other valued features (water, strategic view, etc.). However, about 27 of the early Magdalenian sites and 20 of the late Magdalenian sites had their first human occupation in those respective periods—evidence of real further expansions of settlement and possibly of population density. Virtually every portion of the Cantabrian region was utilized in the Magdalenian in such ways as to leave behind site residues. As in earlier periods, because of steep gradients, the presumably once common open-air sites of this period (especially minor, special-purpose camps and way stations), have been all but totally destroyed by erosion (or deeply buried at footslopes or in river terraces). Caves and rockshelters, probably preferred as residential sites (as well as for many logistical sites) under the still cold or at least very cool conditions of the Tardiglacial, constitute the archeological record of this period. But that in no way conditioned the distribution of sites in the Cantabrian region as far west as Río Nalón, since karstic phenomena are ubiquitous or at least very common. Population pressure, human strategic and tactical choice, and deglaciation were the factors that determined the distribution of Magdalenian sites.

Magdalenian sites are found near the present-day shore (and presumably near the Tardiglacial shore as well), along ridges or in dolinas on the coastal plain (or in hills that descend directly to the coast in Guipúzcoa), and in the relatively broad lower valleys of all the region's rivers. Even more than in the Solutrean, they are found in the mountainous interior (including narrow intermontane valleys, upper valleys, and gorges near the headwater of the principal streams and on the Cordilleran slopes themselves).

As in the Pyrenees, the final "conquest of the mountains" took place in Cantabrian Spain during the Tardiglacial Magdalenian and Azilian. In Asturias, this phenomenon is marked by the repeated utilization of Collubil cave for ibex hunting, at nearly 300 m above present sea level, on extremely steep cliffs at the western end of the Picos de Europa. This site, at the head of a steep, narrow side gorge, is 120 m above the upper course of Río Sella (González Morales 1974). Other mountains sites in Asturias include the art and habitation sites of Trauno, Llonín, and

Coimbre as well as other little-known sites (La Hermida, Cueva de la Peña) and several as yet unexcavated cave art locations of probable Tardiglacial age, all along the steep, narrow gorges of Ríos Cares and Deva in the central and eastern Picos de Europa.

In Santander, the site of Rascaño was first occupied in the early Magdalenian. Located at 275 m above present sea level, this small cave dominates a narrow gorge of Río Miera from 50 m above the valley floor and is on an extremely steep cliff in highly mountainous terrain with nearby peaks up to 1,000 m. Like Collubil and Bolinkoba, Rascaño was utilized almost exclusively for ibex hunting (Straus 1987b). In the same valley lie the Magdalenian sites of Piélago (also Azilian like Rascaño), La Bona (also Solutrean), and, higher still, El Salitre (also Solutrean and Azilian). Further east in Santander, in the upper drainage of the Asón, are numerous high mountain sites that probably are of Magdalenian age. The most spectacular is Becerral, a painted cave dated stylistically to the early Magdalenian and located at 720 m, near the 1,160-m Cordilleran pass of La Sia on the Burgos border. It is from sites like Becerral that, after substantial deglaciation of the Cordillera, humans may have reached the northern Meseta where there are several cave art sites, notably Ojo Guareña, which is only about 20 km to the south and which has yielded torch charcoal dated to 15,600 B.P. (Bernaldo de Quirós et al. 1987). Also in the mountainous eastern area of Santander, not far from Becerral, are the engraved or painted caves of Patatal and Emboscados in Matienzo, Sotarriza, Cullalvera, Covalanas, and Cova Negra near Ramales. None of these have been excavated yet, but all of them probably are Magdalenian (ACDPS 1986).

High-mountain Basque Country sites of Magdalenian age include Silibranka (335 m above present sea level), Bolinkoba (350 m [also used in the Gravettian and Solutrean]), and Lezetxiki (375 m [also used in the Mousterian and Early Upper Paleolithic]). Another, little-known Magdalenian site, Sailleunta, is located at an unknown elevation on slopes of the Sierra de Amboto near Silibranka and Bolinkoba. Several other Basque Magdalenian sites are on steep slopes in very hilly terrain, although at fairly low elevations (Ermittia, Erralla, Ekain, Aitzbitarte). Berroberría and Abauntz are located in northwestern Navarra on the southern edge of the Cordillera. Abauntz is at about 700 m above present sea level; it is another indicator of the increasingly significant use of the Meseta in the early Magdalenian, here dated to 15,800 B.P. (Utrilla 1982).

Although there are Magdalenian sites throughout the Cantabrian region, they are not randomly scattered (Figure 6.2). Distinct clusters of sites exist: 1) along the Nalón valley; 2) along the Sella; 3) in the Posada de Llanes area of coastal Asturias and contiguous hinterland; 4) around

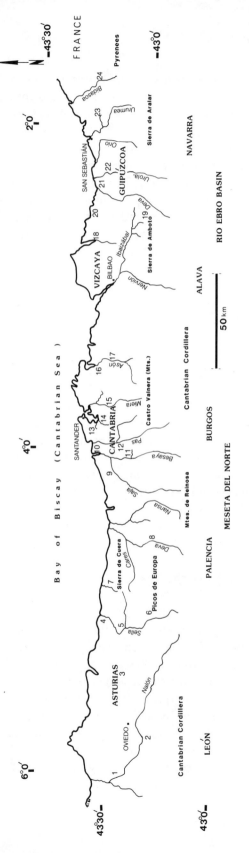

FIGURE 6.2. *Late Magdalenian sites: 1, La Paloma, Sofoxó, Cueva Oscura de Ania; 2, Entrefoces; 3, Peña Ferrán; 4, Tito Bustillo, Viesca, El Cierro, Cova Rosa; 5, Los Azules; 6, Collubil; 7, La Riera, Cueto de la Mina, Bricia; 8, La Hermida; 9, Linar, Cualventi; 10, La Pila; 11, Sovilla; 12, El Castillo; 13, El Pendo; 14, Cueva Morín; 15, El Rascaño, El Piélago; 16, La Chora, El Otero; 17, El Valle; 18, Atxeta, Santimamiñe; 19, Silibranka, Lezetxiki; 20, Lumentxa, Laminak, Abittaga, Goikolau; 21, Urtiaga, Ekain, Ermittia; 22, Erralla; 23, Aitzbitarte, Torre; 24, Berroberría.*

the Bay of Santander and in the interior of central Santander Province (Rios Pas and Miera drainages); 5) along the Río Asón; 6) along the Guernica estuary; and 7) near the coast between Ríos Deva and Urola in Guipúzcoa. These areas must have been centers of preferred Magdalenian residence (core areas of band territories?). There are, however, isolated sites on the peripheries of and between these areas. The latter may represent more occasional utilization of extended territories, perhaps by members of more than one band. Some of the isolated sites may have been logistical camps (like the ibex-hunting camps associated with many of the major site clusters), but others might also be parts of once-important clusters of which the rest have either been lost (to erosion, burial, or sea-level transgression) or not yet been found. One such potential cluster might include the major site of Aitzbitarte IV (plus Aitzbitarte III and Torre) on the edge of the narrow coastal zone around San Sebastian. It might be part of the same settlement system as the cave art and occupation complex of Alkerdi and Berroberría, 25 km to the east, and the chamois-hunting camp of Abauntz, 30 km to the southeast in Navarra. As will be shown later, the Magdalenian habitation site clusters are generally associated with cave art—often including "sanctuaries" of the first order. First, however, Magdalenian interassemblage variability must be examined.

Magdalenian Technology and Systematics

As mentioned above, considerable effort has been expended in recent years to establish the archeological systematics of the Cantabrian Magdalenian (e.g., Moure 1974; GTPC 1979; Utrilla 1981a,b; González Sainz 1989). All specialists seem to agree that Breuil's subdivision scheme for the Magdalenian of southwestern France (as modified by Cheynier and de Sonneville-Bordes to eventually include phases 0, I, II, III, IV, V, VIa, and VIb) cannot be strictly applied to Cantabrian Spain (if anywhere). However, the bulk of recent and present research continues to focus on normative attempts to devise a better subdivision scheme for the region.

Much of this work has focused, in a rather "art historical" way, on analysis of the form and decoration of antler artifacts, notably sagaies and harpoons. With few complete, securely stratified series from recent excavations (Rascaño is an exception, but the remnant deposits we dug at the rear of the cave were very small and peripheral) the _modus operandi_ consists largely of detailed comparisons of selected artifacts and motifs among Cantabrian collections with French "type" collections. The temporal subdivisions that are being proposed are so fine as to exceed

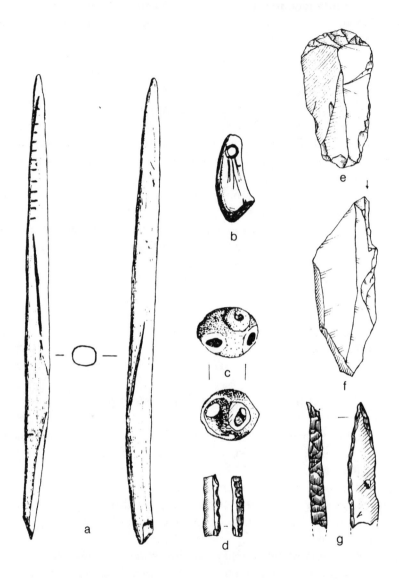

FIGURE 6.3. *Magdalenian artifacts, La Riera Cave: a, engraved "sagaie" with quadrangular cross-section; b, perforated red deer canine; c, perforated* Littorina *shell; d, backed bladelet; e, endscraper on blade; f, angle dihedral burin; g, Gravette point; h, engraved flat bone plaquette fragment with figure of unidentified animal; i, biface. (From Straus and Clark 1986.)*

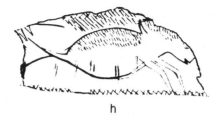

h

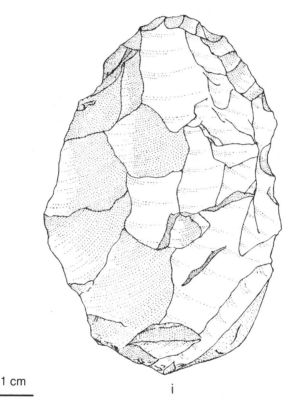

1 cm

i

the level of resolution of most radiocarbon dates within such relatively large blocks of time as the early and the late Magdalenian. The product of recent work along these lines includes the following subdivisions: "Archaic," "Lower," "Middle," "early Upper," and "late Upper" or "Final" Magdalenian (Utrilla 1981a,b; González Sainz 1989).

This maximalist splitting approach does not differ significantly from the Breuil scheme. It is opposed by a simpler (and somewhat older) view in which there would be only two fundamental subdivisions: Lower and Upper Cantabrian Magdalenian (at most dividing the harpoon-bearing assemblages into "Upper" and "Final" stages) (see Moure 1979; GTPC

1979; González Echegaray 1985). The existence of a "Middle" Magdalenian turns on the interpretation of a few worked antler objects ("protoharpoons") in the site of Ermittia whose old stratigraphy is difficult to interpret (Barandiarán and Utrilla 1976; González Sainz 1989) and of newly excavated levels at Rascaño (Utrilla 1981a,b; *pace* Barandiarán and González Echegaray 1981) and Las Caldas (Corchón 1981). Most specialists (e.g., Utrilla, Corchón, González Sainz, González Echegaray) recognize a wide range of variability ("facies") among assemblages within (as well as between) their respective versions of the Magdalenian "temporal" subdivisions. It is this variability that concerns us here, as opposed to the interminable debates about defining supposed phases. Because most of the dated early Magdalenian assemblages in the Cantabrian region were formed under the generally cold, open-vegetation (albeit fluctuating) conditions of Dryas I, it makes sense to consider them as a group.

The Early Magdalenian

Appendix D2 presents the principal lithic tool group indices for the main Magdalenian assemblages that date either radiometrically or stratigraphically to the early period (about 16,500 to 13,000 B.P.). There are essentially two groups of assemblages: those with high percentages (>30%) of backed bladelets, and those with high percentages (>30%) of endscrapers (Figure 6.3). These two axes of variability also define underlying variability among Solutrean substrate (i.e., nonpoints) tool assemblages. Among the early Magdalenian assemblages that have few or no backed bladelets are several from modern excavations with systematic fine screening (i.e., Rascaño, Las Caldas, Altamira [1981 excavation], El Juyo Level 4 "Sanctuary"). Among those with many backed bladelets are several from older excavations (i.e., La Paloma, Urtiaga, Aitzbitarte). Thus, the dichotomy between "many backed bladelets" and "few backed bladelets" is likely to be real and probably functionally significant.

In several sites (particularly in the Basque Country), high backed bladelet indices are associated with high burin indices, which in turn exceed endscraper indices. This phenomenon continues the tradition of "Gravettian-like" assemblages in the Tardiglacial just as in the Last Glacial Maximum, especially in the Basque sites. The microlithization of Magdalenian (and earlier Upper Paleolithic industries) in the region may be due to the small size of available flint nodules. The high percentages of burins in Basque sites could signal more rapid abandonment of these tools, with less resharpening, in an area abundant in flint than

in areas with less readily accessible materials appropriate for burin manufacture (i.e., west-central Santander and Asturias).

Traditionally one of the hallmarks of the "Lower Cantabrian Magdalenian" has been the presence in some assemblages of thick endscrapers,
including many "nucleiform endscrapers." There has been considerable
discussion concerning the nature of the nucleiform endscraper (type 15
in the original Upper Paleolithic typology of Sonneville-Bordes and Perrot
[1954] to the extent that it was omitted from the latest version of the
type list (see Utrilla 1981a:13,1984–1985,1990). A recent microwear study
of "thick endscrapers and nucleiform burins" from El Rascaño and El
Juyo by Keeley (1988) concluded that these pieces were mostly just cores
and that the nibbling retouch along their edges is the result of platform
preparation by hammerstone, with few instances of use on wood or hide.
A microwear study of "type 15—nucleiform endscrapers" from Abauntz
by Mazo (1980, cited in Utrilla 1990:44) also failed to find traces of use
wear. Nonetheless, these objects (whether "endscrapers on cores" or simply unused, exhausted cores, do appear in several early Magdalenian
assemblages—with other endscraper types—in very large quantities, suggesting something specialized about the site occupations.

Keeley's (1988) study (like virtually all of the many others conducted
in France and in northern Europe) confirms that other "endscraper" types
were indeed used mainly (80% to 85%) for hide scraping, whereas virtually all backed bladelets were used as projectile armatures. Perforators were used for boring a wide variety of materials and for fine graving
on bone and antler. Burins were multipurpose tools for working bone
and antler (graving, sometimes scraping, rarely boring). On the basis of
this first microwear study (and common sense), it is possible to argue
for a lot of hide-working at both El Rascaño and El Juyo, with evidence
of large-scale killing of ibex and red deer, respectively (see below).

El Juyo also has significant evidence of bone working—not only in its
relatively high percentages of burins but also in the presence of several
"blanks" and of bones and antlers from which blanks have been removed
by the groove-and-splinter technique for future tool manufacture (Barandiarán 1985). La Riera (or at least the rear vestibule area that remained
for us to dig in 1976–1979) seems to have been a place where much
rearming (and discard of used microlithic armature elements) took place,
judging from the very high proportions of backed bladelets. This also
seems to have been true at Ekain in the early Magdalenian occupation,
where there are few lithic tools other than backed bladelets.

However, it is not yet possible to assign specific functions to the early
Magdalenian sites, beyond general statements based on cave sizes, site
locations, faunas, features/structures, and amounts of debris, combined

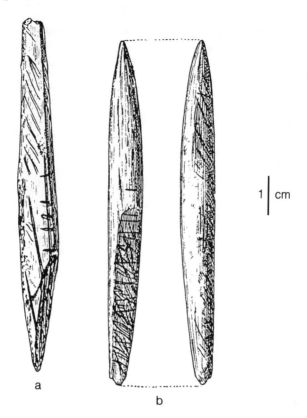

1 cm

FIGURE 6.4. *Magdalenian antler points ("sagaies") and harpoons: a,b, Balmori (from Vega del Sella 1930); c–g, El Rascaño (from Obermaier 1924).*

with impressionistic interpretations of the artifacts. Even supposedly specialized hunting camps such as Rascaño (small, high, uncomfortable, difficult access, heavily dominated by ibex remains) have evidence of other activities (in this case, bone-working, including mobile art pro-duction—reminiscent "secondary" activities at the Eskimo "Mask Site" hunting stand [Binford 1978]). In addition, even the finest archeologically defined levels (as at La Riera) are palimpsests and, in most Cantabrian Upper Paleolithic cave sites, the cultural horizons are very thick, rich, and difficult to subdivide meaningfully or to equate in behavioral terms from cave to cave (Freeman 1988; González Echegaray 1984). Another source of clues as to site function can come from nonlithic artifacts.

One of the hallmarks of "the Magdalenian", in contrast to "the Solu-trean", is the abundance of osseous (mostly antler) artifacts (Figure 6.4). Ornaments and works of mobile art made of bone, antler, or tooth are discussed below, together with those made of stone. However, the main

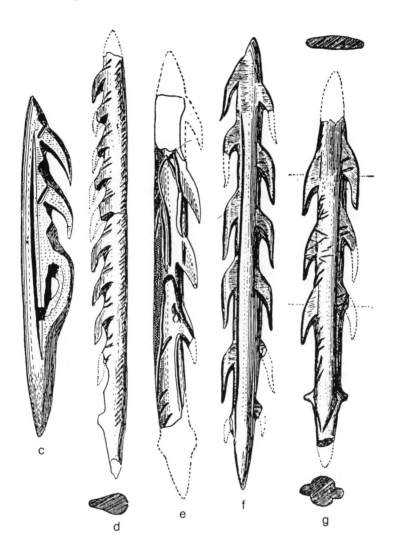

category of osseous artifacts are "sagaies" (point, foreshafts, or linkshafts) whose "decorations" generally include transverse or oblique engraved lines across basal bevels (usually single in this period) to help create a tight bond to other wooden or antler hafted elements. In the early Magdalenian, the majority of sagaies are quadrangular in cross section, and many have apparently real decorative and rather standardized geometric "tectiform" engravings on the side.

It is even more difficult to quantify osseous artifacts than it is to quantify lithic ones (although one backed bladelet element from a multi-component weapon hafted with many such pieces is not equivalent to a large, hand-held endscraper on a blade). An antler sagaie may easily break into many identifiable pieces and, in the absence of positive refits, may be erroneously counted as more than one artifact. Under some soil and micro-environmental conditions (even differing laterally or stratigraphically within an individual cave), antler objects may become weathered into unrecognizable lumps or destroyed altogether (see Utrilla [1982] for such an instance at Abauntz). Fortunately, in the alkaline environments of the limestone caves of this region, faunal and osseous artifact preservation usually is excellent.

In some of the old collections the sagaies and other carved antler objects may have tended to be somewhat preferentially saved during excavation or subsequent curation. On the other hand, they (like Solutrean points) often tended to be the objects stolen from museum displays or storerooms. Appendix D3 lists the numbers of sagaies (I. Barandiarán's [1967] "Group I" in his osseous artifact typology) for the levels whose lithic tool assemblages are given in Appendix D2. Appendix D3 also gives the ratio of lithic tools to antler points for each level. Some of the old collections (El Castillo, Altamira, Cueto de la Mina D) may show an exaggerated importance of sagaies as a result of the differential collection and curation problems, although it is inescapable that very large quantities of antler points were discarded (and probably made at and used near these sites). Sites excavated and curated more recently and carefully are: notably El Juyo 4 and 7, Rascaño 4, Aitzbitarte, and Erralla.

On the other hand, unless caused by unfavorable preservation conditions (as apparently the case at Abauntz), there are several recently excavated sites where these probable weapon tips were hardly abandoned at all for reasons undoubtedly related to site function or to sampling error: Ekain, Entrefoces, La Lloseta, Rascaño 3. Most other assemblages lie in the range of about 11 to 30 lithic tools per sagaie, perhaps suggesting a more balanced set of activities resulting in discard or loss of both antler and stone artifacts. It bears repeating that assemblages with Solutrean points (as throughout the sequence of La Riera Levels 4 through 17) have kinds of sagaies once thought strictly typical of the early Magdalenian (or late Solutrean only): bipointed sagaies with central flattening, sagaies with a single basal bevel covering more than one-third of the object length, quadrangular cross-section sagaies (González Morales 1986). However, there is an overall trend for sagaies (as well as backed bladelets) to increase, ultimately replacing Solutrean points as armatures. Due to the vagaries of functional and disposal variability and of sampling error throughout an individual stratigraphic sequence, this trend may not be apparent at any one site.

Table 6.1 Summary of Major Tool Group Indices for Early and
Late Magdalenian

	Indices		
Period	Endscrapers	Burins	Backed Bladelets
Early (n = 36)			
Range	0.9–59.3	1.3–36.0	0–74.4
Average Percentage	28.9	13.3	20.2
SD	17.5	7.1	22.2
Late (n = 34)			
Range	1.3–41.6	1.6–47.4	0.9–54.7
Average Percentage	14.4	23.7	25.3
SD	11.0	12.2	15.7

The Late Magdalenian

Appendix D4 presents the main tool group indices for the principal assemblages of late Magdalenian date from both old and recent excavations. The former are included with all the usual reservations concerning poor or uneven screening, selective collection, discard or loss from museums, etc. For El Castillo Level 6 ("Magdalenian Alpha") the documented bias is so great that it is not included, despite the great size of the lithic and osseous assemblages from this stratum [González Sainz 1989; Cabrera 1984].)

As opposed to the early Magdalenian assemblages where endscrapers outnumber burins in 63% of the levels, in the late Magdalenian assemblages burins outnumber endscrapers (but often only slightly) in 76% of the levels included in the sample (Table 6.1). As before, and for reasons that might have to do with a less conservative use of abundant local flint (i.e., less resharpening and quicker discard), the relative frequencies of burins generally are highest at sites in the Basque Country.

Like the early assemblages, there is a broad range of variability among the late assemblages in terms of the relative frequency of backed bladelets. And it is not only some older collections that have few of these armatures. In fact, some older collections (La Paloma, Urtiaga, Silibranka) have rather high percentages. But it is clear that in other old excavations they were either not systematically collected or were subsequently lost, as in the cases of Cueto de la Mina, Bricia, and El Valle. Santimamiñe was dug by the same team (Aranzadi and Barandiarán) as Silibranka and

Urtiaga, presumably with the same methods, suggesting that the differences in microlith representation among the three sites may be real. On the other hand, several assemblages from careful, recent excavations are not very rich in backed bladelets (Rascaño 2b, Otero 2, Abittaga) and those with many of these items show percentages that vary significantly from about 15% in many assemblages to around 50% in some levels of La Riera, Tito Bustillo, Ekain, and Erralla.

The fact that within individual multilevel sites there are great variations in the percentage of backed bladelets suggests either a functional or a sampling cause (or both) related to when and where rearming took place among sites, among occupations of a site, or at different places within individual caves through time. Although in both periods there is a wide range of variability in backed bladelets, there is no difference between the two periods; the average percentage in the early Magdalenian is 20.2% ($n = 36$, SD $= 22.2$) and in the late Magdalenian it is 25.3% ($n = 34$, SD $= 15.7$). (In contrast, the average backed-bladelet index in a sample of 26 Solutrean assemblages is 11.65% [SD $= 17.8$], showing the nature of the shift in weapon tip technology.)

As in the Solutrean, both early and late Magdalenian lithic assemblages have variable, but always low, percentages (only once $\pm 7\%$) of perforators. Denticulates/notches are present in virtually all the Magdalenian assemblages (as in the Solutrean), often in non-negligible quantities (up to about 20% in half a dozen instances between both Magdalenian periods) and not restricted to the quartzite-dominated areas of the western end of the region. Sidescrapers are less ubiquitous, and their percentages usually are lower than those for the other "archaic" types, with some tendency to be more abundant in the west, although by far the highest percentage (14.6%) is at Urtiaga (Level F, "early Magdalenian" or "Solutrean") in the flint-rich east. Overall, there is a slight decrease in the representation of sidescrapers in the Magdalenian when compared to the Solutrean.

All these data tend to confirm a lack of clear difference between the early and the late Magdalenian, with the exception of an increase, on average, of burins in the latter period. These data also confirm the general continuity between the Solutrean and Magdalenian in all aspects of lithics, albeit with the disappearance (by definition) of Solutrean points and an overall trend toward an increase in backed bladelets (a functional replacement?) between the two periods.

It could be asked: Is the increase in burins in the late Magdalenian reflected in an increase in the use of osseous materials? For the reasons discussed above, this is not easy to measure (for example, at Silibranka rockshelter, poor preservation conditions are given as the reason for the small inventory of osseous artifacts [González Sainz 1989:113]). For another, despite Keeley's (1988) conclusion that early Magdalenian burins at El Rascaño and El Juyo were often used on bone/antler, there is a large body of microwear evidence (summarized by Akoshima n.d.) that suggests a lack of a one-to-one relationship between burin facets and bone/antler grooving. Appendix D5 shows the numbers of sagaies and harpoons for the levels whose lithic tool assemblages are summarized in Appendix D4. As with the early Magdalenian assemblages, the representation of these antler points is highly variable, a fact that in part may have something to do with site function (as well as preservation and sampling factors).

Even harpoons, the fossil director of the late Magdalenian, are rare of absent in many cases—either because the sites were used not much or at all for fishing or because of sampling factors as in the case of El Pendo where old, small-scale excavations by Carballo yielded harpoons but more recent, large-scale ones in another area of this vast cave uncovered none. However, in some sites harpoons are rare or absent, despite good preservation of fauna, sagaies, and other antler artifacts—even in locations near rivers as in the case of Tito Bustillo. Indeed, two adjacent sites, La Riera and Cueto de la Mina, with penecontemporaneous levels and the same location have greatly different quantities of harpoons (24 from the latter and only 3 from both old and new excavations at the former), a fact suggesting some difference in the activities conducted from the two sites (perhaps of a seasonal nature).

Appendix D5 also shows the ratio of total lithic tools to total antler points for each assemblage. The average ratio of stone tools per antler point, 24.3:1, is only slightly less than the ratio, 28.8:1, for the early assemblages, so it is hard to argue that antler points generally became more abundant in the late Magdalenian. The differences between the two periods that do appear include an overall increase in circular cross-section sagaies versus quandrangular ones and of double-bevel bases versus single-bevel bases. The reasons for these shifts in frequency distributions remain obscure (see Utrilla 1981a; González Sainz 1989; but see González Morales 1986 for the specific case of La Riera which violates these norms). The Magdalenian *as a whole* is characterized by generally abundant osseous industries and is essentially divided temporally by the absence or presence of one element of those industries: circular cross-section harpoons.

As shown by González Sainz (1989), there are both geographic and temporal components to variability within the Magdalenian harpoon group: more of the bilaterally barbed variety in the Basque sites and in the most recent period (ca. 11,500 to 11,000 B.P.)—perhaps a genuine cul-

tural preference or ethnic stylistic marker, whether conscious or unconscious. Just what "Magdalenian" inhabitants of Tardiglacial Cantabrian
Spain were doing with their large, varied, and highly specialized stone
and antler weapons and other tools is the subject of the following discussion of subsistence activities.

Magdalenian Subsistence

There are abundant date to support the view that intensification of subsistence continued apace during the Tardiglacial. Most of the same animal species hunted (or gathered) in the Upper Pleniglacial were also taken
by Magdalenian humans, although by this time the rhinos and mam-
moths were nearing or had reached extinction in northern Spain. The
increasing regularity with which roe deer and boar are present in Magdalenian archeofaunas no doubt is due partly to the increasing frequency
with which thickets and limited woods were part of the Cantabrian vegetation. But, in the case of boar, increased need and sophistication in
hunting tactics and weapons also probably were responsible since earlier periods with some woods had seen few if any of these fast, dangerous suids in the game bags. Otherwise, there are no apparent climatic
trends in the faunal data. Variations among levels and sites are probably
due mostly to differences in site role or to the vagaries of archeological
sampling. Even decreases in limpet size, often thought to have been
caused by increases in ocean temperature, now seem to have been the
result of human overexploitation.

Appendix D6 lists data on the ungulate faunas from early and late
Magdalenian levels in terms of minimum number of individuals (MNI).
All collections from modern and many major old excavations are summarized, except Las Caldas (MNIs were not calculated here but the
Magdalenian yielded 339 and 331 remains of red deer and ibex, respectively, and little else [Soto and Meléndez 1981]) and from El Castillo
(whose Magdalenian fauna were never fully quantified but whose early
level is heavily dominated by red deer and whose late level has a more
even distribution of red deer, bovines, ibex, and chamois. Both levels
are said to contain reindeer remains [Cabrera 1984]). Only MNIs are given
to simplify somewhat an already complex table. Although they over-
state the relative importance of rare species and understate that of major
species, they do give a readily understandable impression of the composition of the Magdalenian game bag. There is no escaping the over-
whelming importance (even if underestimated) of two medium size
ungulates to Tardiglacial subsistence: *Cervus* and *Capra*. To obtain some

idea of that importance, consider a few striking values for number of identified specimens (NISP): *Cervus*, 1,639 in La Riera Level 18 and 1,303 in Level 19, 3,925 in El Juyo Level 4, 2,627 in Level 6/7, and 1,289 in Level 8/9; *Capra*, 1,313 in El Rascaño Level 5 and 1,319 in Level 4b, 2,375 in Erralla Level V. These remarkably large numbers of remains come from limited excavations of thin levels (sometimes from marginal areas of sites) and despite extensive destruction of bones (by human processing and trampling and from the pressure of overburden weight and movement).

The killing of large numbers of red deer and ibex, usually at different times and places (although some sites, like La Riera, were close to preferred habitats of both species and include levels alternately dominated by both), was a regular and key part of Magdalenian subsistence. MNIs of 15, 20, and even 30 or more red deer are now common. Specialized sites such as Rascaño and Erralla (like others in the same period in the Pyrenees [Straus 1987b]) have evidence of the slaughter of ibex, with MNIs of 15 to 36 per level. Bolinkoba continued to be a specialized ibex hunting site in Vizcaya, with 66% of its total Magdalenian NISP being from that species (Altuna 1990d). And old Magdalenian excavations at Collubil in the Picos de Europa yielded similarly specialized ibex faunas (González Morales 1974). One site, El Juyo, stands out as a residential from which truly massive nearby red deer massacres took place and to which substantial parts of the carcasses were brought for secondary processing and consumption in the early Magdalenian. My (Straus 1977b) calculations of MNIs from the original faunal study of the 1955–1957 excavations at El Juyo (Azpeitia 1958) lowered earlier estimates but still arrived at 13 and 20 red deer individuals for Levels VI and IV, respectively. The new excavations by Freeman, González Echegaray, Barandiarán, and Klein have yielded MNIs for *Cervus* of up to 78, according to the latest published count (Freeman et al. 1988). Even an earlier count (after only two seasons of excavation), showed an MNI of 38 for Level 4 by itself (Klein and Cruz-Uribe 1985).

Analyses of *Cervus* molar crown heights at El Juyo (Klein et al. 1981, 1983; Klein and Cruz-Uribe 1985) indicate a catastrophic mortality pattern, suggesting mass hunting practices in which young, old, and especially prime age deer were killed, perhaps in drives or surrounds. At both El Juyo and Tito Bustillo (studied by Altuna [1976]), there are osteological (i.e., antler scarcity) and biometrical (i.e., sexually dimorphic measurements) indications that hunters targeted hind herds, killing mothers and their young. (Red deer stags live separately from the hinds, either alone or in smaller groups and often at higher altitudes, most of the year except at rut in fall. A similar strategy seems to have been followed at Ekain (Altuna and Mariezkurrena 1984), Cueto de la Mina (Castaños 1982), and La Riera (Altuna 1986; Clark and Straus 1983). The hunters of red deer probably took advantage of topographic features to capture or hinder the flight of these gregarious animals. Many Magdalenian (and Solutrean) sites are located at steep-sided cul-de-sac side valleys or dolinas or on narrow gorges. Surrounds and drives (perhaps using portable nets or fences to close narrow gorges and valley mouths) may have been used to force the deer toward the hunters. In winter, deep or lightly crusted snow could have helped immobilize the hind herds to be killed.

A similar focus on the slaughter of female ibex and their young seems to be suggested by the data from Erralla (Altuna and Mariezkurrena 1985), whereas at Rascaño there is evidence of both that strategy and the killing of male herds (Altuna 1981). The systematic hunting of the fast, wary, cliff-dwelling ibex requires careful planning, organization, and execution. One way to accomplish it might involve determining herd location the night before a hunt, positioning of hunters at a crestline above the herd (since the natural flight reaction of ibex is to run upward), and then driving the animals toward the hunters. The first parts require meticulous attention to wind direction, silence, hidden spotter and hunter movements, etc. By Solutrean and Magdalenian times, Cantabrian inhabitants needed to be able to exploit this resource systematically and thus mastered these techniques and developed the weapons to conduct successful large-scale hunts. (The atl-atl was probably part of the repertoire of available Magdalenian propulsion devices [Barandiarán 1972], but positive evidence of the existence of the bow is lacking.)

More than anything else, the successful hunting of red deer and ibex in large quantities is evidence of 1) the need of Late Glacial humans to increase the harvest of available wild food resources; and 2) their skills in the collection and dissemination of information on game location, state, and behavior, in planning group approaches for killing, processing, and sharing large numbers of animals, and in developing effective killing and processing tools.

As indicated in Appendix D6, other large, medium, and small ungulates were taken regularly in the Magdalenian (as in the Solutrean). But remains of bovines (probably mostly bison) and horse usually are scarce and MNIs are very small. Despite their visual and numerical importance in regional cave art, these animals probably were occasional, solitary targets. Nonetheless, when they were killed, they were of great dietary importance because of their large size (especially the bison). Reindeer were present fairly consistently in the Cantabrian region, especially during the colder episodes of the Tardiglacial. Indeed, there seems to have been an overflow from a center of reindeer population in southern

France into northern Spain (especially the Basque Country) during the Dryas II) despite ecological competition from the local and equally flexible cervid, the red deer. However, except at Urtiaga, humans rarely killed reindeer, even if they did paint or engrave it exquisitely at Altxerri (Guipúzcoa), Las Monedas (Santander), and Tito Bustillo (Asturias). In northern Spain (as opposed to Late Glacial France), it too would have been killed individually, not in drives or surrounds.

Chamois was taken regularly and in large numbers at some sites (Urtiaga Level D, Aitzbitarte Level II, Abauntz Level E). It and the roe deer, a frequent but minor game species in the Magdalenian, are small and often were brought back to residential sites substantially whole. For the first time, boar is regularly represented in most sites, a testimony to Magdalenian human skill, courage, and necessity. Seal remains occasionally occur (as in the Solutrean) and may be evidence of the killing or scavenging of beached animals.

Other carnivores are listed in Appendix D7 in terms of numbers of identifiable specimens (NISP) (the counts are so small that use of MNI would consistently overemphasize the importance of most carnivores in the Magdalenian archeofaunas). Ursids and large felids are few and concentrated in only a limited number of sites (mostly in the always bear-rich Basque caves for the former). Hyenas and dholes are virtually absent. Wolf is often present, although usually in small numbers. Mustelids and especially fox are common and sometimes abundant. It is possible that they were trapped for their pelts. Examination of the bones of these small fur-bearers would be useful in testing this hypothesis. Lagomorphs are more common than in earlier periods, a fact that might indicate human trapping for pelts (as opposed to natural death in burrows in caves), but rabbits and hares were never really abundant in Cantabrian Spain, in striking contrast to the situation throughout the Upper Paleolithic in eastern Spain and Portugal.

The large-scale gathering and transport of marine mollusks, initiated during the Last Glacial Maximum at such sites as La Riera, increased and became generalized during the Tardiglacial, even though the ocean level had not yet risen enough to make a significant difference in the distance to the shore from the sites where shellfish are abundant. Besides La Riera (Ortea 1986), such sites include Balmori, Cueto de la Mina, Cova Rosa, La Lloseta (Clark 1976; and pers.obs.), Tito Bustillo (Madariaga 1975,1976), Altamira (Straus 1976–1977; Klein and Cruz-Uribe 1984), El Juyo (Madariaga and Fernández 1985; Klein and Cruz-Uribe 1984), El Otero (Madariaga 1966), La Chora (Madariaga 1963), and Lumentxa (Aranzadi and Barandiarán 1935).

In almost all cases in Asturias and west-central Santander, limpet (mostly *Patella vulgata*) is by far the dominant species, usually followed by periwinkle (mostly *Littorina littorea*). However, oyster (*Ostrea*) is an important mollusk at El Otero and La Chora in coastal eastern Santander in the Magdalenian. Limpets are rare at Lumentxa in Vizcaya; periwinkle seems to be more abundant. Shellfish are present in the Magdalenian deposits at most sites in Guipúzcoa, but these are in the hills and the amounts of mollusks are small. Some Magdalenian deposits at Tito Bustillo, La Riera, and El Juyo are real shell middens, with 10,000 or more shells having been counted from limited excavations in the latter two sites. Beyond the increase in amounts of shells, new species of mollusks were added to the assemblage in Magdalenian times at La Riera, including not only species found in estuaries but also those living at the open, moderately wave-beaten shore.

The size of the limpets also began to decrease, probably as a result of overexploitation of certain stretches of shoreline (down from average lengths of 40 to 45 mm in the Solutrean and early Magdalenian at La Riera, to about 35 mm in the late Magdalenian and 25 to 30 mm in the Azilian and Asturian) (Ortea 1986). This phenomenon had been (and continues to be) observed at other sites but is generally attributed to warming ocean temperatures (see Madariaga 1976; Madariaga and Fernández 1985). Ortea (1986) has shown that large (45 mm) *Patella vulgata* still exist along stretches of coasts in Asturias where people do not currently collect them but in stretches where they are intensively collected for fish soup and appetizers, the average length is around 33 mm. Magdalenian and espeically "epi-Magdalenian" and Mesolithic inhabitants of the Cantabrian coast were putting considerable pressure on the molluscan resource, probably because they were under subsistence stress themselves. Even inland sites, such as El Castillo, are now said to have abundant limpets (Cabrera 1984). This is evidence that it was worth while to make a 40- to 55-km round trip to the shore to collect shells *for food* (while possibly doing other things such as looking for game or acquiring plant foods or flint).

Fish remains are much less well preserved than seashells but, for the first time, fish bones (vertebrae and some jaws) are quite common in Cantabrian sites after appearing in the Solutrean. Most of the fish are salmonids (*Salmo spp.*: salmon, trout, and sea trout), which can be caught by net or harpoon in the streams, rivers, and estuaries of the region. However, in the Magdalenian, for the first time there are references to marine fish, possibly caught from rocks along the outer shore. These include sparids (bream). Sites with published fish remains include La Paloma, Sofoxó, Tito Bustillo, Coberizas, La Riera, Balmori, Altamira, El Juyo, El Rascaño, El Castillo, El Otero, La Chora, Santimamiñe,

Abittaga, Ermittia, Urtiaga, Berroberría, Lumentxa, Erralla, and Ekain (Straus 1977b,1983a; Freeman et al. 1988; Altuna and Mariezkurrena 1984,1985; Menéndez et al. 1986; González Sainz 1989, with references). At least at La Riera, Rascaño, and El Castillo, there seem to be increases in fish in the late Magdalenian levels. At least seven of the other sites have exclusively late Magdalenian levels, and in others (but not all) it is only the late Magdalenian levels that yielded the fish remains. Thus, while fish are present in early Magdalenian (and Solutrean) deposits, fishing seems to have been a more important, regular activity in the late Magdalenian, which probably explains the invention of harpoons (and possibly leisters).

Birds also are a regular (albeit minor) part of the Magdalenian archeofaunas, having been identified at Balmori, Cueto de la Mina, La Riera, Coberizas, Altamira, El Pendo, El Otero, La Chora, Lumentxa, Torre, Erralla, Ekain, Urtiaga, and Aitzbitarte IV. At La Riera, bird bones were found only in the Magdalenian and Azilian levels and were dominated by waterfowl, taken probably for their down as well as for food (Eastham 1986). At both Erralla and Ekain there are many varieties of birds, especially in the early Magdalenian deposits. But most are choughs (which may have died naturally in the cave mouth, a favorite habitat of *Pyrrhocorax*) (Eastham 1984,1985). Nets may have been used to trap birds. This is suggested by the presence of ocean fish and implied as part of the technology useful in driving herd animals. Further, the grid-like signs common in Cantabrian cave art may offer a depiction.

Again, evidence of gathering and consumption of plants for food is usually circumstantial at best in the Tardiglacial. Certainly in temperate oscillations such as Bölling and Alleröd, acorns, hazels, and beechnuts would have been available, along with some tubers, roots, seeds, and berries, but much less than in the Holocene. Macrolithic artifacts, frequent in several Magdalenian deposits such as those at Rascaño, Cueto de la Mina, and La Riera, could have been used for digging, chopping, wood-working, etc. Handstones and anvils are also relatively common in Magdalenian assemblages, and, although some clearly were used for grinding pigments, others could have been used to grind seeds, crack nuts, mash tubers, or cut and soften meat. Only at El Juyo has comprehensive flotation yielded seeds, nuts, berry pits, and other plant parts in relative abundance, though it is hard to be sure how many of these were remains of meals (Freeman et al. 1988; Crowe 1985).

The Magdalenian record is one of continued subsistence intensification, both through specialized red deer and ibex hunting and through marked diversification.

Seasonality and Mobility Strategies

Data on the seasonality of site occupations include studies of juve-
nile ungulate mandibular dental eruption and wear sequences, supplemented in some cases by studies of antlers (only red deer stags have
antlers, which are shed after the fall rut) and of shellfish and salmon
vertebrae. (Attempts to determine the seasonality of mollusk harvest-
ing in the Late Glacial and Tardiglacial at La Riera by oxygen isotope
analysis were stymied by recrystallization.) Naturally, such studies
(with many uncertainties and potential sources of error) can only tell
when humans were present and killing animals at a site. They cannot
guarantee that humans were absent at the other seasons of the year,
especially when samples of precisely aged mandibles are abysmally
small—even in the Magdalenian. With all these caveats, the extant
body of results does give some interesting information for this period.
It paints a picture not of mechanistic, strictly seasonal, altitudinal
transhumance but rather one of residential moves among base camps
in the coastal zone and lower valleys combined with logistical trips
to specialized sites (notably in the mountains) at any season of the year
(see Straus 1986b, n.d.g).

Most of the evidence from Magdalenian levels at La Riera indicates
spring and summer occupations, but there also are deer killed in winter
and fall in Levels 19 and 20, respectively (Altuna 1986). The Magdalenian
levels at the site are more strictly "warm season" than the earlier and
later levels at the site. Even the large (i.e., old) salmon remains found in
the Solutrean levels and thought to indicate winter spawning runs up
the Asturian rivers, are absent in the Magdalenian levels (Menéndez de
la Hoz et al. 1986). And those levels lack winter guest waterfowl that
are present in the succeeding Azilian levels (Eastham 1986). Young red
deer are especially abundant in the upper levels at La Riera, suggesting
slaughters of hind herds soon after spring calving (Altuna 1986). Were a
strict transhumant model to apply to eastern Asturias in the Last Glacial, one would not expect to find evidence of occupations at all seasons during the Solutrean and mostly in the warm season during the
Magdalenian at La Riera. Instead, this lowland site should have had exclusively or mostly cold season indicators.

Similarly, at nearby Tito Bustillo on the coastal plain of eastern
Asturias, Altuna (1976) could determine the season of death for a dozen
deer, killed in fall, winter, summer, and mostly late spring or early summer. Analysis of limpet growth rings gave a similar result: collecting in
all seasons, but with more of a focus on the warm period of the year
(Madariaga 1975). Old collections from the Magdalenian at Cueto de la

Mina, adjacent to La Riera, also included deer killed in spring/summer and late winter (Castaños 1982).

Seasonality data for the Magdalenian of Santander coastal zone come only from El Juyo where red deer were definitely killed in spring (presence of neonates) but where human presence cannot be ruled out (and is indeed possible on the basis of the non-multimodality of crown heights) (see Klein et al. 1983; Klein and Cruz-Uribe 1985). Antlers are rare, a fact that reinforces the hypothesis of hind herd hunting. Rascaño in the nearby mountains produced seasonality data from ibex teeth. Although many were killed in spring and summer (as would be predicted by a strict altitudinal transhumant model), there are also winter and fall kills in Levels 5 and 4 (Altuna 1981). Seashells in this and other sites in the interior of Santander indicate the ease with which trips were made between sites in the coastal zone and those in the mountains.

In Guipúzcoa, recent excavations at Erralla and Ekain, together with analyses of older faunas from Urtiaga, Ermittia, and Aitzbitarte, give some of the best seasonality evidence for the region. Red deer and reindeer dentitions from the Magdalenian levels at Urtiaga, near the present coast, indicated hunting at all seasons, though perhaps less in fall than in the others (Altuna 1972; Altuna and Mariezkurrena 1984). Nearby Ermittia has evidence of early summer and early and late winter hunting of ibex and red deer (Altuna 1972; Altuna and Mariezkurrena 1984). There is a summer reindeer kill at Aitzbitarte on the edge of the coastal zone at the eastern end of the province as well as a shed red deer antler perhaps indicative of late winter/early spring collection by humans.

At Ekain, in the hilly interior, the early Magdalenian fauna is dominated by red deer killed in fall but mostly in June. The late Magdalenian level is dominated by ibex, also killed in June and September (Altuna and Mariezkurrena 1984). At nearby Erralla, the early Magdalenian fauna is dominated by ibex hunted in spring, summer, fall, and possibly winter. Red deer are somewhat more abundant in the small late Magdalenian assemblage whose only seasonality data point to summer hunting (Altuna and Mariezkurrena 1985). The site of Abauntz is located in northern Navarra, near a mountain pass leading to Guipúzcoa and the coast. This small cave had an early Magdalenian occupation specialized in chamois hunting. All seven animals yielding seasonality data were killed in summer or fall, which is not surprising given the elevation of the site, 610 m (Altuna and Mariezkurrena 1982). The Abauntz flint appears to be nonlocal, and there is a seashell pendant testifying to contact (probably direct) with the coast (Utrilla 1982).

Movement between the Tardiglacial coast and sites of the Guipúzcoan interior is attested to directly by the presence of a few marine mollusks in the Magdalenian levels at Ekain and especially Erralla (Leoz and Labadia 1984; Altuna 1985). Although most lithic materials could have been procured very close to these sites, some nonlocal sources were possibly as far as 16 km from Ekain (Altuna and Mariezkurrena 1984) and 12 km from Erralla (Baldeón 1985). All of these facts suggest that the coastal zone Guipúzcoan sites could be utilized throughout the year—albeit not necessarily or likely continuously but with perhaps some tendency for abandonment or less-frequent use in fall.

As in coastal Santander and Asturias, residential moves may have been made from one cave to another in this central, strategically located zone between the glacial shore and the high mountains. Such moves would occur when local resources of food and fuel foraged on a daily basis became scarce or because of social factors (disputes, desire for socialization with other individuals or bands, etc.). In all the coastal zone areas with dense clusters of Magdalenian sites (especially the Ribadesella–Llanes strip of eastern Asturias, the area around the modern Bay of Santander, the Guernica–Lequeitio area of central Vizcaya, and the area between Ríos Deva and Urola in western Guipúzcoa) there are several major residential sites as well as satellite camps (foraging way stations, etc.). All of these clusters are also associated with several hinterland sites, including specialized ibex-hunting sites.

Although based in the coastal zone on average during most of the year (including summer), whole bands or specialized hunting parties would make either residential or logistical trips to the mountain sites, sometimes to pursue a wide variety of subsistence (and other) activities (red deer hunting, fishing, etc.) and sometimes specifically to hunt ibex or chamois. This apparently could go on at any season of the year (except perhaps in the extreme case of Abauntz), although logically in winter it would be more common to send logistical parties into the mountains while the residential groups remained at more sheltered, lowland sites. This is the model suggested by the high Pyrenean site of Les Eglises—a cold season ibex-hunting site with little in the way of residential debris and with flints imported from the lowlands of south-central France (Clottes 1983; Delpech and LeGall 1983; Simonnet 1985; Straus 1987b).

Thus, the core residential areas of the Cantabrian Magdalenian (and Solutrean) were along a strip roughly equidistant between the resources of the glacial shore and those of the Cordillera. Magdalenian subsistence relied on a combination of both foraging around shifting residential bases and collecting by organized logistical parties (*in sensu* Binford [1979, 1980,1982]). The distances between the mountains and the shore were relatively short, and the chief game species (red deer and ibex) are far less extensively migratory than the chief game of the French Magdalenian, reindeer. In an environment of high relief and many contiguous biotopes, with many ecotones and a mosaic of habitats (even or especially under Late Glacial conditions), extensive mobility was not required of human bands. Relatively short residential movements within limited territories could support small human groups that exploited the wild animal (and plant) resources intensively, systematically, and efficiently while avoiding depletion.

Magdalenian Structures

By far the most extensive record of deliberate cave site modification in the Cantabrian region dates to the Tardiglacial. The evidence consists of pits, hearths, pavements, and other features. To date, the most complex have been found and described in detail at El Juyo (Freeman et al. 1988; Freeman and González Echegaray 1984). Level 7 produced two small basin-shaped hearths. Level B had a large dugout filled with shell midden trash. Level 6 had a small (1.4 by 1.3 by 0.25 m), square, dugout with slab and boulder walls and containing pigments, grinding stones, and a stone lamp. Next to it was another, more irregularly shaped dugout (2.5 by 2.25 by 0.25 m) with many red deer skeletal parts. Both of these were dug inside an earlier, larger structure. A paved walkway is said to lead out toward the original El Juyo cave mouth.

Level 4 contained a large number of structures: two small, square, dugouts with rounded corners and a complex of features that has been called "the Sanctuary" and given ritual significance by the excavators (Freeman and González Echegaray 1981). This complex had been reworked at several times by the early Magdalenian inhabitants, beginning with a 6.5-m-long D-shaped dugout with an internal ramp and a pit. The dugout wall was lined with stones. Then, three shallow trenches were dug and covered with mounds. These mounds are said to have been made up of different colored sediments and each had very unusual contents (exotic objects). One had atop it a supposed stone face whose features ("half-human, half-feline") are partially natural and partially engraved and sculpted, according to Freeman and González Echegaray (1981,1984). Finally, the whole Level 4 complex was supposedly "paved" over and two hearths were built on it.

In his recent limited excavation in the Magdalenian excavation at Altamira, Freeman (1988) located two pits with evidence of possible redigging and reuse. Their first use may have been for cooking; they contain ashes, fire-cracked stones, and bones (some burned) and shells.

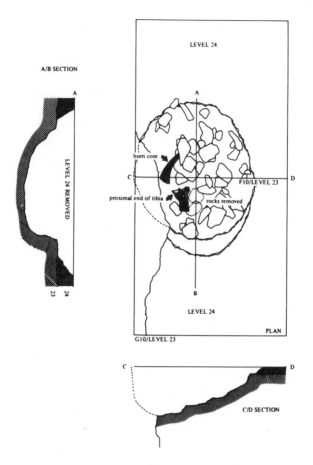

FIGURE 6.5. *Plan and sections of a Magdalenian roasting pit, La Riera (dug into Level 23). G10 and F10 are meter squares. (From Straus and Clark 1986.)*

Then they were used to dispose of trash. At least one grinding stone was found in the fill.

Fire-cracked rock (mostly sandstone) was abundant in many of the La Riera Magdalenian levels (Straus and Clark 1986). Level 19 had a small, shallow pit partially lined with stones. Level 24 had two pit features: one irregular with a sloping bottom and a partial rock fill, and the other oval with a regular basin shape and filled with stones, a horn core, and a stag tibia fragment (Figure 6.5). Neither had clear evidence of burning.

The early Magdalenian of Las Caldas contained a dug-out hearth lined and filled with stones, many fire-cracked (Corchón 1982). The hearth contents include charcoal, artifacts, and triturated faunal remains (many burned).

The early Magdalenian lenses of Level VII in Ekain yielded several simple hearths, made on the surface and sometimes surrounded by stones and ringed and littered with artifacts and bones. There are two small man-made pits, one containing 41 flint artifacts, 2 salmon vertebrae, and charcoal-rich organic dirt. The other one has two sandstone plaquettes sitting upright on its edges and contains only charcoal-rich earth. Level VI (late Magdalenian) also contains small, localized hearths (Altuna 1984). Level V (early Magdalenian) at Erralla has an artificial structure composed of stones and vertical slabs which are associated with several sagaies, a shed antler, other antler tines with cut marks for the removal of splinter blanks, other deer, chamois and ibex remains, and some shells. At another spot in a different lens, there is a second association of an antler, sagaies, bones of the same three species, and shells. The redundancy between these two deposits suggests a ritual function to the excavators (Altuna et al. 1985). The same Erralla level yielded three hearths in separate lenses. The largest of these contained stones and ashes. In another lens, a large block's surroundings contained most of the lens' artifacts and bones, suggesting that the block had served as a seat. The early Magdalenian level at Abauntz contained two dug-out, stone-lined basin hearths with fire-cracked cobbles. Associated with these hearths was a paved area within the cave vestibule. A third hearth, somewhat lower in the stratigraphy (Level G), yielded a Solutrean point (Utrilla 1982).

Charcoal-rich lenses ("hearths") were commonly mentioned in old excavations (as at El Castillo) but were not described in any detail. Fire was used in various ways in the Magdalenian, including its conservation by means of sandstone blocks and quartzite cobbles. Future excavations, based on the precedents set at El Juyo, La Riera, Altamira, Las Caldas, Erralla, and Ekain, will seek out and describe more evidence of elaborate Magdalenian constructions—contemporary with those of Duruthy, Dufaure, Pincevent, Etiolles, Gönnersdorf, and Andernach and so well known in the Tardiglacial literature of France and Germany.

Human Remains

As in the Solutrean, no human burials of Magdalenian age have been discovered in the Cantabrian region, but scattered, isolated remains are more common than in earlier periods. The best known of these are the two frontal bones from the early Magdalenian of El Castillo: both are of robust adult males (Vallois and Delmas 1976; Garralda 1989). Claims that these bones had been fashioned into "cups" are problematic and unconfirmed (Cabrera 1984:422). Another frontal (this one from a child, possibly male) was found in the late Magdalenian of El Pendo (Basabe and Bennassar 1980). Two separate levels of late Magdalenian in La Paloma produced a molar and a mandible fragment with two molars, respectively, as well as possibly other remains including maxillary fragments, according to the excavation journals studied by Martínez Navarrete and Chapa (1980); the actual objects have been lost.

Two loose teeth (an incisor and a premolar) were recovered from Magdalenian deposits at Tito Bustillo (Garralda 1976), an incisor and a portion of skull (occipital and parietal) at Rascaño (possibly from a middle-aged female) (Guerrero and Lorenzo 1981), a milk tooth and a tiny parietal fragment at Morín (Altuna 1971), a molar at Cobalejos (Obermaier 1924), a molar at Santimamiñe (J.M. Barandiarán 1976), a molar and a canine at Erralla (Rua 1985), an adult (male?) maxilla with teeth from the possible early Magdalenian (or Solutrean) of La Pasiega (González Echegaray and Ripoll 1953–1954), and, from Level 2 (very late Magdalenian or Azilian), a maxillary fragment with four teeth in place plus two loose upper molars, and a small mandible fragment with one molar from a second individual (González Echegaray et al. 1963; González Sainz 1989). (The age of human cranial and mandible fragments found several years ago in the undoubtedly Magdalenian cave art site of Becerral is unknown [Bernaldo de Quirós et al. 1987].) Intense abrasion has been observed on all teeth of adults that were studied in recent times (Tito Bustillo, Rascaño, Chora, Erralla). Little else can be said about the Cantabrian Magdalenian *Homo sapiens sapiens* population from a paleontological standpoint.

The well-known crania found in Levels D (late Magdalenian) and C (Azilian) at Urtiaga in the 1930s are now known to be intrusive from overlying Chalcolithic or Bronze Age levels, having been dated by the accelerator radiocarbon method to about 3,500 B.P. (Altuna and Rua 1989). It is not clear whether other human bone fragments (including a sacrum) and loose teeth found in Level D and even as low as Level F might also be the result of mixing or intrusive burials (see González Sainz 1989:162–163).

The larger inventory of isolated human finds may be an indicator of denser regional population. But the fact that people who certainly did regularly dig hearths, pits, and larger structures (as at El Juyo) did not leave behind a single burial may suggest that entombment was simply not a mortuary practice in this region during this period—in sharp contrast to other regions of Europe in the Magdalenian/Epigravettian. Instead of being placed in graves, corpses may have been left to be dismembered by scavengers; when this was done in caves, these sites were simply abandoned for a time by the survivors.

Mobile Art

Cantabrian Magdalenian mobile art is a vast topic, as this region and time period were among the most prolific in the Upper Paleolithic world. Naturally, the term "art" is probably a misnomer in that the majority of decorated objects were certainly practical, technomic artifacts. Magdalenian people put a great deal of effort into decorating sagaies, harpoons, perforated antlers ("bâtons de commandement"—probably shaft-straighteners or thong-softeners), and other antler objects such as "wands" whose functions are unknown but probably were not simply decorative items (handles of some sort?). Even stone "retouching tools" occasionally were exquisitely decorated, as in a notable case at Bolinkoba (Apellániz 1986). Other objects—perforated and carved or engraved bone, ivory, tooth, stone, and shell—may have been made to adorn the body or clothing. Finally, yet other objects (usually deer scapulae or other flat bones and stone plaquettes) were engraved with one or more animal figures in the most spectacular Magdalenian (and Solutrean) works of mobile art— perhaps in the sense closest to our use of the term. Even so, it is quite possible that these objects had magico-religious functions or were used to practice figures to be engraved on cave walls, although we will never know specifically what motivated the artists.

More than 1,200 objects classified as works of mobile art of all sorts are now known from the Cantabrian region (Corchón 1986); the vast majority date to the Magdalenian period. The objective here is not to attempt to recapitulate the information contained in recent catalogue-treatises on Cantabrian mobile art (e.g., Barandiarán 1967,1972; Corchón 1986; Moure 1985) but rather to make a few observations on the distribution, in time and space, of decorated and decorative objects in the Cantabrian Magdalenian context. Cave art is treated in Chapter 7.

The distribution of mobile art objects is very uneven: some caves are true "supersites" (to borrow Paul Bahn's term), whereas most sites are poor or lacking in such artifacts. In quantitative and qualitative terms, the supersites are (from west to east) La Paloma, Tito Bustillo, Cueto de la Mina, Altamira, El Pendo, El Castillo, El Valle, and Urtiaga (see Barandiarán 1972). Three of these supersites (Altamira, El Castillo, and Tito Bustillo) are also among the half-dozen or so richest, most complex cave art sites in the region, but the others have little or no rock art. On the other hand, several major cave art sites that also have significant, excavated cultural deposits are quantitatively very poor in mobile art (notably Ekain and Peña de Candamo). La Pasiega, a major art sanctuary, also lacks significant mobile art but is adjacent to El Castillo which is one of the richest mobile *and* rupestral art sites anywhere.

Many other sites have several decorated sagaies or other pieces. Among them, three of the high-mountain caprid-hunting sites (Collubil, Rascaño, and Bolinkoba) all have a few extraordinary works of art, namely, a rib with an engraving of a chamois in the first site, a perforated antler carved with an ibex head and an ibex scapula engraved with a bison figure in the second, and two stone "compressors" (one engraved with two or possibly three ibex, and the other with a possible chamois) in the third site (Barandiarán 1972,1981; Apellániz 1986). At least in these sites, the relationship between artistic themes and surrounding environment, faunas, and human hunting activities could not be more obvious.

At several other Magdalenian sites, there is only one work of mobile art but that solitary object is extraordinary, leading one to wonder under what (deliberate?) circumstances it may have been abandoned. The most notable of these cases are 1) the unique engraved gannet bone tube from Torre (with fine, diminutive, realistic engravings of a horse, a red deer, a chamois, an aurochs, two rather more stylized ibex, a grotesque anthropomorph, and various signs) (Barandiarán 1971); and 2) the mica-schist sandstone plaquette from Ekain (with figures of two ibex, one red deer, and possibly one horse) (Apellániz 1978). These two pieces very clearly bear the representations of the major Cantabrian Magdalenian game animals. The only figurative art object found in our recent reexcavation of La Riera (in late Magdalenian Level 24) is a small, flat bone fragment intricately engraved with an animal (Figure 6.3h) that is difficult to identify with certainty (González Morales 1986). Even the much larger-scale excavations by Vega del Sella in La Riera yielded no more than a few engraved sagaies and a harpoon.

Other unusual objects include the anthropomorphic head carved from a quartzite cobble in Entrefoces (González Sainz 1989:33) and the supposed anthropomorph/feline stone figure from El Juyo, noted above (Freeman and González Echegaray 1981). Both "heads" date to the early Magdalenian, between 15,000 and 14,000 B.P. by radiocarbon dating.

Recent discoveries of *contours découpés* at La Viña (Fortea 1983), El Juyo (Freeman and González Echegaray 1982), and Tito Bustillo (Moure 1985) show how heretofore unknown types—in this case very similar to items typical of and common in the "Middle Magdalenian" of the French Pyrenees (Clottes 1976)—can suddenly change our perception of the range of artistic variability and chronology in the region. These objects suggest the existence of contacts or down-the-line exchanges with

Pyrenean bands in the period around 14,000 B.P. (as verified by radiocarbon dates from all three sites). This dating is interesting because of the precocious presence of harpoons at Tito Bustillo and their absence in the other two Cantabrian sites as well as in the Pyrenean sites with *contours découpés*. These objects would seem to be good temporal markers in both regions for the period immediately before the widespread adoption of the harpoon. Because *contours découpés* are presumably purely decorative objects (even if they did function as *social* markers), they might in fact be better temporal diagnostics than harpoons whose presence or absence is in part controlled by practical, economic, "technomic" factors.

As noted above, the early Magdalenian (and, to some extent, Solutrean) is known for geometric, tectiform engravings on many sagaies. Other motifs include curvilinear engravings on several late Magdalenian sagaies interpreted as schematic frontal views of ibex (González Sainz 1989). Others are interpreted as stylized cervids. About 55% of the late Magdalenian sagaies and harpoons bear an association of oval and arrow-like signs (Corchón 1986). For structuralists, the "complementary opposition" between signs that could be interpreted as "female" and male" is striking. Both abstract decorations and figurative representations coexist in the mobile art of all three periods: Solutrean and early and late Magdalenian (Barandiarán 1972). However, of the 125 items with realistic representations listed by Barandiarán (1972), almost 90% date to the Magdalenian, and figurative art abruptly and nearly totally disappears with the development of the Azilian (to be replaced by distinctive geometric decorations).

Among the best-known, most characteristic, and significant works of mobile art from the Cantabrian region are the engraved scapula from Altamira and Castillo (Figure 6.6). The significance of these scapulae to the dating of rupestral engravings and the controversy surrounding the dating of the Altamira pieces found by Alcalde del Río in 1904 are dealt with in the chapter on cave art (Chapter 7).

In 1911, Obermaier found 33 engraved scapulae in the early Magdalenian level ("Magdalenian Beta" = Cabrera's Level 8). All are of red deer, except possibly two (one either red deer or bear and one possibly reindeer). It is unknown whether the pieces were found in horizontal and vertical proximity to one another because they are not mentioned in the extant excavation journals (!) (Almagro 1976:11).

After years of vicissitudes, this fabulous series was recuperated, reassembled, and studied at the Museo Arqueológico Nacional in Madrid by its Director, M. Almagro Basch (1976). The technique and style are distinctive: fine outline engravings with the heads and necks of the ani-

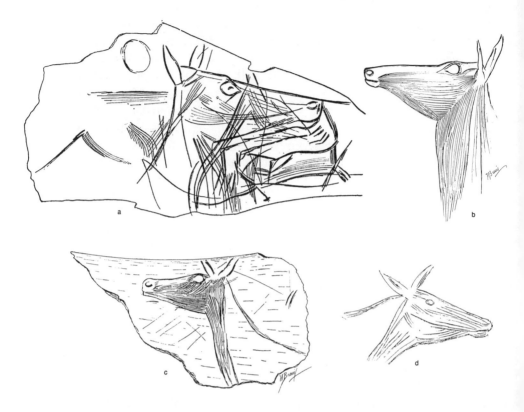

FIGURE 6.6. *Engravings of red deer (hinds) on scapulae and cave walls in El Castillo and Altamira: a, El Castillo, early Magdalenian scapula (from Obermaier 1924); b, El Castillo, cave wall (from Alcalde del Río et al. 1911); c, Altamira, Solutrean scapula (from Breuil and Obermaier 1935); d, Altamira, cave wall (from Breuil and Obermaier 1935). Scales vary; all drawings are by H. Breuil.*

mals filled with myriad subparallel lines for shading. Sometimes, crossed lines were used to show the meaty parts of the body, according to Almagro (1976:69). Several of the scapulae carry superimposed figures, some requiring reorientation of the piece in order to be seen, but in at least one case there is an apparent attempt to show a line of five superimposed hinds in perspective. Of the 68 animals shown, 38% are red deer hinds and 13% are stags. Almost all are figures of only the head. There are two horses and eight horse heads, one bovine, two fish, and four indeterminate quadrupeds. All of these scapulae are very similar, and it is hard to tell whether they were made by one or more artists (if the latter, they were certainly of the same "school") (see Apellániz 1982:44).

Alcalde del Río (1906) claimed to have found the Altamira engraved red deer scapulae in the reddish, clayey Solutrean deposit at the rear of the vestibule of that cave. This layer, like the early Magdalenian one above it, was filled with blocks fallen from the roof, and there was no sterile zone between the two cultural levels. No more engraved scapulae were found in the subsequent excavations by Obermaier. Six of these objects were described by I. Barandiarán (1972:69–71). In total, they carry eight figures of hinds (mostly just heads), a partial bison, and a possible horse. The technique of fine, subparallel and crossed lines filling the outlines of the heads is the same as at El Castillo. The hind heads all are very similar and very realistic depictions of this critical Cantabrian game animal. The similarity of the engraved scapulae from the two sites has struck generations of prehistorians, from Breuil and Obermaier (1935) to Barandiarán (1972), Almagro (1976), and Apellániz (1982). The two sites are 17 km from other another. Both the Solutrean (and Magdalenian) deposit(s) at Altamira and the early Magdalenian deposit at El Castillo were overwhelmingly dominated by red deer remains (Straus 1976–1977; Cabrera 1984). A similar engraved scapula (this one, appropriately, of ibex but with a figure of a bison) was found in disturbed deposits (certainly Magdalenian) at Rascaño, also in central Santander (Barandiarán 1981). This object and most of the Altamira and Castillo scapulae are broken, which is not surprising, given the extreme fragility of these shoulder blades. This fragility adds to the exceptional nature of these objects. Why the scapulae were engraved and why they were discarded? These questions are probably unanswerable, but it does not seem unreasonable to assume that they functioned in the "socio-technic" or "idiotechnic" realm(s) (*in sensu* Binford 1962). These were not practical, technomic artifacts, but they may have been of enormous importance in social or spiritual contexts. But even this vague hypothesis could be wrong, as they could have been works of art for art's sake, even if the chief subject was also the principal food source for the artists.

In addition to these spectacular objects, studied in exhaustive detail with particularistic art historical methods, and the hundreds of engraved Magdalenian sagaies, harpoons, and wands (not only described individually in site reports and catalogues but also treated statistically in terms of cross-section and base form and decorative motifs), there are many perforated and sometimes engraved teeth. These objects (and fewer numbers of perforated small species teeth, such as *Trivia*, used only for decoration) are quite common for the first time in Magdalenian levels. Most of the perforated teeth are red deer upper canines—atrophied, rounded, vestigial teeth that occur irregularly in the deer and look like pearls. The perforations were often made after the roots were thinned by scraping or incising. The perforations generally were made by bipolar boring (see González Morales 1986).

In a 1-m square of Level 2 at the rear of the vestibule of Rascaño, a cave I rediscovered in 1973, I found a cluster of nine perforated red deer canines; five engraved with series of very fine, short, subparallel lines, and four unengraved. This discovery was certainly suggestive of an entire necklace that had been discarded or, more likely, cached and then forgotten in a recess along the cave wall at the back of the inhabited area. These objects, like the perforated *contours découpés*, were highly visible indicators of who the wearer was, in terms of individual persona, achievement, or status or in terms of group membership or identification. Other, more elaborate, subtle (and controversial) analyses by M. Conkey have been done of engravings on Cantabrian sagaies, notably the Altamira collection that I rediscovered in the attic of the old Altamira Museum in 1974 and then helped make available to that student of Paleolithic art.

Conkey (1980) did a detailed analysis of design elements and structural principles on numerous engraved sagaies and other antler objects from Altamira and several other early Magdalenian sites (notably La Paloma, El Cierro, Cueto de la Mina, and El Juyo). The hypothesis that she wished to test was that Altamira (and other sites) was a place where microbands occasionally assembled (or "aggregated") for purposes that may have combined practical activities, such as collective deer hunts, with social and ceremonial activities (see Straus 1976–1977). Perhaps inevitably, there were many weak points in the Conkey study, including the fact that the collections came from old excavations that lumped materials spanning long periods of time. (Chronological control is much better now than at the time of Conkey's study in the mid-1970s, but even today the largest collections of mobile art are the same ones from old excavations. The early excavators targeted the richest sites and dug very large areas of them with cruder methods than today's painstaking excavations of small areas.) Nonetheless, Conkey's results were most interesting and suggestive. She found that the mobile decorations were significantly more diverse at Altamira and Cueto de la Mina than at the other sites in her sample. This might imply that people from different bands (with different engraving styles) came together occasionally at these two supersites and abandoned some of their decorated artifacts at them during their visits. Of course, other explanations are possible, but Conkey's work makes sense in the context of the richness of Altamira and Cueto de la Mina (in fauna and lithics as well as in mobile art and, at Altamira, cave art). They also are consistent with the central location of each of these sites relative to large numbers of other residential sites (and logistical camps) in the coastal zones of central Santander and eastern Asturias, respectively.

It should be noted that although it is not a significant cave art site (with only a few engraved lines that may predate the Magdalenian), Cueto de la Mina, unlike Altamira, is adjacent to several other caves with possible Magdalenian wall paintings and engravings. These include Coberizas, La Riera, Balmori, Quintanal, and Tebellín. The fact that the last of these was discovered only very recently (González Morales 1982b) may suggest that more art remains to be found (or once existed) in the extensive, now partially flooded Llera karstic system. The relationship of major individual art sites (or groups of smaller "sanctuaries" like the one at La Llera in eastern Asturias) to local and regional residential sites and site clusters will be further explored below.

It is interesting to note that although La Paloma is a supersite in terms of the quantity and quality of works of mobile art, its design elements and structural principles are not very diverse and do not show as many similarities to those of the other sites as do Altamira and Cueto de la Mina. La Paloma is located at the extreme western end of the distribution of known Cantabrian sites—not an ideal location for aggregation of bands from the wider territory in terms of providing social contacts, matese, goods, or information (see Wobst 1976). El Cierro and El Juyo are close to (and thus in the social orbit of) Cueto de la Mina and Altamira, respectively. Those two supersites could serve the social needs of Magdalenian bands for information, assistance, and mates over large macroband territories roughly corresponding to the modern provinces of Asturias and Santander, respectively, just as the supersite of Isturitz probably served as the social center for the western Pyrenees/Basque Country.

Clearly, more analyses along the lines innovated by Conkey are needed to test these hypotheses. Now that there are up-to-date catalogues of all the known mobile art material and that many modern excavations have provided new, accurately dated materials, such analyses might prove most fruitful. We return to the anthropological utility of Upper Paleolithic art studies in the following chapter.

Conclusions

There is a wealth of information on the chronology, technologies, settlement patterns, subsistence, and art of the Tardiglacial period in Cantabrian Spain. The Magdalenian is one of the richest, most spectacular archeological periods in European prehistory, but it would be an error to take it as typical of the whole Upper Paleolithic.

The Magdalenian adaptations to this narrow, physically circumscribed, still cold and open but faunally diverse and rich region were the continuation of long processes of subsistence intensification. Ultimately driven by the need to feed more mouths (Cohen 1977; *pace* Bailey 1983b) and required to readapt continually to the frequently changing physically environments of the Tardiglacial, human groups selected both local inventions and innovations acquired through social contacts with bands north of the Pyrenees. Continued increases in the efficiency and breadth of exploitation of terrestrial, aquatic, and avian resources came through both cumulative technological developments (e.g., the atl-atl, harpoon, and, presumably, leister, nets, and traps) and the manipulation of social relations. More formalized, regular social contacts would be important to survival under conditions of relatively high regional population density (in a situation perhaps reminiscent of proto-historic coastal California, but colder). Mutual aid in activities requiring or helped by large-scale, collective effort (such as big game drives), information on resource condition and location, mate exchange, and "social insurance" in the event of local catastrophes all would have been critical reasons for maintaining a fairly intense social life among members of different, fluid microbands.

The regional macroband (or linguistic band) would be the social unit within which the most frequent extrafamilial (or microband) contacts would be maintained. These probably were mediated through visible symbols of membership and through exchanges of objects and were solidified through ceremony and ritual—perhaps the main focus of the hypothesized aggregations at sites like Altamira where cave art may have played some role in the collective activities. It was not some abstract desire to be artistic, some inevitable result of a vitalistic progression towards technical and aesthetic sophistication, that caused the so-called Magdalenian apogee. Humans had been successfully adapting to the conditions of the Cantabrian region for hundreds of generations before the Magdalenian, but to continue to be adapted as the conditions changed, as they rapidly did in the late Last Glacial, significant innovations had to be made and accepted in the realms of technology, settlement, subsistence, and social relations. These built on the knowledge and achievements of the past but continued to break new ground as circumstances (demography, climate, vegetation, resources) both permitted and demanded. It is no accident, in my opinion, that the phenomenon of Franco-Cantabrian cave art occurred when and where it did. Nor can its study be divorced from that of the site locations, artifacts, structures, and faunal remains left behind as the other traces of its makers.

Chapter 7

CANTABRIAN CAVE ART

FROM the discovery of the paintings in Altamira in 1879 until the present, 82 or 83 caves with Upper Paleolithic rupestral art have been found in the provinces of Asturias, Santander, Vizcaya, Guipúzcoa, and northernmost Navarra (Moure 1987). The latest round of systematic cave explorations began in the early 1970s, and now art is being discovered almost every year. Together with the French Pyrenees and the Périgord-Quercy region (Dordogne and Lot river drainages), this geographical concentration of caves constitutes the distinctive area of Franco-Cantabrian art.

The three subareas of Franco-Cantabrian Paleolithic art are roughly equal in numbers of known painted or engraved caves. Each area is separated geographically from the others by areas with few or no art caves and probably corresponded to an area that, for reasons of topography, habitats, and resources, was repeatedly preferred for human habitation during the Upper Paleolithic. There is a close geographical relationship between habitation sites and art caves, of which many (but far from all) are one and the same. Each of the three areas contains dozens of caves with only one or a handful of usually rather unextraordinary painted, drawn, or engraved images. Many other caves have what are called "minor sanctuaries": small concentrations of naturalistic or geometric figures. However, each of the areas includes several major sanctuaries and at least two or three "giants": Lascaux and Font de Gaume in Dordogne, Pech Merle in Lot, Niaux and Trois Frères in Ariège, El Castillo and Altamira in Santander, and Tito Bustillo in Asturias.

In addition to the vast majority of Upper Paleolithic art caves located in the Franco-Cantabrian areas, there are nearby outliers on the Castillian Meseta and in southeastern and west-central France. More distant out-

167

liers, bearing strong thematic, stylistic, and technical similarities to the Franco-Cantabrian art, are found in northern France, Spanish Levante, Andalusia, and Extremadura, and Portugal. Even farther afield, but still identifiably similar in general style and age, are several art caves in Italy, Sicily, Yugoslavia, Romania, and even the southern Urals of Russia (see up-to-date maps and lists in Bahn and Vertut [1988]).

The concentration of Paleolithic rupestral art in the Franco-Cantabrian region would seem to be a real cultural phenomenon, not a reflection of unusual preservation conditions or cave location. This can be stated because karstic areas are common throughout much of Europe as well as in substantial parts of the rest of the Old World, yet these other cave-rich areas either have little evidence of Ice Age art or lack it altogether. It is probable that considerable open-air rock art (engravings and paintings) existed in the Upper Paleolithic, as demonstrated by recent discoveries of engravings at Mazouco (Bragança, Portugal) and Fornols-Haut (Pyrénées-Orientales, France) as well as by the existence of engravings in the exterior of cave mouths or rockshelters such as Chufín, Hornos de la Peña, Venta de la Perra, La Viña, and La Lluera in the Cantabrian region. In fact, in later periods (Neolithic, Chalcolithic), there are explosions of rock art in other regions of Europe where Upper Paleolithic art is rare (e.g., Levantine Spain, southern Portugal).

Dating the Art

Excellent general discussions of the problems of dating cave art can be found in English in Bahn and Vertut (1988) and in Ucko and Rosenfeld (1967). In simple terms, there are ways in which the cave art can be dated to varying degrees of specificity, as follows.

1. Some of the animals depicted either went completely extinct (e.g., mammoth, wooly rhinoceros, giant deer) or were regionally extirpated (reindeer, bison, large felines) by the end of the Last Glacial.

2. Some of the caves with art have been essentially sealed by collapse of the entrance roof for thousands of years (e.g., Tito Bustillo, Altamira, Fontanet).

3. Some of the figures are covered with translucent calcite (not a guarantee of necessarily great antiquity).

4. The art often is found in the same caves as cultural residues of Upper Paleolithic age, and sometimes those residues date to relatively short periods of time within the Upper Paleolithic (e.g., early Magdalenian at Lascaux, Solutrean at Chufín).

5. Sometimes the rock art (either still on the wall or on a block spalled

from the wall) was covered with archeological deposits that provide a *terminus ante quem* date for the art (i.e., the art was made before the sediments and cultural remains were laid down) (e.g., Pair-non-Pair, Teyjat, Isturitz, La Viña, El Conde).

6. In some cases there are very close thematic, stylistic, technical, and proportional similarities between figures on works of mobile art and others on the walls of the same or nearby caves (e.g., the engraved scapulae and walls of Altamira and Castillo).

7. The few deliberate forgeries that have been attempted (e.g., Lledias in Asturias) are obviously very different in style, technique, and proportions and lack the usual "patina."

In the early days of systematic study of cave art by the Abbé Henri Breuil (and, to some extent, still today), subjective, aesthetic criteria of perspective and realism were used to place figures within subdivisions of two great cycles: "Aurignaco-Perigordian" and "Solutreo-Magdalenian" (Alcalde del Río et al. 1911; Breuil 1952). Breuil's scheme also depended on the existence of superpositions of figures of different styles in individual panels and the coexistence of various styles within the same cave—notably at El Castillo.

Subsequent schemes, notably those of Laming-Emperaire (1962), Jordá (1964), and André Leroi-Gourhan (1971), were elaborations on the Breuil subdivisions but took into consideration the fact that superposed figures need not have been made at long-separated times (as Breuil had tended to assume). They made use of the few cases of fairly securely (if relatively) dated art figures as well as stylistic comparisons. Unfortunately, Breuil's scheme and its successors involved the attribution of cave art images to periods that were sometimes not even represented among the archeological levels present in the same sites as the art. For example, some art was assigned to the Aurignaco-Perigordian when there were only Solutrean and or Magdalenian levels in the cave (as at Altamira).

There are few direct indications of the specific age of cave art images in the Cantabrian region. At Isturitz, just over the border in the French Basque Country, early Magdalenian deposits covered engravings of ungulates on a stalagmitic pillar, meaning that the images were made in the Solutrean or Early Upper Paleolithic (EUP)—which are also represented by cultural deposits in the cave (Passemard 1944; Saint-Périer 1952). Numerous engravings of lines, signs, and animals have been discovered recently on the wall of the La Viña rockshelter near Oviedo; these were covered with early Magdalenian deposits (containing the *contours découpés* mentioned in Chapter 6 as indicators of an age of about 14,000 B.P.) and thus were made during the Solutrean (or possibly earlier, as yet unknown, occupations of the site) (Fortea 1981; Fortea et al. 1990). By analogy, Fortea (1989) attributes the similar engravings of the nearby site of La Lluera I to the Solutrean or late Gravettian. A series of deeply engraved lines in the wall of the nearby Cueva del Conde was partially covered by Aurignacian deposits, which unfortunately, are not dated by any chronometric or chronostratigraphic means (Marquez Uría 1981). These may be among the oldest examples of rupestral art in Cantabrian Spain (or anywhere).

The other basis for dating rock art (mainly engravings) in the Cantabrian region depends on the existence of detailed similarities between works of mobile art from archeological contexts and wall art figures. We have already discussed the most significant example, the Altamira and Castillo engraved scapulas, in Chapter 6 in the sections on mobile art, but a word on their stratigraphic contexts is in order since the former were said to have been found in the Solutrean stratum and the latter in the early Magdalenian stratum of the respective sites. Because doubt occasionally has been cast on the Solutrean provenance of the Altamira pieces (e.g., Breuil 1962), both sides of the issue need to be explored. The discoverer, H. Alcalde del Río (in a separately bound text titled "Exploration du Gisement d'Altamira" and dated 1908, although supposedly part of the 1906 book by Cartailhac and Breuil, *La Caverne d'Altamira à Santillana près Santander* [1906]) gives the following account of the find:

> Le niveau inférieur mesure 0m40 à 0m80, il est plus argileux et pétri de fragments calcaires; les coquilles y sont médiocrement abondantes; en revanche, les os y sont assez abondants, bien travailles; on y remarque de nombreuses formes solutréennes; l'outillage en os est maigre et peu varié; pourtant c'est dans cette assise, mais dans sa partie supérieure, qu'ont été trouvées les omoplates gravées de figures de cervidés très habilement exécutées par fines hachures. (Alcalde del Río 1908: 259.)

Further in the text, Alcalde del Río (1908:267,274) stresses that the engraved scapulae were found *in situ* associated with Solutrean points in the lower stratum of the site and that the engravings are similar to ones on the walls and ceiling of the cave. This interpretation of the provenance of the finds was originally accepted by Cartailhac and Breuil in their postscript to Alcalde's text (pp.274–5), as well as by Breuil and Obermaier (1935:159). The fact that Obermaier did not find more such pieces (in either the Solutrean or early Magdalenian level) during his 1924–1925 excavations at Altamira could suggest that Alcalde's finds were highly localized (a cache?). Alcalde's main excavation (20 m²) was toward the rear of the vestibule near the entrance of the "Hall of the Bison" (an area covered in 1925 by a huge stone and cement roof support), whereas Obermaier dug exclusively in a 50 m² area near the front of the vestibule. In neither excavation were the Solutrean and Magdalenian levels separated by a sterile layer, although both excavators cite sedimentological differences between the two strata. The presence of many large roof-fall blocks did make the job of distinguishing the two difficult, however.

Digging in 1981 on the edge of Obermaier's pit near the present mouth of Altamira, Freeman (1988) found evidence of pits dug during early Magdalenian times that could have led to the mixing of deposits from both periods. Like Alcalde and Obermaier, Freeman believes that the front area of the vestibule was heavily utilized for cooking activities (on the basis of the pits, the density of charcoal and ash, and the amounts of ungulate and molluscan food remains as well as stones, some burned). This suggests specialization of activity areas within the vestibule and helps to explain why no engraved scapulae have been found in the front section. As we have seen, there are no specific data on the horizontal or vertical positions of the far more numerous engraved scapulae from the massive early Magdalenian stratum at Castillo.

Ultimately, the fact that the engraved scapulae from the two sites are so similar in all respects simply adds support to the idea that the distinction between "Solutrean" and "early Magdalenian" is totally arbitrary, as shown by overlapping radiocarbon dates and by overlapping antler point types and substrate lithic assemblages.

The enduring fact is that these engravings are extremely similar to ones on the walls and ceilings of both caves, suggesting an age for the rupestral figures centered on 17,000 to 16,000 B.P. Similar engravings (with fine line "shading") have also been found on bones from other "Magdalenian" deposits (e.g., El Rascaño [Barandiarán 1981]) and on cave walls (e.g., Llonín in eastern Asturias [Berenguer 1979]). Other close similarities have been established between engravings on stone plaquettes in the dated late Magdalenian deposit at the original mouth of Tito Bustillo and engravings on walls deeper within the same cave (Moure 1982). Stylized engravings of frontal views of ibex heads on the wall of El Otero Cave (a late Magdalenian living site) are similar to engravings on many mobile art objects from several sites, all dating to the late Magdalenian (González Sainz et al. 1985). At a more general level, resemblances (i.e., not near-identity) have been noted between dated mobile art objects and parietal engravings in different (but not very distant) caves (e.g., early Magdalenian mobile art in Bolinkoba and wall art in Altxerri [Apellániz 1986]).

Another (albeit less specific or secure) line of reasoning that can be used in trying to establish the age of cave art within the Upper Paleolithic is to examine possible relationships to archeological deposits within the same caves. It would seem a reasonable hypothesis that artistic and habitational uses of individual caves were related temporally, even if some art could have been made when the cave was not otherwise used (or when habitations were either very brief or located in areas not yet sampled by excavations). Table 7.1 lists the archeological attributions of materials from sites in caves that also have rupestral art. We have already seen how few EUP sites there are in the Cantabrian region—only 10 with definite or problematical EUP (Chatelperronian, Aurignacian, or Gravettian) levels *and* rupestral art—and all but one of these also have Solutrean or Magdalenian occupation residues. Most of rest of the habitation-*cum*-art caves (a total of 24) are assigned archeologically to the Late Upper Paleolithic (LUP)—some with both Solutrean and Magdalenian deposits and others with just one or the other. A few others have only been excavated in limited fashion, resulting in assignment either to "indeterminate Upper Paleolithic" or, in the case of shallow excavations, only to the Azilian or Asturian. In addition, as noted earlier, there are very few instances of mobile art (or even of ornaments) firmly dated to the EUP in the Cantabrian region, in striking contrast to the situation in the Périgord and even in nearby Isturitz (see Barandiarán 1972; Straus 1987a; González Echegaray 1986). These data suggest that the vast majority of Cantabrian cave art was made in the LUP. In addition, although much of it was indeed done during the period conventionally known as the Magdalenian, a great deal was done in the Solutrean time range (20,500 to 16,500 B.P.), as argued by Jordá (1964) at the 1960 Burg Wartenstein conference, in opposition to the theories of Breuil (1952; also see reply to Jordá's presentation by Breuil [1962]). Thus, the great bulk of the art corresponds to a period of apparently much increased regional population density beginning in the Last Glacial Maximum.

In cases of single-component Upper Paleolithic archeological sites in caves with art, the dating of the art to that one cultural period would seem reasonable. In the case of the complex Tito Bustillo karst in Ribadesella, there are three entrances, each with an archeological site. The connection between the caves of Tito Bustillo (Ardines mouth), La Cuevona, and La Lloseta (El Río) may not have existed or been used in LUP times. Recent interpretations associate most of the art with the Ardines mouth site (late Magdalenian) and at least one separate sanctuary (composed especially of red "vulvas") with the La Cuevona site (early Magdalenian) (González Morales 1987; Moure 1980).

Table 7.1 Cultural/Temporal Attributions of Archeological Materials from Caves with Rupestral Art

Asturias

Peña de Candamo: S	Oscura de Anía: M,Z
El Conde: A	La Lluera: S,M
La Viña: G,S,M	Entrefoces: M
El Buxú: S	La Lloseta: M
Tito Bustillo: M	La Cuevona: M
Coberizas: S,M	Cueto de la Mina: A,G,S,M
La Riera: A?,S,M,Z	Balmori: S,M
Coimbre: M	Llonín: M
El Pindal: Z	La Loja: M

Cantabria (Santander)

Chufín: S	La Meaza: Z
El Linar: M	Altamira: S,M
La Pila: M,Z	Cudón: UP indet.
Hornos de la Peña: A,S,M	La Pasiega: S,M?
El Castillo: A,G,S,M,Z	Santián: UP indet.
El Pendo: C,A,G,S,M,Z	El Juyo: M
Oso/Morín: C,A,G,S,M,Z	El Salitre: A?,S,M,Z
El Otero: A,M	Peña del Perro: Z
La Cullalvera: UP indet.	La Haza: S
Covalanas: UP indet.	

Vizcaya

Arenaza: Z	Santimamiñe: A?,S,M,Z
Goikolau: M	

Guipúzcoa

Ekain: S?,M,Z	Altxerri: UP indet.

Navarra

Alkerdi/Berroberría: M,Z

C = Chatelperronian; A = Aurignacian; G = Gravettian; M = Magdalenian; S = Solutrean; Z = Azilian; UP indet. = indeterminate Upper Paleolithic.

Geographical Distribution

In general terms, art caves are distributed throughout the whole length of the Cantabrian region from the Pyrénées to the Río Nalón (Figure 7.1). However, there are distinct clusters, at least among the decorated caves known at present, and some sectors seem to lack such "sanctuaries." These ".empty quarters" (perhaps analogous to the buffer zone

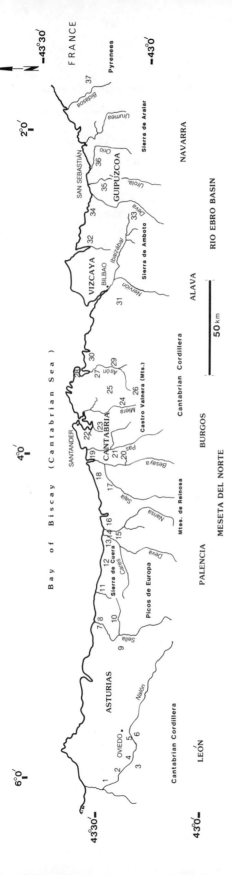

FIGURE 7.1. *Cave art sites of Cantabrian Spain: 1, Peña de Candamo; 2, Cueva Oscura de Ania, Las Mestas, Godulfo; 3, El Conde (Forno); 4, La Lluera I and II; 5, Entrecuevas, Los Murciélagos, La Viña; 6, Entreforces; 7, Les Pedroses, La Lloseta (El Río), Tito Bustillo (El Ramú), La Cuevona; 8, San Antonio; 9, Sidrón; 10, El Buxú; 11, Coberizas, El Tebellín, Cueto de la Mina, La Riera, Samoreli, Quintanal, Balmori (La Ería); 12, Las Herrerías (Bolao), Covarón; 13, Mazaculos (La Franca), El Pindal; 14, La Loja; 15, Los Canes, Trauno, Llonín (El Quesu), Coimbre (Las Brujas); 16, Chufín Micolón, Porquerizo, Traslacueva, Fuente del Salín; 17, La Meaza, Las Aguas, El Linar, Redonda, La Clotilde, Jibosa, La Estación; 18, Altamira; 19, La Pila, Cudón, Las Brujas; 20, Hornos de la Peña; 21, El Castillo, La Pasiega, Las Chimeneas, Las Monedas; 22, Santián, El Pendo, El Juyo; 23, El Oso (lower Cueva Morín); 24, El Salitre; 25, Patatal, Emboscados; 26, Becerral; 27, Cobrantes, El Otero; 28, San Carlos, Peña del Perro; 29, La Cullalvera, La Haza, Covalanas, Sotarriza, Venta del la Perra; 30, Lastrilla, La Hoz, Peña del Cuco; 31, Arenaza, 32, Santamamiñe, 33, Atxuri; 34, Goikolau; 35, Ekain; 36, Altexerri; 37, Alkerdi.*

"game reserves" reported ethnohistorically by Hickerson [1965] in the U.S. Middle West) often also lack Upper Paleolithic residential sites. On the contrary, the main clusters of art caves generally correspond to the main concentrations of living sites (often the same caves). All habitats of the region (coastal zone, coastal foothills, interior valleys, and Cordilleran slopes) have art caves, but the major sanctuaries are located near the present coast (Ekain, Altamira, Tito Bustillo, Peña de Candamo) or in lower valleys of major valleys, sometimes where they cut through the coastal ranges (e.g., the Monte Castillo sanctuaries of El Castillo, La Pasiega, Las Chimeneas, and Las Monedas, as well as Hornos de la Peña).

Recent prospecting by speleologists and archeologists has added several art caves to the once meager roster of mountain sanctuaries. These sites now include Coimbre, Llonín, Los Canes, and Trauno in eastern Asturias; Chufín, Micolón, Porquerizo, and Traslacueva in western Santander; El Salitre in central Santander; Covalanas, La Haza, Cullalvera, Sotarriza, Covanegra, and Becerral in eastern Santander (plus Venta de la Perra right across the border in western Vizcaya); Atxuri in central Vizcaya; and Alkerdi in Navarra. Most, but not all, of these mountain sanctuaries have only a few figures (or, in some cases, just one). They are clearly related to the increasing use of the montane habitats in the LUP. Some are also known to contain archeological sites and, in most cases, the mountain sanctuaries (notably in the Cares valley along the northern face of the Asturian Picos de Europe, in the upper Nansa, Miera, and Asón valleys of Santander, and in the Sierra de Amboto of Vizcaya) are components of larger clusters of sites, testifying to intensive LUP human exploitation of certain sectors of the upland zone. Unfortunately, the difficulty of conducting excavations in the mountain sites (relatively far from the region's cities and research institutions, and generally on steep cliffs) has meant that we have few data on the nature of other human activities related to the production of rupestral art in these habitats (except for the ibex-hunting sites of Collubil, Rascaño, and Bolinkoba).

The coincidence of rupestral art and residential sites is even clearer (and more thoroughly studied) in the coastal zone and along its margins. The westernmost cluster is along the lower and middle course of the Río Nalón, with 11 art caves and rockshelters—most of which are also living sites—plus a few more archeological sites without rock art. The main art site of this cluster is Peña de Candamo. The Sella drainage now has eight known art caves (notably Tito Bustillo) plus several non-art cave sites. In far eastern Asturias there are 11 art caves (only 1 of which, El Pindal, is relatively important, although most are also archeological sites) along a short stretch of the narrow coast platform, a zone also particularly rich in other nondecorated archeological sites.

The art cave of Fuente del Salín on the coast of Santander is geographically associated with this concentration. Then there is another gap (30 km, interrupted only by two minor, isolated art caves, La Meaza and Las Aguas). This area (like the 55-km gap between the Nalón and Sella clusters in Asturias) is also virtually devoid of known archeological sites. Central Santander, from the Saja to Bay of Santander drainages, both on the relatively broad coastal plain and in the valleys of the coastal ranges, is enormously rich in art caves and archeological sites (both major residential and minor, limited-occupation ones). There are 17 of the former just in this small area, including Altamira and the Monte Castillo sites. There are other smaller clusters of minor cave art and living sites near the present coast around Laredo and Castro Urdiales in eastern Santander. The cluster along Río Asón (both near the coast at Laredo and in the mountains at Ramales) is separated from the Bay of Santander cluster by a gap of 20 to 25 km, interrupted by a pair of recently discovered art sites near Matienzo (El Patatal and Los Emboscados).

The situation is very different in the Basque Country where there is a grand total of only eight art sites spread over three provinces. Here, there are no concentrations, and only three of the sites are of modest (Santimamiñe and Altxerri) to relatively great significance (Ekain) in terms of numbers of figures. However, each of the Basque art caves is associated with Upper Paleolithic archeological evidence: both living sites at the mouths of the art caves themselves, and other nearby living sites that could be said to be clustered in most cases around singular art localities. In general, there are almost no clusters of Upper Paleolithic living sites in the entire Cantabrian region that are not closely associated geographically with one or many art sites. The gaps in the distribution of one kind of site are generally matched by gaps in the other kind. The widespread, but discontinuous, distribution of art sites from east to west throughout the region and their presence in all its distinct topographic zones mirror the evidence for rather complete utilization of the region's habitats and resources in the LUP, to which most of the rupestral art certainly dates.

Animals and Art

As in France, most of the Upper Paleolithic cave art in Cantabrian Spain depicts animals—in particular, large and medium-size ungulates (Figure 7.2). As we will see below, the Cantabrian art is different in hav-

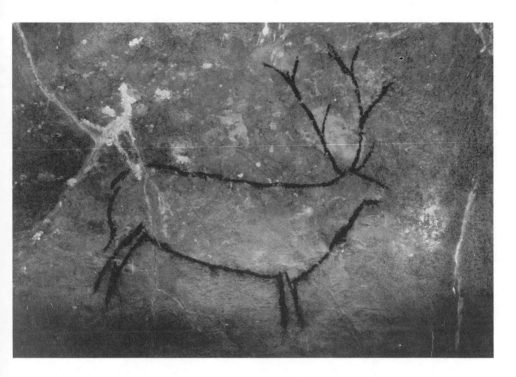

FIGURE 7.2. *Black drawing of a red deer (stag) in Las Chimemeas Cave, Santander.*

ing not only relatively many red deer, as well as other cervids, but also a wealth of "signs" compared with the cave art of France. Nonetheless, bovines (bison and aurochs), horse, cervids, and caprids dominate and are hallmarks of the cave art of both Spain and France. The animalistic nature of the art (and the existence of cases that seem to depict projectiles in, on, or flying toward animals) naturally led to the "hunting magic" theory to explain the art. This theory was espoused by Breuil (1952) and by many others for decades, although Leroi-Gourhan (1958) cast doubt on it as he began to develop his structuralist perspective on the art. Despite legitimate criticisms of the monolithic "hunting magic" theory, it is good to remember that this was art made by people who depended almost totally on animals for their subsistence under Ice Age conditions.

In 1976, I pointed out that at Altamira there are approximately equal representations (ca. 50 each) of bison and red deer (Straus 1976–1977). Horse and ibex lag far behind these two species in terms of numerical representation among the images, and there are at most only three boars (and very possibly none [Freeman, 1978d]). However, the bison images include the many, large, brightly colored paintings of this species in the

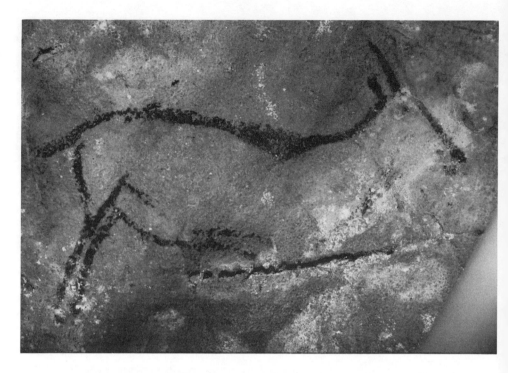

FIGURE 7.3. *Black drawing of an ibex, Las Monedas Cave, Santander.*

Hall of Bison, whereas the red deer images (usually hinds) are mostly smaller, less-visible rock engravings (like those on the scapulae), although the largest figure (2.25 m) on the ceiling of the "polychrome" paintings is in fact a hind. Analyses of the faunas from Obermaier's excavation at Altamira by Altuna and myself (Altuna and Straus 1976; Straus 1976–1977) and from the recent excavation by Freeman and González Echegaray by Klein (in Freeman 1988) show that red deer are by far the dominant food species in the Magdalenian and Solutrean levels, in terms of both number of remains and minimum number of individuals (MNI). The ungulate data from Altamira are summarized in Table 7.2.

If bison carcasses (ca. 400 kg) were as fully represented as red deer carcasses (ca. 100 kg) in the middens they would represent much more fat and meat than the red deer. And, assuming that because of the transport problems posed by such huge carcasses, bison were more extensively butchered at kill sites than red deer, fewer bison *bones* would end up being disposed of at the residential site. Thus, it is possible that bison is actually under-represented in the Altamira archeofaunas in proportion to its contribution to human diet there. Nevertheless, the nearly

Table 7.2 Ungulate Data from the Archeological Site of Altamira (in MNI)

Level	Excavator	Red deer	Bison	Horse	Ibex	Chamois	Roe deer	Boar	Reindeer
Sol.	Obermaier	20	5	8	2	2	1	2	1
Mag.	Obermaier	19	4	4	1	2	2		
Mag.	Freeman & G. Echegaray	14	2	1			3		

MNI = Minimum Number of Individuals

numerical parity but qualitatively differential artistic representation of bison and red deer might be telling us something about the role of both species in human adaptations. The heavy, meaty bison clearly were impressive beasts and sources of food bonanzas when procured. The red deer were the staff of life—less spectacular but critical to daily survival. The fact is that at Altamira there is an apparent relationship (albeit, perhaps not mathematically exact) between species eaten and species represented.

More recently, Altuna (1983) compared the faunal remains and the cave art representations in Tito Bustillo and Ekain. Horse is by far the dominant species *artistically represented* at Ekain and is represented by a slight margin over red deer at Tito Bustillo. At Altxerri, in hilly country not far from Ekain and a cave that has not been excavated, bison is overwhelmingly (67%) dominant among the figures. However, red deer is by far the main *game species* in all levels of the site of Tito Bustillo, with ibex a distant second, followed by horse. Ibex dominates the late Magdalenian fauna of Ekain followed by red deer, which dominates the early Magdalenian fauna (followed by ibex). It is unlikely that many bison were there to be hunted from Altxerri. Altuna (1983:236) concludes that "Paleolithic artists did not render the species that were most often hunted, but that other factors dictated the choice of animals represented in sanctuary contexts."

Similar demonstrations have been made for Lascaux (Leroi-Gourhan and Allain 1979) and for mobile art and fauna from La Madeleine and La Vache (Delporte 1985). But note that although horse is the animal most represented in the mobile art of both La Madeleine (whose fauna is dominated by reindeer) and La Vache (where people mostly hunted ibex), reindeer and ibex are the second most figured animals in the art. The Altamira example discussed above also suggests that, while the relationship between eating and representing may not be clear (and indeed may be absent in some cases such as at Ekain), there might be some residual insight to be gleaned from such comparisons. This has been attempted by Rice and Patterson (1985, 1986), by González Sainz (1988), and by Mithen (1990). These studies have focused not on individual sites but on the art and faunas of regions. This is a sensible approach, as hunters operate in relatively large territories during the course of a year and a lifetime, not just in the environs of a single site. In addition, the statistics on art figure counts from the same single sites can vary as a result of identification problems, new discoveries, etc. (e.g., Freeman 1978d; Clottes 1986–1987).

In analyzing the Cantabrian situation statistically, Rice and Patterson

(1986) confirm that red deer is systematically under-represented and ibex is extremely under-represented in the art, whereas horse and especially bovines preponderate. These authors conclude (1986:665) that, in part, "bigger was better."

> . . . prevalence patterns were essentially descriptors of the faunal resources in local living environments and were the basis for "memories" of those environments. When the memories were transformed into patterns of parietal art, they were distorted but in a patterned way: the relative prevalence of larger species was exaggerated at the expense of smaller species. . . . These findings strongly support the hypothesis findings that the economic contribution of big game animals was the primary stimulus for the art: only those species that are significantly and consistently represented in living site archeofauna are significantly and consistently found in the art. The close art-size relationship suggests artist-hunters must have recognized both the overall importance of the animals to community survival, and the differential importance of different species.

Although Rice and Patterson find ibex under-represented overall in Cantabrian rupestral art, it is worth noting that this small species does come in third in numeric representation at Ekain and Altxerri in the generally very mountainous, ibex-rich Basque Country (Altuna 1983). In that regard, we earlier mentioned the prominence of ibex (and chamois) images in the mobile art of a number of Magdalenian ibex-hunting sites in Asturias, Santander, and the Basque Country.

González Sainz (1988) surveyed parietal and mobile art representations from northern Spain and compared the results with overall statistics for Upper Paleolithic art compiled by André Leroi-Gourhan. Cervids (mostly red deer hinds) make up 46% of the animal images on Cantabrian mobile art (versus 27% overall, mostly reindeer) and 30% to 35% in parietal art (versus 18% overall). The percentages for caprids are 25% and 11% versus 8.5% and 8.6%, respectively, for northern Spain and the whole Franco-Cantabrian art province. These statistics suggest the relative importance of cervids (notably red deer) and caprids (notably ibex) in the lives of the Cantabrian hunter-artists and their lesser importance in France (see also Moure 1988).

González Sainz (1989:51) also makes a germane point in observing that the many stylized caprid images on mobile art from El Pendo need not be concerned with hunting activities directly around that site on the edge of the Santander coastal plain, since the occupants of the site would have made ibex-hunting trips into the adjacent mountains to such specialized sites as Rascaño (about 22 km away). Furthermore, he shows that hinds are absent (and stags rare) in the mobile art of the Basque Country whereas ibex (and chamois) images are more common than in Santander and especially Asturias—a clear reflection of overall habitat and hunting differences also seen in the archeofaunas when compared at a general level by subregions within northern Spain.

González Sainz (1988) also believes that art "tracks" hunting practices on a temporal axis as well as on a geographical one. He shows a decline in stag and especially hind figures in mobile art and an increase in ibex between the early and the late Magdalenian and believes that these robust trends are related to a decline in red deer hunting and an increase in ibex hunting, as reflected by changes in the archeofaunas of several stratified sequences. He explains this shift to be a result of climate change. While he is partially correct about the few specific archeofaunal sequences cited, there was considerable climatic fluctuation throughout the whole Magdalenian time period, not just a single temperature–cold shift. And, although there are some spectacular cases of early Magdalenian red deer slaughter (e.g., El Juyo), there are similar cases in the late Magdalenian (e.g., Tito Bustillo). At specialized mountain sites (e.g., Rascaño), ibex were killed almost exclusively and in large numbers throughout the entire Magdalenian. I do not believe there are enough data as yet from modern excavations of stratified sequences to support a general decline in red deer hunting and artistic representation.

Finally, Mithen (1990) points out the contradiction between the heavy numerical dependence on red deer and ibex in the Upper Paleolithic economies of Cantabrian Spain and their relative under-representation in the cave art of the region. His ingenious, albeit unproven, hypothesis is that the numerically dominant animals in the cave art (bovines and horse) were individually tracked as a back-up subsistence strategy when cyclic or stochastic declines in availability occurred among the deer. Red deer (like the artistically under-represented reindeer in France) were routinely killed by cooperative mass hunting methods (drives, surrounds), especially by LUP times. The art consisted of cues, mnemonic devices for storing and transmitting, among other things, critical back-up survival information, not for the common hunting strategies and tactics but for the less common ones. This was information perhaps little used in any given generation but of crucial value between generations, perhaps passed on through stories, sagas, or legends by old people who used the paintings as aids to memory and instruction.

Mithen (1990:247) puts it thus: ". . . at times of particularly low yields the hunters turned from co-operative game drives to the tracking and stalking of individual animals and the art facilitated the rapid recall of information that had become relevant but which had not been foremost in the mind owing to the co-operative drives." Mithen (1990:254) adds further that the art had

a very specific context in the LUP when hunters acquired functional benefit from their artistic traditions and associated ritual—the failure of co-operative mass hunting and the switch to the stalking of individual animals. This complemented a more general educational role of the art. In essence, the art with its information gathering and information required themes facilitated the recall of information from encyclopaedic memory and creative thought about the future at the transition between these hunting activities.

Although Mithen (1990; see also 1988) has no illusions that *all* the cave art constituted hunting cues, many of his points are highly germane and ring true to the LUP situation in Franco-Cantabrian cave art as we understand it. Indications of game location, condition, seasonal behavior, sounds, spoor, and hunting dangers may be encoded into the art and were eminently practical pieces of information. Mithen shows this against a backdrop of subsistence uncertainty, given demographic and environmental pressures particularly during the rapid, sharp climatic swings of the Tardiglacial. Just a few Cantabrian examples of such cues in cave art would be the roaring stags of El Buxú, Peña de Candamo, and Altamira (indicative of the rut season) and the isolated antlers of El Salitre and Peña de Candamo as well as Freeman's interpretation of the Altamira bison (see below). In the category of animals in action, at La Loja (Asturias) there is an engraved "cameo" scene of a cohesive "herd" of six aurochsen.

Although not the whole story, Mithen's hypothesis does go a long way to satisfy this author. Statistically clearer perhaps in the mobile art, the Cantabrian cave art is a reflection of the hunting activities of late Last Glacial inhabitants. It is just that the relationship is not quite as direct and simple as had been thought, blurred as it may be by the occasional presence of "curious" or "awesome" animals that were rarely if ever hunted (e.g., reindeer, mammoth, bear, felines), by distinctions between the frequency and the meat-yield of kills of medium-size versus large species, and perhaps by distinctions between routinely mass-driven versus occasionally and individually stalked prey.

Signs and Symbols

Geometric figures are found throughout Upper Paleolithic cave art, but they are especially abundant in Cantabrian Spain (Ucko and Rosenfeld 1967) and some Cantabrian caves (e.g., El Castillo) are particularly rich in quantity and diversity of these enigmatic images (Leroi-Gourhan 1982). Although not unique to the Cantabrian region (some are found in Lascaux, for example), quadrilateral or "grid-like" signs are characteristic of this region, particularly in the Monte Castillo caves of El Castillo, La Pasiega, and Las Chimeneas, as well as at Altamira. As a possible indicator of macro-scale intra-regional differences in iconography, there are no signs in the parietal art of the Basque Country (i.e., to the east of the Asón River) (Moure 1988). In this, as in aspects of subsistence and technology, the Basque record during the Solutrean and Magdalenian (and in more recent periods) is distinctive, perhaps because of this area's more totally mountainous topography.

The most spectacular (but little-known) instance of such grids is at Las Herrerías in eastern Asturias, where the only art in the cave is a group of 24 approximately square red-painted "boxes" filled with or formed by 3 to 14 parallel lines (with two modes of 5 and 9 lines and an average of 7.4 lines) (Jordá and Mallo 1972). Similar grids (or ones formed of dots [Figure 7.4]) are found in many other sites in Asturias and Santander (e.g., Chufín, Las Aguas, Tito Bustillo, Llonín, La Riera, El Pindal). Other purely ideomorphic sanctuaries in the Cantabrian region include La Meaza in eastern Santander with a large serpentine figure formed by dots (similar to a figure in Llonín in eastern Asturias) and Santián in central Santander with a unique group of 15 figures interpreted as stylized arms and hands (Alcalde del Río et al. 1911).

As impressive as Las Herrerías in terms of grid signs is the long, low, narrow cave of El Buxú in the mountains of eastern Asturias. In this cave with a small Solutrean site, there are 18 rectangular engraved signs (some with traces of black pigment) accompanied by paintings and engravings of 8 horses, 9 deer (plus 1 set of isolated antlers), 4 ibex, 2 bison, and 5 indeterminate animals (Menéndez 1984). The fascinating aspect of El Buxú is its location. Probably a hunting camp, it is situated near the head of a steep, narrow, cul-de-sac side valley leading up from the east-west intermontane valley that parallels the Picos de Europa. Like other LUP sites (e.g., Las Caldas, Hornos de la Peña), El Buxú would have been at an ideal place for driving game, closing the valley mouth, and slaughtering the animals trying to scramble up the steep sides and end of the cul-de-sac. Many other sites (like those of Monte Castillo)

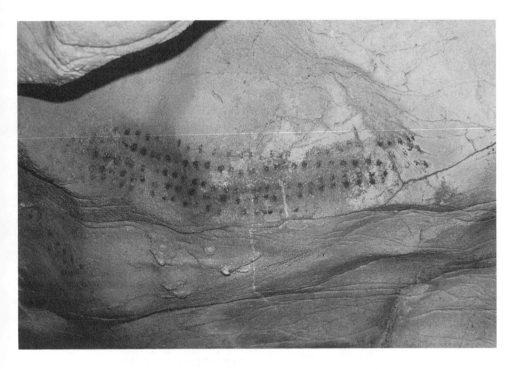

FIGURE 7.4. *Red dot Sign, Cueva Chufín, Santander.*

are located above narrow gorges that would have been easy to close, trapping small herds of animals between cliff walls, a river, hunters, and perhaps fences or nets.

Another type of sign common in Cantabrian sites is the "claviform" (as at La Pasiega, Tito Bustillo, Altamira, El Pindal, Cullalvera, El Tebellín). Some of these are similar to the grids but have one long edge formed by two curved lines coming to a point or peak midway. Many of the grids (as at El Castillo) are quite elongated, as if formed by many individual units that had been joined together. There are also signs that combine a long line crossed by short vertical lines (as at El Pindal).

As a working hypothesis, I suggest a practical explanation for the Cantabrian grid signs, one that is in the spirit of Mithin's view of the art. Rather than (or perhaps as well as) being "spirit houses" (as Breuil [1952] thought) or totemic emblems (as is still argued at times [e.g., Jordá and Mallo 1972]), these signs may represent nets or portable fences used in game surrounds. That this is an old idea (see discussion in Bahn and Vertut 1988:151) does not mean that it is necessarily implausible. When used in narrow valleys or gorges, nets or fences would have been particularly effective in hindering the flight of deer long enough to permit their slaughter by hunters. Thus, they would be part of the technological repertoire of cooperative hunting practices that might be associated with multiband or family aggregations. Use of such fences would require a number of handlers as well as beaters and killers. Whole families, including women, children, and old people as well as adult males, could be mobilized to bring off such drives effectively. Naturally, if the grids do indeed represent actual objects, they could have also included nets or weirs used in catching birds or fish.

One final observation is that such grids are concentrated in the eastern half of Asturias and the western half of Santander, an area where most LUP archeofaunas (except those of the mountain ibex-hunting sites) are dominated by red deer. The grids are scarce or absent in the Basque Country (see Moure 1987), although there are other kinds of linear engravings, sometimes made over or next to animal figures (notably at Altxerri). The suggestion is that the grid "fences" may have been particularly used to help trap deer but not ibex.

Beyond its reliance on common sense, this practical interpretation of some of the geometric figures remains speculative. Other recent approaches to such images include the theory of Lewis-Williams and Dowson (1988) that the geometric figures are representations of universal entoptic phenomena. But this theory cannot explain why such types of figures are more common in the rock art of certain times and places than of others. While it is also possible that images whose origins were in real objects may have been generalized into abstract signs or symbols for ideas, it seems more prudent to start with more modest interpretations rooted in the lives of the people who made the images.

The Great Hall of Altamira

Recent years have seen the suggestion of two interesting but pragmatic interpretations of the polychrome paintings (actually red and black "bichromes") on the ceiling of the "Great Hall" or Hall of Bison of Altamira. This is a rectangular (10 by 20 m) side chamber off the Altamira vestibule. The central group of paintings (most also filled with engravings) consists of 16 to 19 bison all about 1.5 to 2 m long, plus a horse and the large hind mentioned earlier. Freeman (1987) has determined that both male and female bison are represented and that the locations and positions of the two sexes (as well as the presence of one possible copulating couple) suggest representation of the fall rut. (Freeman has also reinterpreted a pair of engraved animals in the low, narrow, terminal gallery of Altamira as representing copulating bison, in line with the supposed emphasis on rut on the ceiling of the Great Hall.) He believes that the Great Hall ceiling was a deliberate composition showing a cohesive herd. Detailed sylistic comparisons by Apellániz (1982) have led him to conclude that the polychrome bison were the work of a single artist—supporting Freeman's notion of a planned composition laden with seasonal, behavioral, and ecological information.

The other recent practical interpretation of the Great Hall bison is that of Kehoe (1990). He argues that: 1) the cul-de-sac hall itself is shaped like a pound or corral into which bison could be driven; 2) the "curled-up" bison in the center of the cluster may be shown as dead (though Mithen (1990) thinks they are wallowing); 3) the external bison are portrayed as still standing, facing outward; 4) The engraved human figures are found mainly on the edge of the bison cluster (Breuil and Obermaier [1935:72–76] reported eight such figures, described them as "masked," and said that they are associated at the end of the hall with 70 scallop- or fan-shaped engraved signs that they interpret as "straw-roofed huts"—all of which they claim, on subjective stylistic grounds, is older than the polychromes); and 5) the claviform signs in and on the edge of the bison cluster could represent bows or atl-atls.

In addition, Kehoe (1990) sees the quadrangular signs as possible representations of corrals (see above) and the lines of dots (as in El Castillo), as drive lines, etc. Rather than seeing juxtaposed male and female symbols (à la Leroi-Gourhan) in the Castillo composition that groups "bell-shaped" signs with a "branched line," Kehoe (1990:184,186) sees corrals and a stand-in for a drive line beater (a "scarecrow", as it were). He has good ethnographic analogies to make his points, but of course that proves nothing per se. The fact is that a structuralist, symbolic explanation is not necessarily better simply because it is more complex. The view of the Upper Paleolithic art as *the art of hunting people* is a fundamentally common-sense approach and one that should not be dismissed in favor of more elaborate formulations.

On the contrary, and to avoid the impression that I advocate a complete return to a monolithic "hunting" hypothesis (if not a "hunting magic" hypothesis), it should be noted that depictions of apparently "wounded" animals (or ones with projectiles sticking into them) are extremely rare in the Cantabrian art—as opposed to the many obvious cases in Les Trois Frères (Bégouën and Breuil 1958) or in the Salon Noir of Niaux, both in the central Pyrenees (Leroi-Gourhan 1982). Two notable exceptions are magnificent engraved stag figures in Peña de Candamo, one showing six "spears" sticking into his flank and the other with one "spear" (Moure 1981, after Hernández-Pacheco 1919).

Masters, Schools, and Styles

We have already mentioned that through art historical analysis Apellániz (1982) concluded the Altamira polychrome bison were the work of a single "master" artist—an exceptional example of identifying the work of an individual human in remote prehistory. Apellániz (e.g., 1982,1991) has also set out to elucidate the existence of other masters or schools in the cave (and mobile) art of the Cantabrian region. In rupestral art, the discovery of detailed stylistic similarities between figures in the same and especially different caves *assumes* that the figures were created contemporaneously. The dangers of circular reasoning are evident, since dating is usually still (per force) done on stylistic grounds. Nonetheless, some of Apellániz's results are highly suggestive because they are so strikingly obvious and because they concern caves located within reasonably close proximity to one another (at least by hunter-gatherer standards).

The clearest of these cases is the "Ramales School," named after the pair of art caves Covalanas and La Haza on cliffs above the town of Ramales on upper Río Asón in eastern Asturias (Apellániz 1978,1982). In these artistically homogeneous caves, in the equally homogeneous Arenaza (about 35 km east of Ramales in Vizcaya), and in the artistically complex cave of La Pasiega (on Monte Castillo, about 45 km west of Ramales) there are large numbers of very small images of red deer hinds (plus a few aurochsen and horses). All were made by dabbing red ochre dots to form simple outlines (Figure 7.5). The figures share many details of perspective, proportions, and pictorial conventions, leading Apellániz to suggest that they were made by a group of acquaintances or even "disciples" of the master artist who drew the Covalanas images. (Although he later changed his mind on the subject, Apellániz [1978 contra 1982] originally included the little, red dot outline deer in El Salitre, midway between Ramales and La Pasiega, in this style cluster, an opinion that I share.)

Close similarities also have been described between figures at Ekain (Guipúzcoa) and Etcheberri (Soule in French Basque Country) and between Ekain and Tito Bustillo, sites 110 and 235 km apart, respectively (Apellániz 1978). At a more general level, Sieveking (1979) detects similarities among many figures (of likely mid-Magdalenian age) throughout the Vasco-Cantabrian and Pyrenean regions: the "black outline group" (Figure 7.6). She even suggests that the "Great Panel" of black drawings in Santimamiñe (Vizcaya) was made by an artist or artists (Apellániz [1982] believes it was one person) who had attempted a rather poor, small-scale copy of elements of the "Salon Noir" at Niaux, almost

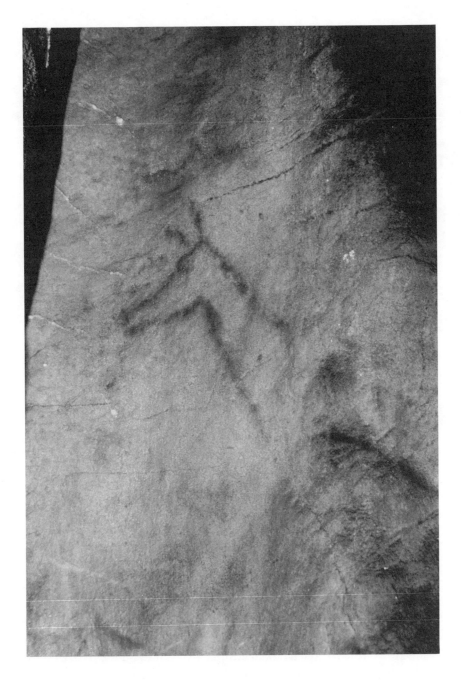

FIGURE 7.5. *Red drawing of a red deer (hind), La Pasiega Cave, Santander.*

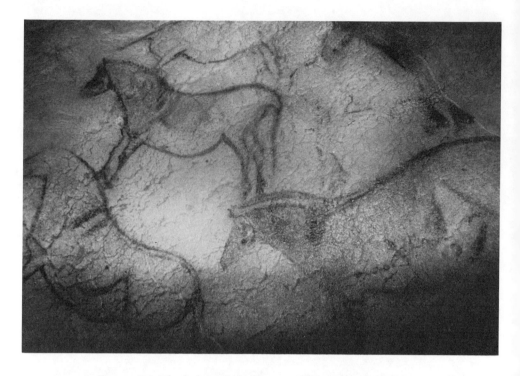

FIGURE 7.6. *Black drawings of horses, Ekain Cave, Guipúzcoa.*

350 km to the east in the central Pyrenees. If true, this would imply at least occasional distant travels by Vasco-Cantabrian regional band members, a possibility not at all unreasonable given what is known about Arctic and Australian hunter-gatherer behavior. Apellániz (1982) makes a convincing case for a single artist responsible for several simple, charming drawings of stags (and perhaps a horse and an ibex) within the "black outline group" in Las Chimeneas on Monte Castillo (Figure 7.2).

Other examples of artistic similarities at the local or regional level include a group of three sites (Chufín, Mazaculos, La Riera) within a 30-km stretch of western Santander and eastern Asturias, each having a natural cavity in the cave wall outlined by red dots, possibly dating to the Solutrean (Straus 1982b). Almagro (1976) and Berenguer (1979) have argued for similarities not only between the shaded engravings on scapulae and on the Altamira and Castillo cave walls but also on walls of Llonín, El Buxú, Peña de Candamo, and Santimamiñe (see above). Thus, there are: 1) some inter-regional similarities linking the Pyrenees with Cantabrian Spain; 2) distinctive characteristics (both stylistic and thematic) of the art in Cantabrian Spain as a definable region; and 3) local peculiarities, styles, and schools *within* that region.

Particular instances of close stylistic similarities at the regional or intra-regional levels may inform us about the existence of prehistoric regional macrobands or linguistic bands and perhaps of local bands (Straus 1982b). Such examples as the Arenaza–Ramales–Pasiega group might define a band territory (if the chronological problem could be resolved). Inter-regional similarities may reflect contacts among participants in adjacent, but ecologically distinct, adaptive systems (Straus 1983c), whereas broad similarities between sanctuaries at geographical extremes of the Cantabrian region itself (e.g., Ekain and Tito Bustillo) might suggest the limits of a regional macroband—limits defined fundamentally by adaptations to the distinctive topography, ecology, and resources of the region.

Concluding Remarks

Owing to the nature of the karstic systems in the Cantabrian region, the caves normally are of moderate size, neither rather small as is usually the case in the Périgord nor vast as is frequent in the Pyrenees. Paleolithic spelunkers did not have to walk or crawl a kilometer or more to get to the deepest recesses of caves to make some of their art (as they did in many Pyrenean caves). On the other hand, some of the Cantabrian art is in rather difficult galleries (e.g., the terminal "Cola de Caballo" gallery at Altamira with its myriad engravings and paintings including nine mysterious mask-like figures and signs [Freeman et al. 1987], or Cullalvera with paintings up to 1,100 m from the entrance [ACDPS 1986]). As in France, there is "public" art, easily visible and adjacent to the mouth and to living areas (e.g., the deep, external engravings of Hornos de la Peña, La Viña, La Lluera, El Conde, Cueto de la Mina, Chufín, and Venta de la Perra or paintings in La Riera, Peña de Candamo, and the Hall of the Bison at Altamira).

But there is much art that may have been seen rarely or, in the case of fine engravings in deep galleries, perhaps only once by the artist alone. Several Cantabrian art caves have both "public" art and "private" or restricted art (e.g., El Castillo, Pasiega, Tito Bustillo, etc.). This clearly complicates the task for anyone trying to defend a monolithic explanation for the phenomenon of Upper Paleolithic art. Undoubtedly, these anatomically and cerebrally modern, complex people had as many motives for making art as we do—ranging from the sacred to the profane, from the illustrative to the decorative, from the idle to the serious. But certainly they did not separate art from the facts of daily existence as modern academics do!

Lest the earlier discussions lead to the impression that ungulates and signs constitute the total content of Cantabrian cave art, it should be said that humanoid or anthropomorphic figures (engraved) are present in several caves, notably Altamira and Hornos de la Peña. As noted earlier, there is a spectacular and anatomically convincing group of red "vulvas" in the La Cuevona end of Tito Bustillo. There are also possible half-human half-animal figures (in El Castillo and Hoz, the Altamira "masks," and the detached stone "head" in El Juyo), and positive and negative painted hands (at El Castillo and the recently discovered Fuente del Salín). Unusual animals represented in Cantabrian cave art include the bears at Ekain, the wolverine at Altxerri, the fish at Altxerri and Pindal, the lagomorph at Altxerri, the auks at El Pendo, etc. Even the reindeer at Las Monedas, Tito Bustillo, and Altxerri can be considered "exceptional" representations in the Cantabrian context.

While there may have been some fundamental symbolic-educational-cybernetic-marking "reason(s)" (possibly unconscious) for much of the art, a great deal of it may lie in the realm of the decorative, fanciful, or individualistic activities of single human beings at particular places and moments in time. That is to say, some of the art could have been done for its own sake and the satisfaction of doing it (see Halverson 1987). We will never explain all the art, just as we obviously will never enter the minds of the long-dead artists to ask emic questions. However, from the etic standpoint it seems reasonable and plausible to suggest that much of the art relates to the conditions of existence and to the adaptations of these hunter-gatherers, with the accent on hunting. For these people, access to resources, reliable social relations, and information was crucial for survival. The exploitation of resources through cooperation, careful planning, sophisticated technology, and profound knowledge of behavior and ecology was the key to success.

The world of cave art is one in which social relations, practical preparations, and magico-religious experiences were integrated, probably with no thought to the kind of separations we have devised in the industrialized world. To say that the art tells us something structurally and symbolically profound about the artists' psyches is not to deny that the same art could have been used to mark band territories, to put the human stamp on certain caves, and to serve as educational tools for the young, foci for ceremonies and *rites de passage* and cues to help organize hunters through tales and legends that passed on the accumulated experiences and wisdom of earlier generations. The art was probably all of these things, and more. Some of it may simply have been beautiful, as the bison were beautiful.

In Cantabrian Spain, as in southwestern France, the LUP was a time of increased regional population density [as argued above, and by Mellars (1973), Straus (1977b), and Jochim (1983)] triggered (or exacerbated) by a concentration of human settlement during the Last Glacial Maximum (Straus n.d.c.). That concentration occurred in the mountainous regions of southwestern Europe bordering the Bay of Biscay/Cantabrian Sea because of the richness of the region's terrestrial (and, secondarily, aquatic) resources. The high relief (thus ecological variability), southerly latitudes (with consequent long growing period), and shores and rivers made the Franco-Cantabrian province ideal for hunting people, despite the cold and stormy climate. But the available land areas were relatively small for mobile foragers, and the conditions were severe.

Thus, both the margin for error in subsistence strategies and the size of available band territories shrank in this period. The needs for information storage and transmission and for territorial partitioning and marking consequently increased. The cave art may be a density-dependent phenomenon. Although there is no single explanation for the Franco-Cantabrian cave art, it is fundamentally related to the animal world, most especially to the subset game species. This overall relationship to hunting activities does not preclude the art sanctuaries from also having been places of assembly and man-made territorial landmarks (on edges or in centers of band-use-ranges). To the contrary, multiple meanings and "uses" of the art are most likely. Luckily, there is both fodder for many other interpretations and food for thought as well as plenty of room for wonder in the topic of Upper Paleolithic cave art of the Franco-Cantabrian region. As argued by Moure (1990), while there is not an *exact, statistical* relationship between art figures and hunted game or paleoenvironments, there is clearly a general relationship, and the art must be seen as reflecting the world and life of these hunting people. This fact should be our basic point of departure in all attempts at understanding the phenomena of Upper Paleolithic art. It is this author's view (and that of many other modern observers) that the art must be observed and discussed in the context of the world and lifeways of the artists and their societies.

Chapter 8

THE PLEISTOCENE–HOLOCENE
TRANSITION: Epipaleolithic and Mesolithic

Abrupt Versus Gradual Change

AND then it was over. Or was it?

The end of the Pleistocene (or, more accurately, the end of the Last Glacial), in its real effect on Cantabrian hunter-gatherers, occurred over a millennium of marked climatic and environmental changes culminating in mild, humid conditions and reforestation. It did not occasion drastic changes in the main game species, nor was it signaled by an immediate rise of the sea to its present level. The glaciers along the Cordillera and Picos de Europa probably had already essentially disappeared by Bölling or at least early Alleröd times. Yet these would not be dense, continuous woodlands until the early Holocene. As we will see, the period between about 11,000 and 9,000 B.P.was one of considerable continuity and significant change, both environmentally and culturally. Even more substantial change seems to have come in the period from 9,000 to 6,000 B.P., by the end of which time some degrees of food production had begun, at least in parts of the Cantabrian region.

The first period has cultural residues that may be characterized as "Epipaleolithic" (Azilian) and that are in many aspects of technology, settlement, and subsistence similar to, overlapping with, and derived from the Magdalenian (although less so in terms of art). The second period, with industries that can be called "Mesolithic" (Asturian, Sauveterrian, Tardenoisian), shows considerable temporal, industrial, settlement, and subsistence overlaps with the Epipaleolithic and the Neolithic.

One of the most interesting aspects of the Pleistocene–Holocene transition in Cantabrian Spain is the sharp contrast with the natural and cultural changes that occurred at the same time in adjacent southwestern France (see Straus 1983c,1985b,1986a,1991,n.d.d,n.d.e,n.d.f,n.d.g). While human bands in the Pyrenean and Aquitaine regions of France seem to have become progressively more dependent on and specialized in reindeer hunting in the late Magdalenian (even until the end of Alleröd, at least along the Pyrenees [Altuna et al. n.d.]), reindeer was never of significant economic importance in Cantabrian Spain, particularly to the west of Guipúzcoa. When reindeer moved north or died out and when reforestation occurred in southeastern France, the human groups were forced to change their adaptations radically and quite rapidly. This happened around 11,000 years ago.

In contrast in Cantabrian Spain, although making heavy use of red deer, human bands had been diversifying their subsistence base since Solutrean times, a process that continued uninterrupted throughout the Magdalenian, Azilian, and Mesolithic. Subsistence intensification, consisting of both specialization (large-scale red deer and ibex hunting) *and* diversification, was a long-term characteristic of Cantabrian adaptations (Straus 1977b). Broad-spectrum "Mesolithic" type subsistence strategies (particularly the exploitation of marine and riverine resources) had begun there in the Last Glacial Maximum. And they had developed space throughout the course of the environmental vicissitudes of the whole Tardiglacial. Thus, because the same main food sources remained available, the fluctuations of Alleröd, Dryas III, Preboreal, and Boreal had little immediate effect on the fundamental adaptations of Cantabrian groups. If anything, they were able to diversify their subsistence base even further as more plant and animal species became available or more abundant under conditions of greater forestation, warmer ocean water, and more estuarine habitats. The further emphasis on marine resources was eventually reflected in the presence of a subregional coastal cultural "facies" known as the Asturian. So successful was this long-lived, highly diversified, broad-spectrum adaptation that food production was adopted only rather late, and then only partially and spottily in the Cantabrian region.

Thus, although it was brusque in southwestern France, the Pleistocene–Holocene transition was gradual in Cantabrian Spain. Two adjacent parts of the same broad prehistoric culture area that were sharing the same sea and mountain chain and the same general Upper Paleolithic industrial and artistic traditions (and hence undoubtedly many social contacts) showed different kinds of adaptive responses to climatic and vegetative changes at the end of the Last Glacial. There was a major break in subsistence strategies and tactics (and presumably in group size, organization, and mobility patterns) in southwestern France in contrast to substantial continuity in most aspects of life in Cantabrian Spain. This was because earlier adaptive trajectories had taken partially but critically different directions through the course of the Upper Paleolithic in the two regions. Cultural evolution proceeds both by "punctuated equilibria" and by "gradualism," depending on the circumstances.

A fascinating aspect of the differences between these two contiguous regional adaptive systems is that in both regions the Magdalenian technology changed into something so similar as to be easily called by the same name, "Azilian," despite the different subsistence changes in the two regions. Thus, the trajectories may have been different, but the material results were very similar. And, despite earlier theories to the contrary, the transformation of the late Magdalenian into the Azilian seems to have taken place slightly earlier in France than in Spain (Fernández-Tresguerres 1980; Straus 1985b; González Sainz 1989), perhaps because people were forced to make changes in equipment on a more urgent basis in France with the abrupt turnover of fauna that occurred in Alleröd. Both in France and in Spain, however, those technological changes were at first only fairly minor, amounting to "tinkering" with a proven thing. In both regions, only later would more profound changes occur, characterized as "Mesolithic" by archeologists.

Another intriguing (and as yet unexplained) similarity between the two halves of the Franco-Cantabrian cultural province at the close of the Last Glacial is the disappearance of cave art and the marked decrease and stylistic changes in mobile art. If indeed closely linked to the nature of the regional hunting economy (as argued above), it would make sense that the art disappear or radically change in southwestern France where the kind of hunting underwent a profound change at the end of the Pleistocene. However, because adaptations do not seem to have changed fundamentally in Cantabrian Spain at about 10,000 B.P., why should the making of art in caves have ended and the decorating of antler and stone have decreased so markedly and changed? We will explore these questions but cannot now propose entirely satisfying answers. First, however, we must outline the chronological and environmental background to the most recent glacial–interglacial transition.

Chronology of the Azilian

Conventional dates for the pollen zones that bracket the Pleistocene–Holocene transition are as follow:

Alleröd: 11,800–10,800 B.P.;
Dryas III: 10,800–10,000 B.P.;
Preboreal: 10,000–9,000 B.P.;
Boreal: 9,000–7,500 B.P.;
Atlantic: 7,500–4,500 B.P.

All of these dates carry a standard deviation of about ± 150 years (Evin 1979) and are uncalibrated. (Only radiocarbon dates from the Atlantic onward now can be calibrated routinely by dendrochronology, so all dates given here will be uncalibrated.) The sharp upward increase in temperatures at about 10,000 B.P. is confirmed in this region by oxygen isotope (O.I.) analyses of deep-sea cores drilled in the Bay of Biscay/ Cantabrian Sea (Duplessy et al. 1981), making the Dryas III–Preboreal boundary a good marker for the beginning of the Holocene interglacial (O.I. Stage 1).

Appendix E1 presents the extant radiocarbon dates for Cantabrian archeological assemblages attributed to the Azilian, Asturian, and other Mesolithic "cultures." The question of definitions will be dealt with below; particularly thorny is the issue of distinguishing terminal Magdalenian assemblages from Azilian ones in the absence of either round or flat cross-section harpoons. Once again, this points to the lack of absolute reality among the classic normative prehistoric cultures and to the weakness of using rare (albeit generally temporally meaningful) artifact types for dating levels, particularly during periods of rapid technological change.

Chronostratigraphy and Environments of the Pleistocene–Holocene Transition

Given internal inconsistency among the three dates from La Riera Level 27 (there is a third of 14,800 B.P., not given here), it is hard to accept the 12,300 B.P. date *if* the assemblage from the base of the level is indeed Azilian (our opinion [Straus and Clark 1986], but one not completely shared by González Sainz [1989]). This was a relatively thick, partially loose, partially concreted midden layer, rich in shells and difficult to excavate stratigraphically. Thus, the 10,600 B.P. date from the top of the level is not inconceivable. Both Level 27 and Level 28 (the latter undated but containing a classic flat cross-section, unilaterally barbed, buttonhole perforated, undecorated harpoon) are considered sedimentologically to be the products of cold, humid conditions attributable to Dryas III (Laville 1986). They are underlain by deposits that include a discontinuous calcium carbonate crust and evidence of erosion, attributable to Alleröd. There is a sharp increase in the arboreal pollen (AP) percentage in Level 26 and then a sharp decrease in Levels 27 and 28, although Leroi-Gourhan (1986) assigned all of these strata to Alleröd. (There are traces of oak, elm, and even walnut in Levels 27 and 28, along with small amounts of birch, beech, and pine.) Nonetheless, a Dryas III age for the

La Riera Azilian seems most likely. Note that Nordic vole makes its last appearance at this site in Level 27 (Altuna 1986).

The Zatoya situation is complicated (see Straus 1985b, with references). The dates from Levels II and Ib of the main excavation at the front of this cave, in Pyrenean Navarra near the French border, are stratigraphically coherent (ca. 11,500 B.P. for II–base and 8,200 B.P. for Ib) but far separated in time. As in La Riera Level 27, no Azilian harpoons or decorated cobbles were found, although the chipped stone assemblage is Azilian-like (Barandiarán 1977,1979b). Level BIII, with dates older than 11,000 B.P., was defined in a separate pit in the cave interior where few artifacts were found. Its stratigraphic relationship to Level II is unknown. It is conceivable that there was a depositional hiatus within Level II, so assignment of the two old dates to the Azilian is problematical. A recent analysis showed low APs associated with the early-dated levels, provisionally assigned to Dryas III. After a hiatus, there is a much higher set of APs associated with the recent-dated levels, provisionally assigned to the Boreal (Isturiz and Sánchez 1990).

Aside from the problems at La Riera and Zatoya, assemblages clearly assignable to the Azilian, in traditional normative terms, do appear around 11,000 B.P. The best stratified sequence is at Los Azules, a small cave with a very deep in-filling, located at the junction of the major west-east intermontane valley of eastern Asturias and the Río Sella valley. Still under meticulous excavation by Juan Fernández-Tresguerres (e.g., 1976a,1979,1980,1981,1983; Blas and Fernández-Tresguerres 1989:85–88), Los Azules is known to have a late Magdalenian level (Level 6) at the base with round cross-section, decorated harpoons. This is followed by a level (Level 5) alternately assigned to the final Magdalenian or to the initial Azilian, with flat cross-section but decorated harpoons. Then there is a sterile clay layer, probably rapidly formed colluvially. The main Azilian stratum (Level 3) is subdivided into seven lenses. The base of Level 3 dates to around 11,000 B.P. and the top, to about 9,400 B.P. Level 2 is also Azilian. These two levels have yielded more than 60 whole or fragmentary flat cross-section, undecorated, perforated harpoons—the funadmental fossil director of the Azilian. Level 1, capping the deposit, is sterile clay.

Only limited preliminary paleo-environmental data have been published on Los Azules (López 1981). Level 4 has AP values up to about 60% and including birch, hazel, pine, oak, and elm. Sedge pollen are abundant in Level 4, testifying to high local humidity. The AP decreases to about 35% in the middle of level 3 (3b inf.) while Graminae increase. The APs briefly increase again to 62% (mainly pine) at the very top of level 3b inf. and then level off between 35% and 50% until the end of the diagram at the base of Level 2. Small percentages of thermophile oak and elm pollen are present throughout Levels 3 and 2.

Fernández-Tresguerres (1980) places upper Level 3 (dated to 9,400 B.P.) in the Preboreal and the evidence of solifluction in Level 2 in the late Preboreal/early Boreal. Although red deer dominates the (as yet unquantified) Level 3 fauna, boar is abundant and other woodland-preferring species (roe deer, wildcat, badger) are present. The top of the Los Azules is Postglacial in age, but the lower part of Level 3 is Dryas III by radiocarbon dating, although this is not seen in the pollen diagram because of the absence of pollen in Levels 3e inf. and med. The total disappearance of periwinkles (*Littorina littorea*) from the malacofaunas of upper Level 3 and Level 2 also suggests a Post-Glacial age for the upper part of the Azilian sequence. No sedimentological studies have been published to date from the key sequence. Unlike the vast cave of le Mas d'Azil, Los Azules is a strangely small cavity to be one of the Azilian supersites of the Cantabrian region.

Another stratified sequence of Azilian levels (actually two separate, apparently parallel sequences in adjacent caves) was recently revealed at El Piélago, just downstream from Rascaño where the Río Miera breaks through the first cliffs of the Cordillera in a narrow gorge (García Guinea 1985). The principal cave (Piélago II) has four levels with Azilian harpoons (Levels 4 to 1), representing a total thickness of about 50 to 70 cm. The basal archeological levels (Levels 6 and 5) were called "Proto-Azilian" by the excavator (García Guinea 1985) but lack harpoons and are tentatively attributed to the terminal Magdalenian on chronostratigraphic grounds by González Sainz (1989:88). Butzer's (1985) sedimentological analysis suggests the hypothesis that Levels 6 and 5b were formed under cold Dryas II conditions, Level 5a during Alleröd, and Levels 4 through 2 during the cold of Dryas III. In combination with the radiocarbon dates from Levels 1 and 4 (10,300 ± 100 and 10,700 ± 100 B.P.), this reconstruction implies that the upper, harpoon-bearing part of the Piélago II sequence is indeed Dryas III. The two radiocarbon dates are in reversed stratigraphic order but lie within two standard deviations of each other, suggesting very rapid deposition of the spall-rich, cryoturbated Levels 4 through 1. There are no palynological data from Piélago. The ungulate faunas (like those of nearby Rascaño) are heavily dominated by ibex remains, but there is a tentative identification of reindeer in the lower part of Level 1 at Piélago II (López-Berges and Valle 1985), which, if correct, would imply the late survival of a few isolated reindeer in Cantabria (as in the Pyrenees).

There is also some chronological and environmental evidence from sites with a single Azilian level (or a very short series of levels). The

Azilian level (Level 1) at Cueva Morín (in which harpoons were found only in the old excavations) is separated by a geological hiatus from the underlying late Magdalenian and is only *terminus ante quem* dated by a radiocarbon determination of 9,000 B.P. on a flowstone directly overlying it. As at nearby Piélago, Butzer (1973) found granulometric evidence of considerable frost weathering that he attributed to the cold conditions of Dryas III. If the pollen spectrum analyzed by Arlette Leroi-Gourhan (1971) is contemporaneous with the formation of Level 1 (a problem in éboulis-rich deposits because of the possibility of downward pollen movement), it shows a low AP (albeit slightly higher than that of Level 2). There are small quantities of hazel, pine, and alder with traces of oak and birch. Ferns are decreased relative to Level 2. Although Leroi-Gourhan (as usual) assigns the Azilian level to Alleröd, the pollen data are not incompatible with Dryas III—with small thickets of trees surviving the cold in refuge habitats in the Cantabrian hills during this still very humid period. There were enough relic woods in the vicinity of Morín to harbor small numbers of roe deer and boar.

Level 1 at Rascaño, dated by two radiocarbon determinations to 10,500 B.P., is assigned to the Azilian although it has never yielded flat cross-section harpoons. The remnant deposit we excavated in 1974 yielded only a very limited artifact assemblage. Sedimentologically, this level is considered to have been formed under cold conditions, based on the presence of large quantities of frost-weathering products. Level 1 is geologically assigned (concordantly with the dates) to Dryas III and is capped by a travertine assigned to the early Holocene (Laville and Hoyos 1981). The AP reaches only 18% and includes relatively many hazel pollens but few of pine, alder, or oak, together with many fern spores. It is attributed by Boyer-Klein (1981), explicitly following the lead of her mentor, Leroi-Gourhan. Again the pollens could have migrated downward through the open rubble of Level 1. This is the only level at Rascaño to have yielded a few boar remains, again pointing to the somewhat ambiguous nature of Dryas III conditions—cold, but with surviving thickets after the millennial temperate conditions of Alleröd.

Levels IV through II at Ekain are archeologically assigned to the Azilian; these are two fragments of a harpoon in Level III (Altuna and Merino 1984). Levels V and III first gave radiocarbon dates of 13,400 and 12,800 B.P., respectively. Suspecting an error, the excavator had more dates run on charcoal samples from Levels IV and III, and both gave dates of 9,500 B.P. The sedimentological analyses from the Azilian levels were interpreted by Areso (1984) as follows:

Level V: very humid and less cold than below;
Level IV: very humid and much more temperate, drying at top;
Level III: still humid but drying; cooler but then more temperature,
with a wet episode at the very top;
Level II: very dry and temperate.

According to Dupré (1984), the AP is very low in Level V, with a modest increase (especially in pine and hazel) at the base of Level IV followed by another decline. APs increase steadily through Levels III and II, and they include many taxa: not only pine, hazel, and alder but also birch, oak, lime, and cypress. Fern spores also dramatically increase, especially in Level III. After the cold oscillation of Dryas III, Dupré sees rapid and significant reforestation, presumably in Preboreal, in line with the "young" dates. Cold climate ungulates and rodents are entirely absent from the Ekain Azilian levels, but boar and roe deer remains are present (Altuna and Mariezkurrena 1984; Zabala 1984).

Two sites in northern Navarra—Abauntz and Berroberría—provide some limited additional data on Azilian chronology and environments. Abauntz Level D dates to 9,500 B.P. Being far inland and high on the south side of the Cordillera, it is not surprising that it lacks harpoons (Utrilla 1982). The AP value ranges between about 60% and 98%, with small percentages of hazel, beech, alder, and oak together with the dominant pine. High humidity is indicated for this Preboreal level by a massive increase in fern spores relative to the underlying Magdalenian (López 1982).

Berroberría is in the valley of the Nivelle that enters the Atlantic at Saint-Jean-de-Luz (France). It now has a radiocarbon date of 10,200 B.P. from Azilian Level D, whose middle part has recently yielded a flat cross-section harpoon (González Sainz 1989). Boyer-Klein (1984) traces a marked increase in the AP (mostly pine, but with some alder and willow) in the Alleröd (presumably corresponding to the terminal Magdalenian lower part of Level D, 11,800 B.P.) and then a sharp decline in AP in Dryas III (the Azilian). During that cold oscillation, Cichoriae increased markedly as open vegetation once again briefly dominated. The top of the Berroberría pollen diagram shows another rapid increase in AP (mostly pine again).

In the cave of Arenaza in western Vizcaya, where a Magdalenian level has recently been found, there is a sequence of Azilian levels, then a stratum with a nongeometric assemblage at the base and a geometric Epipaleolithic assemblage at the top, capped by Neolithic and Eneolithic levels (Apellániz and Altuna 1975; see Straus 1985b). The classic upper

Azilian level has a date of 10,300 B.P. and the nongeometric Epipaleolithic (lithically very similar to the Azilian) has one of 9,600 B.P. None of these have harpoons. Pollen analysis by Isturiz (Isturiz and Sánchez 1990) shows a decline in the AP from the Magdalenian with very low APs throughout the Azilian levels. There are traces of pine, hazel, birch, cypress, and a few other taxa. In the Epipaleolithic level (Level II) there is a rapid increase and diversification in the trees, including many hazel, oak, and alder pollens. This evidence of major reforestation is attributed to the Preboreal and Boreal.

A shell date of 8,700 B.P. from Urtiaga Level C (which had a flat-section harpoon) may be too young (although plausible at plus two standard deviations: 9,000 B.P.). The site has undergone considerable disturbance by badgers and by Chalcolithic or Bronze Age humans who used the cave as an ossuary (see Chapter 6). A recent pollen analysis by Sánchez (1990) shows a marked increase in the AP (9% to 31%) in Urtiaga Level C (compared with low APs suggesting cold, drier conditions below). Oak, hazel, and pine are the major pollen-contributing trees. Xerophiles and heliophiles decline in Level C as reforestation progressed. Sánchez assigns this period to the early Holocene and does not find a date at the Preboreal–Boreal boundary out of line for this Azilian deposit. The warming trend she sees confirms the ungulate faunal evidence (i.e., disappearance of the reindeer once relatively important at this site, and an increase in roe deer and boar, according to Altuna [1979]). In her conclusions, Sánchez (1990) sees evidence of overlap of assemblages labeled "late Magdalenian" and others labeled "Azilian" during Dryas III in the Basque Country and overlap among the "Azilian," "geometric Epipaleolithic," and "Asturian" in the Boreal throughout the Cantabrian region. I am in fundamental agreement with this point of view and will return to its discussion below.

Most of the Azilian finds (including all of the many harpoons) from the vast cave of El Pendo were found in Carballo's early excavations; little is known of their context other than they were discovered *in situ* stratified above late Magdalenian deposits (Carballo 1960). A modest-size lithic assemblage assigned to the Azilian was found in Level I during the Martínez Santa-Olalla excavations recently published by González Echegaray (1980). This level is separated from the terminal Magdalenian (Level II) by a sterile travertine layer (Level Ia). In turn, the Azilian level is overlain by another travertine (Level 0a) and a recent cultural level (Level 0).

The pollen analysis by Leroi-Gourhan (finally published in 1980) is preliminary and incomplete. Level II is low in AP, including pine, hazel, and juniper, with abundant heaths and some sea buckthorn. This spectrum was interpreted by Leroi-Gourhan as suggestive of the transition from Dryas II to Alleröd. No sample was taken from Level I itself, but a sample from the travertine overlying it is very rich in pollen, dominated by trees, including >50% hazel plus beech, oak, ash, and pine as well as *Hedera* (ivy) and *Viburnum* and many fern spores. Leroi-Gourhan assigned this upper travertine to Boreal and argued that the lower travertine would date to Alleröd.

In his sedimentological analysis, Butzer (1980) considers the travertine under Level I as possible evidence of a temperate, humid episode, indeed perhaps attributable to Alleröd. Level I itself, with some frost-weathered spall, was formed under cold, albeit periodically humid, conditions corresponding to Dryas III and earliest Holocene. The Level I fauna, heavily dominated by red deer, includes several remains of roe deer and boar (Fuentes 1980). There are no radiocarbon dates for this level.

At El Castillo, equally undated, Butzer (1981) equates his Level 18 with Obermaier's Azilian layer and, because of its éboulis-rich content, concludes that it was formed under cold conditions with slope instability that he attributes to Dryas III. The discontinuous travertine (Cabrera's Level 5) separating the Azilian and late Magdalenian strata (Cabrera's Levels 4 and 6, respectively) may have formed in Alleröd.

Finally, at El Otero, in eastern Santander, Leroi-Gourhan (1966) did a pollen analysis early in her career. Levels 3 and 2b are late Magdalenian with typical harpoons, although the fragment of one from Level 2b has a somewhat flattened section. The upper part of Level 2 is a stalagmitic layer (Level 2a). Level 1 yielded a tiny, nondescript artifact assemblage (González Echegaray et al. 1966). Although she had no samples from Levels 2 and 3, Leroi-Gourhan analyzed two samples from Level 1. They have very low APs with a few pollens of each of several tree taxa and many fern spores. For no strong reason, she assigned Level 1 to Alleröd, although the excavators preferred assigning Level 2 to that temperate oscillation. There are no radiocarbon dates or sedimentological analyses. Fernández-Tresguerres (1980) suggests an Alleröd age for the stalagmitic layer (Layer 2a) *below* the presumed Azilian Level 1, in a sequence analogous to that of the travertines underlying the Azilian in other Santander caves (El Castillo and El Pendo).

In conclusion, there is now considerable evidence that assemblages classified as Azilian in the Cantabrian region span the period including Alleröd, Dryas III, and Preboreal. Despite Leroi-Gourhan's repeated assignment of Azilian pollen spectra to Alleröd, a thorough analysis of all the data (Straus 1985b) suggests that Alleröd-age Azilian levels in the Cantabrian region are at most fairly rare, in sharp contrast to the situation in

France where they are common. The corpus of radiocarbon dates and paleo-environmental data points to overlap or intergradation between the terminal Magdalenian and Azilian during Alleröd in northern Spain, a fact that we will discuss further below. There also are some indications of survival of late Magdalenian-type artifacts into Dryas III, but here the data and dates are less clear. The Cantabrian region now has numerous dated examples of assemblages that are, by definition, Azilian in the Preboreal, lasting up to and perhaps into the early Boreal in a few cases. This phenomenon also is found in France (as at Dufaure and Duruthy on the edge of the French Basque Country), but it is especially common in northern Spain.

Thus, the Azilian technology and adaptations existed under the relatively temperate, humid, and partially wooded conditions of Alleröd, under the cold, still humid but open vegetation conditions of Dryas III with only isolated thickets, and under the warm, humid, and quickly reforesting conditions of Preboreal—quite an environmental variety within a span of only 2,000 to 2,500 years! Within the limits of resolution of our dating methods, it would seem that the cultural transitions from the late Magdalenian to the Azilian and from the Azilian to the Mesolithic "cultures" were gradual, and not at all disjointed, in the Cantabrian region.

Azilian Site Numbers and Geographical Distribution

At latest count, 35 Cantabrian sites have been assigned on fairly firm grounds (presence of flat cross-section harpoons or decorated cobbles, stratigraphic position above a late Magdalenian, radiocarbon dates, or a combination of these) to the Azilian. In addition, there are five other cases that for various reasons are problematic. Generally not included in these counts are old references that mention mixtures of Magdalenian and Azilian lithic materials; short endscrapers and Azilian points are by no means exclusive to the Azilian and now are known to be found, often in large quantities, in chronologically and artifactually secure late Magdalenian assemblages. The counts are based on data summarized by Fernández-Tresguerres (1980), González Sainz (1989), and Cava (1990). Assuming a 2,000-year span for the Azilian, the 35 sites represent 17 per millennium (or about 16 per millennium for 40 sites over 2,500 years). These values are essentially identical to those for the early and late Magdalenian, suggesting a fairly stable regional population (with all the caveats about such estimates expressed in Chapters 5 and 6).

All but nine of the Azilian deposits overlie known Magdalenian depos-

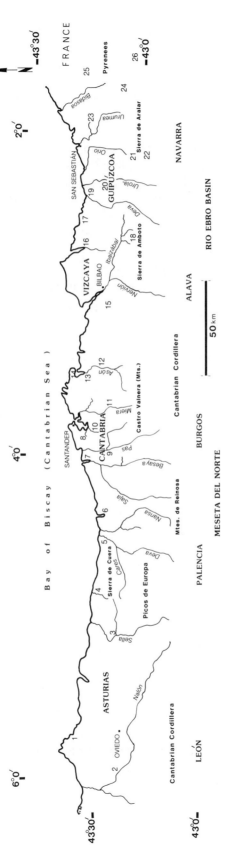

FIGURE 8.1. Azilian sites in Cantabrian Spain: 1, Cueva Oscura de Perán; 2, La Paloma, Cueva Oscura de Ania; 3, Los Azules; 4, La Riera, Balmori; 5, El Pindal; 6, La Meaza; 7, La Pila; 8, El Pendo, Camargo; 9, El Castillo; 10, Cueva Morín; 11, El Rascaño, El Piélago I and II, El Salitre; 12, El Valle; 13, El Otero, La Chora; 14, Peña del Perro; 15, Arenaza; 16, Santimamiñe, Atxeta; 17, Atxurra, Sta. Catalina, Lumentxa, Laminak; 18, Bolinkoba, Silibranka; 19, Urtiaga, Ermittia, Agarre; 20, Ekain, Erralla; 21, Pikandita; 22, Portugain; 23, Aitzbitarte IV; 24, Abauntz; 25, Berroberría; 26, Zatoya.

its (and in some of the nine Azilian sites, excavations have not yet gone below the Azilian levels). Thus, the settlement pattern, shown in Figure 8.1, is essentially identical to that of the Magdalenian. Some sites are located in the coastal zone (Pindal is literally right in the present-day sea cliffs of eastern Asturias), some in valleys of the coastal hill ranges, and some in the intermontane valleys and on the slopes of the Cordillera (including some of the same high-mountain ibex-hunting sites as before, Bolinkoba, Rascaño, Salitre, Piélago, and perhaps Silibranka and Collubil). In every respect, the Azilian settlement pattern is a continuation of the Magdalenian one, suggesting full exploitation of the resources of all of the region's habitats.

There does seem to be a tendency in the extant data for a decrease in sites in Asturias and an increase in the Basque Country, but this may be an illusory pattern. Several of the Basque assemblages classified as Azilian have many characteristics more akin to those of the geometric Mesolithic, but the distinctions often are of a rather semantic nature. This is especially true now that assemblages with abundant geometric microliths, associated with several classic harpoons and dated to about 10,500 B.P., have been published from El Piélago (Garcia Guinea 1985). And the distinctions between the Azilian and the nongeometric Epipaleolithic are especially problematical, which is why I have tended to lump them all together under the rubric of Azilian if they predate the Boreal.

Artifact Assemblages

As noted above, the classic hallmark of the Azilian is the flat cross-section harpoon, unilaterally or occasionally bilaterally barbed, with a basal perforation (either button-hole in shape or, more rarely, round—i.e., cut or bored) (Figure 8.2c). Except for a few sites (notably Los Azules and El Pendo), these harpoons are quite rare. At many sites, only one or two were found (even in old, large-scale excavations). A few assemblages (otherwise reasonably assignable to the Azilian) have yielded no harpoons, probably for reasons of site location and function as well as sampling error. Azilian harpoons are found throughout the whole region (including the Basque Country), especially at sites near rivers or the coast. The Azilian harpoons, in sharp contrast to those of the late Magdalenian, were made quickly, with little elaboration, no decoration, and scant care. Often there are only one or two rapidly cut-out barbs. They give an impression of purely utilitarian functionalism with no concern for the aesthetic qualities so often evident in Magdalenian harpoons, except in the two cases of identically striped flat harpoons from Los Azules and La Lluera (Fortea et al. 1990).

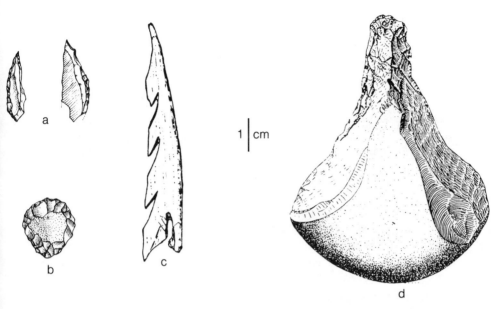

FIGURE 8.2. *Azilian and Asturian artifacts: a, Azilian points; b, thumbnail endscraper; c, Azilian flat cross-section harpoon; d, Asturian pick; a–c from La Riera (Straus and Clark 1986); d from Penicial (Vega del Sella 1916.)*

The other classic hallmark of the Azilian (as first defined by Piette at Le Mas d'Azil in the French Pyrenees in the late nineteenth century) is the painted cobble (or, as at other major French sites such as Rochedane, the engraved cobble). Once again, in the whole Cantabrian region, only Los Azules has ever produced substantial quantities of painted cobbles (>10, plus 2 engraved cobbles). Many of the decorated Los Azules cobbles were found in the context of a burial (described below). One engraved cobble was found at Morín. One painted and one engraved cobble were found in very problematical stratigraphic circumstances at Balmori, as were one painted cobble at El Pindal and one at La Riera (in 1917 and now lost). Two other painted cobbles were found by the early IPH excavation at El Valle (only one of which was *in situ* in the Azilian) (Fernández-Tresguerres 1980). Other cobbles (more likely used to grind ochre) were reported from early excavations in Cueto de la Mina and La Meaza. Significantly, recent work in the Asturian site of Mazaculos has produced two definitely painted cobbles, one from the surface but the other found *in situ* in the *conchero* (shell midden) with Asturian picks (Fernández-Tresguerres 1980:157). The Basque Country lacks painted cobbles (despite its proximity to France, where they are somewhat more widespread), but there is one engraved slate cobble (with a possible poorly drawn animal head) from the Azilian of Arenaza (Apellániz 1982). Other

Table 8.1 Summary of Major Tool Group Indices for the
Cantabrian Azilian

Tool Group	Range	Average Percentage	SD
	(n = 24 Assemblages)		
Endscrapers	0.8–47.5	16.8	11.4
Burins	0.5–27.0	10.1	6.6
Backed bladelets*	23.2–62.5	41.7	12.0

*Includes Azilian and microgravette points.

evidence of artistic activity (at least of kinds that would leave a permanent record) is scant in the Azilian (see below).

With the exception of Los Azules (and, to a lesser extent, Piélago), chipped stone artifact assemblages are generally rather small (Appendix E2) and less diverse than those of the Magdalenian. In a large sample of Cantabrian and Pyrenean Azilian assemblages, an average of only 30 of the 92 de Sonneville-Bordes/Perrot tool types is represented, versus 42 for an equally large sample of late Magdalenian assemblages (Straus 1986a). The decreased diversity may be an effect in part of smaller sample size.

The assemblages not only are simplified in terms of numbers of tool types but also the tools often are very small. Microlithization applies not only to the abundant backed bladelets, points, and geometric pieces but also to endscrapers. Thumbnail and flake endscrapers are relatively abundant (13% to 33% in almost all the Santander and Asturias sites). Perforators, on the other hand, virtually disappear. Assemblages in Asturias and Santander meet the traditional normative criterion of Azilian assemblages established in France by fairly consistently having many more endscrapers than burins (which are mostly of simple angle burin types) (Table 8.1). However, in those Basque sites for which counts are available, burins usually outnumber endscrapers (except at Zatoya and, apparently, Santimamiñe [Cava 1990]). This fact is curious because it indicates a continuation of the long-standing tendency (since Early Upper Paleolithic and Solutrean times) for Basque sites to be particularly rich in burins, as a result of either raw material reasons (as suggested by González Sainz 1989:186) or some as yet unexplained subregional differences in site activities or functions (Straus 1975a,1983b).

Backed bladelets and points make up between a quarter (more usually a third) and a half of the Azilian lithic assemblages. These percentages are comparable to or somewhat higher than those of the late and the early Magdalenian. Included within the backed bladelet percentages given in Appendix E2 are the curved backed Azilian points and straight backed microgravette points. These two types (undoubtedly armatures) together or alone usually make up 5% to 10% of the total assemblages of retouched artifacts (more at Ekain and especially Urtiaga). Such points often are present and sometimes common in late Magdalenian contexts (5.5% in La Riera Level 24). Obviously, if one subtracts the armatures (backed points and bladelets), which probably were used in series (i.e., many mounted together) in multicomponent weapons, the Azilian lithic tool assemblages generally are extremely small—consisting of several endscrapers (or, in the Basque Country, burins) plus a few other miscellaneous pieces.

The effect of subregional raw material differences is apparent in the often presence of more sidescrapers and especially denticulates/notches in the quartzite-rich areas of western Santander and Asturias. The association of many endscrapers and sidescrapers is one that characterizes this subregion throughout the whole Upper Paleolithic. Sagaies and other antler artifacts (aside from the harpoons) are extremely rare. There are simple bone awls and some spatulate objects (of which the decorated ones are mentioned below). In general, both the lithic and bone industries are much simplified, clearly derivative versions of the late Magdalenian but with the addition of some geometric microliths (trapezes, triangles, and circle segments), particularly at Piélago, Ekain, El Valle (11.4% [Cheynier and González Echegaray 1964]) and apparently Santimamiñe (Cava 1990), in several cases in clear association with flat cross-section harpoons.

Azilian Subsistence

Cantabrian Azilian subsistence practices were a continuation of those of the late Magdalenian and the rest of the Late Upper Paleolithic in this region, with the continued addition of more species of animals (and presumably plants as they became available with warmer temperatures and reforestation). Appendix E3 presents the published data on ungulate faunas from both old and modern Azilian (and Epipaleolithic) excavations. All assemblages with substantial numbers of bones are overwhelmingly dominated by red deer—except that those of El Piélago, Rascaño, and Ermittia are dominated by ibex and are located on or at the base of cliffs in mountainous or hilly country. Ibex is relatively important at Arenaza (Levels IV and III) and La Riera (Level 27 lower); both sites are near steep, rocky slopes. Chamois, roe deer, and boar all are quite consistently represented, although roe deer is not present at the ibex-hunting sites. There does seem to be some increase in boar in the more recent, more wooded levels (Preboreal) such as Arenaza II and Urtiaga C. Bovines and horse continue to be present, but in small quantities and inconsistently.

Unfortunately, it is usually impossible to distinguish between *Bos* and *Bison* on the basis of the few (often very fragmented) bovine remains from the Azilian; the few specific identifications that have been made (Altuna 1972; Altuna and Mariezkurrena 1984) show that both were present at this time, although presumably bison was gone from Spain not long after this. Aurochs are last referred to in the Bronze Age, having lasted through the Neolithic when cattle already were domesticated, at least in the Basque Country (Altuna 1980). Wild horse seems to have been replaced by the domestic variety in the late Neolithic or Chalcolithic (K. Mariezkurrena 1990). Carnivores are relatively scarce in Azilian faunas, consisting primarily of small, fur-bearing species (Appendix E4). Seal and lagomorph remains are also very rare. Big cats and cave bear became extinct at this time in Cantabrian Spain.

Because many of the major Azilian sites were dug long ago (e.g., La Paloma, El Valle, Urtiaga, Lumentxa, Santimamiñe, Urtiaga, etc.), there are few data on fish remains (always under-represented because of relatively poor preservation, even when water-screening was used consistently during excavation). Modern excavations at Ekain, La Riera, and Los Azules all found fish remains. At the Ekain they all are of salmon (Altuna and Mariezkurrena 1984); at La Riera they include trout, sea trout, sparids, and various other unidentified marine fish (Menéndez de la Hoz et al. 1986); and at Los Azules, the richest in harpoons, remains of salmon and trout are very abundant (Fernández-Tresguerres 1983). Unidentified fish remains were found in the Azilian of Santimamiñe (Altuna 1972).

Azilian bird remains have only been studied systematically at La Riera (Eastham 1986) and Ekain (Eastham 1984). At La Riera, geese and especially ducks are relatively abundant (Level 25, goose + duck MNI = 1; Level 26, goose + duck MNI = 12–15; Level 27, goose + duck MNI = 3–5), suggesting fairly frequent capture for food and down. Other birds, including partridge, eagle, kestrel, etc., also are present in trace quantities. At Ekain, Levels V through II yielded small numbers of a wide variety of birds including MNIs of 2 to 4 for ducks, 2 for ptarmigan, and 2 to 3 for larks. Bird remains were fairly abundant in the Santimamiñe Azilian deposit (Altuna 1972).

Marine mollusks are common and abundant in Azilian sites near the present coast. (The sea level at the end of Dryas III was still about 60 m below its present level, rising very rapidly during Preboreal and reaching about − 30 m by the beginning of Boreal [Ters 1973].) Current excavations in the rockshelter of La Peña del Perro in eastern Santander are revealing an Azilian layer (with a uniserially barbed harpoon) rich in limpets (*Patella* spp.) and periwinkles (*Littorina* spp.) (González Morales 1990). Santimamiñe and Lumentxa in Vizcaya have unquantified amounts of Azilian seashells—especially *Littorina littorea* but few *Trochus* (= *Monodonta*) at the latter (Altuna 1972), suggesting still cold (Dryas III) ocean waters. The Azilian levels at Ekain (Guipúzcoa) are the only ones at the site to have significant quantities of shellfish, but they are still few in absolute numbers (335) in Level II. They are dominated by warm water *Monodonta lineata* (topshell) with no *Littorina*. There are 72 in Level III, and 2 each in Levels IV and III) (Leoz and Labadia 1984). This is not surprising because the site was still 10 to 12 km from the shore.

The most detailed data on Azilian shellfishing come from La Riera: from Level 26, 545 shells; 8,383 from Level 27, and 3,279 from Level 28. These are identifiable shells only; they do not include unidentifiable fragments. The area of excavated deposits was very small (5, 8, and 3 m^2 for these three levels, respectively), so the amounts of shell studied only give a minimal estimate of the importance of shellfishing. Nonetheless, shell in these levels represents densities of 34, 17, and 40 kg per m^3. According to the analysis by Ortea (1986), the La Riera Azilian malacofaunas are dominated by *Patella vulgata*, but the percentage declines from ⩾90% to 45% as another limpet, *P. intermedia*, increases. The cold-water *Littorina littorea* decreases and is replaced by the warm-water *Monodonta lineata*, replacement between these "snails" being complete in the overlying Asturian deposit. *Monodonta* and *P. intermedia* are less estuarine and more open-littoral in habitat than the species they began to replace in the Azilian.

The decrease in *P. vulgata* size (and in overall limpet size), begun in the Magdalenian, accelerates in the Azilian at La Riera (as at other sites such as El Valle [Madariaga 1971]), probably as a result of intensive human exploitation. Sea urchins and mussels, inhabitants of the rocky, moderately wave-beaten littoral, also were being exploited in the Azilian at La Riera, even though the shore would have still been some 6 to 7 km away. Clearly, people were heavily utilizing the resources of the estuaries and of the open coast, including fishing for ocean fish, probably from outlying rocks (unless they had boats, which is possible but for which we have no evidence). The maxilla and three teeth of a seal were found in La Riera Azilian Level 28 (Altuna 1986). These isolated remains are further testimony to the growing importance of marine resources, even if this was a seal scavenged or clubbed to death while on shore.

The inland Azilian sites of Los Azules, Piélago, El Valle, and El Castillo yielded small but diverse malacofaunas (some, but not all, species used for decoration) (Fernández-Tresguerres 1980; Vega de la Torre 1985; Cabrera 1984). Contact with the coast, now even closer, clearly existed as in Magdalenian and Solutrean times. Land snails are also present, but it is difficult to say whether they were collected by the people or preferred to live in the organic-rich microhabitats of the sites after humans abandoned the caves.

Evidence of plants used as food is mostly indirect, as usual. By Preboreal times, nut and acorn trees, berry bushes, and plants with edible seeds, greens, roots, and tubers would have become abundant for the first time since the Last Interglacial (Acheulean times!). Estuarine resources would be increasing with the rise in sea level (see Clarke 1976). Some of this is evident from the pollen diagrams from Azilian levels, but one can only guess that the resources were being used as part of the ongoing subsistence diversification process seen in the terrestrial, aquatic, and avian faunas of the period. Wood charcoal at Los Azules included oak and plum, as well as pine (Fernández-Tresguerres 1980). Charcoal and nutshell fragments were relatively abundant in the Azilian levels at La Riera, but few were identifiable (oak and olive are possible) (Cushman 1986). Heavy-duty tools (such as choppers in La Riera Level 27 and Ekain Level II) could have been used to collect or process plant foods.

There are few data on Azilian seasonality. At La Riera in Levels 25 through 27 there were remains of 17 animals killed in summer, 2 in fall, 2 in fall or winter, 1 in winter, and 1 in winter or spring. The species include red deer, ibex, and boar. In addition to the large number of young animals, females are significantly over-represented among the remains that could be sexed. Level 28 had one fawn killed in late spring or early summer. Because the only animal that could be sexed is a hind, the tactic of killing hinds and their young seems to have continued. The Azilian levels in general show a considerable focus on hunting young animals and their mothers. Young red deer (MNI in Levels 25 through 27 = 25) outnumber adults (MNI = 20) (Altuna 1986). The emphasis on hunting on the coastal plain of eastern Asturias in the Azilian contrasts with evidence of winter shellfish collection in the Asturian *concheros* at La Riera and other nearby sites (Deith and Shackleton 1986).

The Azilian levels (V through III) at Ekain contain remains of 11 animals killed in summer (and none in other seasons), with a concentration on slaughter of hinds and young soon after calving (Altuna and Mariezkurrena 1984). Summer hunting is also indicated for Level II. There is some evidence of late spring/early summer killing of ibex and red deer at Abauntz in Navarra (Altuna and Mariezkurrena 1982). The winter locale of these Basque Country hunters is unknown but might include major sites such as Urtiaga.

Logistical moves into the mountains for ibex hunting are as clearly indicated for the Azilian (e.g., Piélago, Rascaño) as for the Magdalenian and Solutrean. Trips from near interior sites like Ekain or La Riera to the coast to fish, to gather mollusks and estuarine plants, and to collect information and flints also probably were common. As far as is known, Azilian lithic raw materials generally come from local sources. Thus, a combination of residential and logistical mobility is proposed within fairly limited territories. One intriguing, unique piece of evidence of long-distance contacts is the presence of a Mediterranean shell (*Nassa mutabilis*) in the Azilian of El Castillo (Cabrera 1984:381).

Azilian Features and Burial

The Los Azules Azilian (especially Level 3) is well endowed with hearths consisting of burnt sediments and lenses of ash and charcoal in basin depressions repeatedly dug into the cave fill. A deep pit of unknown function was dug through much of the thickness of Level 3, apparently from Level 2 (Fernández-Tresguerres 1980). Ekain Level V has two hearths: one a simple circular concentration of charcoal; the other is surrounded by rocks and to one side (under the cave wall overhang) there is a concentration of bones and stone artifacts, possibly a specialized dumping area according to Altuna (1984). Level III has another hearth with concentric rings of angular limestone blocks, small cobbles, and slate slabs (Altuna 1984). La Riera Level 27 is particularly rich in fire-cracked rocks, suggesting that there must have been substantial hearths in the front part of the cave dug out by Vega del Sella and subsequent looters (Straus and Clark 1986).

Los Azules produced the oldest clear burial in the Cantabrian region in its Level 3b (between Levels 3a and 3d, dating to 9,400 and 9,500 B.P., respectively, and both intact, as was overlying Level 2). It has been described in detail by Fernández-Tresguerres (1976; 1980). A grave measuring about 2 by 1.3 m, dug to a maximum depth of 40 cm, was found near the low overhanging right wall adjacent to the cave entrance. The skeleton had been disturbed by erosion, and much of the skull is missing. There is enough left to determine that the individual was a young male, about 169.5 cm tall as estimated from the preserved upper and lower limbs, which are robust with marked muscle insertions (Garralda 1982). The floor of the grave was littered with ochre powder and nodules. The skeleton was intimately associated with a deer antler, two harpoons, various retouched lithic tools, large flakes, a hammerstone, a pile of *Modiolus* shells, and a small carnivore skull. All of these objects were in the grave, which was separated from the cave wall by a line of small rocks. The grave was mounded over with dirt and cobbles, including some painted with manganese pigment dots and one with a line incised around its circumference. Slabs had been placed over the lower end of the grave. The head area was delimited by a line of cobbles, and one of these was painted with dots and a line. This burial is similar to one at Le Trou Violet in Ariège (French Pyrenees), also dating to the Azilian.

Virtually no other human remains have been found that date securely to the Azilian. There was a maxilla and teeth from Level 2 at La Paloma, unfortunately not studied and apparently now lost (Fernández-Tresguerres 1980:74). The Urtiaga level C crania are intrusive from the overlying Chalcolithic or Bronze Age, as is the Level D cranium (Rua 1990).

Azilian Art

While there is no proof that rupestral art was made during the Azilian, neither is there absolute proof to the contrary. All significant Azilian sites with cave art also have Magdalenian levels. Breuil believed, without evidence, that in El Castillo and La Meaza caves, some simple signs might have been of Azilian age (Breuil 1952). At Mazaculos there are some red signs, but the only deposit found so far is an Asturian *conchero* with classic picks (despite the presence of painted cobbles). What can be said is that the Azilian period lacks naturalistically engraved and carved stone and osseous mobile art objects. That form of art ended abruptly with the end of the Magdalenian, about 11,000 B.P.

Azilian levels occasionally have small numbers of plain perforated teeth and shells as well as the more rare painted and engraved cobbles (discussed above). There is one artistic area that seems to show clear continuity between assemblages labeled "late Magdalenian" and others labeled "Azilian." This involves bones engraved with long parallel rows of small dots or long parallel lines edged with short tick-marks. In the uppermost Magdalenian level (Level 2) at Rascaño there is a red deer metapodial with the latter kind of decoration on both flat surfaces and a large oval perforation at the proximal end of the bone (Barandiarán 1981). The distal end of this object (probably a "spatula" or pendant) is broken. There are three small fragments of flat bones engraved with the same distinctive geometric motif from the terminal Magdalenian at La Chora in eastern Santander (González Echegaray et al. 1963). Another pendant with the same type of engraved motif has recently been found in the

Azilian of nearby San Juan Cave (González Sainz and González Morales 1986:287–88).

In Azilian Level 3c of Los Azules (below the burial) there was a whole, perforated spatula made of a red deer metapodial like the one at Rascaño. It is 24 cm long and is decorated with the long parallel rows of tiny dots on both flat surfaces as described above, plus short lines across one of the lateral edges.

In Azilian Level 3b of Piélago II, a few hundred meters from Rascaño, a 4 by 2 cm piece of fashioned flat bone was found. It is perforated, and both flat surfaces are decorated with the same motif: three groups of fine parallel lines with little tick-marks along the outer pair of lines of each group. The tick-marks actually are tiny triangles. Other pieces of flat bone and an antler spatula from the Piélago Azilian also bear plain fine parallel striae that seem to have been deliberately engraved (García Guinea 1985).

Recently, another perforated deer (or caprid) metapodial fragment has been identified as probably coming from the Azilian level of Carballo's excavation in Cueva Morín (González Sainz 1982). (There is the possibility of mixture with the late Magdalenian, according to Carballo's description.) The piece bears triple groups of fine, long, parallel lines edged with tick-marks, virtually identical to those of the Rascaño perforated metapodial, the Piélago pendant, or the La Chora bones (one of which has traces of two perforations). Clearly, between the late Magdalenian and Azilian (Alleröd–Dryas III) of Santander and Asturias there exist some strong similarities in forms (perforated bone pendants, notably made of flat bones and metapodials) and in geometric engraved designs (multiple lines of dots or tick-marked striae). In the Azilian of Atxeta (near Santimamiñe and Guernica in Vizcaya), there was a rib with a more complex series of engravings combining lines and short tick marks (Barandiarán 1972:84, Figure 48). González Sainz (1982) noted the existence of black painted lines with tick-marks on the walls of Llonín Cave in eastern Asturias (not far from Los Azules).

The continuity of this form of art between the late Magdalenian and the Azilian is another indicator that there was not an abrupt break between the two archeologically defined concepts, even if the naturalistic art did seem to end. It is likely that figurative art was already fading in popularity and being replaced by geometric art in the period after about 11,000 years ago. These developments are paralleled in the terminal Paleolithic mobile art of France and Italy.

The Azilian thus began as a continuation and simplification of the Magdalenian in terms of lithic and osseous technology and art. It also began as a continuation of the Magdalenian in terms of settlement and subsistence strategies. But, by the end of the Pleistocene, in the Preboreal, major changes were under way that included the continuation and further elaboration of Epipaleolithic/Mesolithic hunting gear *and* the appearance of specialized marine shell dump sites. Such shell middens have traditionally been elevated to the status of an archeological "culture," known as the "Asturian."

Thoughts on the End of the Cave Art

With the amelioration in climate and the significant (if impermanent) reforestation of the Alleröd, Cantabrian hunter-gatherer adaptations changed. Closely attuned to the conditions of a glacial world, highly interdependent on one another in Solutrean and Magdalenian times, the panregional unity and solidarity of the bands may have begun to lessen under the more benign conditions of Alleröd. The margin for error widened after Dryas I and further still after Dryas II. It is entirely possible that the *raisons d'être* for cave art and the elaborate Magdalenian mobile art were already fading by late Magdalenian times, even as conditions warmed and became temporarily more wooded in Bölling. Although we cannot yet explain the cave art boom of the Late Upper Paleolithic, it is clearly correlated in time with both regional population growth and full glacial conditions. When the latter loosened their grip on the Franco-Cantabrian region, the needs and rules of the socio-economic survival game changed. Not surprisingly, the context for creating art and the kinds of artistic expression (as *we* label it) changed, either as a direct result of the changes in the economic and social order or as an indirect consequence thereof. For now, it is the nature of the linkage between the Late Upper Paleolithic art and conditions and the strategies of collective life that eludes us.

As a hypothesis, one could suggest that hunting in the Azilian increasingly took place on small-band territories, emphasizing smaller kills, even of the chief game (red deer), and far greater diversification made possible by the increase in new habitats resulting from deglaciation, reforestation, and sea level rise.

Certainly the Azilian sites (or the surface areas used by Azilian occupants in previously used caves) generally seem to be very small relative to many Magdalenian ones, and most Azilian deposits (except at Los Azules, Piélago, Ekain, and perhaps El Valle) are very thin and poor in features and cultural remains, especially in comparison with the often very thick, rich Magdalenian deposits. The numbers of individual red deer represented by the Azilian archeofaunas are often smaller than those of the Magdalenian. Yet the evidence of boar and roe deer hunting and of shellfish collection seems greater, and the potential for plant food exploitation was undoubtedly so, at least in Alleröd and Preboreal. If hunting were being done on a smaller, more individual scale (perhaps emphasizing encounter tactics more than cooperative drives) and territories of local bands were being reduced as increased possibilities for further subsistence diversification arose, then the need for and frequency of interband contacts may have lessened.

Thus, the social network may have contracted and become attenuated. So too, with improving environmental conditions (even Dryas III was by no means as severe as Dryas I or the Last Glacial Maximum), the need to store and to transmit survival information and cues in permanent form (i.e., in caves used for normal residence, for logistical visits, or for large-scale multiband aggregations) sharply decreased. Social costs may have begun to outweigh survival benefits. As the world that made the art of the caves significant in the lives of hunting peoples changed, the art itself became irrelevant and the memory of its once central role in people's lives faded. Luckily, some of the art itself has remained into the twentieth century to fascinate and baffle us.

Some artistic holdover existed in the realm of bone engraving. With the disappearance of the more characteristic Magdalenian mobile art, often rich in animal imagery, the last Magdalenian art was that of the tick-marked lines on perforated bones—a tradition that continued along the central part of the Cantabrian coast throughout the Azilian.

In the domains of technology, settlement, and food resources (if not social and territorial scale and organization, or cave art), much remained fundamentally the same until the end of Dryas III. Then, once again profoundly different conditions required and instigated new cultural responses, modified adaptations, and rapid changes in the strategies for human survival.

The Asturian Phenomenon

First identified and defined (correctly) as a Postglacial cultural phenomenon by Vega del Sella (1923) in a series of caves along the coast of eastern Asturias, the Asturian represents one important aspect of the adaptations of Preboreal, Boreal, and perhaps even Atlantic human groups: shellfishing. The Asturian is defined by two frequently associated but not necessarily functionally correlated traits: *concheros* (large shell heaps that, because of the subsequent rise in sea level and great potential for erosion on open land surfaces of the coastal plain, survive today only inside the mouths of caves); and simple, unifacial cobble picks (Figure 8.2d).

I, for one, find it hard to believe that these middens—originally containing little beyond hundreds of thousands of limpets and topshells, some animal bones (relatively few, considering the volume of shells), many picks and choppers, some chipping debris, and a limited number of small retouched tools—represent the sum total of the cultural repertoire of human groups inhabiting western Santander and eastern Asturias for two millennia (Straus 1979). Likewise, I find it difficult to accept shells and what are obviously simple, highly expedient implements (the picks) as cultural/ethnic markers in the same way that I might accept a Solutrean concave base point or a Magdalenian style of engraved sagaie as a cultural marker. And, given the relatively small ungulate faunas in the shell heaps, I find it unlikely that the *concheros* represent most of the contemporary human diet in the subregion in which they are found. Ethnographic examples, from Africa and Australia in particular, show that even extensive shellfishing is a supplementary subsistence strategy. So the Asturian is not likely to be a self-contained, self-sufficient adaptive system defined by the distribution of *concheros* and pick-containing sites.

Thus, though I draw from and build on the excellent work of Vega del Sella and of meticulous, recent students of the Asturian (Clark 1976,1983 and González Morales 1982a), I will place a slightly different emphasis on my interpretation of the Asturian within the context of human adaptations prior to, during, and perhaps soon after the introduction and adoption of food production methods in this region.

Asturian Sites and Chronology

Most of the known Asturian sites (some 75 at last count, combining the research of Clark [1976], Gavelas [1980], and González Morales [1982a]) are *concheros* in caves or rockshelters; the rest (notably Ciriego/ Liencres at the eastern end of the site distribution and Bañugues at the western end) consist of open-air finds of picks and other artifacts (Figure 8.3). Asturian-like picks have been found in early Holocene coastal contexts in the French Basque Country and in Portugal, a fact that shows the widespread and purely practical (i.e., nonstylistic) nature of this type of implement.

The vast majority of the classic Asturian *concheros* are found along a 50-km stretch of the coastal plain of eastern Asturias, between Ríos Sella

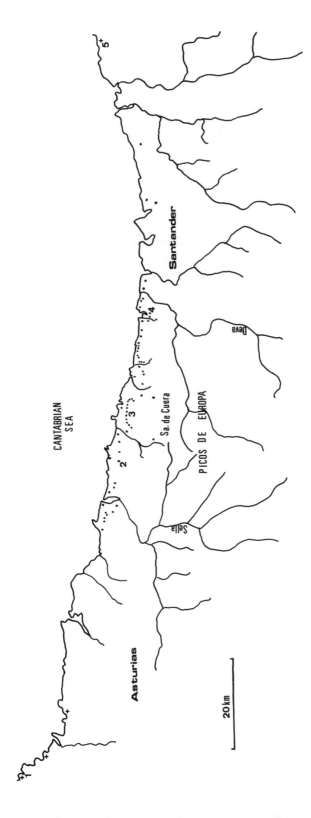

FIGURE 8.3. *Asturian sites: 1, Bañugues; 2, Penicial; 3, Posada de Llanes/"La Llera" Group (La Riera, Balmori, et al.); 4, La Franca Group (Mazaculos, Molino de Gasparín, et al.); 5; Ciriego ("Liencres"). + = open-air find of picks; • = conchero with picks.*

and Deva. The middens are never more than 3 km from the present sea-shore (and usually within 1.5 to 2 km). Under Boreal conditions, the coast would have been about 1 km farther north, whereas under Preboreal conditions it was somewhat farther still; in the Atlantic period the sea was actually slightly higher than it is now along the Asturian littoral (Mary et al. 1975; González Morales 1982a). The densest cluster of *concheros* is located in the center of this strip, along the Llera ridge near Posada de Llanes.

Several instances of picks without *concheros* have been recorded along the shores of Cabo de Peñas in central Asturias (especially at Bañugues, where such finds were made in stratified position without any fauna above the Acheulean deposits ([González Morales 1982a]) as well as one find near the Galician border. At Santimamiñe in Vizcaya, there is a shell midden layer almost exclusively dominated by oyster (*Ostrea*) followed by small mussels (*Tapes*)—in short, malacologically completely different from the *concheros* (Aranzadi et al. 1931:81). Also unlike the latter, the Santimamiñe shell midden is also rich in mammal remains, showing that hunting was also a very important part of subsistence at the site (Aranzadi et al. 1931:84–85). In line with this fact, the level yielded a fairly rich, diverse Epipaleolithic stone tool assemblage with several geometric microliths, backed bladelets, and many Upper Paleolithic burins and endscrapers (Cava 1975). So far, Santimamiñe is an isolated example of heavy utilization of aquatic (estuarine) resources in the early Holocene Basque Country. Although lacking classic picks, the shell midden did yield at least two choppers (Aranzadi et al. 1931:97–98).

Overlying the Azilian layer at La Peña del Perro in eastern Santander (70 km west of Santimamiñe) is a midden deposit composed more of oysters and mussels than of limpets and periwinkles, reflecting the early Holocene rise in sea level to form the present Bay of Santoña. By this time the rockshelter seems to have been used as a shellfishing locus (and dump); the only artifacts are flakes González Morales 1990).

As defined by the presence of characteristic artifacts, there is only one clear case of stratigraphic superposition of an Asturian layer above an Azilian one; it is at La Riera Cave (Vega del Sella 1930; Clark 1976; Straus and Clark 1986). Other possible cases cited by Vega del Sella (e.g., Cueto de la Mina [Vega del Sella 1916] and Balmori [Vega del Sella 1930]) are problematic, due to mixture, lack of stratigraphic clarity, and artificial separation of supposed (but not unequivocal) Azilian artifacts from Magdalenian (Straus 1979c). Subsequent excavations have failed to find other clear examples of an Asturian *conchero* deposit overlying a level with undoubted Azilian artifacts. Nonetheless, Asturian shell middens in general are characterized by molluscan faunas that prefer temperate ocean waters (e.g., *Monodonta lineata*), plus various limpets (*Patella* spp.) and, where estuarine conditions were appropriate, mussels (*Mytilus edulis*) (Vega del Sella 1923; Clark 1976; González Morales 1982a). Despite elaborate efforts to discredit Vega del Sella's good sense and to assign the "crude," heavy-duty picks to the Lower or Middle Paleolithic (e.g., Jordá 1959), radiocarbon dates of samples collected by Clark (1976, 1983; Straus and Clark 1986) and González Morales (1982a) show that these *concheros* with temperate-climate malacofaunas and picks in eastern Asturias date between about 9,300 and 6,500 B.P. or even younger (Appendices E1 and F1).

Asturian Environments

Pollen analyses at Asturian sites and at coastal bogs in the vicinity of *concheros* provide evidence for dense forestation in this period. At La Riera the *conchero* deposit (Level 29) and the flowstone capping it (Level 30) are rich in pollens and show AP values generally ≥50%, with large amounts of hazel as well as oak, birch, pine, elm, linden, willow, alder, and walnut (especially at the top) plus enormous quantities of fern spores (Leroi-Gourhan 1986). The sedimentological reconstruction for the same levels shows increasing warmth and humidity assignable to Preboreal and Boreal (Laville 1986). Similar conditions are recorded in Butzer's (1981) Phases 42 through 44 in an archeologically sterile travertine above Azilian Level 1 (9,000 B.P.) at Cueva Morín. At El Pendo, the uppermost stratum (assigned tentatively to the Boreal) has a pollen diagram similar to that of the top of the La Riera sequence, with a high AP including various thermophiles and hygrophiles (Leroi-Gourhan 1980). A small pollen sample from the *conchero* deposit in Balmori had evidence of pine, chestnut, birch, lime, and oak, with the AP far outnumbering the NAP (Non-Arboreal Pollen index) (Clark 1974–1975). Pollens from the *conchero* at Mazaculos (Preboreal/Boreal) indicate a dense forest of hazels with some pines and some open areas along the coast with ferns, grasses, and composites (Lopez 1986, cited by Dupré 1988).

Sediment samples from a number of Asturian sites (including Liencres and Balmori) were analyzed by Butzer and Bowman (1976) who concluded that they were formed by processes similar to those of the last millennium. Quantitatively poor (and possibly mixed) pollen samples from the open-air site of Liencres yielded high APs including various warmth-loving taxa (as well as the ubiquitous pine pollens) plus heaths, ferns, and grasses, indicative of the site's dunal, shoreside location (Menéndez-Amor 1976). Botanical analysis of Asturian charcoal samples from

Mazaculos near La Riera reveals the presence of at least *Quercus robur* and *Betula* sp. in local firewood (Diaz 1980).

Pollen analysis from the infilling of a sea-cliff cave at Tina Mayor estuary (near the Santander–Asturias border), dating to >10,000 years, shows a spectrum heavily dominated by arboreal pollens (plus fern spores) (Mary et al. 1975). Besides the overproducing pine, there are pollens of oak, olive, hornbeam, and holly. Indications are of temperate, humid conditions of probably Preboreal age. In La Jerra bog in the nearby Oyambre valley, a pollen sample dating to 5,900 B.P. gives spectra dominated by AP with mainly oak plus pine, hazel, and various other trees, again indicating dense, temperate woodlands (of Atlantic age). In another bog of the same valley, there is evidence of deforestation (either natural or anthropogenic) by 5,300 B.P. and then regrowth of trees—notably oak, hazel, and birch (Mary et al. 1975). A terminal Atlantic (4,800 B.P.) bog sample from Río Bederna (also on the coast of easternmost Santander) reveals a dense oak/hazel/elm/alder forest cover under very humid conditions (Mary et al. 1975).

Thus, the latter part of Azilian times and the full span of the accumulation of the "Asturian" *concheros* witnessed the complete reforestation of the Cantabrian region, with substantial wooded areas even reaching upper elevations of the Cordillera as testified by bog pollen cores from its Santander and Galician sectors (see summary of data in González Morales 1982a:60–61). These were environments very different from those of Dryas III or even Alleröd when the Magdalenian–Azilian adaptive change began. In addition to the vegetative changes (replacement of almost all open areas by thick mixed forest), a substantial area of the coastal plain was now submerged. This caused a loss of about 2,800 km^2 of relatively flat land in the period since the Last Glacial Maximum. This loss, occurring mostly during the Preboreal and Boreal, was not fully compensated by the gain of deglaciated high mountain land, although the new estuarine habitats were exceptionally rich.

Asturian Technology

The artifact assemblages associated with Asturian *concheros* (as well as the open-air occurrences in Santander and Asturias) are, to say the least, quantitatively poor and simplified. Appendix E5 lists the retouched tools from modern excavations at Balmori (Clark 1974–1975), La Riera (Clark 1974), Liencres (Clark 1975), and Mazaculos (González Morales et al. 1980). The heavy-duty tools (picks and choppers) and a few of the other pieces (especially denticulates, notches, and sidescrapers) are made on quartzite; the small Upper Paleolithic/Epipaleolithic types are made on flint. Picks make up far higher (or exclusive) percentages of the old collections, either because small implements were not collected or (more likely) were not saved with provenance information in the Museo Arqueológico de Oviedo after Vega del Sella's death. The picks are highly standardized in size (average length, 8.95 cm; SD = 1.36; COV = 0.15; n = 148) according to González Morales (1982a:135–38), with a typically biconcave, elongated but blunt, unifacial, pointed end. The picks were created by only a few large, flake removals made by direct percussion. The base of these cobble tools is always cortical. The tip is generally triangular in cross section (González Morales 1982a). They usually are quite distinct from Acheulean picks.

The function of the picks has been hotly debated for seventy years, although the association with shells or the coast has led most observers to suggest that they were used to knock limpets from the rocks (see discussions in Madariaga [1976b] and González Morales [1982a:198–200], with references). They are too blunt to have been used to pry limpets off, which can be done efficaciously with a sharp bone splinter or flake. And the limpets in the *concheros* are intact, not broken as they would be if struck by such a heavy object. An alternate explanation might be that the picks (and other heavy-duty tools, such as choppers, common in the *concheros*) were used to dig for plant foods in estuarine habitats (in line with suggestions by D.L. Clarke [1976] and consonant with the wear on pick tips mentioned, but not systematically studied, by González Morales [1982a:199]). This would help explain the existence of picks without *concheros* in several sites (although the erosion of open-air shell heaps is quite possible).

It is possible to view the heavy-duty tools as easy-to-make, easy-to-discard (i.e., expedient) tools, made on beach cobbles and removed as obtrusive trash from campsites to nearby cave dumps, along with the noxious, bulky piles of shell and occasional bone. On the other hand, it would rarely be the case that unobtrusive discards such as bladelets or endscrapers would be bulk-loaded off to the dump.

Thus, it is conceivable that the pick–*conchero* association is the result of human disposal practices and not indicative of a functional relationship. Nonetheless, I am mindful that such an association exists between picks or other heavy-duty cobble tools (sometimes called "limpet scoops") along other coasts of Atlantic Europe. So, a partial functional relationship might indeed have existed, even though there are heavy-duty implements in sites far from the coast as well—no doubt used to cut and work wood and to dig.

I have pointed out that, although rare, bladelets (unretouched, retouched, and backed) do exist in Asturian collections. (Unretouched bladelets make up 7.8% of the combined debitage from all of Clark's [1976] excavations of cave and open-air Asturian sites; these pieces cannot all be explained away because of possible mixture at Liencres.) The *concheros* as a group contain not only numerous picks and limited numbers of other retouched stone tools but also hammerstones, grinding stones, unmodified cobbles, cores (mostly for flakes), bladelets, flakes, and a very few blades (Clark 1976,1983). However, in all cases the totals are quite small, indicating that *in situ* knapping was not prevalent at the *concheros*, whereas it may have been more so at Liencres. In addition to the lithic industry, Asturian collections contain small numbers of usually very simple bone points and awls. Mazaculos yielded four bipointed bone objects, reasonably interpreted by González Morales (1982a:105–107) as fish gorges. A similar piece is illustrated by Aranzadi et al. (1931:Plate 31, No.2) from the shell midden layer at Santimamiñe.

Asturian Subsistence

The vast bulk of the classic *concheros* of eastern Asturias is composed of small limpets and topshells. In Level 29 at La Riera, the average length for *Patella vulgata* is only 26.8 mm—down from 42 to 46 mm in the Solutrean at the base of the sequence. The average for all limpets (including the smaller *P. intermedia*) is down to 23.5 mm in Level 29—indicative of heavy human exploitation (Ortea 1986). This is true for all the Asturian *concheros*. Other components of the middens, besides other marine and terrestrial mollusks, are ocean fish (including sole and wrasse), crabs, sea urchins, birds, and ungulates (Ortea 1986; Menéndez et al. 1986; Altuna 1986; Clark 1976,1983; González Morales 1982a). The open littoral and off-shore rocks were being utilized, as were estuaries. The lack or scarcity of salmon remains is interesting in light of their presence with (by definition) Azilian harpoons at other levels/sites in the region.

The modern excavations of *conchero* remnants in La Riera yielded only 194 red deer remains and virtually no other remains of ungulates (Altuna 1972, 1986). Clark's excavation at Balmori disclosed 36 red deer remains out of a total of 58 ungulate bones and teeth (Clark 1974–1975). The *concheros* have collectively produced small amounts of boar and roe deer and traces of aurochs, horse, ibex, and chamois. Bones of fox, bear, mustelids, otter, and wildcat are occasionally present, as are those of lagomorphs and rodents (Clark 1976, 1983). The quantities of ungulate remains are unimpressive, even though it would take thousands of tiny limpets to equal the food value of a single adult red deer!

Oxygen isotope analyses of limited samples of topshells and limpets from the *concheros* La Riera, Penicial, and Mazaculos show that they were collected during the cold season (mostly winter, with some fall) (Deith and Shackleton 1986; Deith 1983). Seasonality information was available from only two red deer in La Riera Level 29: one was killed in spring and the other in winter (Altuna 1986). Thus, there is no evidence of summer *conchero* accumulation, suggesting that intensive shellfish collection was a strategy used to supplement other resources during the winter when plant foods were unavailable and ungulates were scattered and lean. Asturian subsistence was only part of a larger annual subsistence picture.

Asturian Art, Human Remains, Features, and Living Floors

No "art objects" have been found except the two painted cobbles from Mazaculos. A poorly published and little-known burial was found in 1925 by Carballo (1960) in an Asturian deposit at the Molino de Gasparín rockshelter (La Franca, Asturias) (González Morales 1982a:176–179). The individual (an elderly female) was in extended position with three picks by her head. The picks were supposedly surrounded by rocks as was the body. The head lay on stones, and a cervid tibia lay next to the face. There was a mound over the burial, atop which a fire had been built. González Morales (1982a:178) notes great similarities between this Asturian burial and the Azilian burial at nearby Los Azules—one on the coast and the other in the interior.

In a search for evidence of the sexual division of labor, I could make the interesting (perhaps outrageous) suggestion that it might not be purely coincidental that the region's only Azilian burial is a male associated with harpoons and the only Asturian burial is a female associated with picks! Other Asturian human remains include a mandible of an adult male at Mazaculos, the ascending mandibular ramus of a child at Balmori, and a very robust male cranium possibly from the Asturian *conchero* in nearby Cuartamentero Cave (Garralda 1981,1982).

Although fire-cracked rock, cobbles, ash, and charcoal lenses are fairly abundant in *conchero* fills, aside from the Gasparín burial no features have been observed in them. At Mazaculos, the only intact *conchero* (i.e., not earlier dug out for fertilizer or already substantially excavated by Vega del Sella) to have been excavated recently, a living surface was found in the rockshelter at the very base of the 0.8-m-thick stratified shell heap. On this surface, in contact with a clay deposit, there are three "living floor" lenses with scatters of bones, lithic artifacts, and large limestone blocks, some burnt. There is also a diffuse scatter of charcoal and ash and a second concentration of charcoal and ash with burnt stones (a "real hearth" in the words of the excavator, González Morales [1982a:101]). A pick was found lying on the basal living floor, dating to 9,300 B.P. These observations are significant because they show a cave mouth that still had room to harbor an Asturian residential occupation (unlike caves such as La Riera or Balmori where the accumulated Upper Paleolithic fill had left little headroom—just a convenient "hole" for the disposal of shells and other bulk trash. The Mazaculos discovery is also important because it shows cultural activities that are defined (by the pick) as "Asturian" were taking place at a time when other archeological phenomena labeled "Azilian" were still occurring in the same subregion (i.e., at Los Azules, upper Level 3 and Level 2). Thus, there are three kinds of Asturian sites: shell dumps in caves that were not (or no longer) used for habitation, caves at least initially still used for habitation (Mazaculos), and open-air sites with picks and other lithic artifacts but no other remains.

Since Vega del Sella's day (e.g., 1921:165–166), prehistorians have wondered why the caves of eastern coastal Asturias were apparently abandoned in favor of open-air sites for residence in Asturian times. A simple answer might be that it was now generally warmer and more pleasant outside the caves than inside. Camps may have continued to be established near formerly occupied caves (especially along the south face of the Llera ridge in Posada de Llanes) not only for occasional shelter from rain but also because the caves often are in central locations providing shelter from sea winds, high insulation, and easily available fresh water as well as good access to the resources of the now-nearer littoral, the coastal plain, and the coastal mountain range. The same qualities would have applied to fields or terraces in front of cave mouths. As noted above, some of the best-located caves of the Llera group (Cueto de la Mina, La Riera, Tres Calabres, Balmori, etc.) and others (e.g., La Lloseta, El Cierro, etc.) were already substantially filled up by Preboreal times, although they continued to be convenient for bulk garbage disposal. When Vega del Sella (1916:61,1921:165,1930:11–13) discovered La Riera, it was filled to the roof with shells of the Asturian *conchero*. Other *concheros* had already been mined for fertilizer, but their surfaces remained cemented by precipitated carbonates to cave mouth walls and ceilings in many cases.

So, under temperate early Holocene conditions near the shore, Asturian groups seem to have camped mainly outside caves and converted the caves into dumps for shells, bones, some bothersome expedient artifacts, and debris. Such a use rather quickly filled up the remaining openings of cave mouths, usually all the way to the roofs. To date, no campsites associated with these dumps have been found, although this probably is due to a lack of exploration as well as poor preservation and visibility of what probably were very ephemeral, insubstantial, open-air foraging camps. Clark's (1974; Clark and Richards 1978) test trench in the talus directly in front of La Riera Cave in 1969 uncovered Asturian-type artifacts (i.e., three picks) plus such supposedly "unusual" artifacts as bladelets, showing that further such work might prove fruitful.

However, our detailed observations of a substantial gypsy encampment in front of La Riera during the excavations of 1977 show how hard it would be to find any preserved remains from such open-air camps in this environment. Despite the abandonment of substantial amounts of trash, rock and peg features, hearths, etc. by large numbers of inhabitants after one winter's rains and floods (endemic in the karstically drained valleys of Asturias), there was no trace of the gypsy camp at the foot of the low La Riera talus in the following spring.

"Azilian" and "Asturian"

There are various reasons for arguing that the "Asturian" may represent part of a wider adaptive system centered on the subregion of eastern Asturias during the late Preboreal and Boreal. By this I mean that the Asturian sites are specialized aspects of the adaptations of bands during the span of time that is archeologically assigned to the "Azilian." In the early part of its archeological existence ($\geq$9,300 to $\leq$ 8,700 B.P.) the Asturian may represent a functional or activity "pose" of the "Azilian." The apparent temporal relationship between the two archeological units at La Riera may be more a localized successional phenomenon in the use and usefulness of that individual cave than a generalizable phylogenetic order. The bases of my functional argument follow.

1. The Asturian lithic and faunal assemblages are very simple and incomplete; they cannot represent the whole range of human activities and subsistence during late Preboreal and Boreal.

2. Late Azilian and early Asturian radiocarbon dates overlap.

3. Asturian sites are found only right along the coast, whereas Azilian sites are found both there and in the interior.

4. Azilian levels contain both terrestrial and aquatic food remains—the latter include shellfish and fish in early deposits like Levels 26 through 28 at La Riera near the coast and salmonids throughout the geographic range of Azilian sites. All Azilian sites have ample evidence of hunting.

5. Some evidence points to the *concheros* as having been deposited during the cold season only, whereas earlier (Azilian) use of La Riera was mostly in summer as well as in winter, spring, or fall.

6. The Azilian stone and bone industries include many weapon elements (backed bladelets and points, harpoons), whereas the Asturian materials include just a few of the microliths. However, there are enough of them to show that this technology was part of the more general Epipaleolithic technological repertoire.

7. Azilian painted cobbles have been found at the Asturian sites of Mazaculos and El Pindal, where no other Azilian traces have been found (González Morales 1982a:248; Fernández-Tresguerres 1980:155, 157).

8. There are similarities between the Azilian burial at Los Azules and the Asturian at Gasparin.

9. Many of the same sorts of places along the coastal zone used as sites in the Upper Paleolithic (including the Azilian) were also used in the Asturian, so there is a continuity of territorial utilization.

10. Whereas Azilian use of a cave such as La Riera could leave room for Asturian use, the latter would rapidly fill the cave mouth, making it unusable for other purposes and leading to the appearance of a temporal *succession* and the lack of residues from a hunting or salmonid fishing functional pose atop a shellfish dump deposit.

This hypothesis needs to be tested further through more careful excavations and analyses of both kinds of sites and more radiocarbon dates, seasonality studies, and use-wear analyses. It is offered in hope of breaking the gridlock of normative, phylogenetic thinking that sees these different archeological signatures as indications of separate "cultures" sharing the same environment, the same small territory, and, at least partially, the same time period, resources, and technologies. We will return to the Asturian below, because several *concheros* (too many to dismiss now as examples of mixture) have produced ceramics and because at least two have radiocarbon dates that overlap at the recent end of time with the appearance of food production in the region.

Conclusions

The terminal Glacial and early Postglacial periods witnessed dramatic environmental changes: final deglaciation, rapid sea level rise, reforestation, and faunal extinctions. Such changes had happened before with each glacial–interglacial transition, the penultimate of which had been about 128,000 years ago. But this time, the hominid population was relatively dense in the Cantabrian region, and they now were anatomically modern humans. Using equipment derived and simplifed from that of the Magdalenian, with probably greater reliance on the bow and arrow as well as on nets and harpoons, these people adapted to newly forested conditions by continuing to diversify their subsistence. They made increasing use of estuarine, riverine, and marine resources (plants as well as fish and shellfish). They hunted more solitary woodland animals, perhaps using individual encounter tactics more often, even on their old main prey, red deer. Some evidence suggests that the bands stayed within smaller territories, although moves from the coastal zone into the mountains for ibex hunting continued.

The glacial-age context and survival-rooted bases for cave art, and perhaps much of the mobile art, disappeared. The art—in both its social and informational aspects—became less relevant as individual or small group hunting and very restricted territories came about with the environmental changes of Alleröd—and as environments subsequently stabilized. Yet, in certain remnant mobile art objects and motifs there is some evidence of continuity between the late Magdalenian and Azilian, just as there was continuity in settlement and technology. And because the changes in resources and subsistence were far less abrupt or radical even than in southwestern France, the full-blown Azilian phenomenon developed gradually and rather late in Cantabrian Spain.

By late Preboreal times, however, further intensification in the use of marine resources led to the formation of vast but artifactually impoverished shell middens along some sectors of the coast. The Asturian *concheros* can be interpreted as the products of a cold-season tiding-over strategy on the part of groups that continued to be Epipaleolithic hunters and fishers. They simply carried the long-standing Cantabrian trends towards necessary subsistence diversification and specialization one step further along the scale of site-function differentiation. The Asturian is not at all akin to "a culture" (less so than the Azilian); it is a particular activity pose: mollusk gathering. And people continued to collect shells intensively in order to survive, even after they had apparently adopted certain "Neolithic" strategies in addition to hunting and fishing.

All prehistory is change, but the extent and speed of change are clearly focused in this period: first, because it is recent and the data are abundant; second, because it probably really was more dramatic in content and rate at this time than at any other in the prehistory of the Cantabrian region.

Chapter 9

FOOD PRODUCTION AND THE END OF THE STONE AGE

THE finely tuned, highly diversified hunter-gatherer adaptations of the Cantabrian region took the human population well into the Atlantic period before major changes occurred. The Cantabrian bands were no longer innovators. Domesticated livestock and ceramic technology were introduced to the region, probably from the Mediterranean world via the Ebro Valley. Yet the hunter-gatherers of northern coastal Spain did not abandon their ways of life completely or immediately. They grafted the introductions onto their already complex repertoire of food sources and technologies. For millennia there was no radical change. In fact, the region never became a center of cereal agriculture. Pastoralism, fishing, and limited horticulture eventually, but only very gradually, replaced the ancient, deeply rooted mixed hunting-fishing-gathering economy of the Cantabrian coast and mountains. In Upper Paleolithic times this area of Europe had been a center of innovation but had become rather peripheral in the late Neolithic context.

Perhaps because of this peripheral role in the world of the western European Neolithic, little research on this period has been conducted in Cantabrian Spain itself. Instead, researchers have concentrated on the relative wealth of material on the southern side of the Cordillera in the Ebro basin of Alava and Navarra. It is there that we now have an abundant radiocarbon record and several key stratigraphic sequences. In contrast, evidence on the first ceramics and domesticated animals and on the appearance of megalithic monuments becomes increasingly scanty and vague as one goes westward along the Cantabrian coast. Only with the development of the Bronze Age do matters become clearer and the data more abundant, but the establishment of complex societies, even peripheal ones, is beyond the scope of this book. This chapter describes some of what we know (and do not know) about the end of the Stone Age in a region that had been one of the most important centers of late Old Stone Age economic, social, and artistic creativity.

Atlantic Period Environments

Possibly because of continuing tectonic uplift of at least the western sector of the Cantabrian coast, there is evidence of only a slight marine transgression during the Atlantic (Postglacial Optimum): bogs with indicators of ocean incursion at about 5,500 B.P. near the Asturias–Santander border (Mary et al. 1975:17).

Pollen spectra from mountain bogs indicate dense oak forests in the lower elevations, with more pine, hazel, and birch in the higher ones (see summary in González Morales [1982a:60–63]). Various bog deposits along the coast from the French Basque Country to Galicia also have been sampled and analyzed palynologically; these are summarized by Dupré (1988:119–124). In general, the region was densely forested with oaks, hazels, and, varying from area to area and time to time, pines, alder, beech, lime, hornbeam, and elm. The Atlantic was temperate and especially humid, with a drying trend characterizing the subsequent Sub-boreal period.

The archeological site at Abauntz provides a specific example of palynological information. This site is at moderately high elevation in northern Navarra (López 1982). Level C (early Neolithic, 6,900 B.P.), dominated by pine with some hazel, birch, and oak. There is a brief reappearance of open vegetation (deforestation by pastoralism?) before a dramatic increase in hazel in the late Atlantic (Level B4, middle or late Neolithic, 5,400 B.P.). Alder, beech, oak, and lime pollens are present in small quantities. The spectra from the Neolithic open-air site at Herriko Barra in coastal Guipúzcoa (5,800 B.P.) show forest dominated by alder pollens with hazel and pine (Isturiz and Sánchez 1990).

Indications of local deforestation in the Atlantic period are very rare, with more such evidence appearing (especially in sites south of the Basque sector of the Cordillera) in the Sub-boreal (e.g., Berniollo in Alava). The early impact of pastoralism seems to have been slight along the northern face of the Cordillera, although there are some possible indices of anthropogenic deforestation at a few sites and bogs (e.g., Cueto de la Avellanosa, Liencres, and La Jerra in Santander, Sierra del Barbanza and various tumuli in Galicia) (Dupré 1988).

Chronology

Appendix F1 lists uncalibrated radiocarbon dates for late Epipaleolithic/ Mesolithic and Neolithic deposits in the Cantabrian region and the adjacent region of Alava and northern Navarra where neolithic technology seems to have been in place by 6,500 B.P. All the dates from the former region are included, but only ones from the most important stratified sequences are given for the upper Ebro basin. Problems affect the archeological definitions of these sites and levels, just as they do for the earlier periods. In general, an assemblage automatically becomes "Neolithic" if it includes even a few ceramics. Assemblages with only lithics pose a problem when the radiocarbon dates are very recent (e.g., Tarrerón at 5,800 B.P.). Their existence does not mean that other sites of the same human group did not involve the use of ceramics. On the other hand, it is hard to define *concheros* with ceramics—such as Les Pedroses, with a date of 5,800 B.P.

The Basque Late Epipaleolithic and Neolithic

There is considerable continuity between the late Epipaleolithic and Neolithic for the Basque Country in terms of site occupation, location and type (mainly caves and rockshelters), lithic technology, and subsistence. Although there still is no clear chronostratigraphic or cultural sequence for the Basque Epipaleolithic, it is apparent that, by Preboreal times, assemblages of a more pure Azilian type (with antler harpoons, backed bladelets, and Azilian points) were at times being replaced by assemblages with variable quantities of geometric microliths similar to those found in the Mesolithic of southwestern France. I use the terms "Mesolithic" and "late Epipaleolithic" synonymously to refer to lithic assemblages with substantial quantities of geometrics. But even this is not a satisfactory semantic solution, as we have seen, because of the existence at Piélago of assemblages of Dryas III age with both Azilian harpoons and geometrics. Several caves and rockshelters in the Basque Country have stratified sequences of Epipaleolithic levels overlain by Neolithic levels: notably Arenaza and Santimamiñe (Vizcaya), Marizulo (Guipúzcoa), Fuente Hoz (Alava), Montico de Charratu (Treviño), and Abauntz and Zatoya (Navarra). The Epipaleolithic and Neolithic evidence has recently been summarized by Berganza (1990) and Cava (1990), respectively.

Berganza (1990:87) sets the stage for the meeting of the Atlantic and Mediterranean worlds in the early Neolithic by noting the presence of

La Cocina triangles (a type common in Levantine Spain) in Level II of Fuente Hoz and the presence of perforated Mediterranean *Collumbella rustica* shells at the Zatoya, Fuente Hoz, and Padre Areso sites. Cava (1990) claims to see stylistic influences from both southwestern France and Levante among the lithic assemblages of the early Basque Neolithic. The first stage of "Neolithization" seems to have involved the introduction of plain ceramics (or the knowledge of how to make them, although none of the sites has yet provided evidence for *in situ* ceramic firing). This may have occurred by preexisting social networks down the Ebro Valley from the continental Basque provinces (Navarra and Alava) and again via social contacts as well as transhumant hunter-gatherer subsistence movements over the low Cordilleran passes into Guipúzcoa and Vizcaya.

The introduction of domesticated animals is a poorly understood process in this region. Livestock-keeping seems to have been grafted onto the diverse foraging subsistence base of local groups only late and spottily in the coastal Basque Country. This addition of some sheep or goats (or both), cattle, and pigs does not seem to have caused much change in the preexisting settlement types or patterns. Bands continued to inhabit caves (mostly the same ones as before); there are no traces of early Neolithic villages or even huts in the region. The hunting and maintenance technologies do not seem to have changed. Both geometric microliths and nongeometric blade/bladelet and flake-based tools continue to be found in various sites, for reasons that may either be stylistic/cultural (as Cava thinks) or functional. Cardial ceramics (hallmarks of the western Mediterranean early Neolithic world) appear at Peña Larga (Alava) about 6,000 B.P., and, although most sherds continue to be undecorated, incised ceramics do exist in several late Neolithic sites in the Basque Country. That period includes the earliest construction of megalithic monuments in the Cantabrian region (Cava 1990; Gorrochategui and Yarritu 1990; Andres 1990). Solid evidence of cereal agriculture does not appear until the Eneolithic (Chalcolithic) in this region. Thus, a mixed economy of hunting, gathering, fishing, and pastoralism seems to have been practiced in the Basque Neolithic, although not all those activities were conducted at all sites or at all times. What follows is a brief review of the extant artifactual and faunal data for the Basque Neolithic.

The oldest Neolithic evidence from the Basque Country seems to be from Level C in Abauntz Cave: 6,900 B.P. This level, with a small, laminar, nongeometric lithic assemblage (plus a ground stone ax), yielded sherds of crude, thick, undecorated red-brown pottery with coarse temper. It is of "Precardial" type, such as has been found further east in Chaves Cave (Huesca) at a similar date as well as at other sites in Mediterranean Spain (Utrilla 1982). There is no evidence of the presence of domesticated animals in this level. However, Level B4 (5,400 B.P.), which has a similar lithic assemblage and a mixture of simple crude sherds and finer, better fired ones, produced one metatarsal of a domesticated sheep or goat and a pelvis and two teeth of either a young boar or a domesticated pig (Altuna and Mariezkurrena 1982).

Montico de Charratu has a sequence of nongeometric and geometric Epipaleolithic assemblages; the uppermost shows the addition of ceramics without other notable changes in technology (Baldeón et al. 1983). The Neolithic of Los Husos (Alava) is undated, but it underlies an early Eneolithic level dated to 4,700 B.P. The Neolithic ceramics are incised and suggest an age of around 5,000 B.P. (Cava 1990). The Neolithic level (Level IV) has a mixed fauna with 59 remains of sheep or goat, 25 of cattle, 10 of pig, and similar quantities of red and roe deer, aurochs, and boar (plus others that could be either pig or boar and cattle or aurochs) (Altuna 1980).

Arenaza has a sequence of Azilian, geometric Epipaleolithic, early Neolithic, and Eneolithic levels. A polished stone axe was found in the level right below the oldest ceramic level (Level IC1) (Berganza 1990). That early Neolithic level yielded moderate numbers of remains of domesticated cattle, sheep or goat, and pig as well as red deer and traces of roe deer, aurochs, and boar (Altuna 1980). A higher level has decorated pottery; its fauna apparently has not been published. Marizulo (Guipúzcoa) has a single bone of a dog in its Level II which is either terminal Mesolithic or early Neolithic. The overlying level (Level I) yielded a human burial associated with a dog burial, together with 47 sheep or goat remains and many bones of wild animals. The dating of the burials (and possibly the level) is given by a radiocarbon determination as 5,300 B.P.— possibly late Neolithic (Altuna 1980).

Similarly, the early Neolithic of Zatoya (Level I), with a few plain sherds, has only a couple of dog remains. As in Marizulo II, the fauna is dominated by red deer and boar (K. Mariezkurrena 1990). The open-air early Neolithic site at Herriko Barra (coastal Guipúzcoa, 5,800 B.P.) has produced virtually only red deer remains and no domesticated animals (K. Mariezkurrena 1990). In the post-Azilian shell midden at Santimamiñe in Vizcaya (recently reclassified by Cava [1975] as "aceramic Neolithic" with geometric microliths) rare sheep remains had been reported (Aranzadi et al. 1931:87).

Where Is the Santanderine Neolithic?

Very little is known about the post-Azilian period in Santander, except for the appearance of Asturian sites (with or without *concheros*) along the western coast of the province. The small cave site of Tarrerón in the extreme east (right on the border of Vizcaya) has a basal level (Level III) dated to 5,800 B.P. (Apellániz 1971). It lacks ceramics and has a small lithic assemblage dominated by unretouched or simply utilized flakes, blades, and bladelets. There is one short endscraper, a notch, and a circle segment. There is a simple hearth. The presence of marine shells and nonlocal flint suggests that this may have been an ephemeral hunting camp. The unquantified faunal assemblage includes principally long-bone fragments of red deer and bovines. Apellániz (1971:97) suggests that primary butchering took place away from the cave. The site is in the mountainous interior, 20 km from the coast (ca. 28 km via the Ríos Calera and Asón). The upper levels at Tarrerón pertain to the Bronze Age. At La Peña del Perro above the mouth of the Río Asón, the uppermost level (an oyster and mussel shell midden) might pertain to the same period as the lower level at Tarrerón; to date it also lacks ceramics (González Morales 1990). Like other valleys in Santander, the Asón has several poorly dated dolmens.

Aside from a few late Neolithic or Eneolithic megalithic monuments in the mountains of Santander (González Sainz and González Morales 1986), little is known of the origins of domestication in this subregion. Perhaps the Atlantic inhabitants had adopted a few domesticated animals while continuing a mobile hunter-gatherer-fisher way of life, living in very small bands and leaving behind only minimal archeological remains that would be nearly invisible or totally lost if caves were not regularly used for habitation.

Even the succeeding Eneolithic period left few traces of habitation in Santander. A recent rescue excavation in the cave of El Ruso near the city of Santander revealed remnants of a burial with exquisitely decorated bell beaker pottery and stemmed stone arrowheads. This mortuary use of the cave (overlying a travertine and levels of Solutrean and Mousterian) probably dates to between 3,800 and 3,400 B.P. (uncalibrated), by comparison with Eneolithic materials from elsewhere on the Iberian Peninsula (Gavelas 1986). Interestingly, this age corresponds to palynological evidence of a sharp decrease in arboreal pollen percentages around 3,500 B.P. in the mountain bog of Ríofrio in Santander—possibly suggestive of deforestation by pastoralism (González Sainz and González Morales 1986:298). Other mortuary caves include La Peña del Fraile in

Santoña (González Morales 1990). Much work of all sorts is required before we can begin to understand the adoption of pastoralism by the Mesolithic foragers of this area. At present, any statements about this hole in our knowledge are rather speculative. Habitation sites, artifacts, dates, and faunal data all are lacking.

Shellfish and Sheep? The "Neolithic" of Asturias

Massive marine mollusk collection did not end in the Boreal in eastern Asturias. As noted above, there are radiocarbon dates of 5,900 and 4,600 B.P. for *concheros* at Les Pedroses and La Lloseta, respectively (Clark 1976). In addition, ceramics have been found in the *concheros* at Les Pedroses (together with both heavy-duty quartzite artifacts and a few flint blades) (González Morales 1982a). A few sherds also have been found in *concheros* at La Lloseta, Bricia, La Riera (Clark 1976) and at Mazaculos, Pendueles, El Arco, Las Cascaras, El Cueto, Las Lapas, and Recueva (González Morales 1982a). The last five of the *concheros* with ceramics are in western Santander; the other six are in eastern Asturias. The Mazaculos discoveries were made in the course of the modern excavation of a test pit at the entrance of the cave proper. There, an intact *conchero* deposit with an atypical pick and other heavy-duty and smaller tools and debitage yielded three sherds. The pieces of pottery (two of which refit) are thick, black, and handmade with coarse temper. They pertain to the base of a vessel (González Morales 1982a:107). At Pendueles, bowl fragments of black, coarse-tempered, smoothed, fairly fine pottery were recently found cemented onto the top of an Asturian *conchero* (with a classic pick) (González Morales 1982a:207,246). The ceramics found by Clark (1976:167) are described as "handmade", black, and plain (save one obvious intrusive, decorated Bronze Age sherd from Bricia [see Arias et al. 1986]).

The possible relationship between late Asturian *concheros* and coarse ceramics had been suggested by Vega del Sella (1921). He found ceramics at the top of the *conchero* in Cueto de la Mina that have recently been studied by Arias (1986) who suggests that systematic mollusk collection was still going on after the introduction of ceramics in eastern Asturias in poorly defined times between the Neolithic and the early Bronze Age. Asturian-like picks also have been found associated with ceramics in several sites near Biarritz (at the other end of the coast), dated to about 5,500 to 5,000 B.P. (Chauchat 1968, cited by González Morales 1982a:207).

Despite the presence of sherds and the recent dates, González Morales

(1982a:207) argues that the late *concheros* are like those of the late Preboreal and Boreal, with the same molluscan species and ungulates. Unfortunately, these cases have yet to be studied systematically. To my knowledge there is no study of the fauna from the test pit contents in Mazaculos that included the sherds. No domesticated animals have been cited in faunal lists from Asturian deposits (Clark 1976,1983; González Morales 1982a). Although the suid, bovine, and caprid remains *might* include domesticated forms, this has not been argued on any paleontological grounds. One would want to study remains specifically from *conchero* lenses containing pottery to test for the presence of domesticated animals.

The low plateaux along the southern edge of the narrow coastal plain of eastern Asturias, just inland of the string of Asturian *concheros*, are extremely rich in tumuli and open-air sites, recently documented and studied by Pérez and Arias (1979). Sepulchral caves (e.g., Trespando [Arias et al. 1986]) and dolmens (e.g., Santa Cruz [Blas 1979]) are located along the intermontane valley between the Picos de Europa and the coastal mountain range of eastern Asturias (in the same zone as the caves of Los Azules, El Buxú, and Llonín). The chronology of these manifestations is rather vague, although suggestions of Eneolithic and early Bronze Age seem reasonable. None of the tumuli or open-air sites on the coastal plain have been excavated (Pérez and Arias 1979). The open-air sites have yielded varied flint and quartzite assemblages including a few endscrapers, blades (including a so-called sickle element), geometric microliths, arrowheads, and a pick-like chopper (similar to the atypical pick found with the ceramics in nearby Mazaculos Cave). These sites have not produced any ceramics so far (probably for lack of excavation). In tombs excavated during the 1920s in two of the tumuli (next to the prominent "Peña Tu" rock outcrop with enigmatic carvings and paintings), several Asturian picks were found (González Morales 1982a:207–8; Blas 1979:757).

These discoveries strongly suggest that Asturian-type shellfish collection and pick manufacture were still going on when the tumuli were constructed in the immediate vicinity of (virtually overlooking) the coastal middens. Assuming that the builders of the tumuli were late Neolithic or Eneolithic pastoralists (for which there is no *prima facie* evidence), either there were two separate "cultures" living cheek-by-jowl in this very small subregion or, more likely, the "native" late Mesolithic groups of hunter-gatherer-fishers had simply added animal husbandry to their diversified subsistence repertoire. The consequences of that step in terms of changes in social and territorial relations seem manifested by the tumili, sepulchral caves, and dolmens. They are the visible signs of the beginnings of a more complex way of life that is beyond the scope of this book. And by the end of the Eneolithic, about 4,000 B.P. (uncalibrated), metallurgy appears, closing the Stone Age.

Data on the economic transition are scarce in the Basque Country, but they are almost absent in Santander and Asturias. The only subsistence data from Atlantic-age sites available so far indicate continued hunting and gathering. Even the argument that the megalithic monuments along the hills and mountains of those provinces were the work of pastoralists is based on an analogy with little-known phenomena in the Basque Country and Pyrenees. The traditional explanation for the appearance of the megaliths is the "spread" of pastoral people (see discussion in Blas and Fernández-Tresguerres 1989). But the situation in the homeland of the Asturian *concheros* suggests the gradual, *in situ* adoption of new technologies, subsistence, and funerary practices while use of the old diversified subsistence practices continued for several centuries after the introduction of ceramics and (presumably) domesticated animals. Northern Spain has always been known as a pastoral region (especially of goats and cattle) and, for obvious topographic and climatic reasons, not a major cereal-producer. The process of acquiring ceramics, possibly via interband contacts and trade-exchange networks along the coast reaching as far as the Basque Country, may have begun as early as about 6,000 B.P.

The construction of megaliths in western Santander and Asturias, whose presence would imply a major (although not yet total) change in local economy and social organization, may have been begun about 5,000 B.P. If not a wholly independent, local development (which seems unlikely, given the known distribution of megaliths in the Iberian Peninsula [Chapman 1981]), the monuments of Cantabrian Spain may have been emulations by essentially local people of *possibly* earlier monuments in the Ebro Valley and in Portugal (Andres 1990). Whatever the "origins" of the dolmens and tumuli, their implications in terms of the development of stratified societies and of new concepts of territorialism are significant. But, before elaborating complex models borrowed from other regions of megalithic Atlantic Europe, archeologists would do well to obtain hard dates, subsistence data, and evidence of human habitation from the Cantabrian region itself.

Conclusions

The adoption of "Neolithic" traits throughout the Cantabrian region was by no means rapid, simultaneous, or complete. This is probably a measure of the relative success of indigenous subsistence and social arrangements. Under the temperate, humid, densely forested conditions of the Atlantic period, Cantabrian hunter-gatherers continued to exploit the wide diversity of terrestrial, aquatic, and avian resources of the region's many habitats. They probably did so in the social context of small, territorially restricted, largely self-sufficient bands, maintaining informal contacts and relationships of mate exchange with neighboring bands.

Ceramics or knowledge of ceramic manufacturing appeared around 7,000 B.P. in the trans-Cordilleran part of the Basque Country, probably via band-to-band social contacts up the Ebro Valley and thence to the coastal Basque area. Such a route is suggested by the chronological evidence of earlier ceramics in eastern Spain and Mediterranean France (Languedoc-Provence) and by the absence of early Neolithic evidence in extreme southwestern France. Ceramics appear in several Basque sites before the verified appearance of domesticated animals. When domesticated animals do appear in the late Neolithic of several Basque sites, they are sheep or goat, cattle, and pig as well as dog. All of these except sheep, could have been domesticated locally from wild stock (which does not mean that they were). And, not only in late Neolithic contexts but also in the Eneolithic (Chalcolithic) and Bronze Age, wild game (red and roe deer, aurochs and boar) continued to be hunted, sometimes in substantial quantities (Altuna 1980; K. Mariezkurrena 1990). However, the late Neolithic/Eneolithic faunas do show substantial dependence on sheep or goat, followed by cattle. This mixed foraging-cum-pastoral economy seems to have been responsible for the construction of the first megalithic monuments in the Basque region (Andres 1990).

Farther from the apparent "Mediterranean stimuli" (a term I shudder to use) than the Basque Country groups, the hunter-gatherer-fisher bands of western Santander and eastern Asturias seem to have begun to acquire ceramics (through down-the-line contacts and exchanges) perhaps by about 6,000 B.P., although this is entirely vague. It is conceivable that ceramic vessels, both there and in the Basque Country, constituted objects of prestige because of their novelty and rarity. In any event, the appearance of a few pots does not seem to have changed the adaptations of the resident bands who continued collecting plant foods and shellfish (*à la* Asturian) and hunting and fishing (*à la* Azilian) throughout most of the Atlantic, as they had in late Preboreal and Boreal.

The phenomenon of tumuli and dolmens is a widespread one throughout Santander and Asturias (as well as Galicia). Its relationship to late Neolithic or Eneolithic pastoralism is hypothetical but likely. The presence of these monuments by the end of the Atlantic period still did not mean the end of shellfishing and hunting, at least in eastern Asturias.

There, a complementary relationship between late *concheros* and mega-lithic sites seems likely, albeit very poorly understood as is seen in general discussions of the phenomena (González Morales 1982a; González Sainz and González Morales 1986; Blas 1979; Blas and Fernández-Tresguerres 1989). In terms of cereal agriculture and even full-blown pastoralism, northern Spain was clearly a peripheral area of the *Mediterranean* Neo-lithic world. This is a testament to its richly diverse *Atlantic* adaptations, developed in response to changing demographic and physical environments over the course of a long, local Old Stone Age.

After this work was in proof, P. Arias (1991) published a description of human burials associated with an aceramic Epipaleolithic industry in Los Canes Cave, in the intermontane valley of eastern Asturias. Four AMS-radiocarbon dates on human bones range between 6,900 and 6,200 B.P. (Appendix E1), thus overlapping with ones from late Asturian *concheros* at La Riera and Bricia in the nearby coastal zone of the same region, as well as with Neolithic dates from Abauntz and Zatoya in northern Navarra. These important finds confirm the complex variety of adaptive poses that co-existed during the Atlantic period in Vasco-Cantabria.

Chapter 10

REFLECTIONS

IT is my hope that this book has shown the record of human settlement and adaptations in Cantabrian Spain to be long, rich, and complex. Although generally considered part of the larger Franco-Cantabrian cultural province (especially in the Upper Paleolithic), the Cantabrian region has distinctive characteristics in terms of settlement patterns, mobility strategies, lithic technology, faunal exploitation, artistic expression, details and timing of cultural sequence, and so on.

The purpose of this book has been to present a large amount of information from environmental and cultural records that span at least 100,000 years. It has done so by summarizing and synthetisizing the results of more than a century of excavations and analyses by Spanish and other prehistorians and natural scientists. Although by no means complete, the bibliography gives the interested reader a point of entry into the vast (and, in North America and Britain, often difficult to obtain) literature on Cantabrian Spain. The emphasis, obviously, has been on the more recent research, but in the context of solid earlier work.

I hope I have not done too much injustice to the work and opinions of my Spanish colleagues by interspersing my own results and interpretations. Let the reader judge whether my points of view are defensible, or at least plausible. If I have succeeded, readers will at least have another data base for contrast with the well-known, easily accessible record of the Périgord.

This book is but one of many recent attempts to show the points of variability among regional adaptive systems within the European continent—both during specific "time slices" and diachronically. By developing such regional prehistories and increasingly using chronometric dating methods free of the tautologies of "dating-by-the-artifacts," stu-

241

dents of the Stone Age will be able to make comparisons across time and space at the appropriate level, that of regional adaptive systems.

I have struggled to address issues with which I am less comfortable, the Acheulean, the Mousterian, and the Neolithic, because I have had relatively little firsthand experience excavating or analyzing them. I also include cave and mobile art among these issues: although I am very familiar with the phenomena, as a "bones-and-stones" "dirt archeologist", I am leery of grand interpretive schemes that somehow want us to enter into the minds of long-dead people. I hope I have at least provided enough evidence so that readers can grasp the nature of the problems and appreciate some of the main interpretive tendencies of the present and the past. It also will be apparent that my functionalist, cultural-materialist, processual perspective influences most of my interpretations. I have tried to show the importance of social arrangements and relationships in explaining aspects of adaptive change and art, but I must confess that I believe hunter-gatherers and pastoralists are likely to put their stomachs first. Thus subsistence and technology are foundations upon which sociological and ideological phenomena rest, even if these phenomena are crucial in making the whole system run and, perhaps, in justifying or legitimizing it.

Any book of this type—one that simplifies a complex, imperfectly known record to tell a story about human history in a particular region—runs the risk of telling a big lie. That lie is the impression that all adaptations were successes. The countless individuals and human bands that inhabited the Cantabrian region probably more or less continuously at least since the Last Interglacial undoubtedly made many mistakes. Sometimes those failures led to individual or even group extinction. And yet, over the long run human habitation was successful in evolutionary terms. Indeed, the record suggests that over time, in facing new challenges and new permutations of old ones, people developed strategies (no doubt by trial-and-error) for minimizing the risk of failure. These strategies involved increasingly specialized technologies, carefully planned, organized, and timed uses of an increasing variety of the region's diverse resources, social and artistic systems for gathering, storing and transmitting important survival information (cybernetics), and all manner of buffering mechanisms (social, mobility-based, diversity-related).

Lest I leave the impression that I believe in some teleological, vitalistic idea of progress, I hasten to add that the adaptive changes that took place over scores of millennia in this (or any) region tended to have cumulative effects. We see them in retrospect, and they seem to be directional. That is a problem of perspective, particularly because archeologists must focus on material remains of technology and because the Cantabrian region is still occupied by people who are affected by antecedent uses of their distinctive landscape and resources, even in the post-industrial age. Over the course of time and with many false starts that tend to be invisible in the remote archeological record, people did develop fine-tuned ways of living in the physical environments of each major climatic phase of the late Quaternary, given their contemporary levels of population density. I cannot escape that fundamental belief.

Fundamentally this book has told the story of how people continually readjusted to circumstances to survive in the Cantabrian region, given the conditions of each period. Those conditions obviously are better known (and therefore better controlled, analytically) for the recent times. So the reconstructions I present for the Acheulean, the Mousterian, and even the early Upper Paleolithic are clearly more tentative than those I suggest for the late Upper Paleolithic and the Mesolithic. However, it is surprising how little we really know, not about environments but about human economies and societies at the end of the Stone Age, at the time of the appearance of food production. This is a reflection in part of the interests of regional prehistorians over the past century, obviously attracted to the glories of the late Upper Paleolithic.

A final word of explanation concerns my continued use of archeological terms such as "Acheulean," "Solutrean," "Asturian," and "Neolithic." I use them purely for convenience and so that communication be as clear as possible. These culture-stratigraphic unit names, the heritage of de Mortillet and Lubbock, are of unequal value and uncertain reality in terms of actual self-identifying ethnic groups or cultures. I have made my position clear on this issue (Straus 1987c), but I am convinced that the names provide a necessary shorthand for facilitating communication among prehistorians. We may be stuck with them but, so long as we do not believe too firmly in their reality or purely ethnic nature, we can use them to aid in discourse. I have completely eschewed subdivisions of these basic culture-stratigraphic units because I am convinced that they are bereft of *temporal* validity. However, there is a significant amount of roughly contemporaneous interassemblage variability within each of the basic traditional units.

In closing, a few words should be said about what I think needs to be done in continuing Cantabrian paleo-anthropological research. First, it is apparent that there is and will continue to be a certain amount of theoretical tension between the historiographic/art historical/phylogenetic approaches of many regional prehistorians and the social science/natural science/cultural evolution perspectives that characterize others (especially the Anglo-American contributors to the debate). Rather than wishing that one theoretical tendency ("paradigm") triumph over the other, I hope the debate continues. It is natural that the specialists who are closest to the data—the natives—tend to accentuate particularistic and humanistic studies of what they perceive as "their" prehistory. So too is it natural that outsiders view the record from a somewhat more distant, generalizing, comparative point of view. Both approaches are valid. In recent years the theoretical discussion between the two paradigms has led to very fruitful international, interdisciplinary research projects such as those at La Riera and El Juyo as well as long-term individual collaborations (e.g., González Echegaray and Freeman; Altuna and myself). The cross-fertilization of the two paradigms is also apparent in recent volumes, such as the study by González Sainz (1989) of the late Magdalenian and, perhaps, the present book. I hope that the intensity and content of transatlantic communication can be increased and formalized.

At the practical and empirical levels, I make the following specific suggestions.

1. Concerted efforts need to be made to try to locate buried open-air sites (by systematic core-boring and by monitoring road, foundation, gravel pit, and other large-scale excavations). However, because of the high rate of erosion in the region, I am not sanguine that the present massive bias in favor of Paleolithic *cave* sites is likely to change significantly. Nonetheless, the discovery and careful documentation of at least a limited sample of open-air sites would greatly expand our perspectives on prehistoric settlement, activities, mobility, population levels, and so on. Subregional surveys, such as those conducted by the Universidad de Oviedo in the Nalón Valley and by the Sociedad de Ciencias Aranzadi in Guipúzcoa, should be multiplied, and excavations should be coordinated around major thematic problems.

2. Caves ought to be deeply tested (to bedrock if possible), in attempts to augment the current very small samples of early Upper, Middle, and especially Lower Paleolithic sites in the region (or at least, if the results of such tests are negative, to confirm the apparently low densities of regional human population during those periods).

3. More refined and more precise dating methods (e.g., AMS radiocarbon dating of charcoal, individual amino acids from bones, rock art pigments, as well as uranium series dating of travertines) need to be used to try to resolve some of the problems of apparent "cultural overlaps" suggested in this book (E.g., Solutrean/Magdalenian, Magdalenian/Azilian, Azilian/Asturian, Asturian/Neolithic). In addition, with more independent, chronometric dates, we could begin to tackle questions of the rates of adaptive change in different prehistoric periods (the issue of punctuated equilibria versus gradualism in cultural evolution) and differences in rates among regions and subregions. With a more complete

web of dates, the artifact assemblages could be liberated further from their imprecise (and sometimes erroneous) role as temporal indicators. Thus, we could begin to make temporally high-resolution, synchronic comparisons among sites in different habitats to reconstruct more meaningful regional adaptive systems. And we could make diachronic comparisons of changes in system state with greater degrees of confidence that the objects of our comparisons (assemblages from separate sites) indeed pertain to specific target time slices. Furthermore, systematic attempts must continue to date the Mousterian and the Middle Paleolithic–Early Upper Paleolithic transition, especially in light of Bischoff's recent and provocative results from El Castillo and sites in Catalonia.

4. Efforts ought to continue to find and petrographically "fingerprint" lithic raw material sources. This kind of evidence will be crucial to test hypotheses on prehistoric mobility strategies and territories.

5. The application of lithic microwear studies needs to be expanded and made more routine, although, because many of the stone tools are made on quartzite and other nonflint materials, the results may not always be very conclusive.

6. Cadres of faunal analysts of all kinds need to be trained. This would permit the speedier publication of basic identifications *and* the routinization of more in-depth studies of seasonality, hunting strategies and tactics, body parts, and prehistoric economic decision-making.

7. Stable isotope studies need to be done on the few available Paleolithic and Mesolithic human bone scraps to obtain tentative indications of the relative proportions of plant, terrestrial animal, and marine animal contributions to diet at different periods. And such analyses need to be conducted systematically on the more abundant late Neolithic/ Eneolithic and Bronze Age skeletons to monitor the appearance and relative importance (if any) of agricultural products (e.g., cereals) across time and among subregions.

8. An intense effort must be made to locate, excavate, chronometrically date, and thoroughly analyze Neolithic and Eneolithic sites (especially nonfunerary sites, although the tumuli and dolmens really ought to receive more systematic, in-depth attention as well). Little is known about the nature of the process and the extent of adoption of food production economies in the Cantabrian region, or about their socioeconomic consequences in the subsequent Bronze Age.

9. Serious protection must be provided for all cave art sites. Many have been seriously damaged by the effects of tourism (which has led to the closing of some caves and serious restrictions on visitation at Altamira) or by deliberate vandalism. More must be done to make cave art replicas and to interpret the art for the Spanish and international tour-

ist public that increasingly besieges the caves. Continued efforts to ameliorate the relations and coordination of regional speleologists and prehistorians are needed to systematize the search for documentation and protection of art and archeological sites in caves. A panregional center for the protection, documentation, and study of cave art (perhaps under the aegis of the Ministry of Culture) would be most useful, if archeopolitical jurisdictional problems among the autonomous regions of Euskadi, Cantabria, and Asturias can be resolved successfully. Such a center would assemble and curate copies of all extant film and drawn records of the cave art and would arrange for filming and tracing of all figures for which an adequate record does not already exist.

10. Modernization of museum facilities, including laboratories, storage areas, and displays is needed to safeguard their irreplaceable collections, to facilitate research, and to allow the very interested modern regional and international populations to enter the mysterious and fascinating world of the Stone Age Cantabrians and prehistoric archeologists.

Most importantly, these suggested actions must not take place in a theoretical void. Data cannot be meaningfully collected without a fairly explicit justification in terms of significant problems. Thus, the continuing dialogue among researchers (and between them and the interested public) must continue and increase. Even if we all have different perspectives, we all must recognize that the Stone Age archeological record is finite and endangered. So it must be used wisely to provide the greatest possible information relevant to different kinds of research problems and public interests.

The goal of my research in Cantabrian Spain and elsewhere in southwestern Europe—like that of all prehistorians—is to attempt to explain differences and similarities among archeological assemblages and, in so doing, to try to understand the lives of people who can no longer speak for themselves. If I have succeeded here, the reader will agree that the Stone Age inhabitants of Cantabrian Spain produced an unsurpassed record of cultural activity, including phenomena such as the cave art of Altamira, that happily will never lose their aura of mystery and awe—perhaps despite the best efforts of scientific archeology to "explain" them! In this corner of Iberia before the Iberians, there is material enough, if carefully used, for at least another century of archeological research and debate, and for enduring regional pride.

Appendix A1 Mousterian Faunas, by Site and Level

Site:	Morín			El Pendo							
Level:	17	16	15	XVIc	XVIb	XVIa	XV	XIV	XI–XIII	IX	VIIId
Taxa:											
Sus	2(1)	—	—	—	—	—	—	—	—	—	—
Cervus	142(5)	3(1)	6(1)	2(1)	50(4)	185(10)	3(1)	9(1)	10(2)	29(4)	46(1)
Capreolus	15(3)	—	2(2)	—	1(1)	17(?)	—	—	—	—	2(1)
Megaloceros	—	—	—	—	—	9(1)	—	—	—	—	—
Bovini	215(6)	8(1)	2(1)	?(2)	?(3)	24(11)	46(?)	4(1)	6(2)	1(1)	2(1)
Bison	—	—	—	—	—	1(1)	—	—	—	—	—
Capra	1(1)	—	—	—	—	1(1)	—	—	—	—	—
Equus	124(7)	5(1)	1(1)	7(1)	13(3)	67(3)	1(1)	6(1)	4(1)	—	—
Dicerorhinus	4(2)	—	—	—	—	—	—	—	—	—	—
Ursus spelaeus	—	—	—	—	—	—	—	—	—	—	1(1)
Crocuta	2(1)	—	—	—	—	1(1)	—	—	—	—	—
Canis lupus	1(2)	—	—	—	—	—	—	—	—	—	—

Site:	Lezetxiki								Amalda
Level:	VIII	VII	VI	Vb	Va	IVc	IVb	IVa	VII
Taxa:									
Sus	—	—	—	—	—	—	—	—	—
Cervus	—	1(1)	26(2)	11(2)	48(4)	36(4)	21(2)	33(2)	150(5)
Rangifer	—	—	—	—	—	1(1)	—	—	—
Capreolus	—	1(1)	8(2)	—	14(3)	2(1)	1(1)	—	3(3)
Megaloceros	—	—	4(1)	—	—	—	—	—	—
Bovini	28(3)	13(4)	196(6)	—	23(2)	5(1)	6(1)	18(3)	58(3)

(continued)

Appendix A1 Mousterian Faunas, by Site and Level *(continued)*

Taxa	Lezetxiki					Amalda	Axlor VIII	Axlor VII	Axlor VI–V	Axlor IV	Axlor III
Capra	7(2)	4(1)	2(1)	2(2)	—	61(5)	—	—	2(1)	—	—
Rupicapra	9(1)	14(3)	10(1)	7(1)	2(1)	536(16)	—	—	15(2)	—	—
Equus	—	1(1)	—	—	—	48(4)	—	—	12(3)	—	—
Dicerorhinus	2(1)	—	—	—	—	—	1(1)	4(1)	3(1)	—	—
Ursus arctos	1(1)	—	—	—	—	—	—	—	54(2)	—	—
U. spelaeus	21(3)	15(2)	40(4)	334(16)	76(3)	58(5)	99(3)	253(6)	757(13)	—	—
Crocuta	—	—	—	—	—	3(2)	—	—	—	—	—
Cuon	—	—	—	—	—	1(1)	—	—	—	—	—
Canis lupus	2(1)	—	4(2)	9(1)	3(1)	17(3)	—	2(1)	15(2)	—	—
Vulpes	1(1)	—	—	2(1)	—	29(2)	—	—	9(2)	—	—
Meles	—	—	—	—	—	—	—	—	2(2)	—	—
Mustela spp.	2(2)	—	—	—	—	—	—	—	—	—	—
Lynx	—	—	—	—	—	—	—	—	2(1)	—	—
Felis silvestris	—	2(1)	—	2(1)	—	—	—	—	—	—	—
Panthera pardus	9(1)	—	—	—	—	—	—	—	9(1)	—	—
P. spelaea	—	—	—	—	—	3(1)	1(1)	1(1)	128(2)	—	—
Site: Axlor — Level:							**VIII**	**VII**	**VI–V**	**IV**	**III**
Sus							1	—	1	—	—
Cervus							120	23	316	137	18
Rangifer							—	—	—	1	1
Capreolus							1	—	1	—	—

Megaloceros	—	—	—	—	—
Bovini	2	3	61	171	35
Capra	23	22	117	193	38
Rupicapra	13	8	75	12	1
Equus	3	—	23	72	41
Dicerorhinus	—	—	—	—	—
Ursus arctos	—	—	—	—	—
U. spelaeus	—	—	1	3	—
Crocuta	—	—	—	—	—
Cuon	—	—	—	—	—
Canis lupus	—	—	3	1	—
Vulpus	—	—	—	3	—
Meles	—	—	—	1	—
Mustela spp.	—	—	—	—	—
Lynx	—	—	1	—	—
Felis silvestris	—	—	—	—	—
Panthera pardus	—	—	—	—	—
P. spelaea	—	—	—	—	—

Note: numerals are numbers of identified species (NISP); numerals in parentheses are minimum numbers of individuals (MNI).
Sources: Altuna 1971, 1972, 1973, 1989, 1990c; Fuentes 1980.

Appendix A2 Mousterian Lithic Assemblages, by Site and Level

Site:	El Pendo					El Castillo		Flecha	Hornos
Level:	XVI	XIV	XIII	XII–XI	VIIId	22	20	—	—
Flake tools, no.	174	49	49	99	58	3,200	2,360	378	94
Denticulates, %	48.3	12.2	16.3	51.5	37.9	16.3	31.8	57.5	23.4
Sidescrapers, %	26.4	57.1	51.0	13.1	20.7	65.7	43.7	11.6	53.2
True bifaces, no.	1	—	—	—	—	7	31	1	2
Cleavers, no.	—	—	2	—	—	1	303	—	—

Site:	Morín						El Conde	
Level:	17 inf.	17	16	15	14–13	12	E	D
Flake tools, no.	97	377	311	101	91	263	132	386
Denticulates, %	33.7	28.4	20.6	23.2	41.2	40.8	17.2	62.2
Sidescrapers, %	7.5	23.4	36.0	45.0	29.9	5.0	46.9	10.6
True bifaces, no.	—	1	4	—	—	—	1	1
Cleavers, no.	—	12	12	2	—	—	—	—

Site:	Amalda	Lezetxiki			Axlor					
Level:	VII	VI	Vb	IVc	VIII	VII	VI	V	IV	III
Flake tools, no.	180	?	?	?	?	?	47	?	?	?
Denticulates, %	26.5	30.7	26	7	9	15	13	15	10	10.6
Sidescrapers, %	41.1	36.2	36	66	76	65	76	74	77	81
True bifaces, no.	2	?	?	?	?	?	?	?	?	?
Cleavers, no.	1	?	?	?	?	?	?	?	?	?

Note: Flake tools = "essential" count (not including unretouched Levallois flakes or use-nibbled flakes).
Sources: Baldeón 1990a,b; Freeman 1964, 1971, 1973, 1977, 1980; Freeman and González Echegaray 1968.

Appendix B1 Relative Frequencies of Middle Paleolithic Tool Types
Found in Early Upper Paleolithic Levels

El Castillo		El Otero	
Level	Percent	Level	Percent
18	6.82	8	31.25
16	17.44	6	26.46
14	9.02	5	10.81
12	29.85	4	15.08
Morín		**El Pendo**	
Level	Percent	Level	Percent
10	38.10	VIIIb	48.60
9	26.70	VIIIa	39.10
8b	20.30	VIII	59.50
8a	24.90	VII	14.10
8R	32.20	VI	12.30
7	28.47	Vb	8.70
6	22.32	Va	9.80
5l	20.10	V	9.30
5u	14.36	IV	16.60
4	18.80	III	16.10
El Conde		**El Cierro**	
Level	Percent	Level	Percent
4	77.48	7	12.69
2	62.27	6	6.66
1	65.09		
Bolinkoba		**Amalda**	
Level	Percent	Level	Percent
F	7.60	VI	21.41
		V	8.82

Note: This summary includes: Type 74, notch; Type 75, denticulate; Type 77,
sidescraper.

Appendix B2 Relative Frequencies of Upper Paleolithic Lithic
Tool Types Found in Middle Paleolithic Levels

El Pendo			Morín	
Level	Percent		Level	Percent
XVI	13.21		17l	29.40
XIV	20.40		17	22.00
XIII	14.28		16	17.70
XII/XI	20.20		15	13.10
VIIId	13.80		14/13	11.00
			12	20.20
			11	17.00

El Conde			El Castillo	
Level	Percent		Level	Percent
9/8	15.61		22	11.25
6	15.87		20	8.53
4	20.77		Amalda	
			VII	17.75

Note: This summary includes: Type 30, typical endscraper; Type 31, atypical endscraper; Type 32, typical burin; Type 33, atypical burin; Type 34, typical borer; Type 35, atypical borer; Type 36, backed knife; Type 37, atypical backed knife; Type 38, natural backed knife; Type 39, raclette.

Appendix B3 Relative Frequencies of Lithic Raw Material Types in Cantabrian Mousterian and Early Upper Paleolithic Assemblages, by Sites and Levels

Percentages

El Conde

Site:					
Level:	9/8	6	4	2	1
Attribution*:	M	M	A	A	A
Flint	—	—	—	—	—
Quartzite	100.0	100.0	100.0	100.0	100.0
Quartz	—	—	—	—	—
Ophite	—	—	—	—	—

El Cierro

Site:		
Level:	7	6
Attribution:	A	A
Flint	18.75	—
Quartzite	81.25	—

Morín

Site:										
Level:	17	16	15	10	9	8b	7	6	51/u	4
Attribution:	M	M	M	C	A	A	A	A	A/G	G
Flint	67.7	56.8	65.9	78.2	82.3	90.5	93.7	93.7	93.3	77.8
Quartzite	11.6	16.1	14.0	13.4	11.0	5.6	3.4	2.1	2.2	6.0
Quartz	0.1	0.1	0.2	0.6	2.7	3.9	1.7	2.2	3.8	15.7
Ophite	20.6	25.3	17.7	7.9	4.0	—	1.1	1.9	0.5	0.5

Appendix B3 Relative Frequencies of Lithic Raw Material Types in Cantabrian Mousterian and Early Upper Paleolithic Assemblages, by Sites and Levels (continued)

El Pendo

Level:	XVI	XIV	XIII	XII–XI	VIIId	VIIIb	VIIIa	VIII	VII
Attribution:	M	M	M	M	M	A	A	C	A
Flint	79.7	50.9	41.4	51.2	57.9	62.9	86.5	98.7	89.1
Quartzite	15.9	32.5	42.5	35.9	27.6	34.3	16.9	—	5.7
Quartz	0.3	0.3	0.6	1.5	0.7	—	—	—	4.7
Ophite	3.6	16.0	15.5	11.4	13.7	2.9	1.6	1.3	0.5

Level:	VI	Vb	Va	V	IV	III
Attribution:	A	A	G	G	A	A
Flint	97.9	95.7	94.4	93.7	88.9	90.5
Quartzite	2.1	4.3	1.4	6.2	1.0	5.6
Quartz	—	—	4.2	—	10.1	3.9

El Castillo

Level:	22	20	18	16	14	12
Attribution:	M	M	A	A	G	G
Flint	44.5	60.4	41.9	59.2	67.6	93.3
Quartzite	48.4	37.0	51.4	29.6	15.7	3.3
Other	7.1	2.6	6.7	11.1	16.7	3.3

Site:	Amalda		
Level:	VII	VI	V
Attribution:	M	G	G
Flint	85.5	93.2	100
Quartzite	1.7	2.1	—
Quartz	—	0.4	—
Ophite	1.3	1.1	—
Others	7.3	3.2	—

*M, Mousterian; C, Chatelperronian; A, Aurignacian; G, Gravettian.

Appendix B4 Lithic Tool Indices of Cantabrian Early Upper Paleolithic, by Sites and Levels

Site:	El Conde			El Cierro		El Castillo			
Level:	4	2	1	7	6	18	16	14	12
Attribution[a]	A	A	A	A	A	A	A	G	G
Index[b]									
GA	6.32	3.30	5.40	30.20	40.70	28.89	19.76	13.10	6.70
GP	0.60	3.30	0.50	6.30	8.60	2.21	3.49	11.50	6.70
IGA	6.30	3.30	5.20	30.20	40.70	21.27	18.60	9.80	3.70
IB	1.60	10.60	8.90	22.20	6.20	10.41	11.63	25.40	15.70
IBd	1.40	6.20	4.50	15.90	4.90	7.17	9.31	13.10	6.70
IBt	0.00	0.00	1.10	6.30	1.20	1.16	0.00	3.30	4.50
IG	12.90	11.00	14.50	44.40	66.70	35.49	33.71	32.80	12.70
n =	364	273	441	62	81	865	86	122	134

Site:	El Pendo									
Level:	VIIIb	VIIIa	VIII	VII	VI	Vb	Va	V	IV	III
Attribution:	A	A	C	A	A	A	G	G	A	A
Index										
GA	14.30	15.30	6.30	30.40	14.50	10.10	5.60	12.50	12.40	7.20
GP	0.00	8.50	6.30	4.20	5.50	2.90	9.90	37.50	2.80	1.70
IGA	14.30	11.60	2.50	21.20	13.10	8.70	2.80	12.50	11.50	7.20
IB	8.60	11.60	10.10	21.70	46.20	56.50	63.40	21.90	43.50	41.10
IBd	2.90	9.50	5.10	13.30	37.20	40.60	47.90	6.20	32.60	22.80
IBt	2.90	1.10	1.30	4.70	3.40	13.00	9.90	3.10	3.90	7.20
IG	22.90	21.70	16.50	40.00	17.90	14.50	7.00	21.90	21.10	19.40
n =	35	189	79	405	145	69	71	32	356	180

Morín

Index	10	9	8b	8a	8R	7	6	51	5u	4
Level:	10	9	8b	8a	8R	7	6	51	5u	4
Attribution:	C	A	A	A	A	A	A	A	G	G
GA	6.00	11.80	11.90	21.40	12.20	19.40	23.10	16.90	13.70	8.80
GP	7.50	3.40	4.20	0.90	1.70	2.70	3.70	4.80	28.70	20.70
IGA	5.40	9.30	7.60	17.90	11.10	15.00	17.00	12.10	12.30	6.50
IB	12.10	9.30	5.10	8.90	6.00	14.80	11.00	21.20	11.60	13.80
IBd	9.20	5.80	5.10	6.20	5.30	12.20	7.00	15.80	8.90	10.10
IBt	0.60	0.50	0.00	0.90	0.40	1.40	1.10	3.60	2.00	1.80
IG	13.60	25.30	11.90	25.00	22.70	33.30	34.00	30.90	22.50	16.20
n =	520	206	118	112	465	346	618	164	146	217

	El Otero			Amalda		Bolinkoba
Site:						
Level:	6	5	4	VI	V	F
Attribution:	A	A	A	G	G	G
Index						
GA	20.58	2.70	15.90	9.26	2.9	6.99
GP	2.95	0.00	5.66	8.87	37.25	10.18
IGA	14.70	0.00	4.71	3.92	1.96	5.20
IB	8.82	29.72	19.81	41.07	25.5	25.9
IBd	5.88	10.81	10.37	3.21	3.9	6.70
IBT	0.00	10.81	8.49	7.48	15.68	2.07
IG	26.47	10.81	27.35	8.57	2.97	24.14
n =	34	37	106	280	102	670

[a] A = Aurignacian; C = Chatelperronian; G = Gravettian

[b] GA = all characteristically "Aurignacian" tools, or endscrapers, "strangled" blades, and those with scalar, invasive retouch; GP = all characteristically "Périgordian" tools, or blades and bladelets with abruptly backed edges, including Gravette points and Chatelperron knives; IGA = "Aurignacian" types of [thick, keeled, and nosed] endscrapers; IB = all burins; IBd = dihedral burins; IBt = truncation burins, not including the Noailles burins abundant in many of the Basque assemblages; IG is the combined percentage of all endscrapers.

Sources: Freeman 1977; Cabrera 1984; González Echegaray 1978, 1980; Bernaldo de Quirós 1982; González Echegaray, et al. 1966.

Appendix B5 Relative Frequencies of Gravettian and Aurignacian Lithic Tool Types in Cantabrian Early Upper Paleolithic Assemblages, by Sites and Levels

Percents

El Conde

Level:	4	2	1
Attribution[a]:	A	A	A
Type[b]			
Chatelperron knives	—	—	—
Gravettes	—	—	—
Noailles burins	—	—	—
Dufour bladelets	—	—	—

El Cierro

Level:	7	6
Attribution:	A	A
Chatelperron knives	1.6	—
Gravettes	—	—
Noailles burins	—	—
Dufour bladelets	1.6	1.2

Morín

Level:	10	9	8b	8a	8R	7	6	51	5u	4
Attribution:	C	A	A	A	A	A	A	A	G	G
Chatelperron knives	1.9	—	0.8	—	0.4	—	0.2	—	3.4	—
Gravettes	—	—	—	—	—	—	0.2	—	9.6	1.4

	VIIIb	VIIIa	VIII	VII	VI	Vb	Va	V	IV	III
Noailles burins	—	—	—	—	—	—	—	—	—	0.5
Dufour bladelets	0.2	6.3	21.2	15.2	1.9	2.3	4.8	3.0	4.8	0.9

El Pendo

Level:	VIIIb	VIIIa	VIII	VII	VI	Vb	Va	V	IV	III
Attribution:	A	A	C	A	A	A	G	G	A	A
Chatelperron knives	—	2.1	3.8	1.5	0.5	—	—	—	—	—
Gravettes	—	—	—	—	—	—	—	—	—	—
Noailles burins	—	—	—	0.5	—	—	—	—	—	—
Dufour bladelets	—	—	—	0.8	1.4	1.5	—	3.0	1.4	1.1

El Otero

Level:	8	6	5	4
Attribution:	A	A	A	A
Chatelperron knives	—	—	—	—
Gravettes	—	—	—	—
Noailles burins	—	—	—	—
Defour bladelets	—	—	—	0.9

El Castillo

Level:	18	16	14	12
Attribution:	A	A	G	G
Chatelperron knives	0.1	—	—	—
Gravettes	—	—	1.6	—
Noailles burins	—	—	0.8	—
Dufour bladelets	—	—	—	—

(continued)

Appendix B5 Relative Frequencies of Gravettian and Aurignacian Lithic Tool Types in Cantabrian Early Upper Paleolithic Assemblages, by Sites and Levels (*continued*)

Bolinkoba

Level:	F
Attribution:	G
Chatelperron knives	—
Gravettes	5.7
Noailles burins	16.0
Dufour bladelets	—

Amalda

Level:	VI	V
Attribution:	G	G
Chatelperron knives	—	—
Gravettes	0.35	5.88
Noailles burins	3.9	28.2
Dufour bladelets	2.14	—

[a] A = Aurignacian, C = Chatelperronian; G = Gravettian
[b] Tool types: Chatelperronian knives, 46 and 47; Gravettes, 48, 49, 50/51; Noailles burins, 42; Dufour bladelets, 90.

Appendix B6 Early Upper Paleolithic Ungulate and Carnivore Faunas in Vasco-Cantabrian Spain, by Site and Level

Sites:	Riera	Conde			Rascaño			Pendo									Amalda	
Levels:	1	4	3	1	9	8	7	VIIIb	VIII	VII	VI	Vb	Va	V	IV	III	VI	V
Attribution:	?	A	A	A	A	A	A	A	C	A	A	A	G	G	A	A	G	G?
Taxa																		
1. Equus caballus	5	1	1	1	1				1	3	1		1	1	1	3	6	3
2. Capra pyrenaica	4	1	2	3	1	3	2				1						7	8
3. Rupicapra rupicapra	1				1	1											59	35
4. Bos/Bison	4			1	1	1		1		1	1	1	1	1	1	3	4	3
5. Capreolus capreolus	1							1		1	1		1				2	1
6. Cervus elaphus	7		2	2	2			2	1	5	7	1	4	5	8	12	6	5
7. Megaloceros sp.											1							
8. Dama sp.																		
9. Rangifer tarandus																	1	
10. Sus scrofa																		1
11. Dicerorhinus kirchbergensis																1	2	
12. Coelodonta antiquitatis																		
13. Mammuthus primigenius																		
14. Elephas antiquus																		
15. Panthera pardus																	1	1
16. P. leo																		1
17. P. spelaea										1								
18. Felis silvestris														1				
19. Lynx lynx/spelaea											1							
20. Canis lupus			1					1		1	1						3	1
21. Vulpes vulpes																	3	2
22. Alopex lagopus																	1	2
23. Cuon alpinus																	1	1
24. Crocuta crocuta								1		1								
25. Ursus spelaeus										1					1		7	4
26. U. arctos															1			
27. Gulo gulo																		
28. Mustela spp.							1											2

(continued)

Appendix B6 Early Upper Paleolithic Ungulate and Carnivore Faunas in Vasco-Cantabrian Spain, by Site and Level (*continued*)

Sites:	Cueva Morín									Bolinkoba	Lezetxiki		Aitzbitarte	Ekain				Castillo				
Levels:	10	9	8	8	7	6	5i	5s	4	F	IIIA	II	IV	10a	9b	9a	8	18	16	14	13	12
Attribution:	C	A	A	A	A	A	A	G	G	G	?	G	A	C?	?	?	?	A	A	G	?	G
Taxa																						
1. Equus caballus	1	1	3	2	1	2	3	4	4	(32)	2	3	1	2	16	11	2	a	a	a	p	a
2. Capra pyrenaica			1			1	2	3	3	(634)			2	4			5	p	p	p		p
3. Rupicapra rupicapra							1	1		(32)	12	8	5					p	p	p	p	p
4. Bos/Bison	1		3		2	4	3	3	2	(37)			5	4	6	5	1	29	p	11		a
5. Capreolus capreolus		1	1		1	4	6	5	4	(3)	1	2	2					p				1
6. Cervus elaphus	1	1	7		5	4	10	9	10	(26)	8	3	7	5	4	3	5	216	c	10	1	p
8. Dama sp.																			p			
9. Rangifer tarandus																			p			
10. Sus scrofa			2							(4)	1	1						c	p	p		p
11. Dicerorhinus kirchbergensis											1								p		p	
12. Coelodonta antiquitatis											1											
13. Mammuthus primigenius								1														
14. Elephas antiquus																		p				
15. Panthera pardus							1								1			p	p		p	p
16. P. leo																						
17. P. spelaea																		p				1
18. Felis silvestris			1			1	1															
19. Lynx lynx/spelaea									1													
20. Canis lupus			1			1	1		1		2	1	1		2	1	1		p	p	p	p
21. Vulpes vulpes			1			1	1	1			1	2		1	2	1	2		p	p	p	p
22. Alopex lagopus											2				1					p		p
23. Cuon alpinus											7	2			11	6		>10	p			p
24. Crocuta crocuta													1					p				p
25. Ursus spelaeus												1										
26. U. arctos																						
27. Gulo gulo																						
28. Mustela spp.											4	1	3				1					

Note: Abbreviations are: C = Chatelperronian; A = Aurignacian; G = Gravettian. Numbers are minimum numbers of individuals [MNI] except for Bolinkoba where they are numbers of remains.
p, present; c, common; a, abundant.
Sources: Altuna 1971, 1972, 1977, 1981, 1986, 1990c,d; Altuna and Mariezkurrena 1984; Cabrera 1984; Fuentes 1980; Straus 1977b.

Appendix C1 Radiocarbon Dates for the Last Glacial Maximum of
Northern Spain

Site and level	Laboratory no.	Date (B.P.)	Solutrean Phase
Amalda			
IV	I-11435	16,090 ± 240[b]	Upper
IV	I-11428	16,200 ± 380	Upper
IV	I-11355	17,580 ± 440	Upper
V[a]	I-11372	17,880 ± 390	?
V/VI[a]	I-11663	19,000 ± 340	?
Urtiaga			
F base	GrN-5817	17,050 ± 140	?
Lezetxiki			
IIIa[a]	I-6144	19,340 ± 780	?
Aitzbitarte IV			
VIII	GrN-5993	17,950 ± 100	Upper
Ekain			
VIII[a]	I-13005	20,900 ± 450	?
Chufín			
1	CSIC-258	17,420 ± 200	Upper
La Riera			
17	GaK-6445	16,900 ± 200	Upper
17	GaK-6444	17,070 ± 230	Upper
16	GaK-6983	18,200 ± 610	Upper
15	GaK-6449	15,600 ± 570[b]	Upper
15	UCR-1272A	17,225 ± 350	Upper
14	UCR-1271A	15,690 ± 310[b]	Upper
12	GaK-6446	17,210 ± 350	Upper
10	GaK-6447	19,820 ± 390	Upper
8	GaK-6450	15,860 ± 330[b]	Upper
8	GaK-6981	20,690 ± 810	Upper
4	GaK-6984	20,970 ± 620	Upper
1[a]	UCR-1270A	19,620 ± 390	?
1[a]	Ly-1783	20,360 ± 450	?
1[a]	BM-1739	20,860 ± 410	?

(continued)

Appendix C1 Radiocarbon Dates for the Last Glacial Maximum of Northern Spain *(continued)*

Site and level	Laboratory no.	Date (B.P.)	Solutrean Phase
Las Caldas			
3	Ly-2421	18,250 ± 300	Upper
4	Ly-2422	17,050 ± 290	Upper
7	Ly-2423	18,310 ± 260	Upper
9	Ly-2424	19,390 ± 260	Upper
12 top	Ly-2425	19,030 ± 320	Middle
12 base	Ly-2426	19,480 ± 260	Middle
16	Ly-2428	19,510 ± 330	Middle
18[a]	Ly-2429	19,000 ± 280	Middle (?)
Hornos de la Peña			
?	BM-1881	18,230 ± 510	?
?	BM-1882	19,950 ± 300	?
?	BM-1883	20,700 ± 350	?

[a]No Solutrean points found.
[b]Date probably too young, but plausible at + 1 or + 2 SD.

Appendix C2 Ungulates, Carnivores, and Lagomorphs from Old Solutrean Excavations

Taxa	Altamira[a]	Hornos de la Peña[b]	Pasiega[c]	Santimamiñe[d]	Bolinkoba[d]		Ermittia[e]	Aitzbitarte[e]	Caldas[f]
(MNI)									
					E	D			
Cervus elaphus	20	6	12	7	1	2	3	9	6
Capreolus capreolus	1	1	1	1	—	—	1	1	—
Rangifer tarandus	1	—	—	1	—	—	2	1	—
Sus scrofa	2	2	—	1	—	—	1	—	—
Bovini	5	6	3	—	2	3	—	2	—
Rupicapra rupicapra	2	2	1	1	3	2	4	6	—
Capra ibex	2	4	2	3	11	16	8	1	2
Equus caballus	8	—	1	2	2	1	1	3	3
Panthera sp.	—	—	—	—	—	—	—	—	—
Lynx	—	—	—	—	—	—	1	—	—
Mustela spp.	—	—	—	—	—	—	2	5	—
Martes martes	—	—	—	—	—	—	—	—	—
Meles?	—	—	—	—	—	7	—	—	—
Crocuta crocuta	—	—	—	—	—	—	—	—	—
Ursus sp.	5	—	2	—	2	2	—	—	—
Canis lupus	—	—	—	—	—	—	2	—	—
Vulpes vulpes	2	—	2	1	3	6	3	1	—
Lepus europaeus	—	—	—	—	—	—	1	—	—
Phoca	1	—	—	—	—	—	—	—	—

Taxa	Oscura[f]	Cova Rosa[f]	Cierro[f]	Balmori[e]	Coberizas[e]	Cueto de la Mina[g]	
						F	E
Cervus elaphus	7	5	21	3	2	3	17
Capreolus capreolus	—	—	—	—	1	—	1
Rangifer tarandus	—	—	1	—	—	—	1
Sus scrofa	—	1	2	—	1	—	1
Bovini	2	3	—	—	—	1	4
Rupicapra rupicapra	—	1	—	1	1	—	1
Capra ibex	—	1	1	—	1	—	3

(continued)

Appendix C2 Ungulates, Carnivores, and Lagomorphs from Old Solutrean Excavations *(continued)*

Taxa	MNI					
	Oscura[f]	Cova Rosa[f]	Cierro[f]	Balmori[e]	Coberizas[e]	Cueto de la Mina[g]
Equus caballus	3	2	3	1	1	1
Panthera sp.	—	—	—	1	—	3
Lynx	—	—	—	—	—	—
Mustela sp.	—	—	—	—	—	—
Martes martes	—	—	—	—	—	—
Meles?	—	—	—	—	—	—
Crocuta crocuta	—	—	—	—	—	—
Ursus sp.	—	—	—	—	—	1
Canis lupus	—	—	—	—	—	1
Vulpes vulpes	—	—	—	—	—	2
Lepus europaeus	—	—	—	—	—	—
Phoca	—	—	—	—	—	—

[a]From Altuna and Straus 1976
[b]From Straus 1975a.
[c]From Straus 1975b.
[d]From Straus 1974a.
[e]From Altuna 1972.
[f]From Straus 1974b.
[g]From Castaños 1982.

Appendix C3 Ungulates, Lagomorphs, and Carnivores from Modern Solutrean Excavations, by Site and Level

Site:	Amalda	Las Caldas			Morín		La Riera						Buxú
Level:	IV	II–VI	VIII–IX	X–XIV	3	17	16	15	14	13	12	11	Sol.
Cervus	144(8)	65	147	340	51(5)	722(16)	1797(27)	1160(15)	2494(20)	651(11)	286(9)	830(13)	85(12)
Capreolus	1(1)	—	—	—	7(3)	—	2(1)	7(1)	24(3)	3(2)	—	3(1)	—
Rangifer	1(1)	—	—	—	—	—	—	—	—	—	—	—	—
Megaloceros	1(1)	—	—	—	—	—	—	—	—	—	—	—	—
Capra	134(9)	36	29	72	3(2)	171(8)	458(11)	250(7)	559(8)	178(5)	59(5)	74(2)	19(5)
Rupicapra	503(16)	—	—	—	—	—	7(1)	20(2)	12(4)	18(2)	1(1)	17(2)	110(17)
Bovini	9(1)	—	—	—	4(1)	1(1)	1(1)	2(2)	1(1)	—	—	—	—
Sus	5(1)	—	—	—	—	—	—	—	—	—	—	—	—
Equus	2(2)	10	14	66	3(2)	1(1)	7(4)	9(2)	4(2)	—	—	—	—
Oryctolagus	—	—	—	—	—	—	—	—	—	—	—	—	—
Lepus	—	—	—	—	—	—	—	—	1(1)	—	—	—	—
Canis lupus	9(1)	—	—	—	1(1)	—	2(1)	1(1)	—	—	—	—	—
Vulpes	27(3)	—	—	—	—	—	1(1)	1(1)	—	—	—	—	—
Mustela nivalis	—	—	—	—	—	—	1(1)	—	—	—	—	—	—
Ursus spelaeus	35(6)	—	—	—	—	—	—	—	—	—	—	—	—
Phocidae indet.	—	—	—	—	—	—	—	—	—	—	—	—	—

Site:	La Riera									Buxú
Level:	10	9	8	7	6	5	4	2/3	1	Sol.
Taxa:										
Cervus	938(12)	1783(25)	1268(19)	1912(34)	177(3)	512(6)	216(3)	199(3)	44(3)	85(12)
Capreolus	6(2)	48(4)	10(3)	33(4)	1(1)	—	—	1(1)	—	—
Rangifer	—	—	—	—	—	—	—	—	—	—
Megaloceros	—	—	—	—	—	—	—	—	—	—
Capra	185(5)	364(7)	520(6)	5677(14)	125(4)	648(12)	425(6)	362(6)	63(4)	19(5)
Rupicapra	1(1)	13(2)	2(1)	18(2)	—	—	—	1(1)	1(1)	110(17)
Bovini	—	—	—	—	—	—	8(2)	1(1)	19(2)	—
Sus	—	—	—	5(2)	—	—	—	—	—	—
Equus	—	1(1)	9(1)	32(6)	7(1)	18(4)	24(2)	3(1)	126(9)	—
Oryctolagus	—	—	—	11(1)	—	—	1(1)	—	—	—
Lepus	—	—	—	—	—	—	—	—	—	—
Canis lupus	—	—	—	1(1)	—	1(1)	—	—	—	—
Vulpes	1(1)	1(1)	1(1)	—	—	—	—	—	2(1)	—
Mustela	—	—	—	—	—	—	—	—	—	—
Ursus	—	—	—	—	—	—	—	—	—	—
Phocidae indet.	—	—	—	1(1)	—	—	2(1)	—	—	—

n = NISP; (n) = MNI
Sources: Altuna 1971, 1986, 1990c; Soto 1984; Soto and Meléndez 1981.

Appendix C4 Solutrean Lithic Artifact Assemblages

Site and level	Tools (no.)	Debris (no.)	Total (no.)	Debris/ tools	Area (m²)	Artifact density (no./m²)
Riera						
2	7	132	139	18.9	3.2	43.4
3	44	464	508	10.5	5.2	97.7
4	106	1,434	1,540	13.5	5.5	280.0
5	68	1,241	1,309	18.3	5.5	238.0
6	39	1,320	1,359	33.8	4.0	339.8
7	149	2,306	2,455	15.5	8.5	288.8
8	116	2,609	2,725	22.5	9.0	302.8
9	107	2,277	2,384	21.3	8.0	298.0
10	71	2,389	2,460	33.7	7.0	351.4
11	65	1,099	1,164	16.9	5.5	211.6
12	13	376	389	28.9	3.3	117.9
13	52	772	824	14.8	2.3	358.3
14	316	5,844	6,160	18.5	8.0	770.0
15	76	3,011	3,087	39.6	12.0	257.3
Morín						
3	119	1,684	1,803	14.2	4.1	439.8
Amalda						
IV	532	4,729	5,261	8.9	19.0	276.9

Appendix C5 Tool Group Indices of the Main Cantabrian Solutrean Assemblages, by Site and Level

Site and level	Total pieces	Indices (%)								
		IG	IB	IBd	IBt	IP	ID/N	IS/S	I b/b	Sol. pts.
Las Caldas (Corchón)										
Solut. terminal	276	5.8	10.9	8.7	1.4	7.2	19.9	3.6	1.5	2.5
Solut. superior	242	4.2	10.9	6.8	1.4	8.8	18.2	3.5	0.5	13.9
Solut. medio	336	6.6	16.3	7.7	3.6	6.2	14.3	7.1	1.5	12.2
Las Caldas (old coll.)	177	22.7	10.0	8.2	0.6	3.3	22.0	10.7	1.1	17.5
Cueva Oscura	167	22.2	16.2	11.4	1.2	4.2	18.0	7.2	1.8	6.6
Cova Rosa	217	16.1	17.0	14.3	1.8	4.6	14.8	5.1	3.2	17.5
El Cierro IV	337	34.1	10.2	6.6	2.4	6.9	25.2	13.7	0.9	0.9
Cueto de la Mina										
E 1 + 2	242	26.8	7.9	4.5	1.2	4.1	21.9	10.8	5.0	12.8
E 3 + 4	171	29.2	6.5	2.9	1.2	1.2	21.1	11.7	5.3	11.7
F	117	35.0	6.8	4.3	0	0	23.9	8.6	1.7	15.4
La Riera										
17	151	6.0	4.6	4.6	0	1.3	8.6	1.3	70.9	0.7
16	181	7.2	12.7	10.5	0.6	2.8	22.1	3.3	23.8	0
15	76	11.9	6.6	5.3	0	1.3	22.4	7.9	11.8	1.3

(continued)

Appendix C5 Tool Group Indices of the Main Cantabrian Solutrean Assemblages, by Site and Level *(continued)*

Site and level	Total pieces	Indices (%)								
		IG	IB	IBd	IBt	IP	ID/N	IS/S	Ib/b	Sol. pts.
La Riera										
14	316	13.6	11.1	9.2	0.3	2.5	38.9	10.4	2.9	1.0
12/13	65	9.2	10.8	10.8	0	1.5	56.9	6.2	3.1	0
11	65	9.2	12.3	7.7	1.5	3.1	49.2	6.2	3.1	0
10	71	25.4	7.0	7.0	0	4.2	32.4	0	0	7.0
9	107	9.3	14.9	13.1	0.9	2.8	47.7	7.5	0	0.9
8	116	17.2	7.8	5.2	0	4.3	35.4	4.3	4.3	5.2
7	149	13.4	9.4	9.4	0	2.0	25.5	4.7	5.4	18.8
5/6	107	4.7	8.4	7.5	0	0.9	19.6	0	10.3	31.8
4	106	5.7	14.2	12.3	1.9	0.9	11.3	2.8	14.2	26.4
2/3	51	21.6	7.8	5.9	0	2.0	33.3	2.0	2.0	5.9
Chufín	272	24.2	11.1	5.5	2.9	1.8	4.3	8.5	9.9	18.8
Morín 3	138	11.6	10.1	2.2	4.3	3.6	10.9	1.5	13.8	10.9
Altamira (lower)	522	25.1	20.8	11.1	4.0	4.6	12.8	2.9	0.2	13.2
Almalda IV	518	4.2	13.5	4.4	6.0	7.1	8.5	3.5	42.7	1.5
Bolinkoba										
D	527	18.8	28.3	16.2	4.4	3.8	8.5	5.1	5.7	1.3
E	195	20.5	36.4	19.0	5.6	2.1	6.2	3.1	5.1	0.5
Aitzbitarte IV 3	332	15.3	20.7	9.3	5.4	2.6	11.8	6.6	13.1	9.6

Appendix D1 Radiocarbon Dates for the Cantabrian Magdalenian, by Site and Level

Site and level	Laboratory no.	Date (B.P.)	Subdivision
El Castillo			
8	OxA-971	16,850 ± 220	Early
Urtiaga			
F base	GrN-5817	17,050 ± 140	Early
La Riera			
19	GaK-6448	16,420 ± 430	Early
19	Q-2110	15,530 ± 350	Early
19	Q-2116	15,230 ± 300	Early
La Lloseta			
A	GaK-2549	15,200 ± 400	Early
Abauntz			
E	Ly-1965	15,800 ± 350	Early
Altamira			
Mag.	I-12012	15,910 ± 230	Early
Mag.	M-829	15,500 ± 700	Early
Mag.	M-828[a]	13,900 ± 700	Early
El Juyo			
VI	M-830	15,300 ± 700	Early
7	I-10738	14,440 ± 180	Early
4	I-10736	13,920 ± 240	Early
6	I-10737	11,400 ± 300	Early
El Rascaño			
5	BM-1455	16,435 ± 130	Early
4	BM-1453	15,990 ± 190	Early
3	BM-1452	15,175 ± 160	Early
Erralla			
V	I-12540	15,740 ± 240	Early
V	I-12551	16,200 ± 240	Early
V	I-12868	16,270 ± 240	Early
V	I-10803[a]	10,580 ± 270	Early
IV	I-13728	15,800 ± 230	(Sterile)
IV	I-10819	14,570 ± 300	(Sterile)
Ekain			
VIIb	I-8628[a]	7,880 ±	Early
VIIb	I-12020	16,510 ± 270	Early
VIIf	I-12566	16,250 ± 250	Early

(continued)

Appendix D1 Radiocarbon Dates for the Cantabrian Magdalenian, by Site and Level *(continued)*

Ekain			
VIIf	I-10931[a]	13,950 ± 330	Early
VIIb	I-12224	16,030 ± 240	Early
VIIc	I-12225	15,970 ± 240	Early
VIId	I-12226	15,400 ± 240	Early
El Pendo			
—	OxA-977	14,830 ± 170	Early
La Paloma			
—	OxA-974	14,600 ± 160	Early
Entrefoces			
B	Ly-2937	14,690 ± 200	Early
Berroberría			
G	BM-2375	14,430 ± 290	Early
E	BM-2372	13,270 ± 220	Early
Las Caldas			
VIII	Ly-2936	13,310 ± 200	Early
VII	Ly-3318[a]	12,860 ± 160	Early
III	Ly-2427	13,400 ± 150	Early
La Viña			
IV	Ly-3316	13,360 ± 190	Early
IV	Ly-3317	13,300 ± 150	Early
Tito Bustillo			
1a/b	CSIC-155B	15,400 ± 300	Late
1a/b	CSIC-155A	15,180 ± 300	Late
1a/b	CSIC-154	14,250 ± 300	Late
1a/b	CSIC-261	14,220 ± 180	Late
1c	I-8331	13,870 ± 300	Late
1c2	GrN-12753	14,930 ± 70	Late
2	Ly-4212	14,890 ± 410	?
Sanctuary	CSIC-80	14,350 ± 300	?
Sanctuary	(Paleomag.)	14,800 ± 400	?
Sanctuary	Ly-3476	12,890 ± 530	?
Cualventi			
5	GrN-13774	11,270 ± 150	Late
La Paloma			
—	OxA-975	12,750 ± 130	Late
—	OxA-950	12,500 ± 140	Late
—	OxA-951	11,990 ± 140	Late

Cueto de la Mina			
B	OxA-996	11,650 ± 190	Late
B	OxA-989	11,630 ± 120	Late
El Castillo			
6	OxA-972	12,390 ± 130	Late
6	OxA-970	10,310 ± 120	Late
El Pendo			
—	OxA-976	13,050 ± 150	Late
—	OxA-995	12,470 ± 170	Late
—	OxA-952	10,800 ± 200	Late
La Riera			
20	GaK-6980[a]	17,160 ± 440	Late
20	Ly-1645	12,360 ± 670	Late
23	Ly-1646	10,340 ± 560	Late
24	GaK-6982	10,890 ± 430	Late
Erralla			
III	I-13439	12,310 ± 190	Late
Berroberría			
D inf.	OxA-978	11,600 ± 130	Late
D inf.	OxA-949	11,900 ± 130	Late
D inf.	BM-2370	11,750 ± 300	Late
El Rascaño			
2b	BM-1451	12,895 ± 140	Late
2	BM-1450	12,280 ± 160	Late
Ekain			
VIb base	I-9240	12,050 ± 190	Late
Urtiaga			
D	CSIC-64[a]	10,280 ± 190	Late

[a]Questionable date or attribution.
Sources: C. Mariezkurrena 1990; González Sainz 1989; Straus 1983a;
Barandiarán 1988.

Appendix D2 Lower/Middle Magdelenian Tool Group Indices

Tool Groups	Entrefoces Lev. B	La Lloseta — Level II								El Cierro Lev. III
		Layer 4	Layer 5	Layer 6	Layer 7	Layer 8	Layer 9	Layer 10	Layers 10 + 11	
IG	8.2	37.0	35.3	33.6	41.6	53.9	53.3	30.6	39.8	36.5
IB	10.2	6.7	13.4	15.7	9.5	15.6	4.2	12.0	11.2	16.3
IBd	5.7	5.3	11.3	13.1	5.9	9.9	3.3	9.3	9.7	12.5
IBt	2.0	0.4	0	0.8	1.1	0.7	0.8	2.6	1.5	0.9
IP	—	3.3	4.5	3.2	1.1	2.8	4.2	4.0	2.2	2.9
ID/N	11.8	18.4	14.5	16.0	10.7	7.1	11.9	10.7	15.8	21.3
IS/S	1.0	8.2	8.8	8.6	3.6	4.3	9.3	8.0	6.0	8.8
Ib/b	32.8	14.0	9.9	17.2	16.7	2.5	5.1	10.7	9.0	7.0
Total[a]	195	207	283	244	84	141	118	75	136	343

Tool Groups	Las Caldas Sala II	La Paloma		Cueto de la Mina		La Riera				El Juyo 1955–57 (combined)	El Juyo 1978–82			
		Lev. 6	Lev. 8	Lev. C	Lev. D	Lev. 20	Lev. 19	Lev. 20/19	Lev. 18		Lev. 4	Lev. 4S	Lev. 6	Lev. 7
IG	11.6	38.9	53.9	45.8	59.3	6.5	7.3	6.5	6.7	53.2	29.8	19.0	15.4	16.0
IB	13.0	12.8	15.9	36.0	9.8	6.0	7.8	1.3	4.4	12.4	14.0	20.6	11.6	14.1
IBd	8.2	6.4	7.5	23.4	6.2	4.0	6.9	1.3	4.0	9.4	10.6	7.9	8.4	7.7
IBt	1.4	3.2	3.0	2.0	0.9	1.0	0.5	0	0.4	0.6	0.7	4.8	1.3	2.6
IP	9.2	3.0	0.9	1.0	1.4	4.0	1.4	1.3	0.4	5.2	5.5	3.2	5.3	5.8
ID/N	17.9	5.7	7.2	1.9	12.0	6.0	10.5	7.7	8.4	13.1	12.9	9.5	7.4	14.7
IS/S	1.9	5.4	3.9	3.4	6.7	0.5	0.5	1.3	0	1.5	1.6	1.6	0.4	1.9
Ib/b	7.2	17.1	8.1	5.4	4.8	63.1	61.9	74.4	69.3	6.1	10.0	9.5	30.8	13.5
Total	207	596	332	205	417	203	219	78	225	342	877	63	474	156

Tool Groups	Altamira (Magdal.)		Rascaño				Castillo	Aitzbitarte	Abauntz	Ekain	Erralla	Urtiaga
	1924	1981	Lev. 3	Lev. 4	Lev. 4b	Lev. 5	Lev. 8	Lev. III	Lev. E	Lev. VIII	Lev. 5	Lev. F
IG	19.1	38.7	32.4	39.5	43.1	21.3	55.9	25.2	7.4	0.9	7.7	10.8
IB	23.8	13.2	26.5	17.4	32.3	14.5	13.2	11.7	14.6	6.2	9.7	25.4
IBd	18.2	11.3	18.2	8.2	19.2	7.7	6.1	4.6	7.7	4.7	4.1	—
IBt	1.9	—	4.6	3.1	2.3	3.4	2.1	3.1	2.9	1.5	2.5	
IP	4.7	5.7	4.0	5.6	2.3	3.9	7.1	3.1	5.4	1.2	3.1	6.2
ID/N	20.5	?	8.3	4.0	7.7	11.1	9.3	4.6	5.7	2.8	12.2	15.4
IS/S	6.1	?	1.8	2.6	3.1	7.7	4.7	5.3	1.5	2.7	2.6	14.6
Ib/b	0.5	7.6	4.9	6.1	0	3.9	0.3	22.1	41.3	72.1	44.4	18.5
Total	215	106	324	195	130	207	559	131	334	322	196	130

[a]Total numbers of pieces

Sources: Utrilla 1981a, 1982; Straus 1975b; Straus and Clark 1986; Merino 1984; Baldeón 1985; Barandiarán et al. 1985; Freeman 1988; Cabrera 1984; González Sainz 1989.

Appendix D3 Early Magdalenian Antler Points, by Site and Level

Site and level	Sagaies (no.)[a]	Ratio of stone tools/sagaies[b]
Entrefoces B	3	65.0
Caldas II	14	14.8
Paloma 6	17	19.5
Paloma 8	41	14.5
Cueto de la Mina D	48	8.7
Cueto de la Mina C	18	11.4
Lloseta 4-11	41	31.4
Cierro III	14	24.5
Riera 20	9	22.6
Riera 19	19	11.5
Riera 19/20	7	11.1
Riera 18	16	14.1
Juyo (total old)	10	34.2
Juyo 7	12	13.0
Juyo 6	20	23.7
Juyo 4 + 4S	86	10.9
Altamira (old)	37	5.8
El Castillo 8	160	3.5
Rascaño 5	14	14.8
Rascaño 4 + 4b	32	10.2
Rascaño 3	8	40.5
Aitzbitarte 3	18	7.3
Urtiaga F	8	16.3
Abauntz E	3	111.3
Ekain VII	2	161.0
Erralla 5	20	9.8

[a]Group I (types 1–10).
[b]$\bar{x} = 27.36$; SD $= 35.26$; n $= 26$.

Appendix D4 Upper Magdalenian Tool Group Indices

Tool group	Entrefoces Lev. A	La Paloma Lev. 4	Cueto de la Mina Lev. B	La Riera Lev. 24	La Riera Lev. 21–23	Tito Bustillo Lev. 1a&b	Tito Bustillo Lev. 1b–c	Tito Bustillo Lev. 1c	Bricia Lev. C–E
IG	4.9	41.6	40.8	17.3	18.0	10.4	14.4	5.6	21.6
IB	5.3	17.8	19.9	6.9	19.7	20.9	15.6	18.6	29.4
IBd	3.4	12.6	13.6	4.5	14.8	12.4	10.6	10.7	25.5
IBt	0.8	5.1	2.1	1.5	1.6	4.6	1.9	3.0	2.0
IP	6.5	0.9	1.5	0.5	6.6	2.7	2.9	2.0	4.0
ID/N	19.6	7.0	5.7	3.0	19.7	4.4	5.8	1.0	7.9
IS/S	1.1	0	2.6	2.5	0	1.5	1.0	1.3	5.9
Ib/b	16.9	15.9	4.2	54.0	16.4	30.1	24.0	46.0	—
Total[a]	265	214	191	202	61	588	104	393	51

Tool group	El Pendo Lev. II	El Pendo Lev. II a–b	El Pendo Lev. II c–g	Rascaño Lev. 2b	Morín Lev. 2	El Otero Lev. 2	El Otero Lev. 3	La Chora Levs. 1–8	Valle Magdal.
IG	23.4	30.3	19.8	25.5	15.7	16.4	9.1	37.6	24.3
IB	18.2	18.8	26.4	33.2	10.5	19.8	22.7	22.6	21.6
IBd	10.6	7.4	17.4	24.5	3.8	16.4	13.6	15.7	20.3
IBt	4.1	6.6	4.6	4.1	3.2	2.6	6.1	4.8	1.4
IP	5.1	3.3	3.1	3.6	2.9	0.9	3.0	0.6	—
ID/N	12.7	6.6	12.0	8.6	14.5	0	6.1	0	4.0

(continued)

Appendix D4 Upper Magdalenian Tool Group Indices (*continued*)

Tool group	El Pendo			Rascaño	Morín	El Otero		La Chora	Valle
	Lev. II	Lev. II a–b	Lev. II c–g	Lev. 2b	Lev. 2	Lev. 2	Lev. 3	Levs. 1–8	Magdal.
I S/S	4.5	4.9	2.3	0.5	1.3	0	0	1.4	1.4
I b/b	14.4	21.2	20.5	1.5	14.8	0.9	19.7	16.4	—
Total	291	122	258	196	310	66	116	699	74

Tool groups	Urtiaga		Ekain					Santimamine
	Lev. D	Lev. E	VIa	VIb	VIc	VId	VIall	Lev. VI
IG	12.7	7.6	1.3	2.8	4.5	0	2.6	9.2
IB	39.6	40.0	23.5	18.1	9.1	9.4	18.8	31.6
IBd	29.4	24.8	—	—	—	—	—	21.9
IBt	7.6	7.6	—	—	—	—	—	4.2
IP	0.5	0	0.7	2.8	6.8	0	1.8	2.3
I D/N	5.2	11.4	2.0	1.4	2.3	9.4	2.9	16.6
I S/S	2.2	4.8	0	0	0	0	0	—
I b/b	26.7	28.6	43.6	51.4	45.5	54.7	48.7	4.6
Total	1426	105	149	72	44	71	382	768

Tool groups	Abittaga Lev. VII	Erralla Lev. II–III	Aitzbitarte IV		Silibranka			
			Lev. Iinf.	Lev. II	I	II	III	IV
IG	6.8	1.6	14.4	12.5	9.8	11.3	10.5	6.5
IB	34.3	1.6	25.6	22.1	44.3	47.3	47.4	46.8
IBd	22.6	1.6	18.4	12.5	32.8	37.3	30.1	39.0
IBt	10.0	—	4.8	5.3	6.6	8.0	11.3	3.9
IP	—	3.1	2.4	3.8	—	2.0	2.3	1.3
ID/N	11.6	9.4	4.8	6.7	3.3	3.3	3.0	2.6
IS/S	—	7.8	0.8	1.0	—	1.3	—	2.6
Ib/b	3.3	45.3	23.2	22.1	24.6	22.7	23.3	26.0
Total	60	64	125	208	61	150	133	77

[a]Total numbers of pieces.

Sources: González Sainz 1989; Straus and Clark 1986; Marsan 1979; Gonzáez Echegaray et al. 1963, 1966; Baldeón 1985; Merino 1984; Navarrete and Chapa 1980; Moure and Cano 1976; González Echegaray 1980, 1981.

Appendix D5 Late Magdalenian Antler Points, by Site and Level

Site and level	Sagaies (no.)[a]	Harpoons (no.)[b]	Total points (no.)	Ratio of stone tools/ antler points[c]
Entrefoces B	3	0	3	88.3
Paloma 4	144	11	155	1.4
Cueto de la Mina B	62	24	86	2.2
Tito Bustillo 1a-b	44	4	48	12.3
Tito Bustillo 1b/c	4	0	4	26.0
Tito Bustillo 1c	27	1	28	14.0
Riera 24	10	1	11	18.4
Riera 21–23	10	0	10	6.1
Bricia C–E	7	4	11	4.6
Valle	18	13	31	2.4
Pendo II	5	0	5	58.2
Pendo II a–b	7	0	7	17.4
Pendo II c–g	11	0	11	23.5
Chora 1–8	33	8	41	17.0
Morín 2	15	1	16	19.4
Otero 2	1	1	2	33.0
Otero 3	5	11	16	7.3
Rascaño 2b	11	4	15	13.1
Urtiaga D	85	18	103	13.8
Urtiaga E	7	0	7	15.0
Santimaniñe VI	29	5	34	22.6
Aitzbitarte I inf	7	0	7	17.9
Aitzbitarte II	14	4	18	11.6
Abittaga VII	7	3	10	6.0
Ekain VI	7	4	11	34.7
Erralla 2–3	0	0	0	(64)
Silikranka I–IV	4	0	4	105.3

[a]Group I (Types 1–10).
[b]Group XVII (Types 44 and 45).
[c]$\bar{x}$ = 24.3; SD = 25.83; n = 27.

Appendix D6 Magdalenian Ungulate and Seal Faunas, by Site and Level

Site and level	Cervus	Capreolus	Rangifer	Capra	Rupicapra	Bovini	Sus	Equus	Phoca spp.
La Paloma									
8	109	1	1	3	5	1	—	5	—
6	27	1	—	2	1	1	—	2	—
4	30	—	—	3	3	1	—	1	—
Cueto Mina									
D	17	—	—	1	—	3	—	4	—
B	8	1	1	5	1	2	—	1	—
Sofoxó Mag.	6	4	—	5	4	3	1	1	—
Tito Bustillo									
2	13	—	—	2	1	2	—	2	—
1c	17	—	—	3	1	2	—	3	1
1b	15	—	1	6	4	1	—	4	—
1a	9	1	—	6	2	2	—	3	2
La Riera									
18	15	—	—	6	—	—	—	1	—
19	18	1	—	5	1	—	—	1	—
19/20	14	1	—	5	1	—	—	1	—
20	13	—	—	6	1	—	—	1	—
21/23	16	3	2	4	—	—	2	3	—
24	11	3	2	11	2	—	—	2	—
26	13	6	—	5	2	—	1	2	—

(continued)

Appendix D6 Magdalenian Ungulate and Seal Faunas, by Site and Level (*continued*)

Altamira									
(1924) Mag.	19	2	—	1	2	4	—	—	—
(1981) Mag.	14	3	—	—	—	2	1	—	—
El Pendo									
II	15	—	—	2	1	1	1	1	—
II a+b	11	1	—	1	—	1	1	1	—
II c+d	9	—	—	2	—	1	—	1	—
El Juyo									
8–9	17	5	—	1	—	1	—	3	—
6–7	78	4	—	4	—	2	1	1	—
4	44	4	—	2	—	4	1	3	—
El Rascaño									
5	4	—	—	34	—	1	—	2	—
4b	8	—	—	36	—	—	—	1	—
4a	4	—	—	23	1	1	—	1	—
3	4	—	—	20	1	1	—	1	—
2	4	—	—	15	1	—	1	1	—
Morín 2	9	2	1	3	3	1	2	3	—
Ermittia Mag.	3	1	2	13	2	1	2	1	—
Urtiaga									
F	17	9	2	9	4	2	—	1	—
E	6	3	3	3	3	3	—	3	—
D	37	13	7	20	15	3	3	2	—

Aitzbitarte 2	10	3	2	2	8	4	2	2	—
Erralla									
V	5	1	1	22	2	1	—	1	—
III–II	4	2	1	8	4	1	—	1	—
Ekain									
VII	24	3	—	7	4	3	—	3	—
VI	6	2	1	8	1	2	—	—	—
Abauntz E	2	—	2	2	8	2	—	3	—

Note: Shown as MNI.

Sources: Altuna 1971, 1972, 1976, 1981, 1986; Altuna and Mariezkurrena 1982, 1984, 1985; Castaños 1980, 1982; Freeman 1988; Freeman et al. 1988; Fuentes 1980; Straus 1977b.

Appendix D7: Carnivore and Lagomorph Remains from Magdalenian Sites, by Site and Level

Site and level	Canis lupus	Cuon	Vulpes	Ursus spp.	Panthera leo	Lynx	Felix silvestris	Mustelidae	Crocuta	Oryctolagus	Lepus spp.
La Paloma											
8	2	—	1	1	1	—	—	—	—	—	—
6	—	—	—	—	1	—	—	—	—	—	—
4	3	—	3	1	2	—	—	—	—	—	—
Cueto de la Miña											
D	—	—	2	—	—	—	—	—	—	—	—
B	—	—	1	—	—	—	—	—	—	—	—
Sofoxó	—	—	—	—	—	—	—	1	—	—	—
Tito Bustillo											
2	—	—	—	—	—	—	—	1	—	—	—
1c	—	—	1	—	—	1	—	—	—	—	—
1b	—	—	1	—	—	—	—	1	—	—	1
1a	—	—	1	—	—	—	—	—	—	1	—
La Riera											
18	3	1	1	—	—	—	—	—	—	—	—
19	—	—	—	—	—	—	—	—	—	—	—
19/20	2	—	—	—	—	—	—	—	—	—	—
20	1	—	—	—	—	—	—	—	—	—	—
21/23	4	—	1	1	—	—	—	1	—	—	—
24	2	—	4	1	—	—	—	—	—	—	—
Altamira (1981)		—	1	—	1	—	—	—	—	—	—
El Pendo											
II	—	—	—	—	—	—	—	—	—	—	—
II a–b	3	—	2	—	—	—	—	—	—	—	—
II c–g	1	—	3	1	—	—	—	—	—	—	—
El Juyo											
8–9	—	—	1	—	2	—	—	—	—	—	—
6–7	—	—	3	—	—	—	—	1	—	—	—
4	1	—	10	—	—	—	—	—	—	—	—

El Rascaño										
5	—	3	21	—	—	—	—	1	—	2
4b	2	—	29	—	—	—	—	—	—	—
4a	—	—	8	—	—	—	—	1	—	2
3	—	15	4	—	—	2	—	2	1	1
2	—	—	4	—	—	—	—	—	—	3
Morín 2	—	—	—	—	—	—	—	—	—	—
Ermitta Mag.	—	—	3	—	—	—	—	—	—	—
Urtiaga										
F	—	4	67	1	3	1	—	9	—	2
E	—	26	52	5	4	1	—	3	—	3
D	—	—	156	6	—	—	4	12	—	10
Aitzbitarte Mag.	—	—	6	10	—	—	—	36	—	9
Erralla										
V	—	2	14	3	—	—	—	151	—	5
III–II	—	—	—	8	—	—	—	9	1	8
Ekain										
VII	—	2	33	—	—	—	—	17	—	—
VI	—	6	13	—	—	—	—	—	—	1
Abauntz E	—	—	13	—	—	—	1	—	—	17

Note: Shown as NISP.

Sources: Altuna 1971, 1972, 1976, 1981, 1986; Altuna and Mariezkurrena 1982, 1984, 1985; Castaños 1980, 1982; Freeman 1988; Freeman et al. 1988; Fuentes 1980; Straus 1977b.

Appendix E1 Epipaleolithic and Mesolithic Radiocarbon Dates, by Site and Level

Site and level	Laboratory no.	Date (B.P.)	Attribution
La Riera			
27 base	UCR-12750	12,270 ± 400	Azilian (?)
Zatoya			
BIII	Ly-1400	11,840 ± 240	Azilian
BIII	Ly-1458	≥10,940	Azilian
II base	Ly-1599	11,620 ± 360	Azilian
II base	Ly-1399	11,480 ± 270	Azilian
Los Azules			
3e	BM-1877	11,190 ± 350	Azilian
La Riera			
27 top	BM-1494	10,635 ± 120	Azilian (?)
Piélago			
4	OxA-954	10,710 ± 100	Azilian
1	OxA-953	10,280 ± 120	Azilian
Los Azules			
3f	BM-1878	10,720 ± 280	Azilian
3e	BM-1876	10,700 ± 190	Azilian
3e	BM-1875	10,330 ± 190	Azilian
3d/e	BM-1879	10,400 ± 90	Azilian
El Cierro	GaK-2548	10,400 ± 500	?
El Rascaño			
1.2	BM-1451	10,560 ± 245	Azilian
1.3	BM-1449	10,485 ± 90	Azilian
Portugain	GrN-14097	10,370 ± 90	Azilian (?)
Arenaza			
III	CSIC-174	10,300 ± 180	Azilian (?)
Berroberría			
D	BM-2371	10,160 ± 410	Azilian
Arenaza			
IID	CSIC-173	9,600 ± 180	Tardenoisoid
Abauntz			
D	Ly-1964	9,530 ± 300	Azilian
Ekain			
II	I-11666	9,540 ± 210	Azilian
IV	I-9239	9,460 ± 185	Azilian
Los Azules			
3d	CSIC-260	9,540 ± 120	Azilian
3a	CSIC-216	9,430 ± 120	Azilian

Santimamiñe			
7(?)	Gif-130	9,470 ± 400	Azilian (?)
Oscurá			
(Anía) IIA	Ly-2938	9,280 ± 230	Azilian
Mazaculos			
3.3	GaK-6884	9,290 ± 440	Asturian
Morín			
travertine	I-5150	9,000 ± 150	post-Azilian
Urtiaga			
C	CSIC-63	8,700 ± 170	Azilian
La Riera			
29 lower	GaK-2909	8,650 ± 300	Asturian
Penicial *conchero*	GaK-2906	8,650 ± 180	Asturian
Zatoya			
Ib	Ly-1457	8,260 ± 550	Sauveterrian or
Ib	Ly-1398	8,150 ± 170	post-Azilian
Mazaculos			
1.1	GaK-8162	7,280 ± 200	Asturian
Coberizas			
BI	GaK-2907	7,100 ± 170	Asturian
Bricia *conchero*	GaK-2908	6,800 ± 160	Asturian
La Riera			
29 top	GaK-3046	6,500 ± 200	Asturian
Los Canes			
K	AA-6071	6,930 ± 95	Epipaleo.
D	AA-5295	6,860 ± 65	Epipaleo.
D	AA-5296	6,770 ± 65	Epipaleo.
F	AA-5294	6,265 ± 75	Epipaleo.

Sources: Straus, 1985b, 1986a; Straus and Clark 1986; González Sainz 1989;
C. Mariezkurrena 1990; Arias 1991.

Appendix E2 Azilian Tool Group Indices, by Site and Level

Tool groups	La Paloma	La Riera				Los Azules		Morín
	2	28	27	26	2	3A–D	3E	1
IG	47.5	3.1	17.1	11.5	30.4	23.8	23.6	13.6
IP	0	0	1.9	0	1.4	0.3	0.4	1.9
IB	9.0	9.4	7.6	1.9	5.7	5.9	3.0	7.2
I D/N	6.2	9.4	15.2	7.7	8.7	5.8	12.9	13.1
I S/S	3.2	0	3.8	1.9	1.4	0.8	0.5	1.1
I b/b[a]	23.2	62.5	43.8	38.5	33.2	52.1	50.0	28.2
Geom. microl.[b]	0	0	0	0	0	0.1	0.2	1.7
Total[c]	245	32	105	52	69	1,819	761	359

Tool groups	El Pendo	Ekain				Urtiaga	Aitzbitarte	Zatoya
	I	II	III	IV	V	C	I	II
IG	25.2	1.7	0.8	3.4	3.9	6.5	13.9	26.6
IP	2.5	1.1	0.8	0.6	0.5	1.1	1.6	2.3
IB	18.5	1.7	6.2	13.6	19.5	12.2	27.0	9.5
I D/N	10.0	4.5	1.6	4.0	4.9	6.8	5.7	11.3
I S/S	0.8	1.1	0.8	0.6	0	3.0	?	?
I b/b[a]	24.2	60.5	61.2	54.8	37.1	47.5	50.8	36.4
Geom. microl.[b]	0	10.2	5.4	0	0.5	2.3	0	0.7
Total[c]	119	177	129	177	205	263	122	566

Tool groups	Piélago II					Piélago I		El Valle
	1	2	3	4	5–6	2	3	Total
IB	17.0	18.6	20.0	22.6	14.6	12.6	11.0	34.8
IP	1.6	—	0.6	0.7	—	1.3	2.0	?
IB	16.2	11.3	12.6	7.2	6.7	13.9	3.0	10.6
I D/N	—	—	—	—	—	—	—	?
I S/S	—	—	—	—	—	0.8	—	?
I b/b[a]	31.3	36.4	43.6	33.7	30.7	26.4	53.0	41.6
Geom. microl.[b]	9.7	8.1	2.0	—	—	2.5	—	11.4
Total[c]	320	284	350	152	75	236	100	136

[a]Includes Azilian and microgravette points.
[b]Geometric microliths.
[c]Total number of pieces.

Appendix E3 Azilian Ungulate Faunas, by Site and Level

Site and level	Cervus	Capreolus	Bovines	Capra	Rupicapra	Sus	Equus
Zatoya							
IIa	734/-	58/-	18/-	181/-	151/-	258/-	10/-
Ib	107/-	26/-	7/-	32/-	19/-	167/-	1/-
Abauntz							
D	3/2	—	1/1	3/2	2/1	—	—
Ekain							
V–III	261/16	16/5	5/3	69/10	9/3	1/1	2/1
II	13/5	—	—	6/2	—	10/4	—
Aitzbitarte IV							
1	124/6	6/2	17/2	9/2	40/3	1/1	8/2
Urtiaga							
C	335/16	79/9	—	37/3	40/4	37/5	—
Ermittia							
I	24/3	—	1/1	57/6	2/1	4/2	—
Arenaza							
IV–III	6041/-	580/-	4/-	4269/-	100/-	145/-	2/-
II	1331/-	206/-	87/-	61/-	30/-	347/-	—
Morín							
1	77/5	1/1	4/2	1/1	—	2/1	4/1
El Rascaño							
1	82/9	—	—	577/26	6/3	4/1	3/1

Piélago II						
6	16/-	—	—	94/-	17/-	—
5	27/-[a]	—	—	176/-	75/-	—
4	1/-	—	—	7/-	2/-	13/-
3	26/-	—	—	341/-	158/-	—
2	71/-	3/-	—	758/-	273/-	1/-
1	17/-	—	—	155/-	119/-	—
El Pendo						
I	333/11	11/1	7/1	11/1	8/1	12/1
La Riera						
27 lower	586/14	45/4	10/2	131/5	45/3	9/1
27 upper	502/14	29/2	—	47/2	7/3	2/2
28	86/8	18/1	11/2	4/1	1/1	3/1
Cueto de la Mina						
A	18/9	1/1	1/1	1/1	—	1/1
Los Azules						
Comb.	+++	+	—	+	+	++
La Paloma						
2	207/11	8/3	2/1	1/1	1/1	1/1

Notes: Shown as NISP/MNI; n/-, no MNI given; +, present; ++, abundant; +++, very abundant; [a] includes remains of 1 (?) *Rangifer*.

Sources: Altuna and Mariezkurrena 1982, 1984; Altuna 1971, 1972, 1986, 1990d; Fuentes 1980; Straus, et al. 1981; Castaños 1980, 1982; Fernández-Tresguerres 1980; Lopez-Berges and Valle 1985.

Appendix E4 Azilian Carnivore, Seal, and Lagomorph Remains, by Site and Level

Site and level	Canis lupus	Vulpes	Ursus arctos	Lynx	Felis sylvestris	Panthera leo	Genetta	Mustelidae	Halichoerus	Lepus	Oryctolagus
Abauntz											
D	—	—	1	—	2	—	—	1	—	—	—
Ekain											
V–III	208[a]	2	1[b]	—	—	—	—	21	—	1	—
II	—	1	—	—	—	—	—	—	—	1	—
Aitzbitarte IV											
1	1	1	—	—	—	—	—	11	—	—	—
Urtiaga											
C	2	18	—	—	5	—	—	33	—	4	—
Ermitta											
I	—	2	—	—	—	—	—	2	—	—	—
Morin											
1	—	—	—	—	—	—	—	—	—	—	—
El Rascaño											
1	10	—	—	1	—	—	—	—	—	1	—
Piélago II											
6	1	—	—	—	—	—	—	—	—	—	—
5	1	—	—	—	—	—	—	—	—	—	—
4	7	—	—	—	—	—	—	—	—	—	—
3	—	—	—	—	1	—	—	—	—	—	—
2	1	—	—	—	—	—	—	—	—	—	—
1	—	—	—	—	—	—	—	—	—	—	—
El Pendo											
1	—	1	1[b]	—	—	—	1	—	—	—	—
La Riera											
27	1	1	—	—	—	1	—	—	—	—	—
28	—	—	—	—	—	—	—	—	3	—	—
Cueto de la Mina											
A	—	—	1	—	—	—	—	—	—	—	—
Los Azules											
Comb.	—	—	—	—	1	—	—	1	—	—	—
La Paloma											
2	—	—	1	—	—	—	—	—	—	—	1

Note: Shown as NISP.
[a]All from one individual.
[b]*Ursus spelaeus.*
Sources: Altuna and Mariezkurrena 1982, 1984; Altuna 1971, 1972, 1986, 1990d; Fuentes 1980; Straus, et al. 1981; Castaños 1980, 1982; Fernández-Tresguerres 1980; Lopez-Berges and Valle 1985.

Appendix E5 Asturian Stone Tools From Modern Excavations

Tool group	Balmori D1+E1	La Riera A	Liencres Surface + level 1	Mazaculos Levels 1–3
Endscrapers	4	11	33	—
Perforators	2	4	24	—
Burins	5	7	16	1
Denticulates/ notches	6	26	33	4
Sidescrapers	1	3	6	—
Backed bladelets/ points	5	5	5	—
Picks	1	4	5	30
Choppers	1	3	4	26
Others	4	8	28	2
Total	29	71	154	63

Sources: Clark 1976; González Morales 1982a.

Appendix F1 Radiocarbon Dates for the Late Epipaleolithic and Neolithic, by Site and Level

Site and level	Laboratory no.	Date (B.P.)	Attribution
Fuente Hoz	I-12985	8,120 ± 240	Geom. Epipaleo.
	I-13496	7,880 ± 120	Geom. Epipaleo.
	I-12083	7,840 ± 130	Geom. Epipaleo.
	I-12778	7,140 ± 120	Geom. Epipaleo.
La Peña			
D	BM-2363	7,890 ± 120	Geom. Epipaleo.
Abauntz			
C	I-11537	6,910 ± 450	Early Neolithic
Zatoya			
I	Ly-1397	6,320 ± 280	Early Neolithic
Urtao			
Ib	I-14098	6,220 ± 120	Neolithic?
Fuente Hoz			
II	I-12084	6,120 ± 280	Neolithic
Peña Larga			
IV	?	6,150 ± 230	Cardial Neolithic
IV	?	5,830 ± 110	Cardial Neolithic
Les Pedroses			
Conchero	Gak-2547	5,760 ± 185	Asturian w/ceramics
Tarreón			
III	I-4030	5,780 ± 120	Epipaleolithic
Marizulo			
I	GrN-5992	5,585 ± 65	Neolithic
Abauntz			
B4	I-11309	5,390 ± 120	Mid or Late Neolithic
Fuente Hoz			
Ib	I-11589	5,160 ± 110	Final Neolithic
Ia	I-11588	5,240 ± 110	Final Neolithic
Arenaza			
IC1	I-8630	4,965 ± 195	Neolithic
La Lloseta			
Upper *conchero*	Gak-680	4,460 ± 680	Asturian?

Sources: C. Mariezkurrena 1990; González Morales 1982a.

BIBLIOGRAPHY

Abbreviations:

BAR, British Archaeological Reports [Oxford];

BIDEA, Boletín del Instituto de Estudios Asturianos [Oviedo];

BPH, Bibliotheca Praehistorica Hispana [Madrid];

BSPA, Bulletin de la Société Préhistorique de l'Ariège;

BSPF, Bulletin de la Société Préhistorique Française;

CIMAM, Centro de Investigación y Museo de Altamira, Monografías [Santander];

CIPPM, Comisión de Investigaciónes Paleontológicas y Prehistóricas, Memorias [Madrid];

EAE, Excavaciones Arqueológicas en España [Madrid].

ERAUL, Etudes et Recherches Archéologiques de l'Université de Liège

ACDPS (Asociación Cantabra para la Defensa del Património Subterráneo)
    1986 *Las Cuevas con Arte Paleolítico en Cantabria.* Monografías Arqueológicas 2, Santander.

Aguirre, E., J. Arsuaga, J. Bermudez, A. Garcia, I. Martínez, and A. Rosas.
    1989 Human remains from Atapuerca-Ibeas. In *Hominidae,* edited by G. Giacobini, 251-255. Jaca Book, Milan.

Akoshima, K.
    n.d. Analyse tracéologique d'artefacts en silex. In *L'Abri Dufaure,* edited by L. Straus, Mémoires de la Société Préhistorique Française, Paris. In press.

Alcalde Del Rio, H.
    1906a *Las Pinturas y Grabados de las Cavernas Prehistóricas de la Provincia de Santander.* Blanchard y Arce, Santander.
    1906b (= 1908) Exploration du gisement d'Altamira. In *La Caverne d'Altamira à Santillane près Santander,* edited by E. Cartailhac and H. Breuil, pp. 257–275. Imprimerie de Monaco, Monaco.

Alcalde del Rio, H., H. Breuil, and L. Sierra.
    1911 *Les Cavernes de la Région Cantabrique.* A. Chêne, Monaco.

Almagro, M.

1973 Las pinturas y grabados de la Cueva de Chufín. *Trabajos de Prehistoria* 30:3–44.

1976 Los omoplatos decorados de la Cueva de "El Castillo". *Trabajos de Prehistoria* 33:9–99.

1980 *Altamira Symposium.* Ministerio de Cultura, Madrid.

Almagro, M., V. Cabrera, and F. Bernaldo de Quiros.

1977 Nuevos hallazgos de arte rupestre en Cueva Chufín. *Trabajos de Prehistoria* 34:9–29.

Almagro, M. and M. A. García Guinea.

1972 *Santander Symposium.* Patronato de las Cuevas Prehistóricas, Santander.

Altuna, J.

1971 Los mamíferos del yacimiento prehistórico de Morín. In *Cueva Morín: Excavaciones 1966–1968*, edited by J. González Echegaray and L. Freeman, 367–398. Patronato de las Cuevas, Santander.

1972 Fauna de mamíferos de los yacimientos prehistóricos de Guipúzcoa. *Munibe* 24:1–464.

1973 Fauna de mamíferos de la Cueva de Morín. In *Cueva Morín: Excavaciones 1969*, edited by J. González Echegaray and L. Freeman, 281–290. Patronato de las Cuevas, Santander.

1975 *Lehen Euskal Herria.* Mensajero, Bilbao.

1976 Los mamíferos del yacimiento prehistórico de Tito Bustillo. In *Excavaciones en la Cueva de Tito Bustillo*, edited by J. Moure and M. Cano, 149–194. Instituto de Estudios Asturianos, Oviedo.

1977 Fauna de la Cueva del Conde. *BIDEA* 90–91:486–487.

1979 La faune des ongulés du Tardiglaciaire en Pays Basque et dans le reste de la région cantabrique. In *La Fin des Temps Glaciaires en Europe*, edited by D. de Sonneville-Bordes, 85–95. CNRS, Paris.

1980 Historia de la domesticación animal en el Pais Vasco. *Munibe* 32:1–163.

1981 Restos óseos del yacimiento prehistórico del Rascaño. In *El Paleolítico Superior de la Cueva del Rascaño*, edited by J. González Echegaray and I. Barandiarán, 223–269. CIMAM 3.

1983 On the relationship between archaeofaunas and parietal art in the caves of the Cantabrian region. In *Animals and Archaeology*, edited by J. Clutton-Brock and C. Grigson, vol. #1, 227–238. BAR S-163.

1984 Historia de las excavaciones. In *El Yacimiento Prehistórico de la Cueva de Ekain*, edited by J. Altuna and J. Merino, 17–45. Sociedad de Estudios Vascos, San Sebastián.

1985 Los moluscos marinos de Erralla. In *Cazadores Magdalenienses en la Cueva de Erralla*, edited by J. Altuna, A. Baldeón, and K. Mariezkurrena, 119–121. *Munibe* 37.

1986 The mammalian faunas from the prehistoric site of La Riera. In *La Riera Cave*, edited by L. Straus and G. Clark, 237–274, 421–480. Anthropological Research Papers 36, Tempe.

1987 Prehistoria. *Aranzadiana* 107:23–29.

1989 Subsistance d'origine animale pendant le Moustérien dans la région cantabrique. In *L'Homme de Néandertal*, edited by M. Otte, vol. 6, 31–44. *ERAUL* 33.

1990a D. Jose Miguel de Barandiarán. In *Gure Lehen Urratsak. 1990. Odisea en el Pasado*, edited by J. Altuna, J. Apellániz, and A. Baldeón, 2–24. Eusko Kultur Eragintza Etor, San Sebastián.

1990b D. Jose Miguel de Barandiarán: notas biográficas. *Munibe* 42:7–9.

1990c Caza y alimentacíoan procedente de macromamíferos durante el Paleolítico de Amalda. In *La Cueva de Amalda*, edited by J. Altuna, A. Baldeón, and K. Mariezkurrena, 149–192. Sociedad de Estudios Vascos, San Sebastián.

1990d La caza de herbivoros durante del Paleolítico y Mesolítico del Pais Vasco. *Munibe* 42:229–240.

1990e Situación y descripción de la Cueva de Amalda. In *La Cueva de Amalda*, edited by J. Altuna, A. Baldeón, and K. Mariezkurrena, 9–31. Sociedad de Estudios Vascos, San Sebastián.

Altuna, J. and J. Apellániz.

1976 Las figuras rupestres paleolíticas de la Cueva de Altxerri. *Munibe* 28:1–242.

1978 Las figuras rupestres de la Cueva de Ekain. *Munibe* 30:1–151.

Altuna, J., A. Baldeón, and K. Mariezkurrena.

1985 Cazadores Magdalenienses en la Cueva de Erralla. *Munibe* 37:1–206.

1990 *La Cueva de Amalda*. Sociedad de Estudios Vascos, San Sebastián.

Altuna, J., A. Eastham, K. Mariezkurrena, A. Speiss, and L. Straus.

n.d. Magdalenian and Azilian hunting at the Abri Dufaure. *Archaeozoologia*. In press.

Altuna, J. and K. Mariezkurrena.

1982 Restos óseos del yacimiento prehistórico de Abauntz. *Trabajos de Arqueologia Navarra* 3:347–353.

1984 Bases de subsistencia de origen animal en el yacimiento de Ekain. In *El Yacimiento Prehistórico de la Cueva de Ekain*, edited by J. Altuna and J. Merina, 211–280. Sociedad de Estudios Vascos, San Sebastián.

1985 Bases de subsistencia de los pobladores de Erralla. *Munibe* 37:87–117.

Altuna, J., K. Mariezkurrena, A. Armendariz, L. Del Barrio, T. Ugalde, and J. Peñalver.

1982 Carta arqueológica de Guipúzcoa. *Munibe* 34:1–242.

Altuna, J. and J. Merino.

1984 *El Yacimiento Prehistórico de la Cueva de Ekain*. Sociedad de Estudios Vascos, San Sebastián.

Altuna, J. and C. de la Rua.

1989 Dataciones absolutas de los cráneos del yacimiento prehistórico de Urtiaga. *Munibe* 41:23–28.

Altuna, J. and L. Straus.

1976 The Solutrean of Altamira. *Zephyrus* 26–27:175–182.

Andres, M.

1990 El fenómeno dolménico en el País Vasco. *Munibe* 42:141–52.

Apellániz, J.
  1971 El Mesolítico de la cueva de Tarrerón y su datación por el C14. *Munibe* 23:91–104.
  1978 Análisis e interpretación de Ekain. *Munibe* 30:110–150.
  1982 *El Arte Prehistórico del País Vasco y sus Vecinos.* Desclee, Bilbao.
  1986 Análisis de la variación formal y la autoría en la iconografía mueble de Magdaleniense antiquo de Bolinkoba. *Munibe* 38:39–559.
  1991 *Modelo de Análisis de la Autoría en el Arte Figurativo del Paleolítico.* Cuadernos de Arqueología de Deusto 13.
Apellaniz, J. and J. Altuna.
  1975 Excavaciones en la Cueva de Arenaza I. *Noticiario Arqueológico Hispánico, Prehistoria* 4:123–154.
Aranzadi, T. and J.M. de Barandiarán.
  1928 *Exploraciones Prehistóricas en Guipúzcoa en los Años 1924 a 1927.* Diputación de Guipúzcoa, San Sebastián.
  1935 *Exploraciones en la Caverna de Santimamiñe, 3a Memoria; Exploraciones en la Caverna de Lumentxa.* Diputación de Vizcaya, Bilbao.
Aranzadi, T., J.M. de Barandiaran and E. Eguren.
  1925 *Exploraciones de la Caverna de Santimamiñe, la Memoria.* Grijelmo, Bilbao.
  1931 *Exploraciones de la Caverna de Santimamiñe, 2a Memoria.* Diputación de Vizcaya, Bilbao.
Areso, P.
  1984 Sedimentología de los niveles VII a II del yacimiento de Ekain. In *El Yacimiento Prehistórico de la Cueva de Ekain,* edited by J. Altuna and J. Merino, 47–60. Sociedad de Estudios Vascos, San Sebastián.
Areso, P., M. Aranzasti, M. Olaskoaga, and A. Uriz.
  1990 Sedimentología de la Cueva de Amalda. In *La Cueva de Amalda,* edited by J. Altuna, A. Baldeón, and K. Mariezkurrena, 33–48. Sociedad de Estudios Vascos, San Sebastián.
Arias, P.
  1986 La cerámica prehistórica del abrigo de Cueto de la Mina. *BIDEA* 40:805–31.
  1991 *De Cazadores a Campesinos.* Universidad de Cantabria, Santander.
Arias, P., G. Gil, A. Martínez, and C. Pérez.
  1981 Nota sobre los grabados digitales de la Cueva de los Canes. *BIDEA* 35:937–956.
Arias, P., A. Martínez, and C. Pérez.
  1986 La cueva sepulcral de Trespando. *BIDEA* 40:1259–1289.
Arribas, J.
  1990 El Magdaleniense superior/final en el País Vasco. *Munibe* 42:55–63.
Azpeitia, P.
  1958 Estudio de los restos paleontólogicos de la Trinchera I. In *Memoria de las Excavaciones de la Cueva del Juyo,* edited by P. Janssens and J. González Echegaray, 101–117. Patronato de las Cuevas Prehistóricas, Santander.
Bahn, P. and J. Vertut.
  1988 *Images of the Ice Age.* Facts on File, New York.

Bailey, G.

1983a *Hunter-Gatherer Economy in Prehistory*. Cambridge University Press, Cambridge.

1983b Economic change in late Pleistocene Cantabria. In *Hunter-Gatherer Economy in Prehistory*, edited by G. Bailey, 149–165. Cambridge University Press, Cambridge.

Balbin, R. and J. Moure.

1981a *Las pinturas y Grabados de la Cueva de Tito Bustillo*. Studia Archaeológica 66, Valladolid.

1981b La Galería de los Caballos de la cueva de Tito Bustillo. In *Altamira Symposium*, 85–116. Ministerio de Cultura, Madrid.

1982 El panel principal de la cueva de Tito Bustillo. *Ars Praehistorica* 1:47–97.

Baldellou, V. and P. Utrilla.

1985 Nuevas dataciones de radiocarbono de la prehistoria oscense. *Trabajos de Prehistoria* 42:83–95.

Baldeón, A.

1985 Estudio de las industrias lítica y ósea de Erralla. In *Cazadores Magdalenienses en la Cueva de Erralla*, edited by J. Altuna, A. Baldeón, and K. Mariezkurrena, 123–185. *Munibe* 37.

1990a El Paleolítico inferior y medio en el País Vasco. *Munibe* 42:11–22.

1990b Las industrias de los niveles paleolíticos. In *La Cueva de Amalda*, edited by J. Altuna, A. Baldeón, and K. Mariezkurrena, 63–115. Sociedad de Estudios Vascos, San Sebastián.

Baldeón, A., E. Berganza, and E. Garcia.

1983 Estudio del yacimiento de "El Montico de Charratu". *Estudios de Arqueologia Alavesa* 11:121–186.

Barandiarán, I.

1967 *El Paleomesolítico del Pireneo Occidental*. Monografías Arqueológicas 3, Zaragoza.

1971 Hueso con grabados paleolíticos en Torre. *Munibe* 23:37–69.

1972 *Arte Mueble de Paleolítico Cantábrico*. Monografías Arquelógicas 14, Zaragoza.

1977 El proceso de transición Epipaleolítico-Neolítico en la Cueva de Zatoya. *Principe de Viana* 146–147:5–46.

1979a Excavaciones en el covacho de Berroberría. *Trabajos de Prehistoria Navarra* 1:11–60.

1979b Azilien et post-Azilien dans le Pays Basque meridional. In *La Fin des Temps Glaciaires en Europe*, edited by D. de Sonneville-Bordes, 721–732. CNRS, Paris.

1981 Industria ósea. In *El Paleolítico Superior de la Cueva del Rascaño*, edited by J. González Echegaray and I. Barandiarán, 97–164. CIMAM 3.

1985 Industria ósea paleolítica de la Cueva del Juyo. In *Excavaciones en la Cueva del Juyo*, edited by I. Barandiarán, L. Freeman, J. González Echegaray, and R. Klein, 163–194. CIMAM 14.

1988 Datation C1 de l'art mobilier magdalénien cantabrique. *BSPA* 43:63–84.

Barandiarán, I. and J. González Echegaray.
1981 Interpretación cultural y ambiental del deposito arqueológico del Rascaño.
In *El Paleolítico Superior de la Cueva del Rascaño*, edited by J. González
Echegaray and I. Barandiarán, 325–355. CIMAM 3.
Barandiarán, I., L. Freeman, J. González Echegaray, and R. Klein.
1985 *Excavaciones en la Cueva del Juyo*. CIMAM 14.
Barandiarán, I. and P. Utrilla.
1976 Sobre el Magdaleniense de Ermittia. *Sautuola* 1:21–47.
Barandiarán, J. M. de.
1961 Excavaciones en Aitzbitarte IV. *Munibe* 13:183–285.
1976–78 *Obras Completas*. Gran Enciclopedia Vasco, Bilbao.
Barandiarán, J., A. Aguirre, and M. Grande.
1960 *Estación de Kurtzia*. Diputación de Vizcaya, Bilbao.
Basabe, J. and I. Bennassar.
1980 Algunos restos humanos del Paleolítico santanderino. *II Symposium de
Antropología Biológica de España*, 653–666.
Bauchot, M. and A. Pras.
1982 *Guia de los Peces de Mar de Espana y de Europa*. Omega, Barcelona.
Begouen, H. and H. Breuil.
1958 *Les Cavernes du Volp*. Arts et Metiers Graphiques, Paris.
Benito del Rey, L.
1976 La industria lítica musteriense de la capa "Alpha" de la Cueva del Castillo.
Zephyrus 26–27:31–84.
Berenguer, M.
1979 *El Arte Parietal Prehistórico de la Cueva de Llonín*. Instituto de Estudios
Asturianos, Oviedo.
Berganza, E.
1990 El Epipaleolítico en el País Vasco. *Munibe* 42:81–89.
Bernaldo de Quirós, F.
1982 *Los Inicios del Paleolítico Superior Cantábrico*. CIMAM 8.
Bernaldo de Quirós, F., R. Bohigas, and V. Cabrera.
1987 Las pinturas rupestres de la Cueva de los Santos o del Becerral. *Boletín
Cántabro de Espeleología* 8:133–140.
Beyries, S.
1987 *Variabilité de l'Industrie Lithique au Moustérien*. BAR S–328.
Binford, L.
1962 Archaeology as anthropology. *American Antiquity* 28:217–25.
1978 Dimensional analysis of behavior and site structure. *American Antiquity* 43:330–361.
1979 Organization and formation processes. *Journal of Anthropological Research* 35:255–273.
1980 Willow smoke and dog's tails: hunter-gatherer settlement systems and
archaeological site formation. *American Antiquity* 45:4–20.
1982 The archaeology of place. *Journal of Anthropological Archaeology* 1:5–31.

Binford, L. and S. Binford.

1966 A preliminary analysis of functional variability in the Mousterian of Levallois facies. *American Anthropologist* 68 (2, pt.2):238–295.

Bischoff, J., J. Garcia, and L. Straus.

1991 Uranium-series isochron dating at El Castillo Cave (Cantabria, Spain): the "Acheulean"/"Mousterian" question. *Journal of Archaeological Science* 18.

Bischoff, J., R. Julia, and R. Mora.

1988 Uranium-series dating of the Mousterian occupation at Abric Romaní, Spain. *Nature* 332:68–70.

Bischoff, J., N. Soler, J. Maroto, and R. Julia.

1989 Abrupt Mousterian/Aurignacian boundary at ca. 40 ka bp: accelerator radiocarbon dates from l'Arbreda Cave. *Journal of Archaeological Science* 16:553–576.

Blas, M. A.

1979 La decoración parietal del dolmen de la Santa Cruz. *BIDEA* 98:717–757.

1983 *La Prehistoria Reciente en Asturias*. Fundación Pública de Cuevas y Yacimientos Prehistóricos, Oviedo.

Blas, M. A. and J. Fernández-Tresguerres.

1989 *Historia Primitiva en Asturias*. Silverio Canada, Gijón.

Bordes, F.

1953 Essai classification des industries "moustériennes". *BSPF* 50:457–466.

1961 Mousterian cultures in France. *Science* 134:803–810.

1968 *The Old Stone Age*. McGraw-Hill, New York.

1972 *A Tale of Two Caves*. Harper & Row, New York.

1981 Vingt-cinq ans après: le complexe moustérien. *BSPF* 78:77–87.

Bordes, F. and J. Labrot.

1967 La stratigraphie du gisement de Roc de Combe et ses implications. *BSPF* 64:15–28.

Bordes, F. and D. De Sonneville-Bordes.

1970 The significance of variability in Palaeolithic assemblages. *World Archaeology* 2:61–73.

Boyer-Klein, A.

1976 Análisis polínico de la cueva de Tito Bustillo. In *Excavaciones en la Cueva de Tito Bustillo*, edited by J. Moure and M. Cano, 203–206. Instituto de Estudios Asturianos, Oviedo.

1980 Nouveaux résultats palynologiques de sites solutréens et magdaléniens cantabriques. *BSPF* 77:103–107.

1981 Análisis palinológico del Rascaño. In *El Paleolítico Superior de la Cueva del Rascaño*, edited by J. González Echegaray and I. Barandiarán, 217–220. CIMAM 3.

1984 Analyses polliniques cantabriques au Tardiglaciaire. *Revue de Paleobiologie* 1984:33–39.

1985 Analyse pollinique de la grotte d'Erralla. *Munibe* 37:45–48.

Boyer-Klein, A. and A. Leroi-Gourhan.
1985 Análisis palinológico de la Cueva del Juyo. In *Excavaciones en la Cueva del Juyo*, 57–61. CIMAM 14.

Breuil, H.
1913 Les subdivisions du Paléolithique supérieur et leur signification. *XIV Congrès International d'Anthropologie et d'Archéologie Préhistoriques*, vol. 1, 165–238.
1946 Hugo Obermaier. *Anthropos* 37–40:874–876.
1951 Souvenirs sur le Prince Albert de Monaco et son oeuvre préhistorique. *BSPF* 48:287–288.
1952 *Four Hundred Centuries of Cave Art*. Windels, Montignac.
1962 Théories et faits cantabriques relatifs au Paléolithique supérieur et à son art des cavernes. *Munibe* 14:353–358.

Breuil, H. and H. Obermaier.
1912 Les premiers travaux de l'Institut de Paléontologie Humaine. *L'Anthropologie* 23:1–27.
1913 Institut de Paléontologie Humaine: travaux exécutés en 1912. *L'Anthropologie* 24:1–16.
1914 Institut de Paleontologie Humaine: travaux de l'année 1913: II-Espagne. *L'Anthropologie* 25:233–253.
1935 *The Cave of Altamira et Santillana del Mar, Spain*. Tipografía de Archivos, Madrid.

Breuil, H., H. Obermaier, and H. Alcalde del Río.
1913 *La Pasiega à Puente Viesgo*. Vve. A. Chêne, Monaco.

Brodrick, A.
1963 *The Abbé Breuil: Prehistorian*. Hutchinson, London.

Burkitt, M.
1933 *The Old Stone Age*. Cambridge University Press, Cambridge.

Butzer, K.
1971 Comunicación preliminar sobre la geología de Cueva Morín. In *Cueva Morín: Excavaciones 1966–1968*, edited by J. González Echegaray and L. Freeman, 345–356. Patronato de las Cuevas Prehistóricas, Santander.
1973 Notas sobre la geomorfología regional de la parte occidental de la provincia de Santander y la estratigrafía de Cueva Morín. In *Cueva Morín: Excavaciones 1969*, edited by J. González Echegaray and L. Freeman, 267–276. Patronato de las Cuevas Prehistóricas, Santander.
1980 Investigación preliminar de la geología de la Cueva del Pendo. In *El Yacimiento de la Cueva de El Pendo*, edited by J. González Echegaray, 201–213. BPH 17.
1981 Cave sediments, Upper Pleistocene stratigraphy and Mousterian facies in Cantabrian Spain. *Journal of Archaeological Science* 8:133–183.
1985 Observaciones sobre la geología de la cueva de El Piélago II. *Sautuola* 4:19–24.
1986 Paleolithic adaptations and settlement in Cantabrian Spain. *Advances in World Archaeology* 5:201–252.

Butzer, K. and Bowman, D.

1976 Algunos sedimentos de niveles arqueológicos asturienses de yacimientos de la España cantábrica. In *El Asturiense Cantábrico*, by G. A. Clark, 351–355. BPH 13.

Cabre, J.

1915 *El Arte Rupestre en España*. CIPPM 1.

1934 *Las Cuevas de los Casares y de la Hoz*. Archivo de Arte y Arqueologia 30.

Cabrera, V.

1977 El yacimiento solutrense de Cueva Chufín. *XIV Congreso Nacional de Arqueología*, 157–164.

1983 Notas sobre el Musteriense cantábrico: el "Vasconiense," in *Homenaje al Prof. Martin Almagro Basch*, edited by A. Balil, 131–141. Ministério de Cultura, Madrid.

1984 *El Yacimiento de la Cueva de "El Castillo"*. BPH 22.

Cabrera, V. and J. Bischoff.

1989 Accelerator 14C ages for basal Aurignacion et El Castillo Cave. *Journal of Archaeological Science* 16:577–584.

Campbell, J.

1977 *The Upper Palaeolithic of Britain*. Clarendon, Oxford.

Carballo, J.

1923 *Excavaciones en la Cueva del Rey, en Villanueva*. Memoria de la Junta Superior de Excavaciones y Antiguedades 53.

1960 *Investigaciónes Prehistóricas II*. Diputación Provincial, Santander.

Cartailhac, E. and H. Breuil.

1906 *La Caverne d'Altamira, à Santillane, près Santander*. Imprimerie de Monaco, Monaco.

Castaños, P.

1980 La macrofauna de la Cueva de la Paloma. In *La Cueva de la Paloma*, edited by M. Hoyos, M. Martínez Navarrete, T. Chapa, P. Castaños, and F.Sanchíz, 65–100. EAE 116.

1982 Estudio de los macromamíferos del yacimiento de Cueto de la Mina. *BIDEA* 36:43–86.

Cattelain, P.

1989 Un crochet de propulseur solutréen de la grotte de Combe-Saunière I. *BSPF* 86:213–216.

Cava, A.

1975 La industria lítica de los niveles postazilienses de Santimamiñe. *Sautuola* 1:53–73.

1990 El Neolítico en el País Vasco. *Munibe* 42:97–106.

Chaline, J.

1966 Les lagomorphes et les rongeurs. In *Faunes et Flores Préhistoriques*, edited by R. Lavocat, 397–440. Boubée, Paris.

Chapman,R.

1981 The megalithic tombs of Iberia. In *Antiquity and Man*, edited by J. Evans, B. Cunliffe and C. Renfrew, 93–106. Thames and Hudson, London.

Cheynier, A. and J. González Echegaray.

1964 La grotte de Valle. In *Miscelánea en Homenaje al Abate Henri Breuil*, edited by E. Ripoll, vol. 1, 327–346. Diputación Provincial, Barcelona.

Clark, G.A.

1974 La ocupación asturiense en la Cueva de la Riera. *Trabajos de Prehistoria* 31:9–38.

1974–1975 Excavations in the Late Pleistocene cave site of Balmori, Asturias. *Quaternaria* 18:383–426.

1975 *Liencres: Una Estación al Aire Libre de Estilo Asturiense cerca de Santander*. Cuadernos de Arqueología de Deusto 3.

1976 *El Asturiense Cantábrico*. BPH 13.

1983 *The Asturian of Cantabria*. Anthropological Papers of the University of Arizona 41.

Clark, G. A. and L. Richards.

1978 Late and post-Pleistocene industries and fauna from the cave site of La Riera. In *Views of the Past*, edited by L. Freeman, 117–152. Mouton, The Hague.

Clark,G. A. and L. Straus.

1983 Late Pleistocene hunter-gatherer adaptations in Cantabrian Spain. In *Hunter-Gatherer Economy in Prehistory*, edited by G. Bailey, 131–148. Cambridge University Press, Cambridge.

Clarke, D.

1976 Mesolithic Europe: the economic basis. In *Problems in Economic and Social Archaeology*, edited by G. Sieveking, I. Longworth, and K. Wilson, 449–481. Duckworth, London.

CLIMAP

1976 The surface of the Ice-Age earth. *Science* 191:1131–1137.

Clottes, J.

1976 Les civilisations du Paléolithique supérieur dans les Pyrénées. In *La Préhistoire Française*, edited by H. de Lumley, vol. 1, 1214–1231.

1983 La caverne des Églises à Ussat. *BSPA* 38:23–81.

1986–1987 La determinación de las representaciones humanas y animales en el arte paleolítico europeo. *Bajo Aragón Prehistória* 7–8:41–68.

1989 Le Magdalénien des Pyrénées. In *Le Magdalénien en Europe*, edited by J. P. Rigaud, 281–360. *ERAUL* 38.

Cohen, M.

1977 *The Food Crisis in Prehistory*. Yale University Press, New Haven.

Conkey, M.

1978 *An Analysis of Design Structure: Variability among Magdalenian Engraved Bones from North Coastal Spain*. Ph.D. dissertation, Department of Anthropology, University of Chicago.

1980 The identification of prehistoric hunter-gatherer aggregation: the case of Altamira. *Current Anthropology* 21:609–630.

Corbet, G.

1966 *The Terrestrial Mammals of Western Europe*. Dufour, Philadelphia.

Corchón, M. S.

1981 *Cueva de las Caldas*. EAE 115.

1982 Estructuras de combustión en el Paleolítico: a proposito de un hogar a doble cubeta de la Cueva de las Caldas. *Zephyrus* 34–35:27–46.

1986 *El Arte Mueble Paleolítico Cantábrico* CIMAM 16.

Crowe, W.

1985 Tecnicas de recuperación integral de los datos obtenidos en los sedimentos de yacimientos prehistóricos. In *Excavaciones en la Cueva del Juyo*, edited by I. Barandiarán, L. Freeman, J. González Echegaray, and R. Klein, 65–74. CIMAM 14.

Cushman, K.

1986 Macrobotanical remains from La Riera cave. In *La Riera Cave*, edited by L. Straus and G. Clark, 65–66. Anthropological Research Papers 36, Tempe.

Deith, M.

1983 Seasonality of shell collecting, determined by oxygen isotope analysis of marine shells from Asturian sites. In *Animals and Archaeology*, edited by C. Grigson and J. Clutton-Brock, vol. 2, 67–76. BAR S-183.

Deith, M. and N. Shackleton.

1986 Seasonal exploitation of marine molluscs. In *La Riera Cave*, edited by L. Straus and G. Clark, 299–314. Anthropological Research Papers 36.

Delpech, F. and O. Legall.

1983 La faune magdalénienne de la grotte des Eglises. *BSPA* 38:91–118.

Delporte, H.

1985 Réflexions sur la chasse à la période paléolithique. *Jahrbuch des Bernischen Historischen Museums* 63–64:69–80.

1989 Notas sobre el conocimiento de Altamira en Francia. In *Cien Años después de Sautuola*, edited by M. González Morales pp. 157–171. Diputación Regional de Cantabria, Santander.

Diaz, T.

1980 Identificación de restos de madera quemada. In "El Conchero Asturiense de la Cueva de Mazculos II," by M. González Morales et al., 57–60. *Noticiario Arqueológico Hispánico* 9.

Dibble, H.

1987 Reduction sequences in the manufacture of Mousterian implements of France. In *The Pleistocene Old World*, edited by O. Soffer, 33–44. Plenum, New York.

1988 Typological aspects of reduction and intensity of utilization of lithic resources in the French Mousterian. In *Upper Pleistocene Prehistory of Western Eurasia*, edited by H. Dibble and A. Montet-White, 181–196. University of Pennsylvania Museum Monograph 54.

Dumont, J.

1986 Tool form and function: aspects of the Mount Sandel and Star Carr microwear research in relation to other comparable studies. In *The End of the Paleolithic in the Old World*, edited by L. Straus, 31–45. BAR S-284.

Duplessy, J., G. Delibrias, J. Turon, C. Pujol, and J. Duprat.
  1981 Deglacial warming of the northeastern Atlantic Ocean. *Palaeogeography, Palaeoclimatology, Palaeoecology* 35:121–144.
Dupré, M.
  1984 Palinología de los niveles VII a II. In *El Yacimiento Prehistórico de la Cueva de Ekain*, edited by J. Altuna and J. Merino, 61–63. Sociedad de Estudios Vascos, San Sebastián.
  1988 *Palinología Paleoambiente*. Servicio de Investigación Prehistórica de Valéncia, Trabajos Varios 84.
  1990 Análisis polínico de la Cueva de Amalda. In *La Cueva de Amalda*, edited by J. Altuna, A. Baldeón, and K. Mariezkurrena, 49–51. Sociedad de Estudios Vascos, San Sebastián.
Eastham, A.
  1984 The avifauna of the Cave of Ekain. In *El Yacimiento Prehistórico de la Cueva de Ekain*, edited by J. Altuna and J. Merino, 331–344. Sociedad de Estudios Vascos, San Sebastián.
  1985 The Magdalenian avifauna of Erralla cave. *Munibe* 37:59–80.
  1986 The La Riera avifaunas. In *La Riera Cave*, edited by L. Straus and G. Clark, 275–284. Anthropological Research Papers 36.
  1990 The bird bones in the cave of Amalda. In *La Cueva de Amalda*, edited by J. Altuna, A. Baldeón, and K. Mariezkurrena, 239–253. Sociedad de Estudios Vascos, San Sebastián.
Evin, J.
  1979 Réflexions générales et données nouvelles sur la chronologie absolue 14C des industries de la fin du Paléolithique et du début du Mésolithique. In *La Fin des Temps Glaciaires en Europe*, edited by D. de Sonneville-Bordes, 5–13. CNRS, Paris.
Fagnart, J.
  1988 *Les Industries Lithiques du Paléolithique Supérieur dans le Nord de la France*. Revue Archéologique de Picardie, No. Spéc.
Farizy, C.
  1990 *Paléolithique Moyen Récent et Paléolithique Supérieur Ancien en Europe*. Musée de Préhistoire de l'Ile de France, Mémoire 3.
Fernández Gutierrez, J.
  1969 Nota sobre la estratigrafía desconocida de la caverna del Castillo. *Boletín de la Real Sociedad Española de Historia Natural* 67:5–33.
Fernández-Tresguerres, J.
  1976a Azilian burial from Los Azules I, Asturias, Spain. *Current Anthropology* 17:769–770.
  1976b Espátula decorada aziliense. *Trabajos de Prehistoria* 33:331–338.
  1979 L'Azilien de la grotte de Los Azules I, Asturies. In *La Fin des Temps Glaciaires en Europe*, edited by D. de Sonneville-Bordes, 745–752. CNRS, Paris.
  1980 *El Aziliense en las Provincias de Asturias y Santander*. CIMAM 2.

1981 Cantos pintados del aziliense cantábrico. In *Altamira Symposium*, 245–250. Ministerio de Cultura, Madrid.

1983 La Cueva de los Azules. *Arqueología* 4(24):7–14.

Fortea, J.

1981 Investigaciónes en la cuenca média del Nalón, Asturias. *Zephyrus* 32–33:4–16.

1983 Perfiles recortados del Nalón médio. In *Homenaje al Prof. Martin Almagro Basch*, vol. 1, 343–353. Ministerio de Cultura, Madrid.

Fortea, J.

1989 Cuevas de La Lluera. Avance al estudio de sus artes parietales. In *Cien Años después de Sautola*, edited by M. González Morales, 189–202. Diputación Regional de Cantabria, Santander.

Fortea J., M. Corchón, M. Rodríguez, M. Hoyos, H. Laville, M. Dupré, and J. Fernández-Tresguerres.

1990 Travaux récents dans les vallées du Nalón et du Sella. In *L'Art des Objets au Paléolithique*, edited by J. Clottes, vol. 1, 219–243. Ministère de la Culture, Paris.

Freeman, L.

1964 *Mousterian Developments in Cantabrian Spain*. Ph.D. dissertation, Department of Anthropology, University of Chicago.

1966 The nature of Mousterian facies in Cantabrian Spain. *American Anthropologist* 68(2,2):230–237.

1970 El Musteriense cantábrico: nuevas perspectivas. *Ampurias* 31–32:55–69.

1971 Los niveles de ocupación musteriense. In *Cueva Morín: Excavaciones 1966–1968*, edited by J. González Echegaray and L. Freeman, 27–161. Patronato de las Cuevas Prehistóricas, Santander.

1973a El Musteriense. In *Cueva Morín: Excavaciones 1969*, edited by J. González Echegaray and L. Freeman, 15–140. Patronato de las Cuevas Prehistóricas, Santander.

1973b The significance of mammalian faunas from Paleolithic occupations in Cantabrian Spain. *American Antiquity* 38:3–44.

1975 Acheulian sites and stratigraphy in Iberia and the Maghreb. In *After the Australopithecines*, edited by K. Butzer and G. Isaac, 661–744. Mouton, The Hague.

1977 Contribución al estudio de niveles paleolíticos en la Cueva del Conde. *BIDEA* 90–91:447–486.

1978a The analysis of some occupation floor distributions from earlier and middle Paleolithic sites in Spain. In *Views of the Past*, edited by L. Freeman, 57–116. Mouton, The Hague.

1978b Relaciones entre los niveles musterienses de Morín. In *Vida y Muerte en Cueva Morín*, edited by J. González Echegaray and L. Freeman, 313–322. Institución Cultural de Cantabria, Santander.

1978c Mousterian worked bones from Cueva Morín. In *Views of the Past*, edited by L. Freeman, 29–52. Mouton, The Hague.

1978d Mamut, jabalí y bisonte en Altamira. In *Curso de Arte Rupestre Paleo-lítico*, 157–179. Universidad Internacional "Menéndez Pelayo," Santander.

1980 Ocupaciones musterienses. In *El Yacimiento de la Cueva de El Pendo*, edited by J. González Echegaray, 31–74. BPH 17.

1981 The fat of the land: notes on Paleolithic diet in Iberia. In *Omnivorous Primates*, edited by R. Harding and G. Teleki, 104–165. Columbia University Press, New York.

1987 Meanders on the byways of Paleolithic art. In *Altamira Revisited*, edited by L. Freeman, 15–66. Institute for Prehistoric Investigations, Chicago.

1988 The stratigraphic sequence at Altamira, 1880–1981. *Espacio, Tiempo y Forma* 1:149–163.

Freeman, L. and J. González Echegaray.

1968 La industria musteriense de la Cueva de la Flecha. *Zephyrus* 18:43–61.

1979 Aurignacian structural features at Cueva Morín. *Nature* 226:722–726.

1981 El Juyo: a 14,000-year-old sanctuary from northern Spain. *History of Religion* 21:1–19.

1982 Magdalenian mobile art from El Juyo. *Ars Praehistorica* 1:161–167.

1984 Magdalenian structures and sanctuary from the cave of El Juyo. In *Jungpaläolithische Siedlungsstrukturen in Europa*, edited by H. Berke, J. Hahn, and C. J. Kind, 39–49. Institüt fur Urgeschichte, Tübingen.

Freeman, L., F. Bernaldo de Quirós, and J. Ogden.

1987 Animals, faces and space at Altamira. In *Altamira Revisited*, edited by L. Freeman, 179–247. Institute for Prehistoric Investigations, Chicago.

Freeman, L., J. González Echegaray, R. Klein, and W. Crowe.

1988 Dimensions of research at El Juyo. In *Upper Pleistocene Prehistory of Western Eurasia*, edited by H. Dibble and A. Montet-White, 3–39. University of Pennsylvania Museum Monograph 54.

Fuentes, C.

1980 Estudio de la fauna de El Pendo. In *El Yacimiento de la Cueva de El Pendo*, edited by J. González Echegaray, 217–237. BPH 17.

Gamble, C.

1982 Interaction and alliance in Palaeolithic society. *Man* 17:92–107.

1986 *The Palaeolithic Settlement of Europe*. Cambridge University Press, Cambridge.

Gamble, C. and O. Soffer.

1990 *The World at 18,000 BP: Low Latitudes*. Unwin Hyman, London.

García Castro, J. A.

1987 *Arte Rupestre en España*. Arqueología, Madrid.

García Guinea, M. A.

1985 Las cuevas azilienses de el Piélago y sus excavaciones de 1967–1969. *Sautuola* 4:11–154.

Garralda, M.D.

1976 Dientes humanos del Magdaleniense de Tito Bustillo. In *Excavaciones en la Cueva de Tito Bustillo*, edited by J. Moure and M. Cano, 197–199. Instituto de Estudios Asturianos, Oviedo.

1981 Las mandíbulas de Balmori y Mazaculos II. *BIDEA* 103:595–603.

1982 New human remains of the Spanish Mesolithic. *Historical Anthropology* 9:375–378.

1986 Human remains from Solutrean levels at La Riera Cave. In *La Riera Cave*, edited by L. Straus and G. Clark, 323–324. Anthropological Research Papers 36.

1989 Upper Paleolithic human remains fromEl Castillo Cave. In *Hominidae*, edited by G. Giacobini, 479–482. Jaca Book, Milan.

Gates. W. L.

1976 Modelling the Ice-Age climate. *Science* 191:1138–1144.

Gavelas, A.

1980 Sobre nuevos concheros asturienses en los concejos de Ribadesella y Llanes. *BIDEA* 101:675–703, 711–718.

1986 El enterramiento con cerámica campaniforme de la Cueva del Ruso I. *BIDEA* 118:563–588.

Geneste, J. M. and H. Plisson.

1986 Le Solutréen de la grotte de Combe Saunière I. *Gallia Préhistoire* 29:6–27.

González Echegaray, J.

1974 *Las Pinturas y Grabados de la Cueva de las Chimeneas.* Monografías de Arte Rupestre, Barcelona.

1978 Cuevas con arte rupestre en la Región Cantábrica. In *Curso de Arte Rupestre Paleolítico*, 49–77. Universidad Internacional "Menéndez Pelayo," Santander.

1980 El Yacimiento de la Cueva de *"El Pendo."* BPH 17.

1981 Industria lítica. In *El Paleolítico Superior de la Cueva del Rasaño*, edited by J. González Echegaray and I. Barandiarán, 57–94. CIMAM 3.

1984 Reflexiones sobre el momento actual en la investigación del Paleolítico superior cantábrico. In *Scripta Praehistorica Francisco Jordá Oblata*, edited by J. Fortea, 259–269. Universidad de Salamanca, Salamanca.

1985 La industria lítica. In *Excavaciones en la Cueva del Juyo*, edited by I. Barandiarán, L. Freeman, J. González Echegaray, and R. Klein, 123–153. CIMAM 14.

1986 Essai de classification des sanctuaires paléolithiques dans la région cantábrique. *L'Anthropologie* 90:679–684.

González Echegaray, J. and I. Barandiarán.

1981 *El Paleolítico Superior de la Cueva del Rascaño.* CIMAM 3.

González Echegaray, J. and L. Freeman.

1971 *Cueva Morín: Excavaciones 1966–1968.* Patronato de las Cuevas Prehistóricas, Santander.

1973 *Cueva Morín: Excavaciones 1969.* Patronato de las Cuevas Prehistóricas, Santander.

1978 *Vida y Muerte en Cueva Morín.* Institución Cultural de Cantabria, Santander.

González Echegaray, J., M. García Guinea, A. Begines, and B. Madariaga.

1963 *Cueva del la Chora.* EAE 26.

González, Echegaray, J., M. García Guinea, and A. Begines.
1966 *Cueva del Otero*. EAE 53.
González Echegaray, J. and E. Ripoll.
1953–54 Hallazgos en la cueva de La Pasiega. *Ampurias* 15–16:43–61.
González Morales, M.
1974 *La Cueva de Collubil*. Licenciatura thesis, Departamiento de Prehistoria y Arqueología, Universidad de Oviedo.
1978 Excavaciones en el conchero asturiense de la cueva de Mazaculos II. *BIDEA* 93–94:369–383.
1982a *El Asturiense y Otras Culturas Locales*. CIMAM 7.
1982b La cueva del Tebellín y sus pinturas rupestres. *Ars Praehistorica* 1:169–174.
1986 La Riera bone and antler artifact assemblages. In *La Riera Cave*, edited by L. Straus and G. Clark, 209–218, 385–419.
1987 Arte rupestre paleolítico en Asturias. In *Arte Rupestre en España*, edited by J. Garcia Castro, 56–65. Arqueología, Madrid.
1989 El abrigo de Entrefoces. In *Excavaciones Arqueológicas en Asturias 1983–86*, 29–36. Principado de Asturias, Oviedo.
1990 La prehistoria de las Marismas: excavaciones en el abrigo de la Peña del Perro. *Cuadernos de Trasmiera* 2:13–28.
González Morales, M., M. Marquez, T. Díaz, J. Ortea, and K. C. Volman.
1980 El conchero asturiense de la Cueva de Mazaculos II: campañas de 1976 a 1978. *Noticiario Arqueológico Hispánico* 9:37–62.
González Sainz, C.
1982 Un colgante decorado de Cueva Morín. *Ars Praehistorica* 1:151–159.
1988 Le fait artistique à la fin du Paléolithique. *BSPA* 43:35–62.
1989 *El Magdaleniense Superior-Final de la Región Cantábrica*. Tantin, Santander.
González Sainz, C. and M. González Morales.
1986 *La Prehistoria en Cantabria*. Tantin, Santander.
González Sainz, C., E. Muñoz, and C. San Miguel.
1985 Los grabados rupestres paleolíticos de la Cueva del Otero. *Sautuola* 4:155–164.
Gorrochategui, J. and M. Yarritu.
1990 El complejo cultural del Neolítico final-Edad del Bronce en el Pais Vasco Cantábrico. *Munibe* 42:107–123.
GTPC (Groupe de Travail de Prehistoire Cantabrique)
1979 Chronostratigraphie et écologie des cultures du Paleolithique final en Espagne cantabrique. In *La Fin des Temps Glaciaires en Europe*, edited by D. de Sonneville-Bordes, 713–719. CNRS, Paris.
Guerrero, L. and L. Lorenzo.
1981 Antropologia física en Rascaño. In *El Paleolítico Superior de la Cueva del Rascaño*, edited by J. González Echegaray and I. Barandiarán, 279–321. CIMAM 3.

Guinea Lopez, E.
1953 *Geografía Botánica de Santander.* Diputación Provincial, Santander.
Halverson, J.
1987 Art for art's sake in the Paleolithic. *Current Anthropology* 26:83–89.
Harle, E.
1881 La grotte d'Altamira, près de Santander. *Matériaux* 16:275–283.
Harrold, F.
1981 New perspectives on the Chatelperronian. *Ampurias* 43:35–85.
1983 The Chatelperronian and the Middle-Upper Paleolithic transition. In *The Mousterian Legacy*, edited by E. Trinkaus, 123–140. BAR S-164.
1986 Une réevaluation du Châtelperronien. *BSPA* 41:151–169.
1989 Mousterian, Chatelperronian and early Aurignacian in western Europe: continuity or discontinuity? In *The Human Revolution*, edited by P. Mellars and C. Stringer, 677–713. Edinburgh University Press, Edinburgh.
Hernández-Pacheco, E.
1919 *La Cueva de la Peña de Candamo.* CIPPM 24.
1923 *La Vida de Nuestros Antecesores Paleolíticos, Según los Resultados de las Excavaciones en la Caverna de la Paloma.* CIPPM 31.
1959 *Prehistoria del Solar Hispánico: Origenes del Arte Pictórico.* Real Academia de Ciencias Exactas, Físicas y Naturales, Madrid.
Hernández-Pacheco, F.
1944 *Fisiografía, geología y glaciarismo cuaternário de las montañas de Reinosa.* Real Academia de Ciencias Exacts, Físicas y Naturales, Memoria 10.
Hernández-Pacheco, F, N. Llopis, F. Jordá, and J. Martínez.
1957 *INQUA, V Congreso: Guia de la Excursión N2-El Cuaternário de la Región Cantábrica.* Diputación Provincial, Oviedo.
Hickerson, H.
1965 The Virginia deer and intertribal buffer zones in the Upper Mississippi Valley. In *Man, Culture and Animals*, edited by A. Leeds and A. Vayda, 43–65. American Association for the Advancement of Science, Washington.
Hoffecker, J. and C. Wolf.
1988 *The Early Upper Paleolithic.* BAR S-437.
Houston, J.
1967 *The Western Mediterranean World.* Praeger, New York.
Hoyos, M.
1980 Estudio geológico y sedimentológico de la cueva de la Paloma. In *La Cueva de la Paloma*, edited by M. Hoyos, M. Martínez Navarrete, T. Chapa, P.Castaños, and F. Sanchíz, 23–63. EAE 116.
1981 Estudio geológico de la cueva de las Caldas. In *Cueva de las Caldas*, edited by M. Corchón, 11–56. EAE 115.
Hoyos, M. and M. P. Fumanal.
1985 La cueva de Erralla: estudio sedimentológico. *Munibe* 37:29–43.

Hoyos, M., M. Martínez Navarrete, T. Chapa, P. Castaños, and F. Sanchíz.

1980 *La Cueva de la Paloma.* EAE 116.

Hoyos, M. and H. Laville.

1983 Nuevas aportaciones sobre la estratigrafía y sedimentología de los depositos del Paleolítico superior de la cueva del Pendo. *Zephyrus* 34–35:285–293.

Isturiz, M. J. and M. F. Sánchez Goñi.

1990 Investigaciónes palinológicas en la prehistoria vasca. *Munibe* 42:277–285.

Janssens, P. and J. González Echegaray.

1958 *Memoria de las Excavaciones de la Cueva del Juyo (1955–56).* Patronato de las Cuevas Prehistóricas, Santander.

Jochim, M.

1983 Paleolithic art in ecological perspective. In *Hunter-Gatherer Economy in Prehistory,* edited by G. Bailey, 212–219. Cambridge University Press, Cambridge.

1987 Late Pleistocene refugia in Europe. In *The Pleistocene Old World,* edited by O. Soffer, 317–331. Plenum, New York.

Jordá, F.

1955 *El Solutrense en España y sus Problemas.* Diputación Provincial, Oviedo.

1958 *Avance al Estudio de la Cueva de la Lloseta,* Diputación Provincial, Oviedo.

1959 Revisión de la cronología del Asturiense. *Actas del V Congreso Nacional de Arqueología,* 63–66. Zaragoza.

1964 El arte rupestre paleolítico de la región cantábrica: nueva secuencia cronológico-cultural. In *Prehistoric Art of the Western Mediterranean and the Sahara,* edited by L. Pericot and E. Ripoll, 47–81. Viking Fund Publications in Anthropology 39.

1977 *Historia de Asturias. Prehistoria.* Ayalga, Salinas.

Jordá, F. and M. Mallo.

1972 *Las Pinturas de la Cueva de las Herrerías.* Seminário de Prehistoria y Arqueología, Salamanca.

Jordá, F., J. Fortea and M. S. Corchón.

1982 Nuevos datos sobre la edad del Solutrense y Magdaleniense médio cantábrico: las fechas C-14 de la Cueva de las Caldas. *Zephyrus* 34–35:13–16.

Jordá, F., M. Pellicer, P. Acosta, and M. Almagro Gorbea.

1986 *Prehistoria* (Historia de España, vol. 1). Gredos, Madrid.

Julia, R. and J. Bischoff.

1991 Radiometric dating of Quaternary deposits and of the hominid mandible of Lake Banyolas, Spain. *Journal of Archaeological Science* 18.

Julien, M.

1982 *Les Harpons Magdaléniens.* CNRS, Paris.

Keeley, L.

1981 Premiers résultats de l'analyse des micro-traces d'utilisation de quelques objets. In "Le site magdalénien du Buisson Campin à Verberie," by F. Audouze et al., 137–141. *Gallia Préhistoire* 24:99–143.

1988 Lithic economy, style and use: a comparison of three late Magdalenian sites. *Lithic Technology* 17:19–25.

Kehoe, T.

1990 Corraling life. In *The Life of Symbols*, edited by M. Foster and L. Botscharow, 175–193. Westview, Boulder.

Klein, R. and K. Cruz-Uribe.

1984 *The Analysis of Animal Bones from Archeological Sites.* University of Chicago Press, Chicago.

1985 La fauna mamífera del yacimiento de la cueva de "El Juyo." In *Excavaciones en la Cueva del Juyo*, edited by I. Barandiarán, L. Freeman, J. González Echegaray, and R. Klein, 99–120. CIMAM 14.

Klein, R., K. Allwarden and C. Wolf.

1983 The calculation and interpretation of ungulate age profiles from dental crown heights. In *Hunter-Gatherer Economy inPrehistory*, edited by G. Bailey, 47–57, Cambridge University Press, Cambridge.

Klein, R., C. Wolf, L. Freeman, and K. Allwarden.

1981 The use of dental crown heights for constructing age profiles of red deer and similar species in archeological samples. *Journal of Archaeological Science* 8:1–31.

Kopp, K.

1965 Limite de la nieve perpétua y clima de la época glaciar Würmiense en la Sierra de Aralar. *Munibe* 17:3–20.

Kornprobst, P. and P. Rat.

1967 Premiers résultats d'une étude géologique et paléoclimatique du remplissage paléolithique moyen et supérior de Lezetiki. *Munibe* 19:247–260.

Kozłowski, J.

1990 Northern central Europe c. 18,000 BP. In *The World at 18,000 BP*, edited by O. Soffer and C. Gamble, vol. 1, 204–227. Unwin Hyman, London.

Laming-Emperaire, A.

1962 *La Signification de l'Art Rupestre Paléolithique.* Picard, Paris.

Lautensach, H.

1964 *Iberische Halbinsel.* Keysersche Verlagsbuchhandlung, Munich.

Laville, H.

1981 Los depositos solutrenses de la Cueva de la Riera. *Zephyrus* 32–33:57–59.

1986 Stratigraphy, sedimentology and chronology of the La Riera Cave deposits. In *La Riera Cave*, edited by L.Straus and G. Clark, 25–55. Anthropological Research Papers 36.

Laville, H. and M. Hoyos.

1981 Estudio geológico de la Cueva del Rascaño. In *El Paleolítico Superior de la Cueva del Rascaño*, edited by J. González Echegaray and I. Barandiarán, 191–210. CIMAM 3.

Laville, H., J. P. Rigaud, and J. Sackett.

1980 *Rockshelters of the Perigord.* Academic Press, New York.

Laville, H., J. P. Raynal, and J. P. Texier.
1984 Interglaciaire ou déja glaciaire? *BSPF* 81:9–11.
Leoz, I. and C. Labadía.
1984 La malacología del yacimiento de Ekain. In *El Yacimiento Prehistórico de la Cueva de Ekain*, edited by J. Altuna and J. Merino, 287–296. Sociedad de Estudios Vascos, San Sebastián.
Leroi-Gourhan, André.
1958 Le symbolisme des grands signes dans l'art pariétal paléolithique. *BSPF* 55:384–398.
1971 *Préhistoire de l'Art Occidental*. Mazenod, Paris.
1982 *The Dawnof European Art*. Cambridge University Press, Cambridge.
Leroi-Gourhan, André, and Arlette Leroi-Gourhan.
1964 Chronologie des grottes d'Arcy-sur-Cure. *Gallia Préhistoire* 7:1–35.
Leroi-Gourhan, Arlette.
1956 Résultats de l'analyse pollinique de la grotte d'Isturitz. *BSPF* 56:619–624.
1966 Análisis polinico de la Cueva del Otero. In *Cueva del Otero*, edited by J. González Echegaray, M. García, and A. Begines, 83–85. EAE 53.
1971 Análisis polínico de Cueva Morín. In *Cueva Morín: Excavaciones 1966–1968*, edited by J. González Echegaray and L. Freeman, 359–365. Patronato de las Cuevas Prehistóricas, Santander.
1980 Análisis polínico de El Pendo. In *El Yacimiento de la Cueva de "El Pendo"*, edited by J. González Echegaray, 265–266, BPH 17.
1986 The palynology of La Riera Cave. In *La Riera Cave*, edited by L. Straus and G. Clark, 59–64. Anthropological Research Papers 36.
Leroi-Gourhan, Arlette, and J. Allain.
1979 *Lascaux Inconnu*. CNRS, Paris.
Lévèque, F. and B. Vandermeersch.
1980 Découverte de restes humains dans un niveau castelperronien à Saint-Césaire. *Comptes-Rendus de l'Académie des Sciences de Paris* (Série II) 291:187–189.
Lewis-Williams, J. D. and T. Dowson.
1988 The signs of the times: entoptic phenomena in Upper Paleolithic art. *Current Anthropology* 29:209–245.
López, P.
1981 Análisis polínico del yacimiento de Los Azules. *Botanica Macaronesica* 8–9:243–248.
1982 Abauntz: análisis polínico. *Trabajos de Arqueología Navarra* 3:355–358.
López-Berges, M. A. and M. Valle.
1985 Estudio osteológico de la cueva de Piélago II. *Sautuola* 4:113–121.
Lötze, F.
1962 Pleistozäne Vergletscherungen im Ostteil des Kantabrischen Gebirges. *Akademie der Wissenschaften und der Literatur (Mainz), Abhhandlungen der Mathematisch-Naturwissenschaftlichen Klasse* 2(1962): 151–169.
McIntyre, A., and N. Kipp.
1976 Glacial North Atlantic 18,000 years ago: a CLIMAP reconstruction. In

Investigation of Late Quatenary Paleoceanography and Paleoclimatology, edited by R. Cline and J. Hays, 43–75. Geological Society of America Memoir 145.

Madariaga, B.

1963 Análisis paleontológico. In Cueva de la Chora, edited by J. González Echegaray, M. García Guinea, and A. Begines, 53–74. EAE 26.

1971 La fauna marina de Cueva Morín. In *Cueva Morín: Excavaciones 1966–1968*, edited by J. González Echegaray and L. Freeman, 401–155. Patronato de las Cuevas Prehistóricas, Santander.

1972 *Hermilio Alcalde del Río: Una Escuela de Preshistoria en Santander.* Patronato de las Cuevas Prehistóricas, Santander.

1975 Representación malacológica de la cueva de Tito Bustillo o de "El Ramu". In *Primeros Sondeos Estratigráficos en la Cueva de Tito Bustillo*, edited by M. García Guinea, 71–74. Patronato de las Cuevas Prehistóricas, Santander.

1976a Estudio de la fauna marina de la cueva de Tito Bustillo. In *Excavaciones en la Cueva de Tito Bustillo*, edited by J. A. Moure and M. Cano, 209–227. Instituto de Estudios Asturianos, Oviedo.

1976b Consideraciones acerca de la utilización del "pico marisquero" del Asturiense. In *XL Aniversario del Centro de Estudios Montañeses*, vol. 2, 437–451. Institucion Cultural de Cantabria, Santander.

Madariaga, B. and C. Fernández.

1985 Estudio malacológico de la cueva "El Juyo." In *Excavaciones en la Cueva del Juyo*, edited by I. Barandiarán, L. Freeman, J. González Echegaray, and R. Klein, 77–95. CIMAM 14.

Mariezkurrena, C.

1990 Dataciones absolutas para la arqueología vasca. *Munibe* 42:287–304.

Mariezkurrena, K.

1990 Caza y domesticación durante el Neolítico y Edad de los Metales en el País Vasco. *Munibe* 42:241–252.

Marks, A. and D. Friedel.

1977 Prehistoric settlement patterns in the Avdat/Aqev Area. In *Prehistory and Paleoenvironments in the Central Negev*, edited by A. Marks, vol. 2, 131–158. Southern Methodist University, Dallas.

Marquez, Uria M. C.

1974 Trabajos de campo realizados por el Conde de la Vega del Sella. *BIDEA* 83:811–835.

1977 Las excavaciones del Conde de la Vega del Sella en la Cueva del Conde. *BIDEA* 90–91:431–446.

1981 Los grabados rupestres de la Cueva del Conde. In *Altamira Symposium*, 311–317. Ministério de Cultura, Madrid.

Marsan, G.

1979 Les industries du Tardiglaciaire des Pyrénées-Atlantiques et du Guipúzcoa. In *La Fin des Temps Glaciaires en Europe*, edited by D. de Sonneville-Bordes, 667–692. CNRS, Paris.

Martínez Navarrete, M. and T. Chapa.
1980 La industria prehistoria de la Cueva de la Paloma. In *La Cueva de la Paloma*, edited by M. Hoyos, M. Navarrete, T. Chapa, P. Castaños, and F. Sanchíz, 115–204. EAE 116.

Mary, G., J. Medus, and G. Delibrias.
1975 Le Quaternaire de la côte asturienne. *Bulletin de l'Association Française pour l'Etude du Quaternaire* 1975(1):13–23.
1977a Documents sur l'évolution de la flore du littoral nordespagnol au Würm. *Supplément au Bulletin de l'Association Française pour l'Etude du Quaternaire* 50:23–31.
1977b The flora of the north coastline of Spain during the Würm. *Abstracts of the 10th INQUA Congress*, 290.

Mayor, M. and T. Diaz.
1977 *La Flora Asturiana*. Ayalga, Salinas.

Mellars, P.
1973 The character of the Middle-Upper Palaeolithic transition in southwest France. In *The Explanation of Culture Change*, edited by C. Renfrew, 255–276. Duckworth, London.
1989 Major issues in the emergence of modern humans. *Current Anthropology* 30:349–385.
1990 *The Emergence of Modern Humans*. Edinburgh University Press, Edinburgh.

Mellars, P. and C. Stringer.
1989 *The Human Revolution*. Edinburgh University Press, Edinburgh.

Menéndez, M.
1984 La Cueva del Buxú. *BIDEA* 111:143–186; 112:755–801.

Menéndez-Amor, J.
1976 Muestras de polen de Liencres. In *El Asturiense Cantábrico*, by G. Clark, 359. BPH 13.

Menéndez de la Hoz, M., L. Straus, and G. Clark.
1986 The ichthyology of La Riera Cave. In *La Riera Cave*, edited by L. Straus and G. Clark, 285–288. Anthropological Research Papers 36.

Merino, J.
1984 Industria lítica del yacimiento de Ekain. In *El Yacimiento Prehistórico de la Cueva de Ekain*, edited by J. Altuna and J. Merino, 65–175. Sociedad de Estudios Vascos, San Sebastián.

Mithen, S.
1988 Looking and learning: Upper Paleolithic art and information gathering. *World Archaeology* 19(3):297–327.
1990 *Thoughtful Foragers*. Cambridge University Press, Cambridge.

Morales, A. and E. Roselló.
1990 La ictiofauna de la Cueva de Amalda. In *La Cueva de Amalda*, edited by J. Altuna, A. Baldeón, and K. Mariezkurrena, 255–266. Sociedad de Estudios Vascos, San Sebastián.

Moss, E.
1983 *The Functional Analysis of Flint Implements.* BAR S-177.

Moure, J. A.
1974 *Magdaleniense Superior y Aziliense en la Región Cantábrica Española.* Doctoral dissertation, Departamento de Prehistoria y Arquelogía, Universidad Complutense.
1975 *Excavaciones en la Cueva de Tito Bustillo. Campañas de 1972 y 1974.* Instituto de Estudios Asturianos, Oviedo.
1979 Le Magdalénien supérieur de la grotte de Tito Bustillo. In *La Fin des Temps Glaciaires en Europe*, edited by D. de Sonneville-Bordes, 737–743. CNRS, Paris.
1980 *Las Pinturas y Grabados de la Cueva de Tito Bustillo.* Universidad de Valladolid, Valladolid.
1981 La "Galeria de los Caballos" de la cueva de Tito Bustillo. In *Altamira Symposium*, 85–116. Ministerior de Cultura, Madrid.
1982 *Placas Grabadas de la Cueva de Tito Bustillo.* Studia Archaeologica 69, Valladolid.
1985 Nouveautés dans l'art mobilier figuratif du Paléolithique cantabrique. *BSPA* 40:99–129.
1987 Introducción al arte rupestre paleolítico cantábrico. In *Arte rupestre en España*, edited by J. García, 30–37. Arqueología, Madrid.
1988 Composition et variabilité dans l'art pariétal paléolithique cantabrique. *L'Anthropologie* 92:73–86.
1989 La caverne de Tito Bustillo. Le gisement paléolithique. *L'Anthropologie* 93:407–434.
1990 Fauna y medio ambiente en el arte rupestre paleolítico. *Boletín del Seminario de Estudios de Arte y Arqueología* (Universidad de Valladolid) 56:38–52.

Moure, J. A. and M. Cano.
1976 *Excavaciones en la Cueva de Tito Bustillo: Trabajos de 1975.* Instituto de Estudios Asturianos, Oviedo.

Netboy, A.
1968 *The Atlantic Salmon.* Houghton Mifflin, Boston.

Noval, A.
1976 *La Fauna Salvaje de Asturias.* Ayalga, Salinas.

Nussbaum, F. and F. Gygax.
1952 Glazialmorphologische Untersuchengen im Kantabrischen Gebirge. *Jahresbericht Geographische Gesellschaft* 1951–52:54–79.

Obermaier, H.
1914 *Estudio de los Glaciares de los Picos de Europa.* Publicaciones del Museo Nacional de Ciencias Naturales. Serie Geológica, Memoria 9.
1916 *El Hombre Fósil.* CIPPM 9 (1st ed.).
1924 *Fossil Man in Spain.* Yale University Press, New Haven.
1925 *El Hombre Fósil.* CIPPM 9 (2nd ed.).

Obermaier, H. and R. Conde de la Vega del Sella.
  1918 *La Cueva del Buxú*. CIPPM 20.
Ortea, J. A.
  1986 The malacology of La Riera Cave. In *La Riera Cave*, edited by L. Straus and G. Clark, 289–298. Anthropological Research Papers 36.
Otte, M.
  1990 The northwestern European Plain around 18,000 BP. In *The World at 18,000 BP*, edited by O. Soffer and C. Gamble, vol. 1, 54–68. Unwin Hyman, London.
Passemard, E.
  1944 La caverne d'Isturitz en Pays Basque. *Préhistoire 9*.
Pemán, E.
  1985 Aspectos climáticos y ecológicos de los micromamíferos del yacimiento de Erralla. *Munibe* 37:49–57.
  1990 Los micromamíferos de la cueva de Amalda y su significado. In *La Cueva de Amalda*, edited by J. Altuna, A. Baldeón, and K. Mariezkurrena, 225–238. Sociedad de Estudios Vascos, San Sebastián.
Pérez, C. and P. Arias.
  1979 Tumulos y yacimientos al aire libre de la Sierra Plana de la Borbolla. *BIDEA* 98:695–715.
Peterson, R., G. Montfort, and P. Hollom.
  1982 *Guía de Campo de las Aves de España y de Europa*. Omega, Barcelona.
Peyrony, D.
  1933 Les industries aurignaciennes dans le bassin de la Vézère: Aurignacien et Périgordien. *BSPF* 30:543–559.
Phillips, P.
  1975 *Early Farmers of West Mediterranean Europe*. Hutchinson, London.
Polunin, O. and B. Smythies.
  1977 *Guía de Campo de las Flores de España*. Omega, Barcelona.
Pradel, L.
  1979 Puntas de laurel de la Cueva de la Riera. *BIDEA* 96–97; 485–488.
Rasilla, M. de la.
  1990 Le Solutréen cantabrique. In *Feuilles de Pierre: Les Industries à Pointes Foliacées du Paléolithique Supérieur Européen*, edited by J. Kozłowski, 481–484, ERAUL 42.
Raynal, J. P. and J. L. Guadelli.
  1990 Milieux physiques et biologiques: quels changements entre 60 et 30.000 ans à l'ouest de l'Europe. In *Paléolithique Moyen Recent et Paléolithique Supérieur Ancien en Europe*, edited by C. Farizy, 53–61. Mémoires du Musée de Préhistoire d'Ile de France 3.
Rice, P. and A. Paterson.
  1985 Cave art and bones: exploring the interrelationships. *American Anthropologist* 87:94–100.
  1986 Validating the cave art-archeofaunal relationship in Cantabrian Spain. *American Anthropologist* 88:658–667.

Ripoll, E.

1971 *La Cueva de Las Monedas en Puente Viesgo*. Monografías de Arte Rupestre, Barcelona.

Rodríguez, J.

1978 Nota preliminar sobre las excavaciones del yacimiento de Bañugues. *BIDEA* 93–94:357–368.

1983 *La Presencia Humana más Antigua en Asturias*. Fundación Pública de Cuevas y Yacimientos Prehistóricos de Asturias, Oviedo.

Rodríguez, J. and G. Flor.

1979 Estudio del yacimiento prehistórico de Bañugues y su médio de deposito. *Zephyrus* 29:205–222.

1983 Industrias paleolíticas eolizadas en la región del Cabo Peñas. *VI Reunión del Grupo Español de Trabajo del Cuaternário*, 23–46.

Rua, C. de la.

1985 Restos humanos de Erralla. *Munibe* 37:195–198.

1990 Los estudios de paleoantropología en el País Vasco. *Munibe* 42:199–219.

Ruddiman, W. and A. McIntyre.

1981 The North Atlantic Ocean during the last deglaciation. *Palaeogeography, Palaeoclimatology, Palaeoecology* 35:145–214.

Saint-Perier, R. and S. dé.

1952 *La Grotte d'Isturitz III: Les Solutréens, les Aurignaciens et les Moustériens*. Archives de l'Institut de Paléontologie Humaine, Mémoire 25.

Sánchez Goñi, M. F.

1990 Analyse palynologique de sites préhistoriques du Pays Basque. In *The Environment and the Human Society in the Western Pyrenees and the Basque Mountains during the Upper Pleistocene and the Holocene*, 111–130. Universidad del País Vasco, Gasteiz.

1991 *Analyses Palynologiques des Remplissages de Grotte de Lezetxiki, Labeko Et Urtiaga*. Doctoral dissertation, Museum National d'Histoire Naturelle, Institut de Paléontologie Humaine, Paris.

Sanemeterio, M.

1976 Apuntes bibliográficos sobre el descubrimiento de la cueva de Altamira. In *Marcelino Sanz de Sautuola: Escritos y Documentos*, edited by B. Madariaga, 289–343. Institución Cultural de Cantabria, Santander.

Santonja, M. and P. Villa.

1990 The Lower Paleolithic of Spain and Portugal. *Journal of World Prehistory* 4:45–94.

Sanz de Sautuola, M.

1880 *Breves Apuntes sobre Algunos Objetos Prehistóricos de la Provincia de Santander*. T. Martínez, Santander.

Scarre, C.

1983 *Ancient France*. Edinburgh University Press, Edinburgh.

Schmider, B.

1990 The last Pleniglacial in the Paris Basin. In *The World at 18,000 BP*, edited by O. Soffer and C. Gamble, 41–53. Unwin Hyman, London.

Sierra, L.

1908 Notas para el mapa paletnográfico de la Provincia de Santander. *Actas del Primer Congreso de Naturalistas Españolas*, 103–117, Zaragoza.

Sieveking, A.

1979 Style and regional grouping in Magdalenian cave art. *Bulletin of the Institute of Archaeology* 16:95–109.

Simonnet, R.

1985 Le silex du Magdalénien final de la grotte des Eglises dans le Bassin de Tarascon-sur Ariège. *BSPA* 40:71–97.

Soffer, O.

1985 *The Upper Paleolithic of the Central Russian Plain.* Academic Press, New York.

1987 *The Pleistocene Old World.* Plenum, New York.

Soffer, O. and C. Gamble.

1990 *The World at 18,000 BP: High Latitudes.* Unwin Hyman, London.

Sonneville-Bordes, D. Dé.

1960 *Le Paléolithique Supérieur en Périgord.* Delmas, Bordeaux.

1963 Upper Paleolithic cultures in western Europe. *Science* 142:347–355.

1982 L'evolution des industries aurignaciennes. In *Aurignacien et Gravettien en Europe*, edited by M. Otte, 339–360. ERAUL 13-2.

Sonneville-Bordes, D. dé and J. Perrot.

1953 Essai d'application des méthodes statistiques au Paleolithique supérieur. Premiers résultats. *BSPF* 50:356–364.

1954 Lexique typologique du Paléolithique supérieur. *BSPF* 51:327–333.

Soto, E.

1984 Restos faunísticos de la cueva del Buxú. *BIDEA* 112:803–810.

Soto, E. and G. Meléndez.

1981 Fauna de la Cueva de Las Caldas. In *Cueva de las Caldas*, edited by M. Corchón, 261–268. EAE 115.

Straus, L. G.

1974a Le Solutréen du Pays Basque: une esquisse des données. *Munibe* 26: 173–181.

1974b Notas preliminares sobre el Solutrense de Asturias. *BIDEA* 82:483–504.

1975a *A Study of the Solutrean in Vasco-Cantabrian Spain.* Ph.D. dissertation, Department of Anthropology, University of Chicago.

1975b ¿Solutrense o Magdaleniense inferior cantábrico? Significado de las "diferencias." *BIDEA* 86:781–790.

1976 Análisis arqueologico de fauna paleolítica del Norte de la Peninsula Iberica. *Munibe* 28:277–285.

1976–1977 The Upper Paleolithic cave site of Altamira. *Quaternaria* 19: 135–148.

1977a El Solutrense cantábrico. In *XL Aniversario del Centro de Estudios Montañeses*, vol. 3, 309–319. Institución Cultural de Cantabria, Santander.

1977b Of deerslayers and mountain men: Paleolithic faunal exploitation in

Cantabrian Spain. In *For Theory Building in Archaeology*, edited by L. Binford, 41–76. Academic Press, New York.

1977c Pointes solutréennes et l'hypothèse de territorialisme. *BSPF* 74:206–212.

1977d Thoughts on Solutrean concave base point distribution. *Lithic Technology* 6:32–35.

1978 Observaciones preliminares sobre la variabilidad de las puntas solutrenses. *Trabajos de Prehistoria* 35:397–402.

1979a Notas teóricas sobre el Solutrense de Asturias. *BIDEA* 96–97:473–483.

1979b Cantabria and Vascongadas, 21,000–17,000 B.P.: Toward a Solutrean settlement pattern. *Munibe* 31:195–202.

1979c Mesolithic adaptations along the northern coast of Spain. *Quaternaria* 21:305–327.

1979d Norteamericanos en la prehistoria montañesa. In *Santander y el Nuevo Mundo*, 567–571. Institución Cultural de Cantabria, Santander.

1980 The role of raw materials in lithic assemblage variability. *Lithic Technology* 9:68–72.

1981a On the habitat and diet of *Cervus elaphus. Munibe* 33:175–182.

1981b On maritime hunter-gatherers: a view from Cantabrian Spain. *Munibe* 33:171–173.

1982a Carnivores and cave sites in Cantabrian Spain. *Journal of Anthropological Research* 38:75–96.

1982b Observations on Upper Paleolithic art: old problems and new directions. *Zephyrus* 34–35:71–80.

1983a From Mousterian to Magdalenian. In *The Mousterian Legacy*, edited by E. Trinkaus, 73–111. BAR S-164.

1983b *El Solutrense Vasco-Cantábrico: Una Nueva Perspectiva*. CIMAM 10.

1983c Páleolithic adaptations in Cantabria and Gascony. In *Homenaje al Profesor Martin Almagro Basch*, vol. 1, 187–201. Ministerio de Cultura, Madrid.

1985a Stone Age prehistory of northern Spain. *Science* 230:501–507.

1985b Chronostratigraphy of the Pleistocene-Holocene transition: the Azilian problem in the Franco-Cantabrian region. *Palaeohistoria* 27:89–122.

1986a *The End of the Paleolithic in the Old World*. BAR S-284.

1986b Late Würm adaptive systems in Cantabrian Spain. *Journal of Anthropological Archaeology* 5:330–368.

1986c Once more into the breach: Solutrean chronology. *Munibe* 38:35–38.

1986d An overview of the La Riera chronology. In *La Riera Cave*, edited by L. Straus and G. Clark, 19–23. Anthropological Research Papers 36.

1987a The Paleolithic cave art of Vasco-Cantabrian Spain. *Oxford Journal of Archaeology* 6:149–163.

1987b Upper Paleolithic ibex hunting in SW Europe. *Journal of Archaeological Science* 14:163–178.

1987c Paradigm lost: a personal view of the current state of Upper Paleolithic research. *Helinium* 27:157–171.

1990a Human occupation of Euskalherria during the Last Glacial Maximum: the Basque Solutrean. *Munibe* 42:33–40.

1990b The original arms race: Iberian perspectives on the Solutrean phenomenon. *Feuilles de Pierre: Les Industries Foliacées du Paléolithique supérieur Européen*, edited by J. Kozłowski, 425–447. ERAUL 42.

1991 The Epipaleolithic and Mesolithic of Cantabrian Spain and Pyrenean France. *Journal of World Prehistory* 5:83–104.

1991b Southwestern Europe at the last glacial maximum. *Current Anthropology* 32:189–199.

n.d.a The use of quartzite in the Upper Paleolithic of Cantabrian Spain. In *The Role of Quartzite and other Non-Flint Raw Materials in the Iberian Paleolithic*, edited by N. Moloney, L.Raposo and M. Santonja. BAR. In press.

n.d.b The role of raw materials in Upper Paleolithic & Mesolithic stone artifact assemblage variability in SW Europe. In *Raw Material Economy among Prehistoric Hunter-Gatherers*, edited by A. Montet-White and S. Holen. University of Kansas Publications in Anthropology. In press.

n.d.c Human geography of the late Upper Paleolithic in western Europe: present state of the question. *Journal of Anthropological Research* 47. In press.

n.d.d Human adaptations to the reforestation of the south coast of the Bay of Biscay: 13–9 ka bp. *Early Man News*. In press.

n.d.e To change or not to change: the late and post-glacial in SW Europe. *Quaternaria*. In press.

n.d.f *L'Abri Dufaure: Un Gisement Tardiglaciaire en Gascogne*. Mémoires de la Société Préhistorique Française, Paris. In press.

n.d.g An essay at synthesis: Tardiglacial adaptive systems in the Vasco-Cantabria and Pyrenean regions of SW Europe. *Kobie* 18. In press.

Straus, L., J. Altuna, G. Clark, M. González, H. Laville, Arlette Leroi- Gourhan, M. Menendez, and J. Ortea.

1981 Paleoecology at La Riera. *Current Anthropology* 22:655–682.

Straus, L. and G. Clark.

1986 *La Riera Cave: Stone Age Hunter-Gatherer Adaptations in Northern Spain*. Anthropological Research Papers 36.

Straus, L., G. Clark, J. Altuna, and J. Ortea.

1980 Ice Age subsistence in northern Spain. *Scientific American* 242(6):142–152.

Straus, L., G. Clark, J. Ordaz, L. Suarez, and R. Esbert.

1986 Patterns of lithic raw material variation at La Riera. In *La Riera Cave*, edited by L. Straus and G. Clark, 189–208. Anthropological Research Papers 36.

Straus, L. and C. Heller.

1988 Explorations of the Twilight Zone: the early Upper Paleolithic of Cantabria and Gascony. In *The Early Upper Paleolithic*, edited by J. Hoffecker and C. Wolf, 97–133. BAR S-437.

Stuckenrath, R.

1978 Dataciones de Carbono-14. In *Vida y Muerte en Cueva Morín*, edited by J. González Echegaray and L. Freeman, 215. Institución de Cantabria, Santander.

Taborin, Y.

1990 Les prémices de la parure. In *Paléolithique Moyen Récent et Paléolithique Supérieur Ancien en Europe*, edited by C. Farizy, 335–344. Mémoires du Musée de Préhistoire d'Ile de France 3.

Terán, M., and L. Solé Sabarís.

1968 *Geografía Regional de España*. Ariel, Barcelona.

Ters, M.

1973 Les variations du niveau marin depuis 10.000 ans, le long du littoral Atlantique français. In *Le Quaternaire. Géodynamique, Stratigraphie et Environnement. 9ième Congrès International de l'INQUA*, 114–135. CNRS, Paris.

Trinkaus, E.

1983 *The Mousterian Legacy*. BAR S-164.

1986 The Neandertals and modern human origins. *Annual Review of Anthropology* 15:193–218.

Ucko, P. and A. Rosenfeld.

1967 *Palaeolithic Cave Art*. World University Library, London.

UIMP (Universidad Internacional Menéndez Pelayo)

1978 *Curso de Arte Rupestre Paleolítico*. Universidad de Zaragoza, Zaragoza.

Utrilla, P.

1981a *El Magdaleniense Inferior y Médio en la Costa Cantábrica*. CIMAM 4.

1981b El Magdaleniense inferior del Rascaño en el conjunto del Magaleniense cantábrico. In *El Paleolítico Superior de la Cueva del Rascaño*, edited by J. González Echegaray and I. Barandiarán, 167–188. CIMAM 3.

1982 El yacimiento de la cueva de Abauntz. *Trabajos de Arqueología Navarra* 3:203–346.

1984–1985 Reflexiones sobre el origen del Magdaleniense. *Zephyrus* 37–38:87–97.

1986 Nuevos datos sobre el paleolítico inferior y médio de la Rioja. *Cuadernos de Investigación Histórica* 12:171–192.

1989 Los niveles paleolíticos de la Cueva de Chaves. In *Cien Años después de Sautuola*, edited by M. González Morales, pp. 361–377. Diputación Regional de Cantabria, Santander.

1990 La llamada "facies del País Vasco" del Magdaleniense inferior cantábrico. *Munibe* 42:41–54.

Vallois, H. and L. Delmas.

1976 Los frontales de la cueva de El Castillo. *Trabajos de Prehistoria* 33: 113–120.

Van den Brink, F.
  1968 *A Field Guide to the Mammals of Britain and Europe.* Houghton Mifflin, Boston.
Vega del Sella, R. Conde de la.
  1914 *La Cueva del Penicial.* CIPPM 4.
  1915 Avance al estudio del Paleolítico superior en la región asturiana. *Asociación Española para el Progreso de las Ciencias, Congreso de Valladolid,* 139–160.
  1916 *Paleolítico de Cueto de la Mina.* CIPPM 13.
  1921 *El Paleolítico de Cueva Morín y Notas para la Climatología Cuaternária.* CIPPM 29.
  1923 *El Asturiense: Nueva Industria Preneolítica.* CIPPM 32.
  1927 *Teoría de Glaciarismo Cuaternario por Desplazamientos Polares.* CIPPM 35.
  1929 El diagnóstico de las pinturas rupestres. *Memorias de la Real Sociedad Española de Historia Natural* 15:781–789.
  1930 *Las Cuevas de La Riera y Balmori.* CIPPM 38.
Vega de la Torre, J.
  1985 Estudio malacológico de las cuevas de Piélago I y Piélago II. *Sautuola* 4:123–126.
Vega-Toscano, L.
  1990 La fin du Paléolithique moyen au sud de l'Espagne. In *Paléolithique Moyen Récent et Paléolithique Supérieur Ancien en Europe,* edited by C. Farizy, 169–176. Mémoires du Musée d'Ile de France 3.
Vega-Toscano, L., M. Hoyos, A. Ruiz, and H. Laville.
  1988 La séquence de la grotte de la Carihuela. In *L'Homme de Neandertal,* edited by M. Otte, vol. 2, 169–180. ERAUL 29.
Viera, L. and L. Aguirrezabala.
  1990 Estudio geológico del yacimiento prehistórico de la Cueva de Amalda y su entorno. In *La Cueva de Amalda,* edited by J. Altuna, A. Baldeón, and K. Mariezkurrena, 53–61. Sociedad de Estudios Vascos, San Sebastián.
Villa, P.
  1990 Torralba and Aridos: elephant exploitation in Middle Pleistocene Spain. *Journal of Human Evolution* 19:299–309.
Weniger, G. C.
  1990 Germany at 18,000 BP In *The World at 18,000 BP,* edited by O. Soffer and C. Gamble, vol. 1, 171–192. Unwin Hyman, London.
White, R.
  1982 Rethinking the Middle/Upper Paleolithic transition. *Current Anthropology* 23:169–192.
Wobst, H. M.
  1974 Boundary conditions for Paleolithic social systems: a simulation approach. *American Antiquity* 39:147–178.
  1976 Locational relationships in Paleolithic society. *Journal of Human Evolution* 5:49–58.

Zabala, J.
1984 Los micromamíferos del yacimiento de Ekain. In *El Yacimiento Pre-histórico de la Cueva de Ekain*, edited by J. Altuna and J. Merino, 317–330. Sociedad de Estudios Vascos, San Sebastián.

Zilhão, J.
1984 O Solutrense superior de fácies cantábrico de Vale Almoinha. *O Arqueólogo Português* 4(2):15–86.

1987 *O Solutrense da Estremadura Portuguesa.* Trabalhos de Arqueologia 4.

1990a The Portuguese Estremadura at 18000 BP: the Solutrean. In *The World at 18000 BP*, edited by O. Soffer and C. Gamble, 109–125.

1990b Données nouvelles sur la chronologie, le peuplement, et la culture materielle du Solutréen portugais. In *Feuilles de Pierre: Les Industries à Pointes Foliacées du Paléolithique Supérieur Européen*, edited by J. Kozowski, 485–501. *ERAUL* 42.

Zilhão, J., F. Real and E. Carvalho
1987 Estratigrafía e cronologia da estaçao Solutrense de Vale Almoinha. *O Arqueólogo Português* 4(5):21–35.

INDEX

327